U0922540

杭州市统计局
国家统计局杭州调查队 编
杭州市社会经济调查局

中国统计出版社
China Statistics Press

（京）新登字041号

图书在版编目（CIP）数据

杭州统计年鉴. 2011 / 杭州市统计局, 国家统计局杭州调查队编. —北京：中国统计出版社, 2011.8
ISBN 978-7-5037-6295-6/c.2519

Ⅰ. ①杭… Ⅱ. ①杭… ②国… Ⅲ. ①统计资料－杭州市－2011－年鉴

Ⅳ. ①C832.551-54

中国版本图书馆CIP数据核字(2011)第152332号

杭州统计年鉴－2011

作者／杭州市统计局 国家统计局杭州调查队 杭州市社会经济调查局
责任编辑／佘竞雄 郭 栋
责任校对／俞伟锋 陈小国
封面设计／杭州云鼎广告有限公司
出版发行／中国统计出版社
通信地址／北京市西城区月坛南街57号
邮编／100826
办公地址／北京市丰台区西三环南路甲6号
电话／(010)63376907
E-mail／yearbook@gj.stats.cn
印刷／浙江新中商务印刷有限公司
经销／新华书店
开本／880 X 1230 毫米 1/16
字数／85万
印张／26
印数／1-1200册
版别／2011 年 8 月第 1 版
版次／2011 年 8 月第 1 次印刷
书号／ISBN 978-7-5037-6295-6/c.2519
定价／300.00元

《杭州统计年鉴－2011》编委会和编辑人员

Editorial Board and Staff

编者说明

一、《杭州统计年鉴—2011》是一部信息密集的资料工具书。本书通过大量统计数据，真实地记录了在改革开放中杭州的经济、科技、社会的发展变化。本年鉴在前几年年鉴的基础上作了进一步的调整和改进，充实了数据信息量，并与前几年在版本内容、指标数据等方面基本保持连贯性。

二、本年鉴内容包括：综合；人口和从业人员；农业；工业、能源；建筑业；交通运输、邮电；固定资产投资；国内商业；对外经济、旅游；财政、金融、保险；城市建设、环境保护；科技、教育、文化、卫生、体育；人民生活、物价、民政等十三部分。

三、本年鉴辑入的统计数字，以 2010 年为主，为方便读者使用，主要指标还列入了 1978 年以来有关年度的统计数字。

四、2001 年 3 月起，萧山、余杭撤市建区，市区数据为新市区口径，增长速度按同比口径计算。

五、本年鉴表中符号使用说明：“－”表示这一栏没有数字；“…”表示该数字极小，不足计量单位；“#”表示其中的主要项；空白栏表示未掌握资料；“＊”表示表下有注解。

六、读者在使用统计资料时，凡与本年鉴有出入的，均以本年鉴为准。

七、《杭州统计年鉴》公开出版以来，受到了广大读者的关心和支持，对此我们深表谢意。欢迎广大读者对年鉴内容、编排等方面提出宝贵意见，以利于我们进一步提高年鉴的编辑工作水平，更好地为广大读者服务。

Editorial Note

Ⅰ. *Hangzhou Statistical Yearbook 2011* covers comprehensive data series of Hangzhou's social and economic development. Through the statistical data, it reflects the changes and development of Hangzhou's economy, science, technology and society since China adopted the policy of reform and opening to the outside world. This book is adjusted and progressed on basis of last years' books. It enriches the data, and keeps the consistency with last years' book in content and indicators.

Ⅱ. The book contains the following twelve chapters: 1. General Survey; 2. Population and Employment; 3. Agriculture; 4. Industry and Energy; 5. Construction; 6. Transportation, Post and Telecommunication Services; 7. Investment in Fixed Assets; 8. Domestic Trade; 9. Foreign Trade and Tourism; 10. Finance, Banking and Insurance; 11. Urban Construction and Environmental Protection; 12. Science and Technology, Education, Culture, Public Health and Sports; 13. People's Livelihood, Price Indices and Civil Administration.

Ⅲ. The book mainly reflects statistical data in 2010. And it also contains some selected data series in important years after 1978.

Ⅳ. The administrative of area urban district has been adjusted since March 2001, the new administrative area is composed of eight district including Xiaoshan and Yuhang. Data of urban district belong to new administrative area, while indices are calculated at comparable coverage.

Ⅴ. Notations used in this book:"—" indicates that the column has no figure;"…" indicates that the figure is not large enough to be measured with the smallest unit in the table;"blank" indicates that the data not available;"#" indicates the major items of the total;" * " indicates"see footnotes below".

Ⅵ. In any case the data of this book shall be deemed as the authoritative ones.

Ⅶ. Previous editions of Hangzhou Statistical Yearbook have won wide acclaim among the readers. In order to excel, we welcome all candid comments and criticism from our readers.

目　录
Contents

2010 年杭州市国民经济和社会发展统计公报 …………………………………………………………… (1)
Statistical Communique of National Economy and Social Development of Hangzhou,2010

第一篇　综合
Chapter 1　General Survey

1 - 01　行政区划(2010 年末) …………………………………………………………… (21)
Administrative Division(End of 2010)

1 - 02　土地面积和人口密度(2010 年末) …………………………………………………… (22)
Land Area and Population Density(End of 2010)

1 - 03　平均每天主要社会经济活动 ……………………………………………………… (23)
Selected Indicators on Average Daily Social and Economic Activities

1 - 04　国民经济主要指标 ………………………………………………………………… (24)
Major Indicators of National Economy

1 - 05　主要年份全市生产总值及发展指数(1978 年 = 100) ……………………………… (28)
Gross Domestic Product and its Indices in Main Years(Year of 1978 = 100)

1 - 06　主要年份市区生产总值及发展指数(1978 年 = 100) ……………………………… (29)
Gross Domestic Product and its Indices of Urban District in Main Years(Year of 1978 = 100)

1 - 07　主要年份全市生产总值指数(上年 = 100) …………………………………………… (30)
Indices of Gross Domestic Product in Main Years(Preceding Year = 100)

1 - 08　主要年份市区生产总值指数(上年 = 100) …………………………………………… (31)
Indices of Gross Domestic Product of Urban District in Main Years(Preceding Year = 100)

1 - 09　全市生产总值构成(2010 年) ……………………………………………………… (32)
Composition of Gross Domestic Product(2010)

1 - 10　分县(市)生产总值(2010 年) …………………………………………………… (34)
Gross Domestic Product by Region(2010)

1 - 11　主要指标占全省比重(2010 年) …………………………………………………… (35)
Proportion of Main Indicators in Whole Province(2010)

1 - 12　国民经济主要指标人均水平(按户籍) ……………………………………………… (38)
Major Per Capita Indicators of National Economy(Household registered)

1 - 13　企业家信心指数(2010 年) ………………………………………………………… (39)
Expectation Indices of Entrepreneurs(2010)

1 - 14　企业景气指数(2010 年) …………………………………………………………… (40)
Expectation Indices of Enterprises(2010)

1 - 15　市区分月气象概况(2010 年) …… (41)
Monthly Meteorological Conditions in Urban District(2010)
1 - 16　气象概况(2010 年) …… (42)
Meteorological Conditions by Region(2010)
主要统计指标解释 …… (44)
Explanatory Notes on Main Statistical Indicators

第二篇　人口和从业人员
Chapter 2　Population and Employment

2 - 01　历次普查常住人口情况 …… (49)
Long - term Residents in the Past Population Census
2 - 02　主要年份全市总户数与总人口数 …… (50)
Households and Population in Main Years
2 - 03　主要年份市区总户数与总人口数 …… (51)
Urban District Households and Population in Main Years
2 - 04　分地区总户数与总人口数(2010 年末) …… (52)
Households and Population by Region(End of 2010)
2 - 05　分地区户籍人口年龄构成(2010 年末) …… (53)
Age Structure of Household Registered Population by Region(End of 2010)
2 - 06　主要年份全市人口自然变动情况 …… (54)
Natural Changes of Population in Main Years
2 - 07　主要年份市区人口自然变动情况 …… (55)
Natural Changes of Urban Population in Main Years
2 - 08　分地区人口自然变动情况(2010 年末) …… (56)
Natural Changes of Population by Region(End of 2010)
2 - 09　分地区人口机械变动情况(2010 年) …… (57)
Mechanical Changes of Population by Region(2010)
2 - 10　计划生育情况(2010 年) …… (58)
Conditions of Birth Control(2010)
2 - 11　婚姻登记情况 …… (59)
Marriage Registration Conditions
2 - 12　全市城镇单位从业人员数(2010 年) …… (60)
Number of Employed Persons in Urban Units(2010)
2 - 13　全市国有单位从业人员数(2010 年) …… (64)
Number of Employed Persons in State - owned Units(2010)
2 - 14　全市城镇集体单位从业人员数(2010 年) …… (66)
Number of Employed Persons in Urban Collective - owned Units(2010)

2 - 15 全市其他单位从业人员数(2010 年) …… (68)
Number of Employed Persons in Units of Other Types of Ownership(2010)
2 - 16 按三次产业分从业人员人数 …… (70)
Number of Employed Persons by Three Industries
主要统计指标解释 …… (71)
Explanatory Notes on Main Statistical Indicators

第三篇　农业

Chapter 3　Agriculture

3 - 01 农村基本情况 …… (75)
Basic Conditions of Rural Areas
3 - 02 分地区农村基本情况(2010 年) …… (76)
Basic Conditions of Rural Areas by Region(2010)
3 - 03 分地区农村从业人员(2010 年) …… (78)
Rural Labor Force by Region(2010)
3 - 04 主要年份农林牧渔业总产值 …… (80)
Gross Output Value of Farming, Forestry, Animal Husbandry and Fishery in Main Years
3 - 05 主要年份农林牧渔业总产值构成 …… (81)
Composition of Gross Output Value of Farming, Forestry, Animal Husbandry and Fishery in Main Years
3 - 06 主要年份农林牧渔业分项产值 …… (82)
Gross Output Value of Farming, Forestry, Animal Husbandry and Fishery by Branch in Main Years
3 - 07 主要年份农林牧渔业分项产值构成 …… (83)
Composition of Gross Output Value of Farming, Forestry, Animal Husbandry and Fishery by Branch in Main Years
3 - 08 分地区农林牧渔业总产值(2010 年) …… (84)
Gross Output Value of Farming, Forestry, Animal Husbandry and Fishery by Region(2010)
3 - 09 农林牧渔业产值及增加值(2010 年) …… (86)
Value - Added and Commodity Output Value of Farming, Forestry, Animal Husbandry and Fishery(2010)
3 - 10 主要农作物播种面积及产量 …… (88)
Sown Areas and Yield of Major Farm Crops
3 - 11 分地区粮食播种面积及产量(2010 年) …… (90)
Sown Areas and Yield of Grain Crops by Region(2010)
3 - 12 油、菜、茶、蚕、果生产情况(2010 年) …… (92)
Statistics on Rapeseeds, Vegetables, Tea, Silkworm Cocoons and Fruits Production(2010)
3 - 13 分地区畜牧业渔业生产(2010 年) …… (96)
Statistics on Animal Husbanday and Fishery by Region(2010)
3 - 14 分地区林业生产(2010 年) …… (100)
Statistics on Forestry by Region(2010)

3 - 15 分地区灌溉和水利设施情况(2010 年) …… (102)
Irrigation and Water Conservancy Facilities by Region(2010)

3 - 16 分地区主要农机具年末拥有量(2010 年) …… (104)
Possession of Major Agricultural Machinery at the Year - end by Region(2010)

3 - 17 农业机械作业和物资消耗情况(2010 年) …… (106)
Agricultural Mechanization and Material Consumption(2010)

3 - 18 农村经济收入分配(2010 年) …… (108)
Rural Economic Income Distribution(2010)

3 - 19 乡(镇)基本情况(2010 年) …… (110)
Statistics on Towns and Townships(2010)

主要统计指标解释 …… (124)
Explanatory Notes on Main Statistical Indicators

第四篇　工业、能源

Chapter 4　Industry and Energy

4 - 01 主要年份工业企业单位数 …… (129)
Number of Industrial Enterprises in Main Years

4 - 02 主要年份工业总产值 …… (130)
Gross Industrial Output Value in Main Years

4 - 03 分县(市)工业企业单位数(2010 年) …… (132)
Number of Industrial Enterprises by Region(2010)

4 - 04 分县(市)工业总产值(2010 年) …… (134)
Gross Industrial Output Value by Region(2010)

4 - 05 分县(市)工业销售产值(2010 年) …… (136)
Gross Industrial Products Sales by Region(2010)

4 - 06 全市规模以上工业企业主要经济指标(一) …… (138)
Main Economic Indicators of Industrial Enterprises Above Designated Size(Ⅰ)

4 - 07 全市规模以上工业企业主要经济指标(二) …… (144)
Main Economic Indicators of Industrial Enterprises Above Designated Size(Ⅱ)

4 - 08 全市规模以上工业企业主要经济指标(三) …… (150)
Main Economic Indicators of Industrial Enterprises Above Designated Size(Ⅲ)

4 - 09 市区规模以上工业企业主要经济指标(一) …… (156)
Main Economic Indicators of Industrial Enterprises Above Designated Size in Urban District(Ⅰ)

4 - 10 市区规模以上工业企业主要经济指标(二) …… (162)
Main Economic Indicators of Industrial Enterprises Above Designated Size in Urban District(Ⅱ)

4 - 11 市区规模以上工业企业主要经济指标(三) …… (168)
Main Economic Indicators of Industrial Enterprises Above Designated Size in Urban District(Ⅲ)

4 - 12 全市规模以上工业企业主要经济指标按登记注册类型分(2010 年) …… (174)
Main Economic Indicators of Industrial Enterprises Above Designated Size by Status of Registration(2010)
4 - 13 全市规模以上工业企业主要经济指标按经济组织类型分(2010 年) …… (178)
Main Economic Indicators of Industrial Enterprises Above Designated Size by the Type of Ownership(2010)
4 - 14 全市 1998 - 2010 年规模以上工业企业主要经济效益指标 …… (182)
Main Economic Indicators of Industrial Enterprises Above Designated Size(1998 - 2010)
4 - 15 主要工业产品生产量(2010 年) …… (183)
Output of Major Industrial Products(2010)
4 - 16 单位 GDP 能耗降低情况(2010 年) …… (187)
Increase or Decrease of Energy Consumption Per Unit of GDP(2010)
4 - 17 全市工业企业主要能源消费量按行业分(2010 年) …… (188)
Energy Consumption of Industrial Enterprises by Sector(2010)
4 - 18 电力消费量(2010 年) …… (192)
Electricity Consumption(2010)
4 - 19 2001 - 2010 年水资源量和总用水量 …… (193)
Total Water Resources and Water Consumption(2001 - 2010)
主要统计指标解释 …… (194)
Explanatory Notes on Main Statistical Indicators

第五篇　建筑业
Chapter 5　CONSTRUCTION

5 - 01 建筑业总产值(2010 年) …… (199)
Gross Output Value of Construction(2010)
5 - 02 各种分组总专包企业财务汇总表(2010 年) …… (200)
Financial Conditions of Construction Enterprises(2010)
5 - 03 建筑业企业生产情况 …… (204)
Statistics on Production of Construction Enterprises
主要统计指标解释 …… (205)
Explanatory Notes on Main Statistical Indicators

第六篇　交通运输、邮电
Chapter 6　Transportation,Post and Telecommunications

6 - 01 全市主要年份客运量 …… (209)
Total Passenger Traffic in Main Years
6 - 02 全市主要年份货运量 …… (210)
Total Freight Traffic in Main Years

6 - 03 全社会客货运输量(2010 年) …… (211)
Total Passenger and Freight Traffic(2010)

6 - 04 社会机动车辆年末拥有量(2010 年) …… (212)
Total Number of Motor Vehicles End of the Year(2010)

6 - 05 邮政、电信主要指标(2010 年) …… (213)
Post and Telecommunications(2010)

主要统计指标解释 …… (214)
Explanatory Notes on Main Statistical Indicators

第七篇　固定资产投资

Chapter 7　Investment in Fixed Assets

7 - 01 主要年份全市全社会固定资产投资总额 …… (219)
Total Investment in Fixed Assets in Main Years

7 - 02 主要年份市区全社会固定资产投资总额 …… (220)
Total Investment in Fixed Assets of Urban District in Main Years

7 - 03 主要年份全市固定资产投资按三次产业分 …… (221)
Investment in Fixed Assets Grouped by Three Industries in Main Years

7 - 04 主要年份全市固定资产投资房屋建筑面积及造价 …… (222)
Floor Space of Buildings and Their Cost in Main Years

7 - 05 主要年份市区固定资产投资房屋建筑面积及造价 …… (223)
Urban District Floor Space of Buildings and Their Cost in Main Years

7 - 06 分县(市)固定资产投资完成额(2010 年) …… (224)
Investment in Fixed Assets by Region(2010)

7 - 07 分县(市)限额以上工业投资完成额(2010 年) …… (228)
Super - Scale Investment in Industrial Sector by Region(2010)

7 - 08 分县(市)房地产开发投资情况(2010 年) …… (232)
Real Estate Development by Region(2010)

7 - 09 分县(市)限额以上农村固定资产投资完成额(2010 年) …… (234)
Super - Scale Rural Investment by Region(2010)

7 - 10 房屋建筑面积及造价(2010 年) …… (236)
Floor Space of Buildings and Their Cost(2010)

7 - 11 固定资产投资新增生产能力(或效益)(2010 年) …… (238)
The New Productive Capacity or Facilities Created by Investment in Fixed Assets(2010)

主要统计指标解释 …… (239)
Explanatory Notes on Main Statistical Indicators

第八篇　国内商业

Chapter 8　Domestic Trade

8 - 01　主要年份社会消费品零售总额 ……………………………………………… (243)

Total Retail Sale of Consumer Goods in Main Years

8 - 02　主要年份分县(市)社会消费品零售总额 ……………………………………… (244)

Total Retail Sale of Consumer Goods by Region in Main Years

8 - 03　社会消费品零售总额(2010 年) ……………………………………………… (246)

Total Retail Sale of Consumer Goods(2010)

8 - 04　全市限额以上批发零售贸易企业商品销售总额按登记注册类型分(2010 年) ……… (248)

Sales of Wholesale and Retail Trade Above Designated Size by Status of Registration(2010)

8 - 05　全市限额以上批发零售贸易企业商品销售总额按国民经济行业分(2010 年) ……… (249)

Sales of Wholesale and Retail Trade Above Designated Size by Sector(2010)

8 - 06　全市限额以上批发零售贸易企业财务状况按登记注册类型分(2010 年) ………… (250)

Main Financial Indicators of Enterprises Above Designated Size in Wholesale and Retail Sale Trade by Status of Registration(2010)

8 - 07　全市限额以上批发零售贸易企业财务状况按国民经济行业分(2010 年) ………… (254)

Main Financial Indicators of Enterprises Above Designated Size in Wholesale and Retail Sale Trade by Sector(2010)

8 - 08　全市限额以上住宿业和餐饮业财务状况按注册类型、行业分(2010 年) ………… (258)

Main Financial Indicators of Lodging and Catering Services Enterprises Above Designated Size by Status of Registration and Sector(2010)

8 - 09　全市限额以上住宿业和餐饮业经营按登记注册类型分(2010 年) ……………… (262)

Management Conditions of Lodging and Catering Services Enterprises Above Designated Size by Status of Registration(2010)

8 - 10　全市限额以上住宿业和餐饮业经营按国民经济行业分(2010 年) ……………… (263)

Management Conditions of Lodging and Catering Services Enterprises Above Designated Size by Sector(2010)

8 - 11　个体工商业登记注册情况(2010 年末) ……………………………………… (264)

Statistics of Individual Owned Business(End of 2010)

8 - 12　私营企业登记注册情况(2010 年末) ………………………………………… (266)

Statistics of Private Owned Business(End of 2010)

主要统计指标解释 ……………………………………………………………… (268)

Explanatory Notes on Main Statistical Indicators

第九篇　对外经济、旅游

Chapter 9　Foreign Trade and Tourism

9 - 01　主要年份外商直接投资情况 ……………………………………………… (273)

Foreign Direct Investment in Main Years

9－02　外商直接投资分行业情况(2010 年) ……… (274)
Foreign Direct Investment by Sector(2010)
9－03　外商投资企业分国别(地区)情况(2010 年) ……… (275)
Foreign－Funded Enterprises by Region or Territory(2010)
9－04　外商直接投资分区县(市)情况 ……… (276)
Foreign Direct Investment by Region
9－05　国内招商引资分区县(市)情况 ……… (277)
Domestic Attract Investment by Region
9－06　国家级开发区建设发展情况(2010 年末) ……… (278)
The Construction of National－Class Development Zones(End of 2010)
9－07　主要年份进出口情况 ……… (279)
Imports and Exports in Main Years
9－08　进出口情况(2010 年) ……… (280)
Imports and Exports(2010)
9－09　外贸出口分区县(市)情况(2010 年) ……… (281)
Export of Foreign Trade by Region(2010)
9－10　出口企业自营出口前 20 位排名(2010 年) ……… (282)
The List of First Twenty Export Enterprises(2010)
9－11　外贸出口主要国别(地区)情况 ……… (283)
Export of Foreign Trade by Main Country or Territory
9－12　主要年份旅游事业发展情况 ……… (284)
Development of Tourism in Main Years
9－13　主要年份境外旅游者人数 ……… (285)
Number of International Tourists in Main Years
9－14　接待境外游客及旅游外汇收入情况 ……… (286)
Number of International Tourists and Foreign Exchange Earnings
9－15　接待境外游客分国别(地区)情况 ……… (287)
Number of International Tourists by Country or Territory
主要统计指标解释 ……… (288)
Explanatory Notes on Main Statistical Indicators

第十篇　财政、金融、保险

Chapter 10　Finance, Banking and Insurance

10－01　主要年份财政收入及支出 ……… (293)
Financial Revenue and Expenditure in Main Years
10－02　分县(市)财政收入(2010 年) ……… (294)
Local Financial Revenue by Region(2010)

10 - 03 分县(市)财政支出(2010 年) …… (296)
Local Financial Expenditure by Region(2010)

10 - 04 主要年份全市金融机构存、贷款余额 …… (298)
Balance of Deposits and Loans of Financial Institutions in Main Years

10 - 05 主要年份市区金融机构存、贷款余额 …… (299)
Balance of Deposits and Loans of Financial Institutions of Urban District in Main Years

10 - 06 金融机构本外币存、贷款余额(2010 年末) …… (300)
Balance of Deposits and Loans of Financial Institutions(End of 2010)

10 - 07 金融机构人民币存、贷款余额(2010 年末) …… (302)
Balance of RMB Deposits, RMB Loans of Financial Institutions(End of 2010)

10 - 08 城乡居民储蓄存款余额(2010 年) …… (304)
Balance of Savings Deposits of Rural and Urban Residents(2010)

10 - 09 保险业务情况(2010 年) …… (305)
Development of Insurance Business(2010)

主要统计指标解释 …… (306)
Explanatory Notes on Main Statistical Indicators

第十一篇 城市建设、环境保护

Chapter 11 Urban Construction and Environmental Protection

11 - 01 主要年份市区城市公共交通 …… (311)
Urban Public Transportation in Main Years

11 - 02 主要年份市区城市供电、供水 …… (312)
Urban Electricity and Water Supply in Main Years

11 - 03 主要年份市区市政建设 …… (313)
Public Utilities in Urban District in Main Years

11 - 04 主要年份市区园林绿化 …… (314)
Urban Forestation in Main Years

11 - 05 工业“三废”排放及处理率(2010 年) …… (315)
Discharge and Disposal Rate of Industrial "Three Waste"(2010)

主要统计指标解释 …… (316)
Explanatory Notes on Main Statistical Indicators

第十二篇 科技、教育、文化、卫生、体育

Chapter 12 Science and Technology, Education, Culture, Public Health and Sports

12 - 01 分县(市)城镇单位年末人才资源 …… (321)
Trained Personnel Resource of Urban Units by Region

12-02 分行业城镇单位专业技术人员(2010 年末) …… (322)
Technical Personnel of Urban Units by Sector(End of 2010)
12-03 按经济类型分的城镇单位专业技术人员(2010 年末) …… (323)
Technical Personnel of Urban Units by Ownership(End of 2010)
12-04 文化事业单位数(2010 年) …… (324)
Number of Institutions for Culture(2010)
12-05 分县(市)艺术表演团体演出情况(2010 年) …… (324)
Basic Statistics on Performance of Art Troupes by Region(2010)
12-06 全市专利申请及授权情况(2010 年) …… (326)
Patent Application and Granted(2010)
12-07 主要年份市区文化事业单位数 …… (327)
Cultural Institutions of Urban District in Main Years
12-08 主要年份高等学校基本情况 …… (328)
Basic Statistics on Regular Institutions of Higher Education in Main Years
12-09 主要年份中等专业学校基本情况 …… (329)
Basic Statistics on Specialized Secondary Schools in Main Years
12-10 主要年份高中基本情况 …… (330)
Basic Statistics on Senior High Schools in Main Years
12-11 主要年份初中基本情况 …… (331)
Basic Statistics on Junior Middle Schools in Main Years
12-12 主要年份小学基本情况 …… (332)
Basic Statistics on Primary Schools in Main Years
12-13 主要年份幼儿园基本情况 …… (333)
Basic Statistics on Kindergartens in Main Years
12-14 高等学校基本情况(2010 年) …… (334)
Basic Statistics on Regular Institutions of Higher Education(2010)
12-15 普通中学及职业中学基本情况(2010 年) …… (336)
Basic Statistics on Senior,Junior High Schools and Vacational Schools(2010)
12-16 小学、幼儿园及特殊教育基本情况(2010 年) …… (338)
Basic Statistics on Primary Schools,Kindergartens and Special Education(2010)
12-17 各级成人教育基本情况(2010 年) …… (340)
Basic Statistics on Various Adult Education(2010)
12-18 主要年份医疗卫生机构数 …… (342)
Number of Health Institutions in Main Years
12-19 主要年份医疗病床数 …… (343)
Number of Beds in Health Institutions in Main Years
12-20 医疗卫生机构数(2010 年) …… (344)
Number of Health Institutions(2010)
12-21 医疗病床数(2010 年) …… (346)

Number of Beds in Health Institutions(2010)

12 - 22　卫生事业人员数(2010 年) …… (348)

Number of Medical Technical Personnel(2010)

12 - 23　主要年份卫生技术人员 …… (350)

Number of Medical Technical Personnel in Main Years

12 - 24　体育运动情况(2010 年) …… (351)

Basic Statistics on Sports Activities(2010)

主要统计指标解释 …… (352)

Explanatory Notes on Main Statistical Indicators

第十三篇　人民生活、物价、民政

Chapter 13　People's Livelihood, Price Indices and Civil Administration

13 - 01　主要年份市区城镇住户调查情况 …… (357)

Basic Conditions of Urban Households in Main Years

13 - 02　市区城镇居民家庭平均每人全年现金收支 …… (358)

Per Capita Annual Cash Income and Expenditure of Urban Residents

13 - 03　2010 年市区城镇居民家庭人均现金收支(按收入水平分组) …… (359)

Per Capita Annual Cash Income and Expenditure of Urban Residents in 2010(Grouped by Income Level)

13 - 04　主要年份市区城镇居民家庭人均消费性支出 …… (360)

Per Capita Annual Living Expenditure of Urban Residents in Main Years

13 - 05　2010 年市区城镇居民家庭人均全年消费性支出(按收入水平分组) …… (361)

Per Capita Annual Living Expenditure of Urban Residents in 2010(Grouped by Income Level)

13 - 06　主要年份市区城镇居民家庭平均每百户耐用消费品拥有量 …… (362)

Number of Major Durable Consumer Goods Owned Per 100 Urban Households in Main Years

13 - 07　主要年份全市农村住户调查情况 …… (363)

Basic Conditions of Whole Municipality Rural Households in Main Years

13 - 08　主要年份全市农村居民家庭人均纯收入 …… (364)

Per Capita Annual Gross and Net Income of Whole Municipality Rural Households in Main Years

13 - 09　主要年份全市农村居民家庭人均支出 …… (365)

Per Capita Gross Expenditure of Whole Municipality Rural Households in Main Years

13 - 10　主要年份全市农村居民家庭平均每百户耐用消费品拥有量 …… (367)

Number of Major Durable Consumer Goods Owned Per 100 Rural Households in Main Years

13 - 11　主要年份全市城镇单位在岗职工工资总额 …… (368)

Total Wages of Fully Employed Staff and Workers in Main Years

13 - 12　主要年份市区城镇单位在岗职工工资总额 …… (369)

Total Wages of Fully Employed Staff and Workers of Urban District in Main Years

13 - 13　主要年份全市城镇单位在岗职工年平均工资 …… (370)

Average Annual Wages of Fully Employed Staff and Workers in Main Years

13－14　主要年份市区在岗职工年平均工资 …………………………………………………………………（371）

Average Annual Wages of Fully Employed Workers of Urban District in Main Years

13－15　全市城镇单位从业人员劳动报酬(2010 年) ……………………………………………………………（372）

Laborers´Remuneration of Employed Persons in Urban Units(2010)

13－16　全市国有单位从业人员劳动报酬(2010 年) ……………………………………………………………（374）

Laborers´Remuneration of Employed Persons for State－owned Units(2010)

13－17　全市城镇集体单位从业人员劳动报酬(2010 年) ………………………………………………………（376）

Laborers´Remuneration of Employed Persons for Collective－owned Units(2010)

13－18　全市其他单位从业人员劳动报酬(2010 年) ……………………………………………………………（377）

Laborers´Remuneration of Employed Persons for Other Ownership Units(2010)

13－19　主要年份市区消费价格指数 ………………………………………………………………………（379）

Consumer Price Indices of Urban District in Main Years

13－20　市区居民消费价格指数(2010 年) ……………………………………………………………………（380）

Consumer Price Indices in Urban District(2010)

13－21　市区零售价格指数(2010 年) ………………………………………………………………………（382）

Retail Price Indices in Urban District(2010)

13－22　主要工业品出厂价格分类指数 ………………………………………………………………………（384）

Ex－Factory Price Indices of Industrial Products in Main Years

13－23　主要原材料、燃料、动力购进价格分类指数 ……………………………………………………………（386）

Purchasing Price Indices of Raw Materials,Fuels and Power in Main Years

13－24　房地产销售价格指数 …………………………………………………………………………………（387）

Sales Price Indices of Houses in Main Years

13－25　房地产租赁价格指数 …………………………………………………………………………………（388）

Rental Price Indices of Houses in Main Years

13－26　社会办福利院情况(2010 年) ………………………………………………………………………（389）

Basic Statistics on Welfare Homes(2010)

13－27　优抚对象人员情况(2010 年) ………………………………………………………………………（390）

Number of Persons Enjoying Public Subsidies(2010)

13－28　市、县级社会团体机构情况(2010 年) ………………………………………………………………（392）

Basic Statistics on Institutions and Organizations at County Level(2010)

13－29　社会保障分县(市)情况(2010 年) …………………………………………………………………（394）

Social Security by Region(2010)

13－30　近年来社会保障情况 …………………………………………………………………………………（395）

Social Security in Recent Years

主要统计指标解释 ………………………………………………………………………………………………（396）

Explanatory Notes on Main Statistical Indicators

2010 年杭州市国民经济和社会发展统计公报

杭 州 市 统 计 局
国家统计局杭州调查队
杭州市社会经济调查局
（2011 年 2 月）

2010 年，我市认真贯彻落实科学发展观，突出加快转变经济发展方式这条主线，深入实施“六大战略”，积极推进“一化七经济”，努力破解“七难问题”，促进了经济稳步发展，社会和谐进步，民生不断改善，圆满完成“十一五”规划确定的各项主要目标任务，为“十二五”发展打下了坚实的基础。

一、综　　合

经济总量

初步核算，2010 年，全市实现生产总值（GDP）5949.17 亿元，按可比价格计算，比上年增长 12%，连续 20 年保持两位数增长。其中：第一产业增加值 208.41 亿元，增长 2.5%；第二产业增加值 2844.07 亿元，增长 12.5%；第三产业增加值 2896.69 亿元，增长 12.3%。全市按常住人口计算的人均 GDP 为 69828 元，按户籍人口计算的人均 GDP 为 86691 元，分别增长 8.7% 和 11.1%，按国家公布的 2010 年平均汇率折算，分别达到 10314 美元和 12804 美元。“十一五”时期，全市生产总值年均增长 12.4%，三次产业结构由 2005 年的 5.0∶50.8∶44.2 调整为 2010 年的 3.5∶47.8∶48.7，形成以现代服务业为主导的“三二一”产业结构。

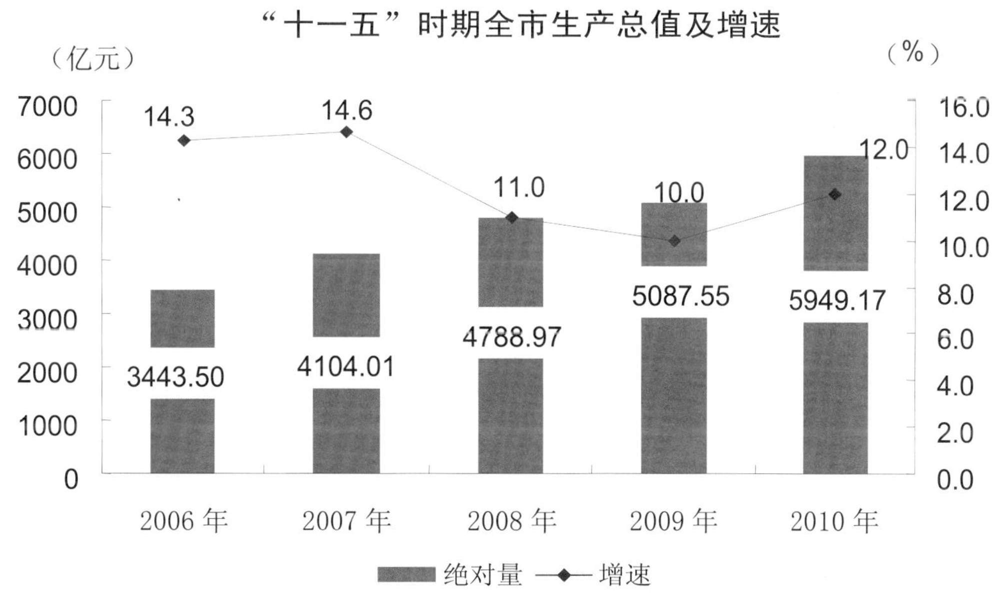

非公经济

初步测算，在全市生产总值中，非公有制经济所占比重已达到 66%，比上年提高 1.5 个百分点。个体私营经济持续活跃。年末，全市共有私营企业 16.17 万户，增长 14.7%，从业人员 145.59 万人，增长 11.2%；个体工商户 29.88 万户，从业人员 65.31 万人，分别增长 5% 和 15.3%。

财政收支

全年完成财政总收入1245.43亿元，比上年增长22.2%，其中地方财政一般预算收入671.34亿元，增长28.9%。在税收收入中，增值税356.92亿元，增长4.2%；营业税221.31亿元，增长25.4%；企业所得税248.08亿元，增长32.8%；个人所得税98亿元，增长22.1%。全年地方财政支出616.58亿元，比上年增长23.8%。其中：教育、科学技术支出134.73亿元，增长24.3%；社会保障和就业支出63.94亿元，增长31.7%；医疗卫生支出41.71亿元，增长28.9%；环境保护支出13.86亿元，增长42.2%；城乡社区事务支出98.29亿元，增长29%。

市场价格

市区居民消费价格总水平比上年上涨3.9%。八大类商品和服务项目价格呈“六升二降”格局(见下表)。

市区居民消费价格指数(上年=100)

项　　目	2010年	2009年
市区居民消费价格指数	103.9	98.6
1.食品	107.3	101.7
2.烟酒及用品	101.9	100.7
3.衣着	98.0	100.6
4.家庭设备用品及维修服务	103.6	100.9
5.医疗保健和个人用品	105.5	100.6
6.交通和通信	99.8	95.2
7.娱乐教育文化用品及服务	102.2	96.9
8.居住	105.8	91.8

全市工业品出厂价格上涨4.9%；原材料、燃料、动力购进价格上涨12.1%。

劳动就业

全年新增城镇就业人员26.01万人；失业人员实现再就业15.54万人；再就业培训6.97万人。年末城镇登记失业率由上年的2.99%下降为2.19%。

二、人口、人民生活和社会保障

人口

2010年末，全市常住人口870.54万人，比上年末增加37.14万人，其中户籍人口689.12万人，比上年末增加5.74万人。在户籍人口中，农业人口323.88万人，非农业人口365.24万人。按公安部门统计的全市人口出生率为10.14‰，人口自然增长率为3.41‰。

人民生活

据抽样调查，全年市区城镇居民人均可支配收入30035元，比上年增长11.8%，扣除价格因素，实际增长7.6%。其中人均工资性收入21075元，增长12.3%，财产性收入和经营性收入分别为2189元、1651元，增长2%和3.4%，转移性收入8896元，增长13.7%；人均生活消费性支出20219元，比上年增长8.7%。全市农村居民人均纯收入13186元，比上年增长11.5%，扣除价格因素，实际增长7.3%，人均生活消费性支出10267元，增长13.3%。“十一五”时期，市区城镇居民人均可支配收入年均增长12.6%，全市农民人均纯收入年均增长11.5%。

市区城镇居民人均住房建筑面积30.86平方米，每百户居民家庭拥有家用汽车23辆、空调器214台、移动电话193部、家用电脑99台、微波炉79台、淋浴热水器99台。全市农村居民人均居住面积71.22平方米。每百户农村居民家庭拥有家用汽车16辆、空调器111台、移动电话213部、家用电脑44台、微波炉29台、淋浴热水器84台、洗衣机85台、电冰箱98台。

年末城乡居民储蓄存款余额达4990.97亿元，比上年末增长16.4%。

社会保障

年末全市参加（纳入）养老保险（保障）人数达490.27万人，其中60周岁以上城乡老年居民不缴费直接享受基础养老金52.39万人；参加基本医疗保险753.56万人，增加38.46万人；参加失业、工伤、生育保险人数分别达243.98、314.95、228.53万人，比上年末净增28.3、40.8、28.73万人。全市新增廉租住房保障4188户，其中市区3188户。市区经济适用住房覆盖面扩大到上年度人均可支配收入80%以下的住房困难家庭，公开销售经济适用房7742套，建筑面积50.2万平方米。市区最低月工资标准为1100元，失业保险金最低标准为880元/月，分别比上年提高140元和112元。

社会福利

年末全市拥有各类福利院、敬老院216所（不含社会办农村敬老院），比上年增加8所，床位23215张，收养人员12437人，分别增长3.5%和6.0%。全市城镇享受最低生活保障人数14964人，农村享受最低生活保障人员73609人。农村五保户和城镇“三无”人员集中供养率分别为95.9%和99.6%。开展第十次“春风行动”，共募集社会帮扶资金4493.18万元。

三、城市建设、环境保护和安全生产

城市基础设施建设

2010年，地铁一期24个车站完成主体结构施工，盾构区间工程已有33段隧道安全贯通，累计掘进58.5公里。沪杭高铁开通，杭甬、宁杭、杭长高铁和东站枢纽工程进展顺利。市区钱江铁路新桥主桥合龙。秋石快速路一期、留石快速路二期等快速路建成通车，半山隧道完成主体结构，九堡大桥成功合龙，庆春路过江隧道建成通车。完成144条背街小巷、305个庭院1335幢房屋庭院改善项目，实现了路平、水畅、灯明、环境整洁舒适。全年完成基础设施投资645.22亿元，比上年增长7.2%。

公用事业

全年杭州电网建设投入35亿元。新开工110千伏及以上项目30项，投产43项，变电容量为320万千伏安，线路154公里。至2010年底，杭州电网拥有110千伏以上变电所215座，变电容量4159万千伏安。全年用电量达到521.93亿千瓦时，比上年增长13.5%，其中城乡居民生活用电63.5亿千瓦时，增长12.4%。市区自来水日供水能力达到320万立方米。年末市区居民家庭天然气用户62.85万户，比上年末增长21.2%；城区新辟公交线路15条，更新公交车508辆，公交空调车比例达95%。主城区与五县（市）实现了公交一体化。至年末，市区免费单车布点2419个，投放自行车由上年末的5万辆增加至6.06万辆。

环境保护

全市化学需氧量和二氧化硫排放量较上年分别减少4.43%和6.10%；工业废气二氧化硫排放达标率、工业废水排放达标率分别达到99.2%和96.9%。全市城市污水集中处理率由上年的89.3%提高到93.3%；主要水系监测断面水质三类以上比例由上年的60.7%提高为75.0%。市区空气质量达到二级和好于二级的天数达到314天。至年末，市区人均公园绿地面积15.12平方米，建成区绿化覆盖率为40.0%。

安全生产

全市发生四大类事故次数、死亡人数、受伤人数和直接经济损失分别比上年下降5.7%、5.1%、2.7%和4.0%。亿元GDP安全生产事故死亡人数为0.15人，比上年下降15.3%。全市流通领域食品快速检测合格率为99.1%。

四、农　　业

2010年，全市完成农林牧渔业总产值316.34亿元，比上年增长9.2%，“十一五”时期年均增长7.6%。其中，农业产值169.88亿元，林业产值32.93亿元，牧业产值70.56亿元，渔业产值34.90亿元，分别比上年增长9.1%、8.9%、9.8%和7.2%，“十一五”时期年均分别增长8.4%、7.2%、7.3%和5.2%。全年粮食总产量100.25万吨，比上年下降6.5%；水产品产量20.89万吨，肉类31.79万吨，禽蛋14.77万吨，水果77.71万吨，分别比上年增长3.0%、2.8%、3.2%和0.6%。

全年茶叶、花卉苗木、水产品、节粮型畜禽、蔬菜和竹业等“六大优势产业”实现产值179.58亿元，水果、干果、蚕桑、药材和蜂业等“五大特色产业”实现产值39.98亿元，分别比上年增长11.0%和7.8%，合计占农林牧渔业总产值比重由上年的68.7%提高到69.4%。

五、工业和建筑业

工业生产

2010年，全市实现工业增加值2502.09亿元，按可比价计算增长12.8%，“十一五”期间年均增长11.1%。实现规模以上工业销售产值10951.31亿元，增长24.2%，“十一五”期间年均增长15.8%。在规模以上工业中：轻工业实现销售产值4510.28亿元，增长20.3%，重工业实现销售产值6441.03亿元，增长27.0%。全年规模以上工业实现新产品产值2131.65亿元，增长36.0%，新产品产值率由上年的16.7%提高到19.2%。

工业效益

全市规模以上工业企业实现主营业务收入10843.24亿元，比上年增长20.1%；实现利税1224.48亿元，比上年增长38.7%，其中利润764.47亿元，增长49.6%。工业产品产销衔接良好，全年规模以上工业产品产销率为98.83%。

建筑业

全年实现建筑业增加值341.98亿元，比上年增长10.0%，“十一五”期间年均增长9.6%。全市有总承包和专业承包资格的建筑企业1331家，完成施工产值2568.91亿元，比上年增长25.8%；房屋建筑施工面积22650万平方米，增长16.5%；房屋建筑竣工面积8220万平方米，增长24.4%。

六、固定资产投资和房地产开发

固定资产投资

2010年，完成全社会固定资产投资2753.13亿元，其中限额以上固定资产投资2651.88亿元，分别比上年增长20.1%和20.8%。在限额以上固定资产投资中，第一产业投资4.2亿元，比上年增长33.9%；第二产业投资687.58亿元，增长12.4%；第三产业投资1960.1亿元，增长24%。“十一五”时期，全社会固定资产累计投资10170.15亿元，年均增长13.1%。

房地产业

全市完成房地产开发投资956.2亿元，比上年增长35.7%，“十一五”期间年均增长15.6%。房屋施工面积6227.05万平方米，比上年增长20.9%；竣工面积1100.18万平方米，增长31.5%。全年商品房销售面积988.34万平方米，比上年下降32.1%，其中住宅销售797.59万平方米，下降39.3%。

七、国内贸易

2010年，全市实现社会消费品零售总额2146.08亿元，比上年增长19.9%。其中城镇消费品零售额2074.24亿元，增长20%；乡村消费品零售额71.84亿元，增长17.6%。分行业看，批发零售贸易业零售额1917.12亿元，增长20.1%；住宿餐饮业零售额228.96亿元，增长18.4%。“十一五”时期，全市社会消费品零售总额年均增长17.0%。

八、对外经济

对外贸易

2010年，全市完成外贸进出口总额523.55亿美元，比上年增长29.5%。其中进口总额170.18亿美元，增长28.6%；出口总额353.37亿美元，增长30.0%。出口总额中，机电产品出口136.6亿美元，增长32.7%；高新技术产品出口44.77亿美元，增长38.9%。按贸易方式分，一般贸易出口277.97亿美元，比上年增长31.4%；加工贸易出口74.58亿美元，增长26.3%。出口国别和地区中，对欧盟出口98.16亿美元，增长27.8%；对日本出口31.47亿美元，增长26.8%；对美国出口71.41亿美元，增长23.7%。“十一五”时期，全市进出口总额累计达2231.75亿美元，其中出口1523.25亿美元，年均分别增长11.9%和12.3%。

对外合作

至2010年末，全市累计设立各类境外投资企业（机构）599个，其中非贸易企业200个。全年境外协议出资16.94亿美元，其中非贸易性投资15.13亿美元，比上年分别增长10.1倍和13.3倍。完成对外承包工程和劳务合作营业额3.57亿美元,比上年下降3.5%。离岸服务外包合同执行额15.53亿美元,比上年增长69%。

利用外资

全年批准外商直接投资545项,合同利用外资77.09亿美元,比上年增长10.7%;实际到位外资43.56亿美元,增长8.5%。全市新批总投资3000万美元以上项目147个,总投资84.32亿美元,合同外资54.15亿美元,分别占全市总额的71%和70.2%。至2010年末,共有82家世界500强企业来杭投资130个项目。

引进内资

全年共引进内资项目5847个,协议资金1490.66亿元,比上年增长15.8%;到位资金650.27亿元,比上年增长16%。

开发区建设

杭州经济技术开发区、杭州高新技术产业开发区、萧山经济技术开发区和杭州之江国家旅游度假区等4个国家级开发区全年合同引进外资25.96亿美元,实际利用外资15.84亿美元,分别占全市的33.7%和36.4%。全年实现技工贸总收入4253亿元,比上年增长29.5%;实现利税340亿元,比上年增长1.2倍。

九、交通运输、邮电和旅游

交通运输

2010年,全社会货物运输总量2.59亿吨,比上年增长15.8%;旅客运输量3.38亿人次,比上年增长12.1%。至年末,萧山国际机场已开通航线160条,其中国际航线30条,港、澳、台航线8条;全年民航旅客进出港达到1706.86万人次,比上年增长14.2%。道路建设快速发展。全年新增公路里程153千米,至年末,全市境内公路总里程达到15266千米,其中高速公路502千米。全市行政村客运班车通达率由上年的98.5%提高到99.1%。机动车辆持续增长,年末全市社会机动车拥有量达183.25万辆,其中私人汽车94.24万辆,比上年末分别增长16.1%和31.1%。

邮电通讯

全市完成邮政业务收入11.47亿元,比上年增长16.6%。邮政特快专递辐射98个国家和地区,全年完成国内特快业务1300.29万件,比上年增长11.3%;国际特快业务30.04万件,比上年下降35.1%。完成电信业务收入132.59亿元,比上年增长5.1%。年末固定电话用户为368.57万户,比上年下降5.6%,移动电话用户为1061.80万户,增长4.9%;计算机宽带用户达到217.89万户,比上年增长34.2%。

旅游业

全年接待入境旅游者275.71万人次,比上年增长19.7%;接待国内游客6304.89万人次,增长23.8%。旅游总收入达到1025.7亿元,增长27.7%,其中旅游外汇收入16.9亿美元,增长22.5%。市民出境旅游人数为70万人次,比上年增长67.9%。旅游基础设施日趋完善。至年末,全市各类旅行社达504家,比上年增长18%;星级宾馆达到236家,其中五星级酒店18家,增加2家;A级景区30个,其中5A景区2个,新增1个。“十一五”时期,全市旅游总收入年均增长17.1%。

十、金融、证券和保险

金融

2010 年末，全市金融机构本外币存款余额 17084.35 亿元，比上年末增长 19.6%；贷款余额 15078.73 亿元，比上年末增长 15%，其中个人消费贷款余额 2426.46 亿元，比上年末增长 23.3%。“十一五”期间本外币存款余额、贷款余额年均分别增长 20.4%、22.2%。

资本市场

全年新增上市公司 19 家，共募集资金 258.27 亿元。至年末，全市上市公司累计 83 家，实现上市融资 818.6 亿元。

保险

全市保费收入 202.94 亿元，比上年增长 27.1%，其中，财产险保费收入 82.11 亿元，增长 34.7%，人身险保费收入 120.83 亿元，增长 22.4%。共支付各类保险赔款 48.98 亿元，下降 1.8%，其中财产险 35.06 亿元，增长 14.1%，人身险 13.92 亿元，下降 27.3%。“十一五”期间全市保费收入年均增长 22.8%。

十一、教育和科技

教育

2010 年末，全市共有小学 408 所，在校学生 45.39 万人；初中 245 所，在校学生 23.6 万人；普通高中 72 所，在校学生 11.7 万人。学前三年幼儿入园率为 98.3%，小学入学率和初中升学率均达到 100%，初中毕业生升入各类高中比例由上年的 99.1% 提高到 99.3%，其中优质义务教育、优质高中招生比例分别由上年的 70%、78.5% 上升到 75.9% 和 81.2%。普通高等院校 37 所，在校学生 43.48 万人，其中在校研究生 3.9 万人，比上年分别增长 1.2% 和 9.3%。高等教育毛入学率由上年的 53.6% 提高到 55.7%。全市义务教育阶段接纳在读进城务工人员子女 19.25 万人。全年义务教育免收杂费、课本费、作业本费 3.69 亿元。

科技

全市研发经费支出 166.87 亿元，占 GDP 2.8%。专利申请量 29732 件，专利授权量 26483 件，分别比上年增长 14.0% 和 70.8%。全年新增高新技术企业 594 家，累计达到 3776 家；累计培育认定研发中心 637 家，其中省级 228 家；企业技术中心 501 家，其中国家级 18 家，省级 136 家。年内新增 10 个中国驰名商标，累计已达 88 个。

十二、文化、卫生和体育

文化

2010 年末，全市有各类专业艺术表演团体 21 个，公共图书馆 16 个，文化馆 13 个，博物馆、纪念馆 70 个，全国重点文物保护单位 24 处（群）。全年获国家级和省级文艺、广播影视、动漫类奖 82 项。年末全市有线电视用户 215.21 万户，其中数字电视 134.79 万户，分别比上年末增长 5.7% 和 29.1%。电视、广播综合覆盖率分别达到

99.88%和99.92%。广播电视“村村通”实现全覆盖。成功举办第六届中国国际动漫节、第十二届西湖博览会等重大文化活动。

卫生

年末,全市拥有各类医疗卫生机构2819个(其中医院151个),拥有床位4.28万张(其中医院床位3.61万张),分别增长4.9%和6.5%。有各类专业卫生技术人员6.11万人,其中执业(助理)医师2.43万人,注册护士2.34万人,分别增长8.5%、6.6%和11.4%。农村卫生服务得到改善。农村自来水普及率由上年的99.7%提高到99.9%,自来水受益人数达437.66万人。新型农村合作医疗参合率为99.3%,乡镇覆盖率达100%。全市婴儿死亡率及5岁以下儿童死亡率分别由上年的3.81‰、5.1‰下降到3.37‰、4.36‰,每十万孕产妇死亡率由上年的7.26人下降为6.8人。

体育

杭州籍运动员获第十六届亚运会9金3银1铜奖牌。成功举办“冲浪中国”嘉年华系列赛、横渡钱塘江、世界汽车飘移大赛、驻华外交官休闲赛、世界电子竞技大师赛,西湖国际马拉松赛等有影响力的大型赛事。群众体育活动深入开展。全年新增全民健身点474个,新安装器材5837件。积极发挥体育社团的作用,组织承办或协办第六届全国传统武术邀请赛、第七届杭州市老年人运动会等活动60余次。

国民经济和社会发展存在的主要困难和不足:经济增长持续平缓,城市竞争力面临周边城市的严峻挑战;自主创新能力不强,转型升级受到多方面的制约;城乡、区域发展不平衡,统筹城乡协调发展难度较大;物价持续上涨,停车难行路难尚未得到根本缓解。这些困难和问题需要采取更加有效的措施加以解决。

公报注释:

本公报中增加值为现价,增加值增长速度按可比价格计算。

Statistical Communique of National Economy and Social Development of Hangzhou, 2010

Hangzhou Municipal Bureau of Statistics
Hangzhou survey office of National Bureau of Statistics
Hangzhou Socio - Economic Investigation Bureau

February, 2011

In 2010, the city implemented the scientific concept of development earnestly, highlighted the theme of accelerating economic development transformation, carried out the "six strategies" in depth, actively promoted the "one into seven economy", made great effort to solve the "seven hard problems", promoted the steady development of economy, along with the social progress and harmony. Improved the people's livelihood constantly, the completion of the main objectives and tasks which determined by "Eleventh Five - Year Plan" was successful, laid a solid foundation for the development of "Twelfth Five - Year".

I. General Situation

Economic Aggregate

According to the preliminary statistics, the Gross Domestic Product (GDP) of Hangzhou was 594.917 billion yuan, up by 12% over the previous year at comparable price, which had maintained a double - digit growth for 20 consecutive years. Of the total, the added value of primary industry was 20.841 billion yuan, up by 2.5%; the added value of secondary industry was 284.407 billion yuan, up by 12.5%; the added value of tertiary industry was 289.669 billion yuan, up by 12.3%. The city's per capita GDP (by the resident population) was 69,828 yuan, the city's per capita GDP (by household registered population) was 86,691 yuan, up by 8.7% and 11.1% respectively, according to the average exchange rate in 2010 which published by the country, reached $10,314 and $12,804 respectively. During the "Eleventh Five - Year" period, the average annual growth rate of the city's GDP was 12.4%, the structure of the three industries was adjusted from 5.0:50.8:44.2 in 2005 to 3.5:47.8:48.7 in 2010, formed the "tertiary, secondary, primary" industrial structure which was modern service - oriented.

Figure 1: The city's GDP and its annul growth rate, 2006 - 2010

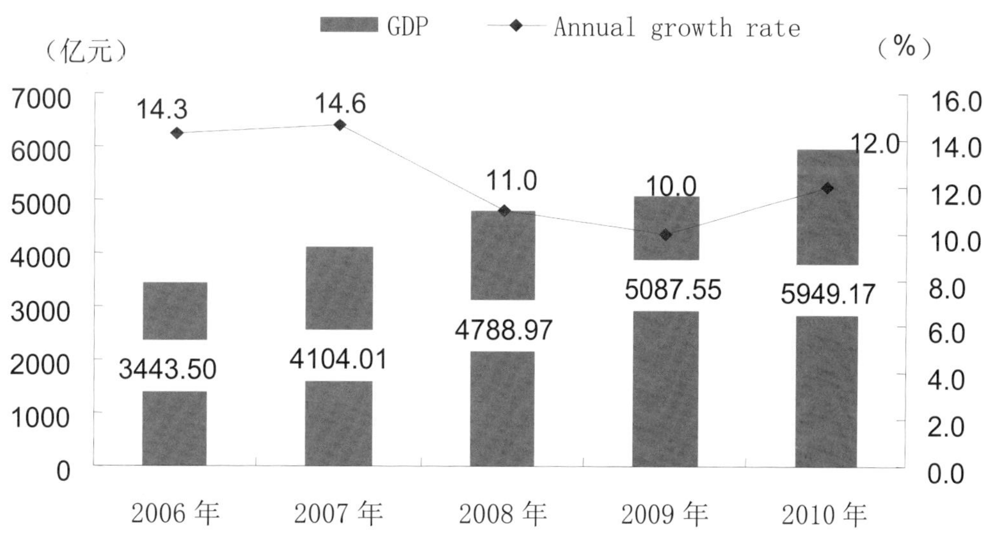

Non – State – Owned Economy

According to the preliminary statistics, the non – state – owned economy accounted for 66% of the city's GDP, increased 1.5 percentage points over the previous year. The private economy continued to be active. At the end of the year, the total private enterprises of the city reached 161,700, increased 14.7%, employed 1.4559 million workers, up by 11.2% over the previous year; The total individual businesses reached 298,800, employed total 653,100 practitioners, up by 5.0% and 15.3% respectively.

Fiscal Revenue and Expenditure

The general fiscal revenue of the city totaled 124.543 billion yuan, up by 22.2% over the previous year. Of the total, the general budgetary revenue of the local government was 67.134 billion yuan, up by 28.9%. In the tax income, the value – added tax amounted to 35.692 billion yuan, up by 4.2%; the business tax numbered 22.131 billion yuan, up by 25.4%; the enterprises' income tax was 24.808 billion yuan, up by 32.8%; the individual income tax reached 9.8 billion yuan, up by 22.1%. The fiscal expenditure of the local government was 61.658 billion yuan for the whole year, up by 23.8%. Of which, the expenditure for education, science& technology numbered 13.473 billion yuan, up by 24.3%; the expenditure for the social security and employment amounted to 6.394 billion yuan, up by 31.7%; the expenditure for health and hygiene reached 4.171 billion yuan, up by 28.9%; the expenditure for the environment protection totaled 1.386 billion yuan, up by 42.2%; The expenditure for urban and rural community services reached 9.829 billion yuan, up by 29%.

Commodity Price

In 2010, the general level of consumer prices in urban area up by 3.9% compared with the previous year. The prices of 8 major kinds of commodity and service items presented the layout of "6 Raising and 2 Dropping".

Table1 : Urban consumer price index(previous year = 100) Unit: %

Item	2010	2009
The general level of consumer prices in urban area (the previous year = 100)	103.9	98.6
1. Food	107.3	101.7
2. Tobaccos and Alcohols	101.9	100.7
3. Clothing	98.0	100.6
4. Household Appliances and Services	103.6	100.9
5. Medical, Health and Personal Articles	105.5	100.6
6. Transportation and Telecommunications	99.8	95.2
7. Recreational, Educational, Cultural Articles and Services	102.2	96.9
8. Housing	105.8	91.8

The producer prices for manufactured goods up by 4.9%; The purchasing prices for raw materials, fuels and power up by 12.1%.

Employment

In 2010, the net increase of job positions reached 260,100 and a total of 155,400 unemployed people were re – employed,

69,700 persons took the re - employment training. The year - end registered urban unemployment rate dropped from 2.99% of the previous year to 2.19%.

II. Population, Living Conditions and Social Security

Population

By the end of 2010, the total number of permanent residents in Hangzhou reached 8.7054 million, gain an increase of 371,400 person over the end of the previous year. Of the total, the household registered population reached 6.8912 million, gain an increase of 57,400 person over the previous year. In the household registered population, the agriculture population amounted to 3.2388 million and the non - agriculture population reached 3.6524 million. The data from the public security department show that the birth rate was 10.14 per mill and the natural growth rate was 3.41 per mill.

Living Conditions

According to the sampling survey, the disposable income per capita for urban residents was 30,035 yuan, up by 11.8% over the previous year, after deducting the price factors, the actual increase was 7.6%. In which: the wage income per capita was 21,075 yuan, up by 12.3%, the property income per capita was 2,189 yuan, the operating income per capita was 1,651 yuan, up by 2.0% and 3.4% respectively. The transferred income per capita was 8,896 yuan, up by 13.7%; The living expense per capita for urban residents was 20,219 yuan, up by 8.7%. The net income per capita for rural residents in Hangzhou was 13,186 yuan, up by 11.5% over the previous year, after deducting the price factors, the actual increase was 7.3%, the living expense per capita for rural residents was 10,267 yuan, up by 13.3%. During the "Eleventh Five - Year" period, the average annual growth rates of disposable income per capita for urban residents and rural residents were 12.6% and 11.5% respectively.

The housing construction area per capita for urban residents was 30.86 square meters, for every 100 urban households, there were 23 family cars, 214 sets of air conditioners, 193 mobile phones, 99 home computers, 79 microwave ovens, and 99 water heaters for shower. The living space per capita for rural residents was 71.22 square meters. For every 100 rural households, there were 16 family cars, 111 sets of air conditioners, 213 mobile phones, 44 home computers, 29 microwave ovens, 84 water heaters for shower, 85 washing machines, and 98 refrigerators.

At the end of the year, the balance of savings deposits of urban and rural residents reached 499.097 billion yuan, up by 16.4% over the previous year.

Social Security

By the end of 2010, a total of 4.9027 million people participated in the pension programs, in which 523,900 urban and rural residents who over 60 years old got direct access to the basic pension without payment; 7.5356 million people participated in the basic medical insurance, increased 0.3846 million; a total of 2.4398 million people participated in the unemployment insurance programs, a total of 3.1495 million people participated in the work accident insurance programs, a total of 2.2853 million people participated in the birth insurance programs, increased 0.283 million, 0.408 million, 0.2873 million persons compares with the previous year respectively. Increased 4,188 new households of low - cost housing security, of which 3,188 households in the urban. The coverage of affordable housing extended to the families whose disposable income per capita lower than 80% of the number in urban in last year, open sale 7,742 affordable housing units, the construction area reached 502,000 square meters. The minimum monthly wage in urban was 1,100 yuan, the minimum unemployment insurance was 880 yuan/month, increased 140 yuan and 112 yuan compared to last year respectively.

Social Welfare

By the end of the year, there were 216 welfare institutions and old people's institutions of various kinds, increased 8 institutions compared to last year, providing 23,215 beds and accommodating for 12,437 inmates, up by 3.5% and 6.0% over the previous year respectively. A total of 14,964 urban residents and a total of 73,609 peasants benefited from the minimum living relief system. The centralized support rate for 5 kinds of rural perfected households and 3 kinds of urban non – working – ability residents reached 95.9% and 99.6% respectively. Carried out the tenth "Spring Action", a total of 44.9318 million yuan social funds raised.

III. Urban Construction, Environment Protection and Work Safety

Urban Infrastructure Construction

In 2010, 24 stations of Metro Phase I completed the main structure construction, in the shield zone project, 33 sections of the tunnel has been through safely, total tunneling 58.5 km. Shanghai – Hangzhou high – speed railway was opened, Hangzhou – Ningbo, Nanjing – Hangzhou, Hangzhou – Changsha high – speed railway and east station hub project were in progress smoothly. The main bridge of Qianjiang railway new bridge had been closured. The Qiushi road phase I, Liushi road phase II were opened to traffic, the main structure of Mid – tunnel was completed, the Jiubao bridge was closured successfully, the cross – river tunnel of Qingchun road was opened to traffic. Completed the improvement projects of 144 streets and lanes, 305 courtyards and 1,335 buildings, achieved the aim of clean and comfortable environment which the road was flat, the water was smooth and the lights were bright. Completed 64.522 billion yuan on infrastructure investment in the whole year, up by 7.2% over the previous year.

Public Utilities

In 2010, a total of 3.5 billion yuan was invested on the construction of power grids. 30 new construction projects which over 110 kV were went into operation, 43 projects put into production, the power transmission capacity was 320 KVA, and the electrical wiring was 154 km. By the end of 2010, there were 215 substations which over 110 kv in Hangzhou, the power transmission capacity reached 41.59 million KVA. The electricity consumption in the whole year reached 52.193 billion kwh, up by 13.5% over the previous year, of which the consumption of residents in urban and rural was 6.35 billion kwh, up by 12.4% over the previous year. The capacity of daily water supply in urban reached 3.2 million cubic meters. By the end of the year, the number of households used pipeline coal – gas reached 628,500, up by 21.2% compared with the end of the previous year. 15 new bus routes were opened in urban area, 855 buses were updated and the proportion of air – conditioned car in urban district public transport reached 95%. The main districts of the city and the five counties (cities) to achieve the integration of the public transportation. By the end of the year, 2,419 free bicycle service networks were launched, the number of delivered public bicycles were increased from 50,000 of the end of last year to 60,600 in 2010.

Environment protection

In 2010, the amount of the total emission of industrial chemical oxygen demand (COD) and that of the sulfur dioxide discharge was dropped 4.43% and 6.10% compared with the previous year respectively. 99.2% of the sulfur dioxide discharge in the industrial emissions and 96.9% of the industrial wastewater comprehensive discharge reached the standard respectively. The centralized disposal rate of city sewage rose from 89.3% of the previous year to 93.3%; The proportion of supervised water quality sections which above third level was rose from 60.7% of the previous year to 75.0%. The number of days which air quality in the urban area reached II – level or above II – level were 314. By the end of the year, the green land area of urban gardens and parks per capita in the urban area reached 15.12 square meters. The green coverage rate of built – up area was 40.0%.

Production safety

In 2010, the number of accidents, the death toll, the injuring toll and the direct economical loss of accidents decreased

5.7%, 5.1%, 2.7% and 4.0% compared with the previous year respectively. The death toll in production safety accidents per 0.1 billion yuan GDP was 0.15, down by 15.3% over the previous year. The passed rate of food rapid detection in city's circulation area was 99.1%.

IV. Agriculture

In 2010, the total output value of farming, forestry, animal husbandry and fishery achieved 31.634 billion yuan, up by 9.2% over the previous year, the average annual growth rate in "eleventh five - year" period was 7.6%. Of the total, the output value of farming was 16.988 billion yuan, the output value of forestry was 3.293 billion yuan, the output value of animal husbandry was 7.056 billion yuan, the output value of fishery was 3.49 billion yuan, up by 9.1%, 8.9%, 9.8% and 7.2% over the previous year respectively, the average annual growth rate in "eleventh five - year" period was 8.4%, 7.2%, 7.3% and 5.2% respectively. The total output of grain in 2010 was 1.0025 million tons, down by 6.5% over the previous year; the output of aquatic products was 0.2089 million tons, that of meat was 0.3179 million tons, that of poultry and eggs was 0.1477 million tons, that of fruit was 0.7771 million tons, up by 3.0%, 2.8%, 3.2% and 0.6% over the previous year respectively.

The "6 Advantageous Industries" of tea, seedling plants, aquatic products, grains - saving livestock & poultry, vegetables and bamboos achieved an output value of 17.958 billion yuan, up by 11.0% over the previous year. The "5 Featured Industries" of fresh fruits, dried fruits, silkworm cocoons&mulberry, medicinal materials and honey achieved an output value of 3.998 billion yuan, up by 7.8%. The proportion of the output value of both "6 Advantageous Industries" and "5 Featured Industries" which accounted in the total agricultural output value was rose from 68.7% of last year to 69.4% this year.

V. Industry and Construction

Industry Production

In 2010, the total Industrial added value was 250.209 billion yuan, up by 12.8% over the previous year at comparable price, the average annual growth rate in "eleventh five - year" period was 11.1%. The total sales value of the industrial enterprises above designated size reached 1,095.131 billion yuan, up by 24.2%, the average annual growth rate in "eleventh five - year" period was 15.8%. In the industrial enterprises which above designated size, the sales value of light industry numbered 451.028 billion yuan, up by 20.3% and that of heavy industry amounted to 644.103 billion yuan, up by 27.0%. The output value of new products of the industrial enterprises above designated size achieved 213.165 billion yuan in the whole year, up by 36.0%, the proportion of output value of new products which accounted in the total output value of the industrial enterprises above designated size was rose from 16.7% of the previous year to 19.2% of this year.

Industrial efficiency

The sales income of the industrial enterprises above designated size achieved 1,084.324 billion yuan, up by 20.1% over the previous year; the amount of their profits & taxes were 122.448 billion yuan, up by 38.7% over the previous year, of which the amount of profits reached 76.447 billion yuan, up by 49.6% over the previous year. The production and marketing situation was good and the sales rate of industrial enterprises above designated size reached 98.83%.

construction industry

The total value - added of the construction industry achieved 34.198 billion yuan in the whole year, up by 10.0% over the previous year, the average annual growth rate in the" eleventh five - year" period was 9.6%. The number of construction enterprises with the qualification of general contract and special contract was 1,331 and the construction value amounted to 256.891 billion yuan in the whole year, up by 25.8% ; The floor space under construction was 226.50 million square meters, up by 16.5% and the completed floor space was 82.20 million square meters, up by 24.4%.

VI. Investment in Fixed Assets and Investment in Real Estate

Investment in Fixed Assets

In 2010, the completed investment in fixed assets was 275.313 billion yuan and of which, the super – scale investment in fixed assets was 265.188 billion yuan, increased 20.1% and 20.8% over the previous year respectively. According to the direction of the super – scale investment in fixed assets, the investment in the primary industry was 0.42 billion yuan, up by 33.9%. The investment in the secondary industry was 68.758 billion yuan, up by 12.4%. The investment in the tertiary industry was 196.01 billion yuan, up by 24.0%. During the "eleventh five – year" period, the total investment in fixed assets was 1.017015 trillion yuan, the average annual growth rate was 13.1%.

Investment in Real Estate

In 2010, the development investment of real estate in the whole year totaled 95.62 billion yuan, up by 35.7% over the previous year, the average annual growth rate in the "eleventh five – year" period was 15.6%. The total floor space of the commercial buildings under construction reached 62.2705 million square meters, up by 20.9% and that of completed commercial buildings amounted to 11.0018 million square meters, up by 31.5%. In the whole year, the total area of commercial housing sales was 9.8834 million square meters, down by 32.1% over the previous year, in which the area of residential housing sales was 7.9759 million square meters, down by 39.3%.

VII. Domestic Trade

In 2010, the total retail sales of the consumer goods in the whole city achieved 214.608 billion yuan, up by 19.9% over the previous year. Of the total, that of the urban area was 207.424 billion yuan, up by 20.0% and that of the rural area reached 7.184 billion yuan, up by 17.6%. In terms of the different sectors, the retail sales value of whole sale and retail sector was 191.712 billion yuan, up by 20.1% ; that of the accommodation and catering industry retail sales was 22.896 billion yuan, up by 18.4%. During the "eleventh five – year" period, the average annual growth rate of the total retail sales of the consumer goods in the whole city was 17.0%.

VIII. Foreign Economy

International Trade

In 2010, the value of import and export totaled 52.355 billion US dollars, up by 29.5% over the previous year. Of the total, the total value of import reached 17.018 billion US dollars, up by 28.6% and that of export amounted to 35.337 billion US dollars, up by 30.0%. In the total exports, the export of electromechanical products was $13.66 billion, up by 32.7% over the previous year; the export of high – tech products was $4.477 billion, up by 38.9%. In terms of trading type, the total value of general trading stood at $27.797 billion, up by 31.4% and that of processing trading numbered $7.458 billion, up by 26.3%. In terms of exporting countries, the export value to EU was $9.816 billion, up by 27.8% , that to USA was $7.141 billion, up by 23.7% and that to Japan was $3.147 billion, up by 26.8%. In the "Eleventh Five – Year" period, the city's import and export volume totaled $223.175 billion, of which the exports was $152.325 billion, the average annual growth rate was 11.9% and 12.3% respectively.

International Cooperation

By the end of 2010, the number of establishment enterprises (or institutions) by foreign investment accumulated to 599,

Of which the number of non – trading enterprises reached 200. The contractual value of the foreign investment reached 1.694 billion US dollars and of which the value of non – trading investment was 1.513 billion US dollars, increased 10.1 times and 13.3 times over the previous year respectively. The turnover of foreign contracted projects and labor cooperation reached $357 million, down by 3.5% over the previous year. The delivery of offshore outsourcing contract reached $1.553 billion, up by 69% over the previous year.

Utilization of Foreign Capital

There were 545 new foreign direct – funded projects signed in year 2010. The contractual value of foreign investment totaled 7.709 billion US dollars, up by 10.7% over the previous year and the foreign investment actually utilized reached 4.356 billion US dollars, up by 8.5%. The number of new approved projects which the total investment of each over $30 million amounted to 147, the total investment reached $8.432 billion, the contracted foreign capital was 5.415 billion U.S. dollars, accounted for 71% and 70.2% of the whole city's foreign investment. By the end of 2010, there were 130 projects built in Hangzhou funded by 82 companies of the World Top 500 Companies.

Utilization of Domestic Capital

The number of domestic investment projects was 5,847 throughout the year, the contractual value of the domestic investment was 149.066 billion yuan, up by 15.8% and the actually utilized investment was 65.027 billion yuan, up by 16.0%.

Development Zone Construction

In 2010, the contractual value of the foreign investment in 4 state – level development zones (such as Hangzhou Economic and Technological Development Zone, Hangzhou High – Tech Development Zone, Xiaoshan Economic & Technological Development Zone and Hangzhou Zhijiang National Holiday Resort Zone) reached 2.596 billion US dollars and the actually utilized investment was 1.584 billion US dollars, accounted for 33.7% and 36.4% of the whole city respectively. The total revenue of technology, industry and trade from the 4 development zones achieved 425.3 billion yuan throughout the year, up by 29.5% over the previous year, the taxes and profits achieved 34 billion yuan, up by 1.2 times over the previous year.

IX. Transportation, Post & Telecommunications and Tourism

Transportation

In 2010, the annual transported cargo totaled 259 million tons, up by 15.8% over the previous year. The volume of passenger transportation in the whole year reached 338 million person – trips, up by 12.1% over the previous year. By the end of the year, there were 160 flight routes built in the Xiaoshan International Airport, including 30 international routes and 8 routes of Hongkong, Macau and Taiwan. The volume of passenger transportation handled by civil aviation amounted to 17.0686 million person – trips, up by 14.2%. The construction of roads sped up. The increased length of roads totaled 153 kilometers. By the end of 2010, the total length of roads within Hangzhou reached 15,266 kilometers, including 502 kilometers expressway. The accessible rate of passenger buses to administrative villagers in the whole city rose from 98.5% of the previous year to 99.1%. The motor vehicles of the city continued to increase drastically. The year – end amount of motor vehicles reached 1.8325 million and of which the private cars were 942,400, up by 16.1% and 31.1% over the previous year respectively.

Post & Telecommunications

The volume of post totaled 1.147 billion yuan, up by 16.6% over the previous year. The radiant network of EMS reached

98 countries and regions. During the whole year, 13.0029 million items of domestic EMS were completed and 300,400 items of international EMS were delivered, up by 11.3% and down by 35.1% over the previous year respectively. The revenue of telecommunications totaled 13.259 billion yuan, up by 5.1%. By the end of 2010, local telephone users numbered 3.6857 million and there were 10.618million mobile phone users, down by 5.6% and up by 4.9% over the previous year respectively. The registered users in international internet amounted to 2.1789 million, up by 34.2%.

Tourism

In 2010, the number of oversea visitors to Hangzhou totaled 2.7571 million person – trips, up by 19.7% over the previous year and the domestic tourists to Hangzhou reached 63.0489 million person – trips, up by 23.8%. The income from tourism totaled 102.57 billion yuan, up by 27.7%. Of which the tourism foreign exchange earnings was 1.69 billion US dollars, up by 22.5%. The number of Hangzhou visitors went abroad was 700,000 person – trips, up by 67.9%. The tourist infrastructure facilities had been further perfected. By the end of the year, there were 504 travel agencies of various kinds in the city, up by 18.0%; The number of star – level hotels reached 236, including 185 – star hotels, increased 25 – star hotels compare to last year; There were 30 sceneries above A – level in urban and of which, 2 scenery were AAAAA – level, increased 1 compare to last year. During the "Eleventh Five – Year" period, the city's average annual growth rate of total tourism income was 17.1%.

X. Banking, Securities and Insurance

Banking

By the end of 2010, the saving deposits of RMB and foreign exchange from all financial institutions in Hangzhou amounted to 1,708.435 billion yuan, up by 19.6% compared with the end of the previous year and loans of RMB and foreign exchange from all financial institutions stood at 1,507.873 billion yuan, up by 15.0%. Of which, the loans for individual consumption reached 242.646 billion yuan, up by 23.3%. During the "Eleventh Five – Year" period, the average annual growth rates of the saving deposits of RMB and foreign exchange and loans of RMB and foreign exchange were 20.4% and 22.2% respectively.

Capital Marketing

In 2010, the city increased 19 listed companies, raising a total of 25.827 billion yuan fund. By the end of the year, the number of listed companies in Hangzhou accumulated to 83 and money raised through stock markets totaled 81.86 billion yuan.

Insurance

In 2010, the premiums of insurance companies in the city gained 20.294 billion yuan, up by 27.1% over the previous year. Of the total, the property insurance premiums were 8.211 billion yuan, up by 34.7% and the life insurance premiums were 12.083 billion yuan, up by 22.4%. The insurance companies paid an indemnity worth of 4.898 billion yuan, down by 1.8%. Of which, the indemnity for the property insurance was 3.506 billion yuan, up by 14.1%, and that for the life insurance was 1.392 billion yuan, down by 27.3%. During the "Eleventh Five – Year" period, the average annual growth rate of the premiums of insurance companies in the city was 22.8%.

XI. Education, Science and Technology

Education

By the end of the year 2010, the number of elementary schools totaled 408 in the city with 453,900 students, 245 junior middle schools with 236,000 students as well as 72 senior secondary schools with 117,000 students. The enrollment rate of the kindergartens for the children who 3 years younger than the school age reached 98.3%, the enrollment rates of primary school and junior high school all reached 100% , the students from junior middle schools enrolled into senior secondary schools of various sorts rose from 99. 1% of the previous year to 99. 3% and of which, the enrollment proportion of excellent senior secondary schools rose from 78. 5% of the previous year to 81. 2% , the enrollment proportion of quality compulsory education rose from 70% of the previous year to 75. 9% . The number of general colleges and universities was 37, a total of 434,800 students were studying in the universities(or colleges) , of which 39,000 were graduate students, up by 1. 2% and 9. 3% over the previous year respectively. The gross enrollment rate of general colleges and universities rose from 53. 6% of the previous year to 55. 7% . In the whole city, 192,500 children of non – local workers were admitted into the compulsory education. The exempted fee of incidental expenses, textbook expenses and homework – book expenses by the compulsory education stood at 369 million yuan.

Science and Technology

In 2010, the R&D expenditure was 16. 687 billion yuan, accounted for 2. 8% of GDP. A total of 29,732 patent applications were submitted and 26,483 patents were authorized, up by 14. 0% and 70. 8% over the previous year respectively. New added 594 high – tech enterprises throughout the year, accumulated to 3,776; The authorized R&D centers added up to 637, including 228 provincial – level centers; The number of enterprise technology centers reached 501, including 18 state – level and 136 provincial – level. New added 10 well – known trademarks in China throughout the year, and reached a total of 88.

XII. Culture, Public Health and Sports

Culture

By the end of the year 2010, there were 21 performing art ensembles, 16 public libraries, 13 cultural stations, 70 museums & memorial halls and 24 state – level protection units of key cultural relics. Hangzhou won 82 awards in arts, radio & television and Cartoon of provincial – level or state – level in the whole year. By the end of the year, the number of cable TV subscribers reached 2. 1521 million households and of which the number of using digital television was 1. 3479 million households, up by 5. 7% and 29. 1% over the previous year respectively. The coverage rate of TV and that of radio reached 99. 88% and 99. 92% respectively. The coverage rate of the rural broadcasting and television project of "Extending Radio and TV Coverage to Every Village" reached 100% . Successfully hosted the Sixth China International Cartoon and Animation Festival, the Twelfth West Lake Expo and other major cultural events.

Public Health

By the end of 2010, there were altogether 2,819 medical treatment institutions of various kinds (including 151 hospitals) and a total of 42,800 beds (including 36,100 hospital beds), up by 4. 9% and 6. 5% respectively. There were 61,100 health workers in the city, including 24,300 licensed doctors and 23,400 registered nurses, up by 8. 5% , 6. 6% and 11. 4% respectively. The condition of health care in rural area was improved. The popularization rate of tap water in the rural area rose from 99. 7% of the previous year to 99. 9% , supplying 4. 3766 million benefited people. The participating rate of new – type rural medical cooperative service was 99. 3% and the coverage rate in township reached 100% . The mortality rate of newborns and that of children under 5 years old dropped from 3. 81‰ and 5. 1‰ of the previous year to 3. 37‰ and 4. 36‰. The death toll per 100,000 pregnant women dropped from 7. 26 persons of the previous year to 6. 8 persons.

Sports

Hangzhou citizenship athletes won 9 gold, 3 silver and 1 bronze medals in the Sixteenth Asian Games. Successfully hosted the "Surf China" Carnival series, crossed the Qiantang River, the world's car drift competition, casual games for foreign diplomats, the World e – Sports Masters and West Lake International Marathon and other influential large – scale events. Carried out the mass sports in depth. New added 474 fitness points and newly installed 5,837 equipments in the whole year. Actively play the role of sports associations, organized or co – hosted the Sixth National Traditional Wushu Tournament, the Seventh Hangzhou aged people games and other activities more than 60 times.

The main difficulties of national economy and social development: the economic growth continued to moderate, facing the harsh urban competitiveness challenges from the surrounding cities; The ability of independent innovation was weak, the transformation and upgrading was subjected to many constraints; The regional development was uneven, the coordination of urban and rural developmen was difficult; The commodity prices continued to rise, the parking problem and the traffic jams have not been fundamentally alleviated. We need to take more effective measures to solve these difficulties and problems.

Notes:

Gross domestic product (GDP) and value – added as quoted in this Communique are calculated at current prices, whereas their growth rates are at comparable prices.

第一篇
CHAPTER-1

综　合

General Survey

综　　合
General Survey

主要统计指标
Major Statistical Indicators

全市生产总值	Gross Domestic Product	5949.17	亿元	(100 million yuan)
为上年	As Compared with the Preceding Year	112.0	%	(%)
第一产业	Primary Industry	208.41	亿元	(100 million yuan)
为上年	As Compared with the Preceding Year	102.5	%	(%)
第二产业	Secondary Industry	2844.07	亿元	(100 million yuan)
为上年	As Compared with the Preceding Year	112.5	%	(%)
# 工业	Industry	2502.09	亿元	(100 million yuan)
为上年	As Compared with the Preceding Year	112.8	%	(%)
第三产业	Tertiary Industry	2896.69	亿元	(100 million yuan)
为上年	As Compared with the Preceding Year	112.3	%	(%)
全市户籍人均生产总值	Per Capita GDP	86691	元	(yuan)
为上年	As Compared with the Preceding Year	111.1	%	(%)
生产总值构成	Composition of Gross Domestic Product	100	%	(%)
第一产业	Primary Industry	3.5	%	(%)
第二产业	Secondary Industry	47.8	%	(%)
# 工业	Industry	42.1	%	(%)
第三产业	Tertiary Industry	48.7	%	(%)

1－01 行政区划(2010年末)
Administrative Division(End of 2010)

单位:个 (unit)

地 区	Region	乡镇 Towns and Townships	#镇 Towns	街道 Subdistrict Offices	村、居委会 Villages and Neighborhood Committees	#村 Villages
全 市	**Whole Municipality**	**128**	**97**	**73**	**3024**	**2081**
市 区	Urban District	38	37	59	1501	678
上城区	Shangcheng	–	–	6	54	–
下城区	Xiacheng	–	–	8	72	–
江干区	Jianggan	4	4	6	151	6
拱墅区	Gongshu	–	–	10	92	–
西湖区	Xihu	2	2	10	196	58
高新(滨江)区	Hi－Tech(Binjiang)	–	–	3	43	15
萧山区	Xiaoshan	17	17	11	569	411
余杭区	Yuhang	15	14	5	324	188
桐庐县	Tonglu	11	7	3	202	183
淳安县	Chun'an	23	11	–	436	425
建德市	Jiande	13	12	3	271	232
富阳市	Fuyang	21	15	4	302	276
临安市	Lin'an	22	15	4	312	287

1－02　土地面积和人口密度(2010 年末)
Land Area and Population Density(End of 2010)

地　区	Region	土地面积（平方公里）Land Area (sq. km)	年末总人口（万人）Population (10000 persons)	人口密度（人/平方公里）Population Density (person/sq. km)
全　市	**Whole Municipality**	**16596**	**689.12**	**415**
市　区	Urban District	3068	434.82	1417
上城区	Shangcheng	18	32.68	18156
下城区	Xiacheng	31	40.1	12935
江干区	Jianggan	210	44.71	2129
拱墅区	Gongshu	88	31.1	3534
西湖区	Xihu	263	62.95	2394
高新(滨江)区	Hi－Tech(Binjiang)	73	15.2	2082
萧山区	Xiaoshan	1163	121.98	1048
余杭区	Yuhang	1222	86.1	705
桐庐县	Tonglu	1780	40.25	226
淳安县	Chun'an	4452	45.43	102
建德市	Jiande	2364	51.02	215
富阳市	Fuyang	1808	65.02	360
临安市	Lin'an	3124	52.59	168

1-03 平均每天主要社会经济活动

Selected Indicators on Average Daily Social and Economic Activities

指标 Item	1995	2000	2005	2006	2007	2008	2009	2010
全市生产总值（万元）Gross Domestic Product (10000 yuan)	20877	37878	80621	94288	112333	130991	139385	162991
工业增加值（万元）Value-Added of Industry (10000 yuan)	10023	16670	36427	42715	50752	58630	57565	68550
规模以上工业企业利税总额（万元）Total Pre-tax Profits of Industrial Enterprises above Designated Size (10000 yuan)	1728	4428	12347	15432	20010	21976	24181	33324
农林牧渔业总产值（万元）Gross Output Value of Farming, Forestry, Animal Husbandry and Fishery (10000 yuan)	2730	4182	6013	6175	6771	7500	7938	8667
全社会固定资产投资（万元）Total Investment in Fixed Assets (10000 yuan)	6365	14123	37991	40015	46138	54260	62785	75428
住宅竣工面积（平方米）Floor Space of Residential Buildings Completed (sq. m)	8751	11501	19327	15876	21153	24472	15949	21981
社会消费品零售总额（万元）Total Retail Sales of Consumer Goods (10000 yuan)	8201	14101	26724	30476	35515	42695	49450	58797
城乡居民储蓄新增额（万元）The Increased Amount of Residents´Savings Deposits (10000 yuan)	2819	1223	9767	9961	2181	23062	22195	43512
财政收入合计（万元）Total Financial Revenue (10000 yuan)	1510	3914	14268	17109	21601	24947	27930	34121

注:本表按当年价计算。2003 年起城乡居民储蓄新增额为本外币合并数据。

a) Figures in value terms in this table are calculated at current prices. The increased amount of residents´savings deposits include both RMB and foreign currencies.

1－04 国民经济

Major Indicators of

指　　标		Item	
年末常住人口	（万人）	Long－term Residents（End of 2010）	（10000 persons）
年末户籍人口	（万人）	Honsehold Registration Population（End of 2010）	（10000 persons）
#非农业人口	（万人）	Non－agriculture Population	（10000 persons）
年末从业人员数	（万人）	Total Number of Employed Persons（End of 2010）	（10000 persons）
全市生产总值	（亿元）	Gross Domestic Product	（100 million yuan）
第一产业	（亿元）	Primary Industry	（100 million yuan）
第二产业	（亿元）	Secondary Industry	（100 million yuan）
第三产业	（亿元）	Tertiary Industry	（100 million yuan）
人均生产总值（户籍）	（元）	Per Capita GDP（Household）	（yuan）
人均生产总值（常住）	（元）	Per Capita GDP（Long－term）	（yuan）
主要农产品产量		Output of Major Farm Products	
粮食	（万吨）	Grain	（10000 tons）
棉花	（吨）	Cotton	（ton）
油菜籽	（吨）	Rapeseeds	（ton）
茶叶	（吨）	Tea	（ton）
蚕茧	（吨）	Silk－worm Cocoons	（ton）
猪年末存栏	（万头）	Hogs in Stock at Year End	（10000 heads）
肉类产量	（万吨）	Output of Meat	（10000 tons）
淡水产品产量	（吨）	Freshwater Aquatic Products	（ton）
规模以上工业总产值	（亿元）	The Output Valne of Industrial Enterprises Above Designated Size	（100 million yuan）
规模以上工业企业利税总额	（亿元）	Total Pre－tax Profits of Industrial Enterprises Above Designated Size	（100 million yuan）
全社会交通运输客运量	（万人次）	Total Passenger Traffic	（10000 person－times）
全社会交通运输货运量	（万吨）	Total Freight Traffic	（10000 tons）
限额以上固定资产投资	（亿元）	Total Investment in Fixed Assets Above Designated Size	（100 million yuan）
社会消费品零售总额	（亿元）	Total Retail Sales of Consumer Goods	（100 million yuan）

注：1. 交通运输客货运输量1990年起为全社会数，1990年以前为交通系统数。

2. 境外旅游者人数1995年开始为全市数，1994年及以前系市区数。

3. 规模以上工业的计算口径，从1997年开始改为全部国有和年销售收入500万元及以上的非国有企业数，1996年以前系乡及乡以上数。

主要指标
National Economy

1980	1985	1990	1995	2000	2005	2006	2007	2008	2009	2010
		583.21		701.7	771.3	789.4	807	820.2	833.4	870.54
515.53	543.05	574.78	597.96	621.58	660.45	666.31	672.35	677.64	683.38	689.12
128.88	153.46	169	191.43	226.99	297.54	309.78	323.75	340.76	354.48	365.24
293.98	330.37	363.49	422.55	408.11	481.1	512.21	533.09	569.16	597.47	626.33
40.65	90.49	189.62	762.01	1382.56	2943.84	3443.50	4104.01	4788.97	5087.55	5949.17
8.15	15.97	30.94	69.25	103.96	148.21	154.86	163.47	179.83	190.51	208.41
25.36	52.08	96.17	410	709.32	1494.36	1728.39	2045.88	2372.58	2387.12	2844.07
7.14	22.44	62.51	282.76	569.28	1301.27	1560.25	1894.66	2236.56	2509.92	2896.69
791	1675	3310	12797	22342	44871	51908	61315	70948	74761	86691
					38542	44128	51416	58861	61533	69828
151.74	180	189.56	174.5	153.08	103.5	107.07	106.93	110.16	107.24	100.25
8007	6704	6693	8038	2112	1038	935	912	957	959	929
46621	51849	60683	61446	80436	70733	67395	69501	78058	80081	76676
18880	22742	26429	19824	24810	25551	26939	28207	29623	30204	30500
6165	7980	11085	13240	9308	16339	18384	20389	18987	17870	15637
190.16	166.1	159	147.58	172.16	165.28	152.47	151.94	170.43	178.61	192.53
9.53	11.16	14.93	19.21	25.24	30.74	29.25	26.68	29.52	30.92	31.79
14080	30400	47588	63294	91626	147800	157300	175944	182098	196520	208945
61.79	128.59	292.26	1020.03	1543.57	5441.13	6975.46	8351.4	9379.58	9390.73	11081.04
13.6	24.81	31.54	63.05	161.61	450.68	576.51	730.5	802.13	882.62	1224.48
3905	6724	8119	16620	18607	24124	25810	28026	29084	30116	33772
2070	2488	6522	10347	11459	19909	20924	22569	22550	22372	25915
4.58	14.19	22.92	156.63	376.65	1277.8	1373.45	1583.78	1882.29	2195.17	2651.88
20.54	47.81	98.17	299.35	514.68	978.43	1119.19	1308.29	1577.59	1804.93	2146.08

a) Since 1990 the data on passenger traffic and freight traffic included non - transportation system, while data for previous years only included transportation system.
b) Since 1995 the data on foreign tourists included whole municipality, while data for previous years only included urban district.
c) The data on pre - tax profits of industrial enterprises included all state - owned enterprises and non - state - owned industrial enterprises with annual sales income of over 5 million yuan, before 1997, refer to enterprises at township and above level.

1-04 续表

指 标		Item	
境外旅游者人数	(万人次)	Number of Foreign Tourists	(10000 person - times)
财政总收入	(亿元)	Total Financial Revenue	(100 million yuan)
财政支出合计(预算内)	(亿元)	Total Financial Expenditure	(100 million yuan)
金融机构存款余额	(亿元)	Deposits of Financial Institutions	(100 million yuan)
金融机构贷款余额	(亿元)	Loans of Financial Institutions	(100 million yuan)
城乡居民储蓄余额	(亿元)	Residents´Savings Deposit	(100 million yuan)
城镇以上单位在岗职工工资总额	(亿元)	Total Wages of Fully Employed Staff and Workers in Urban Units	(100 million yuan)
城镇以上单位在岗职工平均工资	(元)	Average Wage of Fully Employed Staff and Workers in Urban Units	(yuan)
市区居民消费价格指数	(以1978年为100)	Consumer Price Index in Urban District	(Year of 1978 = 100)
市区商品零售价格指数	(以1978年为100)	Retail Price Index in Urban District	(Year of 1978 = 100)
市区居民年人均可支配收入	(元)	Per Capita Annual Disposable Income in Urban District	(yuan)
农村居民年人均纯收入	(元)	Per Capita Annual Net Income in Rural Areas	(yuan)
高等学校在校学生数	(人)	Student Enrollment in Institutions of Higher Education	(person)
中等专业学校在校学生数	(人)	Student Enrollment in Secondary Specialized Schools	(person)
普通中学在校学生数	(人)	Student Enrollment in Secondary Schools	(person)
小学在校学生数	(人)	Student Enrollment in Primary Schools	(person)
卫生机构数	(个)	Number of Health Institutions	(unit)
#医院	(个)	Number of Hospitals	(unit)
卫生技术人员	(人)	Number of Medical Technical Personnel	(person)
#执业(助理)医师	(人)	Number of Certified Doctors(Include Assistant Doctors)	(person)
床位数	(张)	Number of Beds in Health Institutions	(unit)
#医院	(张)	Beds in Hospital	(unit)

注:2002年起医院数据不包括卫生院。

continued

1980	1985	1990	1995	2000	2005	2006	2007	2008	2009	2010
12.5	23.84	38.83	44.13	70.71	151.36	182.02	208.60	221.33	230.40	275.71
11.85	18.65	25.25	55.13	142.85	520.79	624.49	788.42	910.55	1019.43	1245.43
2.17	5.77	11.82	24.91	73.43	238.33	275.48	335.72	419.67	490.40	616.58
18.1	48.5	133.77	707.97	2088.47	6748.72	7855.55	9310.96	11333.35	14284.21	17084.35
17.34	58.01	162.27	567.2	1686.64	5545.3	6603.86	8430.68	10069.05	13113.30	15078.73
4.04	15.96	69.75	342.34	788.56	2191.66	2555.24	2634.83	3476.59	4286.92	4990.97
6.79	13.01	27.79	89.05	126.75	297.02	381.17	495.48	641.64	754.91	933.06
777	1266	2382	7156	14257	31069	32791	36496	40193	43947	48772
109.24	140.21	246.68	503.06	611.07	623.07	630.55	652.62	684.60	675.00	701.33
110.28	142.61	256.45	476.99	504.42	470.47	471.41	486.02	515.18	507.97	526.76
521	1026	1985	6301	9668	16601	19027	21689	24104	26864	30035
250	624	1171	3012	4894	7655	8515	9549	10692	11822	13186
23545	36996	39866	63124	122386	351918	373563	392770	409559	429774	434811
9453	16527	23564	42784	45238	20344	12540	8927	5514	4016	3999
247734	244399	199940	257071	342533	362257	359704	361191	364758	359956	352997
560244	414839	460514	513988	485679	458942	459529	456152	452143	445132	453897
1381	1582	1738	1712	1599	2196	2570	2607	2544	2687	2819
425	404	440	414	396	127	134	138	141	144	151
21110	25593	30990	34245	35487	42353	45375	49780	52379	56270	61117
8311	11503	14483	16465	16317	17833	18831	20701	21223	22753	24345
16317	19637	24121	26684	27166	33251	33972	36928	38114	40226	42828
13478	15010	18879	21360	23303	25907	27186	29987	31416	33094	33611

a) From 2002, figures of hospitals exclude health centers.

1-05 主要年份全市生产总值及发展指数(1978年=100)

Gross Domestic Product and its Indices in Main Years(Year of 1978=100)

单位:万元 (10000 yuan)

年 份 Year	全市生产总值(当年价格) Gross Domestic Product (Current Price)	第一产业 Primary Industry	第二产业 Secondary Industry	第三产业 Tertiary Industry	人均生产总值(元)(按户籍) Per Capita GDP (yuan)	全市生产总值指数(%) Indices of Gross Domestic product(%) (1978=100)	第一产业 Primary Industry	第二产业 Secondary Industry	第三产业 Tertiary Industry
1978	284046	63372	169344	51330	565	100.00	100.00	100.00	100.00
1979	335285	83852	194132	57301	659	113.33	114.23	114.00	110.01
1980	406508	81524	253545	71439	791	135.65	105.63	151.06	130.71
1981	468206	90955	287632	89619	904	154.04	108.74	172.17	162.30
1982	501854	108769	294725	98360	957	165.12	129.80	177.73	176.31
1983	558947	101106	334413	123428	1054	183.63	115.62	203.10	219.86
1984	694690	126443	405535	162712	1298	225.25	140.10	245.38	283.68
1985	904897	159684	520853	224360	1675	268.85	139.90	300.80	352.81
1986	1053589	177589	601277	274723	1917	299.88	145.01	335.28	409.85
1987	1260162	204366	718892	336904	2276	338.38	148.69	382.23	471.62
1988	1525427	256838	855305	413284	2717	363.26	145.46	419.82	497.15
1989	1662945	282746	896736	483463	2928	352.06	145.10	396.51	508.97
1990	1896216	309404	961673	625139	3310	372.37	154.40	422.20	528.01
1991	2279545	334024	1131088	814433	3952	439.77	161.12	492.38	669.52
1992	2900690	349033	1487838	1063819	4996	540.48	161.61	637.53	814.80
1993	4247094	419364	2264440	1563290	7263	703.16	171.15	878.66	1004.65
1994	5855239	575131	3143430	2136678	9924	888.09	185.01	1161.59	1225.67
1995	7620055	692510	4100008	2827537	12797	1064.82	198.15	1434.56	1445.06
1996	9066133	839985	4776225	3449923	15095	1203.25	208.85	1644.01	1621.36
1997	10363299	913611	5415017	4034671	17113	1360.88	223.05	1852.80	1861.32
1998	11348899	960558	5879589	4508752	18611	1513.30	244.02	2071.43	2060.48
1999	12252795	975821	6307510	4969464	19961	1667.66	257.44	2280.64	2287.13
2000	13825616	1039641	7093233	5692742	22342	1867.78	272.11	2565.72	2563.87
2001	15680138	1114569	7935809	6629760	25074	2095.65	292.25	2891.60	2884.40
2002	17818302	1146388	9018225	7653689	28150	2372.28	304.23	3276.18	3308.41
2003	20997744	1265890	10757812	8974042	32819	2732.87	322.48	3885.55	3725.27
2004	25431796	1322341	13182254	10927201	39293	3142.80	338.93	4534.44	4257.98
2005	29438430	1482145	14943581	13012704	44871	3551.36	350.45	5037.76	4956.29
2006	34434972	1548594	17283905	15602473	51908	4059.54	364.71	5672.80	5820.31
2007	41040117	1634719	20458811	18946588	61315	4651.74	372.78	6483.45	6761.14
2008	47889748	1798300	23725807	22365641	70948	5165.17	386.73	7062.80	7705.13
2009	50875529	1905093	23871200	25099237	74761	5680.15	398.74	7521.81	8799.61
2010	59491687	2084144	28440693	28966850	86691	6361.77	408.71	8462.04	9881.96

注:1. 2008年为经济普查正式数。

2. 2005-2007已按经济普查数调整。

a) The data of 2008 were numbers of 2008 economic cencus.

b) The data of 2005 to 2008 had been adjusted auording to 2008 economic cencus.

1－06 主要年份市区生产总值及发展指数(1978 年＝100)

Gross Domestic Product and its Indices of Urban District in Main Years(Year of 1978＝100)

单位:万元 (10000 yuan)

年 份 Year	生产总值(当年价格) Gross Domestic Product (Current Price)	第一产业 Primary Industry	第二产业 Secondary Industry	第三产业 Tertiary Industry	人均生产总值(元)(按户籍) Per Capita GDP (yuan)	生产总值指数(%) Indices of Gross Domestic product(%) (1978＝100)	第一产业 Primary Industry	第二产业 Secondary Industry	第三产业 Tertiary Industry
1978	141995	5215	106663	30117	1389	100.00	100.00	100.00	100.00
1979	167206	6527	126517	34162	1555	116.40	109.40	118.10	111.60
1980	208220	5943	159161	43116	1863	145.30	94.00	150.90	133.90
1981	229243	6165	171946	51132	2005	159.90	90.30	163.90	157.20
1982	248297	7327	183284	57686	2125	173.70	107.30	176.00	175.60
1983	282171	5938	200334	75899	2369	197.90	83.10	193.80	229.50
1984	353781	8469	244445	100867	2919	245.40	114.90	235.50	298.40
1985	448574	11233	293579	143762	3633	289.90	120.70	270.10	382.20
1986	513639	12245	324585	176809	4042	317.30	122.60	287.70	445.10
1987	605234	15408	370668	219158	4724	353.20	137.10	313.80	517.40
1988	708474	19602	425319	263553	5441	370.80	136.00	332.70	534.00
1989	772208	23869	435847	312492	5848	347.00	146.70	296.70	545.20
1990	896496	23919	470844	401733	6722	366.50	147.60	314.60	573.60
1991	1096628	25767	547949	522912	8158	426.00	151.40	356.30	691.10
1992	1413278	27611	712697	672969	10420	535.30	153.10	447.40	877.80
1993	2086571	36208	1052187	998176	15196	687.60	157.70	583.70	1117.40
1994	2788314	48257	1395127	1344931	19945	870.90	172.30	779.60	1335.30
1995	3697794	57784	1866784	1773226	25969	1041.60	183.50	945.70	1574.30
1996	4727377	110881	2356408	2260088	28552	1194.90	194.70	1103.60	1769.50
1997	5414265	130062	2630349	2653853	32227	1354.90	214.20	1230.30	2052.60
1998	5905726	134320	2786159	2985247	34620	1482.50	230.70	1337.20	2266.10
1999	6317335	145242	2915614	3256479	36394	1599.30	254.50	1431.10	2467.80
2000	7111586	145715	3278310	3687561	40127	1785.50	255.50	1596.70	2763.90
2001	12260891	582492	6026353	5652046	32607	2017.20	275.70	1805.30	3126.00
2002	14042278	605433	6901224	6535621	36640	2300.80	290.00	2038.60	3607.40
2003	16647332	665083	8343138	7639111	42675	2664.80	302.20	2448.40	4058.30
2004	20362738	664676	10368453	9329609	51241	3077.40	313.10	2873.90	4630.50
2005	23495459	732463	11582930	11180067	57934	3461.24	318.17	3141.49	5406.57
2006	27483121	755663	13254773	13472684	66731	3955.94	320.48	3493.88	6399.62
2007	32738842	773208	15546960	16418675	78541	4525.33	322.73	3948.39	7455.84
2008	38139834	830741	17926048	19383045	90400	5018.47	324.83	4266.45	8505.21
2009	40698687	874987	18120921	21702778	95342	5539.47	332.99	4563.27	9686.26
2010	47407788	941591	21452228	25013969	109708	6204.21	337.31	5124.56	10867.99

注:1. 2008 年为经济普查正式数。

2. 2005－2007 已按经济普查数调整。

3. 从 2001 年起市区数据包括萧山区和余杭区。

a) The data of 2008 were numbers of 2008 economic census.

b) The data of 2005 to 2008 had been adjusted according to 2008 economic census.

c) Data in this table include Xiaoshan and Yuhang district since 2001.

1－07 主要年份全市生产总值指数(上年＝100)

Indices of Gross Domestic Product in Main Years(Preceding Year＝100)

年 份 Year	生产总值 Gross Domestic Product	第一产业 Primary Industry	第二产业 Secondary Industry	第三产业 Tertiary Industry	人均生产总值 (按户籍) Per Capita GDP (Household registered)
1978	120.2	119.1	123.7	111.6	119.0
1979	113.3	114.2	114.0	110.0	112.1
1980	119.7	92.5	132.5	118.8	118.4
1981	113.6	102.9	114.0	124.2	112.6
1982	107.2	119.4	103.2	108.6	105.9
1983	111.2	89.1	114.3	124.7	109.9
1984	122.7	121.2	120.8	129.0	121.6
1985	119.4	99.9	122.6	124.4	118.2
1986	111.5	103.7	111.5	116.2	110.3
1987	112.8	102.5	114.0	115.1	111.3
1988	107.4	97.8	109.8	105.4	105.8
1989	96.9	99.8	94.4	102.4	95.8
1990	105.8	106.4	106.5	103.7	104.9
1991	118.1	104.4	116.6	126.8	117.3
1992	122.9	100.3	129.5	121.7	122.1
1993	130.1	105.9	137.8	123.3	129.1
1994	126.3	108.1	132.2	122.0	125.2
1995	119.9	107.1	123.5	117.9	118.8
1996	113.0	105.4	114.6	112.2	112.0
1997	113.1	106.8	112.7	114.8	112.1
1998	111.2	109.4	111.8	110.7	110.5
1999	110.2	105.5	110.1	111.0	109.4
2000	112.0	105.7	112.5	112.1	111.1
2001	112.2	107.4	112.7	112.5	111.1
2002	113.2	104.1	113.3	114.7	111.8
2003	115.2	106.0	118.6	112.6	114.0
2004	115.0	105.1	116.7	114.3	113.7
2005	113.0	103.4	111.1	116.4	111.5
2006	114.3	104.1	112.6	117.4	113.0
2007	114.6	102.2	114.3	116.2	113.6
2008	111.0	103.7	108.9	114.0	110.1
2009	110.0	103.1	106.5	114.2	109.1
2010	112.0	102.5	112.5	112.3	111.1

注:1.本表按可比价格计算。

2.2005－2008已按经济普查数调整。

a) The indices in this table are calculated at comparable prices.

b) The data of 2005 to 2008 had been adjusted according to 2008 economic census.

1-08 主要年份市区生产总值指数(上年=100)

Indices of Gross Domestic Product of Urban District in Main Years(Preceding Year=100)

年份 Year	生产总值 Gross Domestic Product	第一产业 Primary Industry	第二产业 Secondary Industry	第三产业 Tertiary Industry	人均生产总值(按户籍) Per Capita GDP (Household registered)
1978	120.1	118.8	122.3	113.6	118.0
1979	116.4	109.4	118.1	111.6	111.4
1980	124.8	85.9	127.8	120.0	119.7
1981	110.1	96.1	108.6	117.4	107.6
1982	108.6	118.8	107.4	111.7	106.3
1983	113.9	77.5	110.1	130.7	111.7
1984	124.0	138.2	121.5	130.0	121.8
1985	118.2	105.0	114.7	128.1	116.0
1986	109.4	101.6	106.5	116.7	107.4
1987	111.3	111.8	109.1	116.0	109.4
1988	105.0	99.2	106.0	103.2	103.3
1989	93.6	107.9	89.2	102.1	92.2
1990	105.6	100.6	106.0	105.2	104.6
1991	116.2	102.6	113.3	120.5	115.3
1992	125.7	101.1	125.6	127.0	124.5
1993	128.5	103.0	130.5	127.3	126.9
1994	126.6	109.3	133.6	119.5	124.4
1995	119.6	106.5	121.3	117.9	117.4
1996	114.7	106.1	116.7	112.4	105.3
1997	113.4	110.0	111.5	116.0	104.7
1998	109.4	107.7	108.7	110.4	107.8
1999	107.9	110.3	107.0	108.9	106.0
2000	111.6	100.4	111.6	112.0	109.3
2001	113.0	107.9	113.1	113.1	111.2
2002	114.1	105.2	112.9	115.4	111.9
2003	115.8	104.2	120.1	112.5	113.8
2004	115.5	103.6	117.4	114.1	113.4
2005	112.5	101.6	109.3	116.8	110.2
2006	114.3	100.7	111.2	118.4	112.5
2007	114.4	100.7	113.0	116.5	113.0
2008	110.9	100.7	108.1	114.1	109.5
2009	110.4	102.5	107.0	113.9	109.1
2010	112.0	101.3	112.3	112.2	110.7

注:1. 本表按可比价格计算。
2. 2005-2008 已按经济普查数调整。

a) The indices in this table are calculated at comparable prices.

b) The data of 2005 to 2008 had been adjusted according to 2008 economic census.

1－09 全市生产
Composition of

单位：万元

行　业	Sector	全 Whole 2010	为上年（%） As Compared with the Preceding Year（%）
全市生产总值	Gross Domestic Product	59491687	112.0
第一产业	Primary Industry	2084144	102.5
第二产业	Secondary Industry	28440693	112.5
工业	Industry	25020925	112.8
建筑业	Construction	3419768	110.0
第三产业	Tertiary Industry	28966850	112.3
交通运输、仓储及邮政业	Transportation, Storage and Post	1608078	104.8
批发和零售业	Wholesale & Retail Trade	5123311	113.0
住宿和餐饮业	Lodging and Catering	1000438	106.6
金融业	Banking and Insurance	6060266	114.1
房地产业	Real Estate	4372904	105.9
科学研究、技术服务和地质勘查业	Scientific Research, Technical Service and Geological Prospecting	1170727	119.7
居民服务和其他服务业	Service for the Residents and Other	515662	104.6
教育	Education	1836953	112.2
卫生、社会保障和社会福利业	Health Care, Sports & Social Welfare	950709	116.3
文化、体育和娱乐业	Culture, Sports and Entertainment	409204	112.1
公共管理和社会组织	Public Management and Social Organizations	2033181	109.2

注：本表绝对数按当年价格计算，为上年（%）按可比价格计算。

总值构成(2010 年)

Gross Domestic Product(2010)

(10000 yuan)

市 Municipality		其 中:市 区 Urban District			
比 重 (%) Proportion(%)		2010	为上年(%) As Compared with the Preceding Year(%)	比 重 (%) Proportion(%)	
2010	2009			2010	2009
100.0	100.0	47407788	112.0	100.0	100.0
3.5	3.8	941591	101.3	2.0	2.2
47.8	46.9	21452228	112.3	45.2	44.5
42.1	41.3	18654637	112.6	39.3	38.7
5.7	5.6	2797591	110.0	5.9	5.8
48.7	49.3	25013969	112.2	52.8	53.3
2.7	2.9	1246328	103.3	2.6	2.9
8.6	8.7	4450518	113.2	9.4	9.4
1.7	1.8	837328	106.5	1.8	1.9
10.2	10.2	5392137	114.0	11.4	11.3
7.4	7.5	3693754	103.0	7.8	8.2
2.0	1.9	1129028	119.9	2.4	2.3
0.9	1.0	397473	103.9	0.8	0.9
3.1	3.2	1486293	111.7	3.1	3.2
1.6	1.6	805540	116.0	1.7	1.7
0.7	0.7	371786	112.1	0.8	0.8
3.4	3.6	1637245	109.6	3.5	3.6

a) Absolute figures in this table are calculated at current prices, while indices are calculated at comparable price.

1－10 分县(市)生产总值(2010年)

Gross Domestic Product by Region(2010)

单位:万元 (10000 yuan)

地区	Region	生产总值总计 Gross Domestic Product	第一产业 Primary Industry	第二产业 Secondary Industry	工业 Industry	建筑业 Construction	第三产业 Tertiary Industry	人均GDP(按户籍)(元) Per Capita GDP (Household) (yuan)
全市	**Whole Municipality**	**59491687**	**2084144**	**28440693**	**25020925**	**3419768**	**28966850**	**86691**
市区	Urban District	47407788	941591	21452228	18654637	2797591	25013969	109708
萧山区	Xiaoshan	12200352	472211	7522773	6978401	544372	4205368	100427
余杭区	Yuhang	6287728	384518	3391118	3028390	362728	2512092	73567
桐庐县	Tonglu	1979313	160028	1214008	1089087	124921	605276	49287
淳安县	Chun'an	1174832	218432	498652	384657	113996	457747	25906
建德市	Jiande	1896478	207552	1071715	984949	86766	617211	37054
富阳市	Fuyang	4156687	286661	2521415	2358037	163378	1348611	64101
临安市	Lin'an	2876590	269880	1682674	1549557	133117	924036	54702

1-11 主要指标占全省比重(2010年)
Proportion of Main Indicators in Whole Province(2010)

指标 Item		全省 Zhejiang Province	杭州市 Hangzhou Municipality	杭州市占全省(%) Proportion of Hangzhou in Zhejiang(%)
年末常住人口 Long-term Residents(End of 2010)	(万人) (10000 persons)	5446.51	870.54	16.0
年末户籍人口 Household Registration Population(End of 2010)	(万人) (10000 persons)	4748	689.12	14.5
#非农业人口 Non-agriculture Population	(万人) (10000 persons)	1469	365.24	24.9
年末从业人员数 Total Number of Employed Persons	(万人) (10000 persons)	3617.40	626.33	17.3
生产总值 Gross Domestic Product	(亿元) (100 million yuan)	27226.75	5949.17	21.9
第一产业 Primary Industry	(亿元) (100 million yuan)	1360.71	208.41	15.3
第二产业 Secondary Industry	(亿元) (100 million yuan)	14121.27	2844.07	20.1
第三产业 Tertiary Industry	(亿元) (100 million yuan)	11744.77	2896.69	24.7
常住人均生产总值 Per Capita GDP of Long-term Residents	(元) (yuan)	52059	69828	-
农林牧渔业总产值 Gross Output Value of Farming, Forestry, Animal Husbandry and Fishery	(亿元) (100 million yuan)	2173.2	316.34	14.6
主要农产品产量 Output of Major Farm Products				
粮食 Grain	(万吨) (10000 tons)	770.67	100.25	13.0
棉花 Cotton	(万吨) (10000 tons)	2.94	0.1	3.4
蚕茧 Silk-worm Cocoons	(万吨) (10000 tons)	6.39	1.56	24.4
生猪年末存栏 Hogs in Stock at Year End	(万头) (10000 heads)	1248.4	192.53	15.4
猪牛羊肉产量 Output of Pork, Beef & Mutton	(万吨) (10000 tons)	134.90	31.79	23.6
淡水产品总产量 Freshwater Aquatic products	(万吨) (10000 tons)	96.7	20.89	21.6

1－11 续表1 continued 1

指 标 Item		全 省 Zhejiang Province	杭州市 Hangzhou Municipality	杭州市占全省(%) Proportion of Hangzhou in Zhejiang(%)
规模以上工业企业利税总额 Total Pre－tax Profits of Industrial Enterprises above Designed Size	(亿元) (100 million yuan)	5099.92	1224.48	24.0
主要工业产品产量 Output of Major Industrial Products				
发电量 Electricity	(亿千瓦时) (100 million kwh)	2496.2	176.22	7.1
氢氧化钠(烧碱)(折100%) Caustic Soda(100% discount)	(万吨) (10000 tons)	104.61	14.0	13.4
碳酸钠(纯碱) Soda Ash	(万吨) (10000 tons)	11.92	11.92	100.0
合成氨 Synthetic Ammonia	(万吨) (10000 tons)	49.49	8.99	18.2
水泥 Cement	(万吨) (10000 tons)	11275.3	2021.01	17.9
平板玻璃 Plate Glass	(万重量箱) (10000 weight cases)	4090.89	437.52	10.7
钢材 Steels	(万吨) (10000 tons)	2832.6	888.6	31.4
化学纤维 Chemical Fiber	(万吨) (10000 tons)	1366.1	530.75	38.9
纱 Yarn	(万吨) (10000 tons)	214.9	53.63	25.0
丝织品 Silk Products	(亿米) (100 million meters)	3.29	0.95	28.9
自行车 Bicycles	(万辆) (10000 units)	1424.88	639.61	44.9
彩色电视机 Colour TV Sets	(万台) (10000 units)	477.03	215.6	4.5
电冰箱 Household Refrigerator	(万台) (10000 units)	889.72	107.63	12.1
洗衣机 Washing Machine	(万台) (10000 units)	1765.02	328.48	18.6
全社会交通运输客运量 Total Passenger Traffic	(万人次) (10000 person－times)	228017	33772	14.8

1－11 续表2 continued 2

指 标 Item		全 省 Zhejiang Province	杭州市 Hangzhou Municipality	杭州市占全省(%) Proportion of Hangzhou in Zhejiang(%)
全社会交通运输货运量 Total Freight Traffic	(万吨) (10000 tons)	170518	25915	15.2
限额以上固定资产投资 Total Investment in Fixed Assets	(亿元) (100 million yuan)	11564.41	2651.88	22.9
社会消费品零售总额 Total Retail Sales of Consumer Goods	(亿元) (100 million yuan)	10163.2	2146.08	21.1
出口额 Total Exports	(亿美元) (100 million USD)	1804.8	353.37	19.6
实际利用外资 Foreign Capital Actually Used	(亿美元) (100 million USD)	110.02	43.56	39.6
境外旅游者人数 Number of International Tourists	(万人次) (10000 person－times)	685	275.71	40.2
财政总收入 Total Financial Revenue	(亿元) (100 million yuan)	4895.4	1245.43	25.4
地方财政预算内收入 Financial Revenue	(亿元) (100 million yuan)	2608.5	671.34	25.7
地方财政预算内支出 Financial Expenditure	(亿元) (100 million yuan)	3208.4	616.58	19.2
金融机构存款余额(本外币) Deposits of Financial Institutions	(亿元) (100 million yuan)	54478.09	17084.35	31.4
金融机构贷款余额(本外币) Loans of Financial Institutions	(亿元) (100 million yuan)	46938.54	15078.73	32.1
城乡居民储蓄存款余额 Residents´Savings Deposits	(亿元) (100 million yuan)	21093.62	4990.97	23.7
城镇单位在岗职工平均工资 Average Wage of Fully Employed Staff and Workers of Urban Units	(元) (yuan)	41505	48772	–
城镇居民人均可支配收入 Per Capita Annual Disposable Income in Urban District	(元) (yuan)	27359	30035	–
农民人均纯收入 Per Capita Annual Net Income in Rural Areas	(元) (yuan)	11303	13186	–
高等学校在校学生数 Number of Institutions of Higher Education	(万人) (10000 persons)	93.29	43.48	46.6
中等专业学校在校学生数 Number of Secondary Specialized Schools	(万人) (10000 persons)	10.62	0.40	3.8
普通中学在校学生数 Number of Secondary Schools	(万人) (10000 persons)	255.15	35.3	13.8
小学在校学生数 Number of Primary Schools	(万人) (10000 persons)	333.33	45.39	13.6

1-12 国民经济主要指标人均水平(按户籍)
Major Per Capita Indicators of National Economy(Household registered)

指标 Item	1995	2000	2005	2006	2007	2008	2009	2010
全市生产总值 (元) Gross Domestic Product (yuan)	12797	22342	44871	51908	61315	70948	74761	86691
规模以上工业总产值 (元) Gross Industrial Output Value above Designatted Size (yuan)	17131	24943	82936	105150	124773	138958	137995	161310
农林牧渔业总产值 (元) Gross Output Value of Farming,Forestry,Animal Husbandry and Fishery (yuan)	1673	2467	3345	3398	3693	4056	4258	4610
社会消费品零售总额 (元) Total Retail Sales of Consumer Goods (yuan)	5027	8317	14869	16768	19368	23087	26523	31273
财政总收入 (元) Financial Revenue (yuan)	926	2308	7938	9414	11780	13490	14980	18148
#地方财政预算内收入 (元) Financial Revenue of Local Government (yuan)	387	1118	3818	4543	5851	6746	7653	9783
地方财政预算内支出 (元) Financial Expenditure (yuan)	418	1187	3633	4119	5016	6217	7026	8985
城镇居民可支配收入 (元) Annual Disposable Income in Urban District (yuan)	6301	9668	16601	19027	21689	24104	26864	30035
城镇居民消费性支出 (元) Annual Living Expenditure in Urban District (yuan)	5559	7790	13438	14472	14896	16719	18595	20219
农民纯收入 (元) Annual Net Income in Rural Area (yuan)	3012	4894	7655	8515	9546	10692	11822	13186
农民消费性支出 (元) Annual Living Expenditure in Rural Area (yuan)	2373	3393	6004	6674	7568	8446	9065	10267

1－13 企业家信心指数(2010 年)
Expectation Indices of Entrepreneurs(2010)

单位:点 (point)

指 标	Item	第一季度 1st. Quarter	第二季度 2nd. Quarter	第三季度 3rd. Quarter	第四季度 4th. Quarter
全市	**Total**	**134.24**	**130.48**	**131.75**	**131.08**
按行业分	**Grouped by Sector**				
工业	Industry	135.35	136.18	131.68	132.92
建筑业	Construction	148.88	127.16	138.16	134.72
交通运输、仓储及邮电通信业	Transportation, Storage and Post	100.00	108.00	104.00	100.00
批发零售贸易业	Wholesale and Retail Trade	140.10	122.47	141.07	141.11
房地产业	Real Estate	114.85	83.56	111.96	111.70
社会服务业	Social Services	129.98	129.98	126.16	119.59
信息传输、计算机服务和软件业	Information Transmission, Computer Service and Software	149.76	168.13	151.07	144.27
住宿和餐饮业	Lodging and Catering	126.86	134.88	140.91	131.82
按经济类型分	**Grouped by Status of Registration**				
国有企业	State－owned	133.69	126.55	135.66	138.94
集体企业	Collective－owned	116.67	116.67	133.33	118.18
有限责任公司	Limited－liability Companies	127.63	128.66	125.43	120.51
股份有限公司	Share Holding Ltd. Companies	151.80	137.09	152.29	159.87
港、澳、台投资企业	Enterprises With Investment from Hong Kong, Macao and Taiwan	140.00	150.00	130.00	119.60
外商投资企业	Enterprises With Foreign Investment	147.41	142.62	141.76	142.20
按企业规模分	**Grouped by Size of Enterprises**				
大型企业	Large	161.81	149.16	156.70	159.14
中型企业	Medium	124.67	130.24	131.28	126.05
小型企业	Small	117.16	114.20	116.47	116.57

1－14　企业景气指数(2010 年)
Expectation Indices of Enterprises(2010)

单位:点　　　　(point)

指　标	Item	第一季度 1st. Quarter	第二季度 2nd. Quarter	第三季度 3rd. Quarter	第四季度 4th. Quarter
全市	**Total**	**131.01**	**130.14**	**129.36**	**129.43**
按行业分	**Grouped by Sector**				
工业	Industry	131.19	129.41	127.54	127.81
建筑业	Construction	136.24	131.18	127.66	132.51
交通运输、仓储及邮电通信业	Transportation,Storage and Post	96.00	116.00	104.00	100.00
批发零售贸易业	Wholesale and Retail Trade	140.56	130.03	140.28	141.64
房地产业	Real Estate	113.82	99.30	111.96	115.40
社会服务业	Social Services	135.60	133.01	138.33	136.42
信息传输、计算机服务和软件业	Information Transmission, Computer Service and Software	155.33	175.18	161.89	165.81
住宿和餐饮业	Lodging and Catering	134.09	155.81	150.00	129.55
按经济类型分	**Grouped by Status of Registration**				
国有企业	State－owned	122.14	130.20	128.99	133.16
集体企业	Collective－owned	125.00	101.54	118.20	118.18
有限责任公司	Limited－liability Companies	126.83	131.81	127.96	118.74
股份有限公司	Share Holding Ltd. Companies	157.60	145.08	148.27	166.72
港、澳、台投资企业	Enterprises With Investment from Hong Kong,Macao and Taiwan	130.00	150.00	123.52	141.67
外商投资企业	Enterprises With Foreign Investment	137.05	132.05	141.91	129.83
按企业规模分	**Grouped by Size of Enterprises**				
大型企业	Large	159.87	144.58	154.34	161.07
中型企业	Medium	122.31	130.92	129.86	126.51
小型企业	Small	111.76	120.12	115.88	112.43

1－15　市区分月气象概况(2010年)
Monthly Meteorological Conditions in Urban District(2010)

月　份	Month	平均气温(度) Average Temperature(℃)	日照时数(小时) Sunshine Hours(hours)	降雨天数(天) Rainfall Days (day)	降水量(毫米) Precipitation(mm.)
全　年	**Annual Total**	**17.4**	**1689.3**	**157**	**1728.1**
1　月	January	5.8	98.1	9	37.1
2　月	February	7.8	96.1	15	151.2
3　月	March	10.3	118.5	15	300.4
4　月	April	14	129.7	18	127.9
5　月	May	21.6	152.5	19	65.1
6　月	June	24.2	109.6	16	163.3
7　月	July	28.8	169.9	16	256.5
8　月	August	30.6	256.5	9	164.6
9　月	September	25.8	135.3	15	212.9
10　月	October	18.3	121.9	8	158
11　月	November	13.3	124.1	8	25.5
12　月	December	8.2	177.1	9	65.6

1－16 气 象

Meteorological

指 标	Item	市 区 Urban District	#萧山区 Xiaoshan
一、气 温	**The Atmospheric Temperature**		
全年平均气温 (度)	Annual Average Temperature (℃)	17.4	17.3
极端最高气温 (度)	The Highest Temperature of the Year (℃)	39.5	40.2
出现日期 (日/月)	Date (d/m)	13/8	12/8
极端最低气温 (度)	The Lowest Temperature of the Year (℃)	－3.6	－3.5
出现日期 (日/月)	Date (d/m)	16/12	14/1
二、降 雨	**Rainfall**		
本年降雨日数 (日)	Total Rainy Days (day)	157	165
全年降雨总量 (毫米)	Annual Rainfall (millimeters)	1728.1	1672.3
最长连续降雨日数 (日)	Longest Consecutive Days of Rain (day)	11	10
最长连续降雨总量 (毫米)	Rainfall (millimeters)	34.8	68.2
最长连续降雨起止日期 (日/月)	Start/End (d/m)	13－23/5	6－15/4
日最大降雨量 (毫米)	Maximum Daily Rainfall (millimeters)	112.5	148.7
出现日期 (日/月)	Date (d/m)	11/9	11/9
三、全年日照总时数 (小时)	**Total Sunshine Hours (hours)**	**1689.3**	**1897.7**
四、霜 雪	**Frost & Snow**		
全年降霜日数 (日)	Annual Frost Days (day)	24	24
初霜日期 (日/月)	Start Date (d/m)	18/11	3/11
终霜日期 (日/月)	End Date (d/m)	11/3	11/3

概　　况(2010年)
Conditions by Region(2010)

桐庐县 Tonglu	淳安县 Chun'an	建德市 Jiande	富阳市 Fuyang	临安市 Lin'an
17.1	17.2	16.8	17.2	16.4
40.3	38.4	40.9	39.3	40.2
4/8	15/8	3/8	3/8	13/8
-4.2	-3	-4.2	-4.5	-5.9
14/1	16/12	17/12	14/1	14/1
162	163	167	158	150
1709.2	1845	1991.1	1510.6	1545.1
11	9	10	10	11
73.9	252.8	155	77.9	42.8
13-23/5	1-9/3	6-15/4	6-15/4	13-23/5
76.6	75.4	64.2	69.6	76.6
15/7	25/2	8/7	15/7	2/3
1614.7	**1827.7**	**1802.8**	**1679**	**1836.7**
24	23	24	29	27
4/12	18/11	3/11	3/11	3/11
11/3	12/3	11/3	11/3	11/3

主要统计指标解释

生产总值(GDP)　指一个国家(或地区)所有常住单位在一定时期内生产活动的最终成果。生产总值有三种表现形态,即价值形态、收入形态和产品形态。从价值形态看,它是所有常住单位在一定时期内生产的全部货物和服务价值超过同期中间投入的全部非固定资产货物和服务价值的差额,即所有常住单位的增加值之和;从收入形态看,它是所有常住单位在一定时期内创造并分配给常住单位和非常住单位的初次收入分配之和;从产品形态看,它是所有常住单位在一定时期内最终使用的货物和服务价值与货物和服务净出口价值之和。在实际核算中,生产总值有三种计算方法,即生产法、收入法和支出法。三种方法分别从不同的方面反映生产总值及其构成。

三次产业　是根据社会生产活动历史发展的顺序对产业结构的划分,产品直接取自自然界的部门称为第一产业,对初级产品进行再加工的部门称为第二产业,为生产和消费提供各种服务的部门称为第三产业。它是世界上较为通用的产业结构分类,但各国的划分不尽一致。我国的三次产业划分是:

第一产业:农业(包括种植业、林业、牧业、渔业和农林牧渔服务业)。

第二产业:工业(包括采矿业,制造业,电力、燃气及水的生产和供应业)和建筑业。

第三产业:除第一、第二产业以外的其他各业。由于第三产业包括的行业多、范围广,根据我国的实际情况,第三产业可分为两大部分:一是流通部门,二是服务部门。具体又分为四个层次:

第一层次:流通部门,包括交通运输、仓储及邮电通信业,批发和零售贸易、餐饮业。

第二层次:为生产和生活服务的部门,包括金融、保险业,地质勘查业、水利管理业,房地产业,社会服务业,农、林、牧、渔服务业,交通运输辅助业,综合技术服务业等。

第三层次:为提高科学文化水平和居民素质服务的部门,包括教育、文化艺术及广播电影电视业,卫生、体育和社会福利业,科学研究等。

第四层次:为社会公共需要服务的部门,包括国家机关、政党机关和社会团体以及军队、警察等。

降水量　从天空降落到地面的液态或固态(经融化后)降水,未经蒸发、渗透、流失而在水平面上积聚的深度。降水量以毫米为单位。

空气的温度(简称气温)　表示空气冷热程度的物理量。

日照时数　太阳在一地实际照射地面的时数。

Explanatory Notes on Main Statistical Indicators

Gross Domestic Product (GDP) refers to the final products of all resident units in a country (or a region) during a certain period of time. Gross domestic product is expressed in three different forms, i. e. value, income, and products respectively. The form of value refers to the total value of all products and services produced by all resident units during a certain period of time minus total value of intermediate input of materials and services of the nature of non – fixed assets or the summation of the value – added of all resident units; the form of income includes all the income created by all resident units and distributed primarily to all resident and non – resident units; the form of products refers to the value of all final goods and services for final use by all resident units plus the value of net exports of goods and services during a given period of time. In the practice of national accounting, gross domestic product is calculated with three approaches, i. e. production approach, income approach, and expenditure approach, which reflect gross domestic product and its composition from different aspects.

Three Industries Industry structure has been classified according to the historical sequence of development. Primary industry refers to extraction of natural resources; secondary industry involves processing of primary products; and tertiary industry provides services of various kinds for production and consumption. The above classification is universal although it varies to someextent from country to country. Industry in China comprises:

Primary industry: agriculture (including farming, forestry, animal husbandry and fishery and services for agriculture sector)

Secondary industry: industry (including mining and quarrying, manufacturing, production and supply of electricity, water and gas) and construction.

Tertiary industry: all other industries not included in primary of secondary industry.

Due to the fact that tertiary industry involves in a large variety of industries in China, it is divided into two sectors: circulation sector and service sector and further into four levels:

The first level: circulation sector, including transportation, storage, postal and telecommunications, wholesale and retail trade and catering trade.

The second level: service sector providing services for production and consumption, including banking, insurance, geological survey, water conservancy management, real estates, service for residents, service for agriculture, forestry, animal husbandry, fishery, subsidiary services for transportation and communications, comprehensive technical services, etc.

The third level: service sector for upgrading scientific, educational and cultural level of the people, including education, culture and arts, broadcasting, movies, television, public health, sports, social welfare and scientific research, etc.

The fourth level: sector providing services for public needs, including government agencies, political parties, social organizations, military and police service.

Precipitation refers to the depth of rainfall onto the ground (as well as liquefied from solid forms) from above the air prior to its vaporization, seepage, running off.

It is calculated in the unit of millimeter (mm).

Air Temperature refers to the physical quantity reflecting the extent of coldness and hotness of the air.

Duration of sunshine refers to the real time for the ground to receive sunshine at a certain place.

第二篇
CHAPTER-2

人口和从业人员
Population And Employment

人口和从业人员
Population and Employment

主要统计指标
Major Statistical Indicators

年末总户数	Total Households(year-end)	216.51	万户	(10000 Subscribers)
为上年	As Compared with the Preceding Year	100.6	%	(%)
年末总人口	Total Population(year-end)	689.12	万人	(10000 persons)
为上年	As Compared with the Preceding Year	100.8	%	(%)
#男性	Male	346.56	万人	(10000 persons)
为上年	As Compared with the Preceding Year	100.6	%	(%)
#非农业人口	Non-agriculture Population	365.24	万人	(10000 persons)
为上年	As Compared with the Preceding Year	103.0	%	(%)
年末市区总人口	Population of Urban District(year-end)	434.82	万人	(10000 persons)
为上年	As Compared with the Preceding Year	101.3	%	(%)
#男性	Male	217.65	万人	(10000 persons)
为上年	As Compared with the Preceding Year	101.0	%	(%)
#非农业人口	Non-agriculture Population	307.52	万人	(10000 persons)
为上年	As Compared with the Preceding Year	103.3	%	(%)
人口自然增长率	Natural Growth Rate	3.41	‰	(‰)
年末从业人员	Number of Employed Persons(year-end)	626.3	万人	(10000 persons)
为上年	As Compared with the Preceding Year	104.8	%	(%)

2-01 历次普查常住人口情况

Long-term Residents in the Past Population Census

单位:万人 (10000 person)

地 区 Region		第一次人口普查 1953.7.1 the First Population Census (1953.7.1)	第二次人口普查 1964.7.1 the Second Population Census (1964.7.1)	第三次人口普查 1982.7.1 the Third Population Census (1982.7.1)	第四次人口普查 1990.7.1 the Fourth Population Census (1991.7.1)	第五次人口普查 2000.11.1 the Fifth Population Census (2000.11.1)	第六次人口普查 2010.11.1 the Sixth Population Census (2010.11.1)
杭州市	**Hangzhou**	**301.13**	**421.90**	**526.05**	**583.21**	**687.87**	**870.04**
杭州市区	Urban District	172.26	243.65	305.77	346.76	450.23	624.20
上城区	Shangcheng	-	-	-	21.10	33.51	34.46
下城区	Xiacheng	-	-	-	25.66	41.24	52.61
江干区	Jianggan	-	-	-	36.12	56.54	99.88
拱墅区	Gongshu	-	-	-	29.34	42.93	55.19
西湖区	Xihu	-	-	-	35.40	59.33	82.00
高新(滨江)区	Hi-Tech(Binjiang)	-	-	-	-	11.59	31.90
萧山区	Xiaoshan	56.32	82.34	106.11	113.06	123.33	151.13
余杭区	Yuhang	52.28	64.96	80.50	86.08	81.77	117.03
桐庐县	Tonglu	19.73	26.20	34.83	37.66	37.81	40.64
淳安县	Chun'an	27.49	38.66	42.03	43.55	38.23	33.68
建德市	Jiande	26.42	38.15	43.64	47.63	47.31	43.08
富阳市	Fuyang	29.22	39.66	54.13	58.07	62.86	71.77
临安市	Lin'an	26.01	35.57	45.65	49.55	51.42	56.67

2-02 主要年份全市总户数与总人口数
Households and Population in Main Years

年 份 Year	总户数（万户） Total Households (10000 households)	总人口数（万人） Total Population (10000 persons)	#非农业人口（万人） Non-agriculture Population (10000 persons)	按性别分 By Sex 男（万人） Male (10000 persons)	女（万人） Female (10000 persons)
1978	117.89	505.55	116.06	260.74	244.81
1979	116.61	511.83	124.60	263.97	247.86
1980	119.11	515.53	128.88	266.02	249.51
1981	125.96	520.73	134.56	268.69	252.04
1982	131.53	528.06	139.94	272.72	255.34
1983	135.55	533.06	143.34	275.64	257.41
1984	139.24	537.49	147.46	278.04	259.45
1985	145.23	543.05	153.46	281.11	261.94
1986	151.59	549.53	157.19	284.57	264.96
1987	157.66	557.63	161.12	288.70	268.93
1988	164.41	565.04	164.87	292.21	272.83
1989	169.09	570.98	167.28	295.15	275.83
1990	171.94	574.78	169.00	297.02	277.76
1991	174.78	578.73	171.25	298.85	279.88
1992	177.68	582.40	174.03	300.63	281.77
1993	179.17	587.10	179.11	303.03	284.07
1994	180.65	592.93	186.50	306.00	286.93
1995	182.55	597.96	191.43	308.25	289.71
1996	184.33	603.22	196.68	310.76	292.46
1997	186.28	607.96	204.39	313.02	294.94
1998	187.80	611.64	210.52	314.69	296.95
1999	191.60	616.05	219.05	316.63	299.42
2000	193.48	621.58	227.00	319.09	302.49
2001	195.56	629.14	237.77	322.78	306.36
2002	198.27	636.81	252.02	326.62	310.19
2003	201.12	642.78	263.67	329.04	313.74
2004	204.52	651.68	282.58	332.62	319.06
2005	207.42	660.45	297.54	336.12	324.33
2006	209.91	666.31	309.78	338.23	328.08
2007	211.99	672.35	323.75	340.50	331.85
2008	213.74	677.64	340.76	342.45	335.19
2009	215.28	683.38	354.48	344.51	338.87
2010	216.51	689.12	365.24	346.56	342.56

注：按公安户籍人口统计。

a) Figures in this table are based on the Public Security Bureau.

2－03 主要年份市区总户数与总人口数
Urban District Households and Population in Main Years

年份 Year	总户数(万户) Total Households (10000 households)	总人口数(万人) Total Population (10000 persons)	#非农业人口(万人) Non－agriculture Population (10000 persons)	按性别分 By Sex 男(万人) Male (10000 persons)	女(万人) Female (10000 persons)
1978	25.52	104.53	78.73	53.95	50.58
1979	26.23	110.50	85.05	57.09	53.41
1980	27.23	113.08	87.93	58.56	54.52
1981	29.88	115.59	90.53	59.96	55.63
1982	31.24	118.05	92.72	61.28	56.77
1983	32.69	120.13	94.94	62.43	57.70
1984	34.07	122.29	97.34	63.63	58.66
1985	35.36	124.67	100.01	64.96	59.71
1986	37.02	127.07	102.59	66.29	60.78
1987	38.70	129.16	104.09	67.38	61.78
1988	40.05	131.26	107.30	68.46	62.80
1989	41.19	132.84	108.88	69.28	63.56
1990	42.26	133.89	109.97	69.75	64.14
1991	42.98	134.97	111.20	70.33	64.64
1992	43.63	136.30	112.70	71.08	65.22
1993	44.55	138.33	115.13	72.22	66.11
1994	45.04	141.27	118.48	73.82	67.45
1995	46.06	143.52	121.38	74.91	68.61
1996	52.39	166.73	128.76	87.15	79.58
1997	53.14	169.29	131.76	88.53	80.76
1998	53.92	171.89	134.62	89.86	82.03
1999	54.64	175.27	139.29	91.65	83.62
2000	55.34	179.18	143.69	93.64	85.54
2001	115.81	379.49	193.26	194.59	184.90
2002	117.11	387.01	205.98	198.47	188.54
2003	119.01	393.19	216.13	201.14	192.05
2004	120.56	401.59	233.08	204.43	197.16
2005	122.02	409.52	245.56	207.70	201.82
2006	123.31	414.18	256.42	209.45	204.73
2007	124.40	419.50	269.30	211.59	207.91
2008	125.56	424.30	285.11	213.54	210.76
2009	126.92	429.44	297.83	215.56	213.88
2010	128.43	434.82	307.52	217.65	217.16

注:从 2001 年起市区数据包括萧山区和余杭区。

a) Figures in this table include Xiaoshan and Yuhang district since 2001.

2－04　分地区总户数与总人口数(2010 年末)

Households and Population by Region(End of 2010)

地　区 Region	总户数 (万户) Total Households (10000 households)	总人口数 (万人) Total Population (10000 persons)	#非农业人口(万人) Non－agriculture Population (10000 persons)	按性别分 By Sex 男(万人) Male (10000 persons)	女(万人) Female (10000 persons)
全　市 Whole Municipality	**216.51**	**689.12**	**365.24**	**346.56**	**342.56**
市　区 Urban District	128.43	434.82	307.52	217.65	217.16
上城区 Shangcheng	11.53	32.68	32.68	16.45	16.22
下城区 Xiacheng	12.56	40.10	40.10	20.38	19.73
江干区 Jianggan	11.65	44.71	42.10	22.45	22.26
拱墅区 Gongshu	10.56	31.10	31.10	15.82	15.28
西湖区 Xihu	16.51	62.95	56.12	32.37	30.57
高新(滨江)区 Hi－Tech(Binjiang)	3.99	15.20	13.98	7.71	7.49
萧山区 Xiaoshan	37.60	121.98	47.65	60.06	61.92
余杭区 Yuhang	24.03	86.10	43.79	42.41	43.69
桐庐县 Tonglu	14.96	40.24	12.18	20.29	19.96
淳安县 Chun'an	14.93	45.43	7.78	23.25	22.18
建德市 Jiande	17.33	51.02	12.95	26.12	24.90
富阳市 Fuyang	21.97	65.02	13.80	32.92	32.11
临安市 Lin'an	18.89	52.59	11.01	26.33	26.25

2-05 分地区户籍人口年龄构成(2010 年末)

Age Structure of Household Registered Population by Region (End of 2010)

地 区 Region	18 岁以下 under 18 years old		18-35 岁 18~35 years old		35-60 岁 35~60 years old		60 岁以上 over 60 years old	
	人数(万人) Number of people (10000 person)	占总人口% of the total population	人数(万人) Number of people (10000 person)	占总人口% of the total population	人数(万人) Number of people (10000 person)	占总人口% of the total population	人数(万人) Number of people (10000 person)	占总人口% of the total population
全 市 Whole Municipality	**104.76**	**15.2**	**178.54**	**25.9**	**287.8**	**41.8**	**118.02**	**17.1**
市 区 Urban District	64.11	14.7	118.65	27.3	175.79	40.4	76.27	17.5
上城区 Shangcheng	3.27	10.0	8.28	25.3	13.39	41.0	7.73	23.7
下城区 Xiacheng	4.47	11.1	12.61	31.4	15.02	37.5	7.99	19.9
江干区 Jianggan	6.14	13.7	15.86	35.5	15.85	35.5	6.86	15.3
拱墅区 Gongshu	3.75	12.1	8.37	26.9	12.63	40.6	6.35	20.4
西湖区 Xihu	9.01	14.3	23.17	36.8	21.96	34.9	8.81	14.0
高新(滨江)区 Hi-Tech(Binjiang)	2.75	18.1	5.06	33.3	5.45	35.9	1.95	12.8
萧山区 Xiaoshan	21.23	17.4	26.15	21.4	52.9	43.4	21.71	17.8
余杭区 Yuhang	13.49	15.7	19.15	22.2	38.59	44.8	14.87	17.3
桐庐县 Tonglu	6.37	15.8	9.44	23.5	17.59	43.7	6.85	17.0
淳安县 Chun'an	7.40	16.3	10.57	23.3	20.28	44.6	7.19	15.8
建德市 Jiande	7.95	15.6	11.96	23.4	22.19	43.5	8.91	17.5
富阳市 Fuyang	11.34	17.4	15.4	23.7	28.17	43.3	10.11	15.5
临安市 Lin'an	7.59	14.4	12.52	23.8	23.78	45.2	8.69	16.5

2-06 主要年份全市人口自然变动情况
Natural Changes of Population in Main Years

年份 Year	出生 Birth		死亡 Death		自然增长 Natural Growth	
	人数(人) Birth Population (person)	出生率(‰) Birth Rate(‰)	人数(人) Death Population (person)	死亡率(‰) Death Rate(‰)	人数(人) Natural Growth Population (person)	自然增长率(‰) Natural Growth Rate(‰)
1978	73550	14.63	29928	2.95	43622	8.68
1979	71442	14.04	29500	5.80	41942	8.24
1980	52145	10.15	30727	5.98	21418	4.17
1981	73015	14.09	31352	6.05	41663	8.04
1982	82910	15.81	30805	5.87	52105	9.94
1983	69940	13.18	33598	6.33	36342	6.85
1984	60091	11.23	33070	6.18	27021	5.05
1985	66757	12.36	33715	6.24	33042	6.12
1986	84702	15.50	33576	6.15	51126	9.35
1987	94127	17.00	33238	6.00	60889	11.00
1988	85472	15.23	35356	6.30	50116	8.93
1989	81048	14.27	34031	5.99	47017	8.28
1990	76579	13.37	34977	6.11	41602	7.26
1991	66144	11.47	33534	5.81	32610	5.66
1992	61708	10.63	34681	5.97	27027	4.66
1993	62465	10.68	34127	5.84	28338	4.84
1994	63580	10.78	35099	5.95	28481	4.83
1995	62586	10.51	36186	6.08	26400	4.43
1996	63680	10.60	25417	5.90	28263	4.70
1997	58471	9.65	34663	5.72	23808	3.93
1998	53951	8.85	38302	6.28	15649	2.57
1999	59085	9.63	36866	6.01	22219	3.62
2000	62300	10.07	40218	6.50	22082	3.57
2001	52088	8.33	33827	5.41	18261	2.92
2002	53064	8.38	35867	5.67	17197	2.72
2003	51420	8.04	36662	5.73	14758	2.31
2004	59940	9.26	34078	5.27	25862	3.99
2005	57233	8.72	35417	5.39	21816	3.33
2006	57790	8.71	38892	5.86	18898	2.85
2007	60296	9.01	37833	5.65	22463	3.36
2008	61332	9.09	42648	6.32	18684	2.77
2009	62441	9.18	39159	5.76	23282	3.42
2010	69606	10.14	46193	6.73	23413	3.41

注:本表按公安部门统计。

a) Figures in this table are based on the Public Security Bureau.

2-07 主要年份市区人口自然变动情况
Natural Changes of Urban Population in Main Years

年份 Year	出生 Birth		死亡 Death		自然增长 Natural Growth	
	人数(人) Birth Population (person)	出生率(‰) Birth Rate(‰)	人数(人) Death Population (person)	死亡率(‰) Death Rate(‰)	人数(人) Natural Growth Population (person)	自然增长率(‰) Natural Growth Rate(‰)
1978	11923	11.56	6449	6.25	5474	5.31
1979	13184	12.26	5808	5.40	7376	6.86
1980	9708	8.68	6511	5.82	3197	2.86
1981	14938	13.06	6599	5.77	8339	7.29
1982	18092	15.49	6494	5.56	11598	9.93
1983	17107	14.36	6949	5.84	10158	8.52
1984	16257	13.41	6892	5.69	9365	7.72
1985	15824	12.81	7403	6.84	8421	6.82
1986	17120	13.60	6865	5.45	10255	8.15
1987	18701	14.60	7070	5.52	11631	9.08
1988	18503	14.21	7503	5.76	11000	8.45
1989	15868	12.02	6985	5.29	8883	6.73
1990	14085	10.56	7490	5.62	6595	4.94
1991	10195	7.58	7025	5.22	3170	2.36
1992	9994	7.37	7259	5.35	2735	2.02
1993	10099	7.35	7196	5.24	2903	2.11
1994	9918	7.09	7082	5.06	2836	2.03
1995	9806	6.89	7367	5.17	2439	1.72
1996	12098	7.80	8221	5.30	3877	2.50
1997	12304	7.32	8630	5.13	3674	2.19
1998	11714	6.87	9060	5.31	2654	1.56
1999	13694	7.89	8148	4.69	5546	3.20
2000	15058	8.50	10996	6.20	4062	2.30
2001	30902	8.22	19439	5.17	11463	3.05
2002	33156	8.65	19922	5.20	13234	3.45
2003	29019	7.44	21176	5.43	7843	2.01
2004	34858	8.77	19445	4.89	15413	3.88
2005	34056	8.39	21310	5.25	12746	3.14
2006	33260	8.08	21156	5.14	12104	2.94
2007	37029	8.88	20051	4.81	16978	4.07
2008	38703	9.17	21428	5.08	17275	4.09
2009	40293	9.44	22178	5.20	18115	4.24
2010	47052	10.89	25404	5.88	21648	5.01

注:从2001年起市区数据包括萧山区和余杭区。

a) Figures in this table include Xiaoshan and Yuhang district since 2001.

2-08 分地区人口自然变动情况(2010年末)
Natural Changes of Population by Region(End of 2010)

地区 Region	出生 Birth		死亡 Death		自然增长 Natural Growth	
	人数(人) Birth Population (person)	出生率(‰) Birth Rate(‰)	人数(人) Death Population (person)	死亡率(‰) Death Rate(‰)	人数(人) Natural Growth Population (person)	自然增长率(‰) Natural Growth Rate(‰)
全市 Whole Municipality	**69606**	**10.14**	**46193**	**6.73**	**23413**	**3.41**
市区 Urban District	47052	10.89	25404	5.88	21648	5.01
上城区 Shangcheng	2611	8.01	1953	5.99	658	2.02
下城区 Xiacheng	3703	9.26	2219	5.55	1484	3.71
江干区 Jianggan	5617	12.63	1920	4.32	3697	8.31
拱墅区 Gongshu	3464	11.20	1790	5.79	1674	5.41
西湖区 Xihu	7650	12.27	2878	4.62	4772	7.65
高新(滨江)区 Hi-Tech(Binjiang)	2313	15.59	617	4.16	1696	11.43
萧山区 Xiaoshan	12222	10.06	8220	6.77	4002	3.29
余杭区 Yuhang	9472	11.08	5807	6.79	3665	4.29
桐庐县 Tonglu	4043	10.07	3009	7.50	1034	2.57
淳安县 Chun'an	4131	9.11	4104	9.05	27	0.06
建德市 Jiande	3494	6.82	5595	10.93	-2101	-4.11
富阳市 Fuyang	6313	9.74	4129	6.37	2184	3.37
临安市 Lin'an	4573	8.70	3952	7.52	621	1.18

2－09 分地区人口机械变动情况(2010年)
Mechanical Changes of Population by Region(2010)

单位:人 (person)

地 区 Region	本年迁入人数 Number of the Persons Moved in(person)		本年迁出人数 Number of the Persons Moved Out(person)		本年净迁入人数 Net Persons Moved in
	省 内 From Zhejiang Province	省 外 From Other Provinces	省 内 To Zhejiang Province	省 外 To Other Provinces	
全 市 Whole Municipality	**50507**	**59028**	**50200**	**21195**	**38140**
市 区 Urban District	34097	49177	31806	17705	33763
上城区 Shangcheng	2138	2484	582	915	3125
下城区 Xiacheng	3776	4609	2470	1936	3979
江干区 Jianggan	6927	10326	11458	5110	685
拱墅区 Gongshu	3018	2228	2562	634	2050
西湖区 Xihu	8219	13218	8355	5974	7108
高新(滨江)区 Hi－Tech(Binjiang)	2898	2743	3093	742	1806
萧山区 Xiaoshan	2989	5523	1483	1274	5755
余杭区 Yuhang	4132	8046	1803	1120	9255
桐庐县 Tonglu	1367	1560	1433	663	831
淳安县 Chun'an	3081	2021	3193	332	1577
建德市 Jiande	4388	2002	4706	762	922
富阳市 Fuyang	3964	2185	3661	781	1707
临安市 Lin'an	3610	2083	5401	952	－660

2－10 计划生育情况(2010年)
Conditions of Birth Control(2010)

单位:% (%)

地 区	Region	综合避孕率 Contraception Rate	计划生育率 Rate of Birth Under Control	独生子女领证率 The Only－child Certification Rate
全 市	**Whole Municipality**	**86.96**	**98.10**	**40.78**
市 区	Urban District	85.35	98.82	48.29
上城区	Shangcheng	82.26	98.74	67.60
下城区	Xiacheng	81.54	99.03	55.50
江干区	Jianggan	86.87	99.15	58.25
拱墅区	Gongshu	83.36	98.58	55.03
西湖区	Xihu	86.14	98.48	41.72
高新(滨江)区	Hi－Tech(Binjiang)	83.87	99.77	36.11
萧山区	Xiaoshan	85.87	98.47	42.04
余杭区	Yuhang	87.01	99.04	48.73
桐庐县	Tonglu	89.56	96.96	27.82
淳安县	Chun'an	91.44	95.54	29.51
建德市	Jiande	89.93	96.10	29.02
富阳市	Fuyang	89.15	96.55	27.19
临安市	Lin'an	87.53	97.53	32.80

2－11 婚姻登记情况
Marriage Registration Conditions

地 区 Region	2010			2009		
	准予登记结婚对数 Marriages Legally Registered(couples)	#再婚人数 Re－married (person)	离婚对数 Divorces (couples)	准予登记结婚对数 Marriages Legally Registered(couples)	#再婚人数 Re－married (person)	离婚对数 Divorces (couples)
全 市 Whole Municipality	**70046**	**17988**	**14912**	**70003**	**20114**	**14512**
市 区 Urban District	47045	11126	9303	49271	12680	9022
萧山区 Xiaoshan	9660	2780	1837	8287	2595	1704
余杭区 Yuhang	8125	1585	1685	8236	2612	1740
桐庐县 Tonglu	3426	1482	1067	3060	1164	997
淳安县 Chun'an	3946	1099	808	3991	1237	703
建德市 Jiande	5849	1053	996	4058	1378	1004
富阳市 Fuyang	5463	1608	1403	5283	1963	1545
临安市 Lin'an	4317	1620	1335	4340	1692	1241

2－12 全市城镇单位

Number of Employed

单位:人

地区、行业	Region Sector	年末单位从业人员 Employed Persons in Urban Units (year－end)	#女性 Female	在岗职工 Fully Employed Staff & Workers
全市总计	**Total**	**2327045**	**796340**	**1940849**
其中:企业	Enterprises	1940593	621115	1598192
事业	Institutions	266693	141345	232754
机关	Agencies & Organizations	99195	24107	92154
民间非营利组织	Non－profit Organizations	9198	5627	7310
其他	Other	11366	4146	10439
市区总计	**Urban District**	**2023066**	**681601**	**1676416**
其中:企业	Enterprises	1717274	539828	1407010
事业	Institutions	212990	114676	184459
机关	Agencies & Organizations	74465	18529	69265
民间非营利组织	Non－profit Organizations	7899	4809	6086
其他	Other	10438	3759	9596
上城区	Shangcheng District	171088	66901	145496
下城区	Xiacheng District	211748	84554	168342
江干区	Jianggan District	151969	35629	133623
拱墅区	Gongshu District	170893	47485	117491
西湖区	Xihu District	345027	100269	247598
高新(滨江)区	Hi－Tech(Binjiang) District	159257	52571	140126
萧山区	Xiaoshan District	457545	156581	432656
余杭区	Yuhang District	182206	69236	169202
桐庐县	Tonglu County	46678	20895	42364
淳安县	Chun'an County	30774	11338	28756
建德市	Jiande City	39644	14808	36465
富阳市	Fuyang City	110318	38272	85241
临安市	Lin'an City	76565	29426	71607

从业人员数(2010年)
Persons in Urban Units(2010)

(person)

其他从业人员 Other Employed Persons	单位平均从业人数 Annual Average Number of Employed Persons in Urban Unit	在岗职工 Fully Employed Staff & Workers	其他从业人员 Other Employed Persons
386196	**2284323**	**1913110**	**371213**
342401	1903518	1574626	328892
33939	262586	229722	32864
7041	98018	91250	6768
1888	8991	7266	1725
927	11210	10246	964
346650	**1990678**	**1649655**	**341023**
310264	1689389	1383486	305903
28531	209778	182166	27612
5200	73488	68520	4968
1813	7722	6065	1657
842	10301	9418	883
25592	169089	143889	25200
43406	212096	165028	47068
18346	143418	125284	18134
53402	167140	117857	49283
97429	336263	239277	96986
19131	153438	135978	17460
24889	461429	437641	23788
13004	179591	167407	12184
4314	46382	42290	4092
2018	30502	28990	1512
3179	39216	36136	3080
25077	101961	85064	16897
4958	75584	70975	4609

地区、行业	Region　Sector	年末单位从业人员 Employed Persons in Urban Units (year - end)	#女性 Female	在岗职工 Fully Employed Staff & Workers
按国民经济行业分组	**Grouped by Sector**			
农、林、牧、渔业	Farming, Forestry, Animal Husbandry & Fishery	1514	415	1441
采矿业	Mining & Quarrying	2682	430	2507
制造业	Manufacturing	759048	312009	674283
电力、煤气及水的生产和供应业	Production & Supply of Electricity, Gas & Water	21923	5331	18379
建筑业	Construction	474914	27319	321905
交通运输、仓储和邮政业	Transportation, Storage, Post & Telecommunications	87822	22034	74197
信息传输、计算机服务和软件业	Information Transmission, Computer Services and Software	64913	25759	54844
批发与零售业	Wholesale & Retail Trade	128502	62300	113273
住宿和餐饮业	Lodging and Catering	80985	46366	70303
金融业	Banking and Insurance	75194	41477	59500
房地产业	Real Estate	60487	23161	54624
租赁与商务服务业	Renting and Business Service	74213	20725	65193
科学研究、技术服务与地质勘查业	Scientific Research, Technical Service and Geological Prospecting	85177	23581	73891
水利、环境和公共设施管理业	Water Conservancy, Environment and Public Utility	43779	15934	32200
居民服务和其他服务业	Service for the Residents and Other	8345	3621	6484
教育	Education	144132	78663	128171
卫生、社会保障和社会福利业	Health Care, Sports & Social Welfare	77577	48472	66123
文化、体育与娱乐业	Culture, Sports and Entertainment	20264	9285	15638
公共管理与社会组织	Public Management and Social Organizations	115574	29458	107893

continued (person)

其他从业人员 Other Employed Persons	单位平均从业人数 Annual Average Number of Employed Persons in Urban Unit	在岗职工 Fully Employed Staff & Workers	其他从业人员 Other Employed Persons
73	1507	1466	41
175	2646	2482	164
84765	749843	668839	81004
3544	22129	18633	3496
153009	469479	323214	146265
13625	87014	74189	12825
10069	60878	51686	9192
15229	125368	110519	14849
10682	76682	66081	10601
15694	72438	56135	16303
5863	58419	52741	5678
9020	72306	63411	8895
11286	82452	71467	10985
11579	43913	32734	11179
1861	7408	6126	1282
15961	142544	127187	15357
11454	75126	64141	10985
4626	19936	15357	4579
7681	114235	106702	7533

2－13 全市国有单位

Number of Employed Persons

单位:人

地区、行业	Region Sector	年末单位从业人员 Employed Persons in Urban Units (year－end)	#女性 Female	在岗职工 Fully Employed Staff & Workers
总　　计	**Total**	**545330**	**214924**	**471321**
按隶属关系分	**Grouped by Subordination**			
中央属	Central	86431	27719	68730
省　属	Provincial	152661	60674	131468
市　属	City	87036	33584	74230
县及县以下	County and Lower Levels	214446	90834	192656
其　他	Others	4756	2113	4237
按企业、事业、机关分	**Grouped by Enterprises, Institutions & Agencies**			
企业	Enterprises	196468	59531	161792
事业	Institutions	247374	130134	215951
机关	Agencies & Organizations	99195	24107	92154
民间非营利组织	Non－profit Organizations	1867	974	1012
其他	Others	426	178	412
按国民经济行业分组	**Grouped by Sector**			
农、林、牧、渔业	Farming, Forestry, Animal Husbandry & Fishery	693	112	672
采矿业	Mining & Quarrying	105	8	105
制造业	Manufacturing	19039	4512	18549
电力、煤气及水的生产和供应业	Production & Supply of Electricity, Gas & Water	12531	2949	9410
建筑业	Construction	17838	3131	15545
交通运输、仓储和邮政业	Transportation, Storage, Post & Telecommunications	46791	11271	39685
信息传输、计算机服务和软件业	Information Transmission, Computer Services and Software	8683	4081	5853
批发与零售业	Wholesale & Retail Trade	9656	3960	8194
住宿和餐饮业	Lodging and Catering	9911	5274	8464
金融业	Banking and Insurance	13499	7791	10339
房地产业	Real Estate	5332	2110	4690
租赁与商务服务业	Renting and Business Service	29908	6720	24006
科学研究、技术服务与地质勘查业	Scientific Research, Technical Service and Geological Prospecting	35652	11116	31361
水利、环境和公共设施管理业	Water Conservancy, Environment and Public Utility	19762	8805	14223
居民服务和其他服务业	Service for the Residents and Other	4165	1656	2907
教育	Education	124287	66640	110822
卫生、社会保障和社会福利业	Health Care, Sports & Social Welfare	66157	41540	56265
文化、体育与娱乐业	Culture, Sports and Entertainment	16623	7446	12241
公共管理与社会组织	Public Management and Social Organizations	104698	25802	97990

从业人员数(2010 年)

in State - owned Units(2010)

(person)

其他从业人员 Other Employed Persons	单位平均从业人数 Annual Average Number of Employed Persons in Urban Unit	在岗职工 Fully Employed Staff & Workers	其他从业人员 Other Employed Persons
74009	**538402**	**465946**	**72456**
17701	86748	69417	17331
21193	149181	128772	20409
12806	86999	73758	13241
21790	211366	190293	21073
519	4108	3706	402
34676	194539	159900	34639
31423	243819	213384	30435
7041	98018	91250	6768
855	1599	999	600
14	427	413	14
21	694	673	21
–	105	105	–
490	18887	18490	397
3121	12737	9662	3075
2293	18708	14943	3765
7106	46886	39973	6913
2830	8358	5736	2622
1462	9718	8236	1482
1447	9861	8521	1340
3160	13161	10156	3005
642	5230	4637	593
5902	29305	23435	5870
4291	34549	30369	4180
5539	19969	14526	5443
1258	3255	2562	693
13465	122875	110113	12762
9892	64121	54658	9463
4382	16480	12140	4340
6708	103503	97011	6492

2-14 全市城镇集体

Number of Employed Persons

单位:人

地区、行业	Region Sector	年末单位从业人员 Employed Persons in Urban Units (year-end)	#女性 Female	在岗职工 Fully Employed Staff & Workers
总　计	**Total**	**52067**	**18292**	**47473**
按企业、事业分	**Grouped by Enterprises, Institutions**			
企业	Enterprises	37115	9499	34295
事业	Institutions	14348	8558	12636
机关	Agencies & Organizations	-	-	-
民间非营利组织	Non-profit Organizations	214	142	156
其他	Others	390	93	386
按国民经济行业分组	**Grouped by Sector**			
农、林、牧、渔业	Farming, Forestry, Animal Husbandry & Fishery	140	62	140
采矿业	Mining & Quarrying	812	114	811
制造业	Manufacturing	4678	1914	4475
电力、煤气及水的生产和供应业	Production & Supply of Electricity, Gas & Water	203	26	203
建筑业	Construction	2454	480	1610
交通运输、仓储和邮政业	Transportation, Storage, Post & Telecommunications	7166	849	6836
信息传输、计算机服务和软件业	Information Transmission, Computer Services and Software	379	188	294
批发与零售业	Wholesale & Retail Trade	1922	713	1839
住宿和餐饮业	Lodging and Catering	2908	1718	2733
金融业	Banking and Insurance	23	15	23
房地产业	Real Estate	1396	480	1095
租赁与商务服务业	Renting and Business Service	13406	2199	12940
科学研究、技术服务与地质勘查业	Scientific Research, Technical Service and Geological Prospecting	1069	315	844
水利、环境和公共设施管理业	Water Conservancy, Environment and Public Utility	2479	1217	2194
居民服务和其他服务业	Service for the Residents and Other	636	238	577
教育	Education	5515	3710	4805
卫生、社会保障和社会福利业	Health Care, Sports & Social Welfare	6655	3937	5861
文化、体育与娱乐业	Culture, Sports and Entertainment	104	77	78
公共管理与社会组织	Public Management and Social Organizations	122	40	115

单位从业人员数(2010 年)

in Urban Collective - owned Units(2010)

(person)

其他从业人员 Other Employed Persons	单位平均从业人数 Annual Average Number of Employed Persons in Urban Unit	在岗职工 Fully Employed Staff & Workers	其他从业人员 Other Employed Persons
4594	**51203**	**46947**	**4256**
2820	36481	33948	2533
1712	14135	12472	1663
-	-	-	-
58	199	143	56
4	388	384	4
-	140	140	-
1	809	808	1
203	4499	4295	204
-	210	210	-
844	2377	1849	528
330	7328	6970	358
85	383	298	85
83	1901	1816	85
175	2938	2764	174
-	23	23	-
301	1408	1099	309
466	12788	12319	469
225	1043	836	207
285	2466	2179	287
59	764	708	56
710	5424	4713	711
794	6475	5723	752
26	102	79	23
7	125	118	7

2-15 全市其他单位

Number of Employed Persons

单位:人

地区、行业	Region Sector	年末单位从业人员 Employed Persons in Urban Units (year-end)	#女性 Female	在岗职工 Fully Employed Staff & Workers
总　计	**Total**	**1729648**	**563124**	**1422055**
按登记注册类型分组	**Grouped by Registration**			
1. 内资	Domestic Funded	1174944	304991	944806
2. 港澳台投资经济	Funded by Entrepreneurs from Hong Kong, Macao & Taiwan	232295	111504	207205
3. 外商投资经济	Foreign Funded	322409	146629	270044
按企业、事业分	**Grouped by Enterprises, Institutions**			
企业	Enterprises	1707010	552085	1402105
事业	Institutions	4971	2653	4167
民间非营利组织	Non-profit Organizations	7117	4511	6142
其他	Others	10550	3875	9641
按国民经济行业分组	**Grouped by Sector**			
农、林、牧、渔业	Farming, Forestry, Animal Husbandry & Fishery	681	241	629
采矿业	Mining & Quarrying	1765	308	1591
制造业	Manufacturing	735331	305583	651259
电力、煤气及水的生产和供应业	Production & Supply of Electricity, Gas & Water	9189	2356	8766
建筑业	Construction	454622	23708	304750
交通运输、仓储和邮政业	Transportation, Storage, Post & Telecommunications	33865	9914	27676
信息传输、计算机服务和软件业	Information Transmission, Computer Services and Software	55851	21490	48697
批发与零售业	Wholesale & Retail Trade	116924	57627	103240
住宿和餐饮业	Lodging and Catering	68166	39374	59106
金融业	Banking and Insurance	61672	33671	49138
房地产业	Real Estate	53759	20571	48839
租赁与商务服务业	Renting and Business Service	30899	11806	28247
科学研究、技术服务与地质勘查业	Scientific Research, Technical Service and Geological Prospecting	48456	12150	41686
水利、环境和公共设施管理业	Water Conservancy, Environment and Public Utility	21538	5912	15783
居民服务和其他服务业	Service for the Residents and Other	3544	1727	3000
教育	Education	14330	8313	12544
卫生、社会保障和社会福利业	Health Care, Sports & Social Welfare	4765	2995	3997
文化、体育与娱乐业	Culture, Sports and Entertainment	3537	1762	3319
公共管理与社会组织	Public Management and Social Organizations	10754	3616	9788

从业人员数(2010 年)

in Units of Other Types of Ownership(2010)

(person)

其他从业人员 Other Employed Persons	单位平均从业人数 Annual Average Number of Employed Persons in Urban Unit	在岗职工 Fully Employed Staff & Workers	其他从业人员 Other Employed Persons
307593	**1694718**	**1400217**	**294501**
230138	1153032	934081	218951
25090	228041	203265	24776
52365	313645	262871	50774
304905	1672498	1380778	291720
804	4632	3866	766
975	7193	6124	1069
909	10395	9449	946
52	673	653	20
174	1732	1569	163
84072	726457	646054	80403
423	9182	8761	421
149872	448394	306422	141972
6189	32800	27246	5554
7154	52137	45652	6485
13684	113749	100467	13282
9060	63883	54796	9087
12534	59254	45956	13298
4920	51781	47005	4776
2652	30213	27657	2556
6770	46860	40262	6598
5755	21478	16029	5449
544	3389	2856	533
1786	14245	12361	1884
768	4530	3760	770
218	3354	3138	216
966	10607	9573	1034

2-16 按三次产业分从业人员人数
Number of Employed Persons by Three Industries

单位:万人　　(10000 persons)

指标名称	Item	2010 年末 (End of 2010)	2009 年末 (End of 2009)
全市总计	**Total**	**626.33**	**597.47**
第一产业	Primary Industry	75.70	80.21
第二产业	Secondary Industry	286.26	277.98
第三产业	Tertiary Industry	264.37	239.28
市　区	**Urban District**	**455.07**	**435.49**
第一产业	Primary Industry	25.59	26.97
第二产业	Secondary Industry	215.8	209.76
第三产业	Tertiary Industry	213.68	198.76

主要统计指标解释

人口数 指一定时点、一定地区范围内的有生命的个人的总和。

年度统计的年末人口数是指每年 12 月 31 日 24 时的人口数。

出生率(又称粗出生率) 指一定时期内(通常为一年)平均每千人所出生的人数的比率,一般用千分率表示。计算公式:

$$出生率 = \frac{年出生人数}{年平均人数} \times 1000‰$$

出生人数是指活产婴儿,即胎儿脱离母体时(不管怀孕月数),有过呼吸或其他生命现象。

年平均人数是年初、年底人口数的平均数,也可用年中人口数代替。

死亡率(又称粗死亡率) 指一定时期内(通常为一年)一定地区的死亡人数与同期平均人数(或期中人数)之比,一般用千分率表示。计算公式:

$$死亡率 = \frac{年死亡人数}{年平均人数} \times 1000‰$$

人口自然增长率 指一定时期内(通常为一年)人口自然增加数(出生人数减死亡人数)与该时期内平均人数(或期中人数)之比,一般用千分率表示。计算公式:

$$人口自然增长率 = \frac{本年出生人数 - 本年死亡人数}{年平均人数} \times 1000‰$$

人口自然增长率 = 人口出生率 - 人口死亡率

从业人员 指从事一定社会劳动并取得劳动报酬或经营收入人员,包括各级机关企事业单位从业人员、个体户主、个体从业人员、农村从业人员及其他未包括的从业人员(包括宗教职业者、现役军人等)。

单位从业人员 是指在各级国家机关、政党机关、社会团体及企业、事业单位中工作,并取得劳动报酬的全部人员。包括在岗职工、再就业的离退休人员、民办教师、在各单位中工作的外方人员和港、澳、台方人员以及聘用的外单位下岗职工、兼职人员、从事第二职业人员、使用的劳务派遣人员和服务外包人员。各单位的从业人员反映了实际参加生产或工作的全部劳动力。

在岗职工 指在本单位工作并由单位支付劳动报酬的人员,以及在本单位有工作岗位,但由于学习、病伤产假等原因暂未工作,仍由单位支付劳动报酬的人,包括本单位临时性用工并支付劳动报酬的人员。

Explanatory Notes on Main Statistical Indicators

Total Population refers to the total number of people alive at a certain point of time within a given area. The annual statistics on total population is taken at midnight, the 31st of December.

Birth Rate (or Crude Birth Rate) refers to the ratio of the number of births to the average population during a certain period of time (usually a year), which is often expressed in ‰. The following formula is used:

$$\text{Birth Rate} = \frac{\text{Number of Births}}{\text{Average Number of Population}} \times 1000‰$$

Number of births refers to live births, i. e. the births when babies had showed any vital phenomena regardless of the length of pregnancy.

Annual Average Number of Population is the average of the number of population at the beginning of the year and that at the end of the year. Sometimes it is substituted for with the mid – year population.

Death Rate (or Crude Death Rate) refers to the ratio of the number of deaths to the average population (or mid – year population) during a certain period of time (usually a year), which is often expressed in ‰. The following formula is used:

$$\text{Death Rate} = \frac{\text{Number of Deaths}}{\text{Annual Average Number of Population}} \times 1000‰$$

Natural Growth Rate of Population refers to the ratio of natural increase in population (number of births minus number of deaths) in a certain period of time (usually a year) to the average population (or mid – year population) of the same period, which is often expressed in ‰. The following formulas are applied:

$$\text{Natural Growth Rate of Population} = \frac{\text{Number of Births} - \text{Number of Deaths}}{\text{Average Number of Population}} \times 1000‰$$

Natural Growth Rate of Population = Birth Rate – Death Rate

Employed Persons refer to persons who are engaged in social labour and receive remuneration payment or earn business income, including all employees of government, enterprises and institutions, self – employed workers, employed persons in the rural areas and other employed workers (including religious professionals, servicemen, etc.).

Persons Employed in Various Units refer to all the persons who are working in government agencies of various levels, political and party organizations, social organizations, enterprises, institutions, and receiving wages or other forms of payment. Including fully employed staff and works, re – employed retirees, teachers in schools run by the local people, foreigners and Chinese compatriots from Hong Kong, Macao, and Taiwan working in various units, part – time employees, employees of other units working temporarily, employees holding the second job, dispatch personnels and outsourcing staff. Persons Employed in various units reflect the actual total labor force which are engaged in the production or work.

Fully Employed Staff and Workers refer to persons who work in, and receive wages from their working units, as well as persons who have their work posts, but are temporarily absent from work for reasons of study or on sick, injury or maternal leave and still receive wages from their working units. including persons who are engaged in temporary employment and receive remuneration payment.

第三篇
CHAPTER-3

农　业

Agriculture

农　　业
Agriculture

主要统计指标
Major Statistical Indicators

农村机械总动力	Total Power of Agricultural Machinery	330.75	万千瓦	(10000 kw)
为上年	As Compared with the Preceding Year	102.6	%	(%)
农村经济总收入	Total Rural Economic Income	12982.33	亿元	(100 million yuan)
为上年	As Compared with the Preceding Year	116.3	%	(%)
农村从业人员数	Total Employees in rural areas	261.77	万人	(10000 persons)
为上年	As Compared with the Preceding Year	100.9	%	(%)
农林牧渔业总产值	Gross Output Value of Farming,Forestry,Animal Husbandry and Fishery	316.34	亿元	(100 million yuan)
为上年	As Compared with the Preceding Year	109.2	%	(%)
粮食总产量	Total Output of Grain Crops	100.25	万吨	(10000 tons)
为上年	As Compared with the Preceding Year	93.5	%	(%)
肉类产量	Total Output of Meat	31.79	万吨	(10000 tons)
为上年	As Compared with the Preceding Year	102.8	%	(%)

3－01 农村基本情况
Basic Conditions of Rural Areas

指 标		Item		1995	2000	2005	2006	2007	2008	2009	2010
农村基层组织		**Rural Grassroots Units**									
乡镇政府	（个）	Number of Township & Town Governments	（unit）	230	234	149	141	136	136	130	128
#镇政府	（个）	Number of Town Governments	（unit）	134	140	110	108	105	105	99	97
村民委员会	（个）	Number of Villagers´Committees	（unit）	4681	4616	3681	3660	2501	2120	2113	2098
村民小组	（万个）	Villager Group	（10000 units）	3.61	3.53	3.43	3.43	3.40	3.29	3.24	3.26
农村户数、人口、从业人员		**Rural Households, Population & Labor Force**									
农村常住户数	（万户）	Resident Households in Rural Areas	（10000 households）	121.23	118.11	139.85	137.01	136.89	131.87	131.46	131.82
农村常住人口数	（万人）	Resident Population in Rural Areas	（10000 persons）	402.77	395.00	447.36	444.27	443.49	433.39	429.13	431.34
农村从业人员数	（万人）	Labor Force in Rural Areas	（10000 persons）	257.70	247.11	267.05	266.68	266.32	260.16	259.32	261.77
按性别分		Grouped by Sex									
男性	（万人）	Male	（10000 persons）	137.57	130.37	141.43	140.75	140.03	137.16	136.86	138.18
女性	（万人）	Female	（10000 persons）	120.13	116.74	125.62	125.93	126.29	123.00	122.46	123.59
按行业分		Grouped by Sector									
农林牧渔业	（万人）	Farming, Forestry, Animal Husbandry & Fishery	（10000 persons）	136.65	116.05	88.82	83.99	79.96	78.08	75.79	73.24
工 业	（万人）	Industry	（10000 persons）	63.40	59.27	85.50	88.65	93.58	89.91	90.75	93.70
建 筑 业	（万人）	Construction	（10000 persons）	12.04	13.02	16.51	16.98	17.66	17.70	18.10	18.68
交通运输、仓储业及邮电通讯业	（万人）	Transportation, Storage, Post & Telecommunications	（10000 persons）	8.67	9.29	11.22	11.64	11.66	11.65	11.52	11.48
批发、零售贸易、餐饮业	（万人）	Wholesale, Retail Trade & Catering Services	（10000 persons）	7.28	10.62	18.03	18.74	19.57	19.58	20.10	20.76
其它非农行业	（万人）	Other Non－agricultural Trades	（10000 persons）	29.66	38.86	46.97	46.68	43.89	43.24	43.06	43.91
#外出临时工、合同工	（万人）	Contract or Temporary Workers Going Outside	（10000 persons）	15.40	22.01	23.89	23.55	22.57	24.05	23.08	24.21
在农村从业人员中：外出	（万人）	Among the Total Rural Labor Force: Going Outside	（10000 persons）	19.14	35.73	43.22	44.12	47.26	–	–	–
#出省的	（万人）	Going to Other Provinces	（10000 persons）	2.06	4.47	5.66	5.08	5.62	–	–	–

注：2002 年起农村住户数、农村人口包括农村居委会户数、人口和农村外来户户数、人口。

a) From 2002, rural households and population in rural areas includes the natives and from the outside.

3－02 分地区

Basic Conditions of

指　标	Item	全市 Whole Municipality	市区 Urban District	#江干区 Jianggan	#拱墅区 Gongshu
农村基层组织	**Rural Grassroots Units**				
乡镇政府 （个）	Number of Township & Town Governments (unit)	128	38	4	－
#镇政府 （个）	Number of Town Governments (unit)	97	37	4	－
农村街道办事处 （个）	Sub－district office in Rural Areas (unit)	38	25	－	3
村民委员会 （个）	Number of Villagers´Committees (unit)	2098	687	6	9
村民小组 （万个）	Villagers´Group (10000 unit)	3.26	1.2	0.01	0.01
农村户数、人口、从业人员	**Rural Households, Population & Labor Force**				
农村常住户数 （万户）	Resident Households in Rural Areas (10000 households)	131.82	64.16	1.86	0.73
农村常住人口数 （万人）	Resident Population in Rural Areas (10000 persons)	431.34	223.38	7.68	2.79
农村从业人员数 （万人）	Practitioners in Rural Areas (10000 persons)	261.77	131.83	3.78	1.38
农村基础设施水平	**Public Facilities in Rural Areas**				
自来水受益村数 （个）	Number of Villages with Access to Tap Water (unit)	2097	687	6	9
通汽车村数 （个）	Number of Villages with Highways (unit)	2098	687	6	9
通电话村数 （个）	Number of Villages with Telephone Communication (unit)	2098	687	6	9

农村基本情况(2010 年)
Rural Areas by Region(2010)

#西湖区 Xihu	#高新(滨江)区 Hi-Tech(Binjiang)	#萧山区 Xiaoshan	#余杭区 Yuhang	桐庐县 Tonglu	淳安县 Chun'an	建德市 Jiande	富阳市 Fuyan	临安市 Lin'an
2	-	17	15	11	23	13	21	22
2	-	17	14	7	11	12	15	15
2	3	11	4	2	-	3	4	4
49	15	411	188	183	425	232	284	287
0.07	0.02	0.72	0.36	0.26	0.4	0.47	0.47	0.46
4.2	2.74	36.22	18	10.4	11.76	12.53	17.24	15.73
15.61	9.85	117.08	69.4	31.24	36.65	39.72	54.31	46.04
8.6	5.56	67.24	44.78	20.74	23.1	24.28	33.15	28.67
49	15	411	188	183	425	232	284	286
49	15	411	188	183	425	232	284	287
49	15	411	188	183	425	232	284	287

3－03 分地区

Rural Labor Force

单位:万人

指　　标	Item	全　市 Whole Municipality	市　区 Urban District	#江干区 Jianggan	#拱墅区 Gongshu
总　　计	**Total**	**261.77**	**131.83**	**3.78**	**1.38**
#女	Female	123.59	63.26	1.8	0.64
农、林、牧、渔业	Farming, Forestry, Animal Husbandry & Fishery	73.24	24.32	0.65	0.05
#农业	Farming	55.68	19.46	0.64	0.05
牧业	Animal Husbandry	7.3	1.32	0.01	-
工　业	Industry	93.7	57.99	1.43	0.52
建筑业	Construction	18.68	11.14	0.22	0.05
交通运输、仓储业及邮电通讯业	Transportation, Storage, Post & Telecommunications	11.48	6.34	0.32	0.14
批发、零售贸易、餐饮业	Wholesale, Retail Trade & Catering Services	20.76	11.63	0.59	0.31
其它非农行业	Other Non－agricultural Trades	43.91	20.41	0.57	0.31
#外出临时工、合同工	Contract or Temporary Workers Going Outside	24.21	9.02	0.19	0.09

农村从业人员(2010 年)
by Region(2010)

(10000 persons)

#西湖区 Xihu	#高新(滨江)区 Hi-Tech(Binjiang)	#萧山区 Xiaoshan	#余杭区 Yuhang	桐庐县 Tonglu	淳安县 Chun'an	建德市 Jiande	富阳市 Fuyan	临安市 Lin'an
8.6	**5.56**	**67.24**	**44.78**	**20.74**	**23.1**	**24.28**	**33.15**	**28.67**
4.13	2.73	32.59	21.12	9.93	10.3	11.33	15.26	13.51
2.12	0.31	12.21	8.75	7.06	11.81	10.5	10.79	8.76
1.52	0.27	9.91	6.84	5.88	8.06	8.85	8.73	4.7
0.07	0.01	0.8	0.43	0.63	2.35	1.03	0.95	1.02
1.63	2.57	31.96	19.86	6.97	1.53	5.25	11.75	10.21
0.77	0.58	6.61	2.9	1.31	1.18	1.75	2.04	1.26
0.69	0.31	2.92	1.94	0.97	0.36	0.74	1.64	1.43
0.86	0.78	5.43	3.51	1.4	0.93	1.42	2.67	2.71
2.53	1.01	8.11	7.82	3.03	7.29	4.62	4.26	4.3
1.3	0.28	3.07	4.07	1.39	6.92	2.8	2.64	1.44

3－04 主要年份农林牧渔业总产值

Gross Output Value of Farming, Forestry, Animal Husbandry and Fishery in Main Years

单位:万元 (10000 yuan)

年份 Year	农林牧渔业总产值 Gross Output Value	#农业产值 Farming	#种植业产值 Planting	林业产值 Forestry	牧业产值 Animal Husbandry	渔业产值 Fishery
1978	85922	67365	64378	3430	14474	653
1979	115649	84727	81989	4629	25216	1077
1980	112377	79006	76059	7262	25015	1094
1981	120792	87354	81659	8309	23799	1330
1982	150606	107566	103346	8912	31801	2327
1983	148878	103685	96272	9800	32693	2700
1984	177029	122567	115286	14769	35922	3771
1985	212961	136893	126026	19095	50110	6863
1986	238285	150803	138254	19990	58197	9295
1987	281326	173080	155960	26427	70129	11690
1988	358500	208838	187648	31434	101013	17215
1989	386805	225969	201389	27857	113952	19027
1990	421045	260031	233055	26962	113424	20628
1991	463578	284275	254834	37763	117458	24082
1992	497915	300828	256833	35589	133867	27631
1993	600760	365124	300736	47476	154766	33394
1994	812473	496392	415366	58627	217217	40237
1995	996440	620057	526328	81321	244054	51008
1996	1173294	740202	617573	95740	271652	65700
1997	1287650	797812	665172	114510	294153	81175
1998	1367578	845106	701850	121197	289085	112190
1999	1414737	876685	737406	126000	293495	118557
2000	1526530	903322	754311	136848	331563	154797
2001	1649978	965005	816884	149264	362303	173406
2002	1685036	932995	886285	162227	391844	197970
2003	1890129	991556	949138	182595	417798	232599
2004	1982683	1010947	972594	206787	457619	234080
2005	2194799	1136559	1103981	233039	495900	270810
2006	2253822	1224822	1191816	267748	490448	206082
2007	2471427	1308047	1279758	294707	585536	222601
2008	2737605	1408124	1374083	320212	636633	309270
2009	2897371	1497362	1462791	362317	642892	325626
2010	3163392	1698775	1673470	329278	705596	349011

注:本表按当年价格计算;从 2003 年起农林牧渔总产值包括农林牧渔业服务业产值(下同)。

a) Data in this table are calculated at current prices. From 2003, Gross Output Value includes the value of service for the farming, forestry, animal husbandry and fishery sector.

3-05 主要年份农林牧渔业总产值构成

Composition of Gross Output Value of Farming, Forestry, Animal Husbandry and Fishery in Main Years

单位:% (%)

年份 Year	农林牧渔业总产值 Gross Output Value	#农业产值 Farming	#种植业产值 Planting	林业产值 Forestry	牧业产值 Animal Husbandry	渔业产值 Fishery
1978	100.0	78.4	74.9	4.0	16.8	0.8
1979	100.0	73.3	70.9	4.0	21.8	0.9
1980	100.0	70.3	67.7	6.5	22.2	1.0
1981	100.0	72.3	67.6	6.9	19.7	1.1
1982	100.0	71.4	68.6	5.9	21.1	1.6
1983	100.0	69.6	64.7	6.6	22.0	1.8
1984	100.0	69.2	65.1	8.3	20.3	2.2
1985	100.0	64.3	59.2	9.0	23.5	3.2
1986	100.0	63.3	58.0	8.4	24.4	3.9
1987	100.0	61.5	55.4	9.4	24.9	4.2
1988	100.0	58.2	52.3	8.8	28.2	4.8
1989	100.0	58.4	52.1	7.2	29.5	4.9
1990	100.0	61.8	55.4	6.4	26.9	4.9
1991	100.0	61.3	55.0	8.2	25.3	5.2
1992	100.0	60.4	51.6	7.2	26.9	5.5
1993	100.0	60.8	50.1	7.9	25.8	5.5
1994	100.0	61.1	51.1	7.2	26.7	5.0
1995	100.0	62.2	52.8	8.2	24.5	5.1
1996	100.0	63.1	52.6	8.2	23.1	5.6
1997	100.0	62.0	51.7	8.9	22.8	6.3
1998	100.0	61.8	51.3	8.9	21.1	8.2
1999	100.0	62.0	52.1	8.9	20.7	8.4
2000	100.0	59.2	49.4	9.0	21.7	10.1
2001	100.0	58.5	52.2	9.0	22.0	10.5
2002	100.0	55.4	52.6	9.6	23.3	11.7
2003	100.0	52.5	50.2	9.7	22.1	12.3
2004	100.0	51.0	49.1	10.4	23.1	11.8
2005	100.0	51.8	50.3	10.6	22.6	12.3
2006	100.0	54.3	52.9	11.9	21.8	9.1
2007	100.0	52.9	51.8	11.9	23.7	9.0
2008	100.0	51.4	50.2	11.7	23.3	11.3
2009	100.0	51.7	50.5	12.5	22.2	11.2
2010	100.0	53.7	52.9	10.4	22.3	11

注:本表按当年价格计算。

a) Figures in value terms in this table are calculated at current prices.

3-06 主要年份农林牧渔业分项产值

Gross Output Value of Farming, Forestry, Animal Husbandry and Fishery by Branch in Main Years

单位:万元 (10000 yuan)

指　　标	Item	1995	2000	2005	2006	2007	2008	2009	2010
农林牧渔业总产值(现价)	**Gross Output Value (Current Price)**	**996440**	**1526530**	**2194799**	**2253822**	**2471427**	**2737605**	**2897371**	**3163392**
#一、农业产值	**Farming**	**620057**	**903322**	**1136559**	**1224822**	**1308047**	**1408124**	**1497362**	**1698775**
1. 种植业产值	Planting	526328	754311	1103981	1191816	1279758	1374083	1462791	1673470
粮食	Grain	262321	208546	178981	187293	194032	217705	217895	215990
油料	Oil-bearing Crops	19675	19583	21608	20111	22987	28809	30796	31137
棉花	Cotton	11829	2205	1146	1012	1058	1126	1155	1255
麻类	Fiber Crops	3863	384	176	115	97	55	30	42
甘蔗	Sugarcane	14274	23815	19075	17028	18697	18942	20074	18756
烟叶	Tobacco	1	5	7	2	3	1	1	1
药材类	Crude Drugs	1725	6005	15800	20428	23901	23432	35546	42927
蔬菜	Vegetables	151614	303583	357734	382697	415720	447147	454890	535623
茶、桑、果	Tea, Mulberry & Fruits	48599	106727	254379	285994	306954	330717	360120	484261
其他	Others	12427	83458	255075	277136	296309	306149	342284	343478
2. 其他农业产值	Other Farming	93729	149011	32578	33006	28289	34041	34571	25305
二、林业产值	**Forestry**	**81321**	**136848**	**233039**	**267748**	**294707**	**320212**	**362317**	**329278**
人造林木生长	Artificial Forestry	11286	18226	23140	22474	22376	24053	26310	27964
林产品	Forest Products	45123	89914	168348	185455	203082	225872	260694	184740
竹木采伐	Lumbering	24912	28708	41551	59819	69249	70287	75313	82063
采集野生植物	Wild Plant collected								34511
三、牧业产值	**Animal Husbandry**	**244054**	**331563**	**495900**	**490448**	**585536**	**636633**	**642892**	**705596**
牲畜	Livestock Raising	143879	175732	292025	283198	366339	390789	387278	430193
家禽饲养	Poultry Raising	35302	65548	68631	50444	61077	72229	72167	70201
活的畜禽产品	Livestock Products	37197	44098	68143	62467	76374	94738	97739	109625
捕猎野兽野禽	Hunting Wild Beast and Wild Fowl	491	2102	2856	3050	3222	3620	4058	4455
其他动物饲养	Other Animals Raising	27185	44083	64245	91289	78524	75257	81650	91122
四、渔业产值	**Fishery**	**51008**	**154797**	**270810**	**206082**	**222601**	**309270**	**325626**	**349011**

注:从2010年开始,茶、桑、果中包含坚果类产值,种植业中的"采集野生植物"产值归入到林业里。

a) Since 2010, the output value of nuts was included in Tea, Mulberry & Fruits, Nuts the output value of "Collecting wild plants" was included in Forestry.

3－07 主要年份农林牧渔业分项产值构成

Composition of Gross Output Value of Farming, Forestry, Animal Husbandry and Fishery by Branch in Main Years

单位:% (%)

指　标	Item	1995	2000	2005	2006	2007	2008	2009	2010
农林牧渔业总产值(现价)	**Gross Output Value (Current Price)**	**100**	**100**	**100**	**100**	**100**	**100**	**100**	**100**
#一、农业产值	**Farming**	**62.2**	**59.2**	**51.8**	**54.3**	**52.9**	**51.4**	**51.7**	**53.7**
1.种植业产值	Planting	52.8	49.4	50.3	52.9	51.8	50.2	50.5	52.9
粮食	Grain	26.3	13.7	8.2	8.3	7.9	8	7.5	6.8
油料	Oil Plants	2.0	1.3	1.0	0.9	0.9	1.1	1.1	1
棉花	Cotton	1.2	0.1	0.1	–	–	–	–	–
麻类	Fiber Crops	0.4	–	–	–	–	–	–	–
甘蔗	Sugarcane	1.4	1.6	0.9	0.8	0.8	0.7	0.7	0.6
烟叶	Tobacco	–	–	–	–	–	–	–	–
药材类	Crude Drugs	0.2	0.4	0.7	0.9	1	0.9	1.2	1.4
蔬菜	Vegetables	15.2	19.9	16.3	17.0	16.8	16.3	15.7	16.9
茶、桑、果	Tea, Mulberry & Fruits	4.9	7.0	11.6	12.7	12.4	12.1	12.4	15.3
其他	Others	1.2	5.4	11.5	12.3	12.0	11.1	11.9	10.9
2.其他农业产值	Other Farming	9.4	9.8	1.5	1.4	1.1	1.2	1.2	0.8
二、林业产值	**Forestry**	**8.2**	**9.0**	**10.6**	**11.9**	**11.9**	**11.7**	**12.5**	**10.4**
人造林木生长	Artificial Forestry	1.2	1.2	1.1	1.0	0.9	0.9	0.9	0.9
林产品	Forest Products	4.5	5.9	7.6	8.2	8.2	8.2	9	5.8
竹木采伐	Lumbering	2.5	1.9	1.9	2.7	2.8	2.6	2.6	2.6
采集野生植物	Wild Plant collected								1.1
三、牧业产值	**Animal Husbandry**	**24.5**	**21.7**	**22.6**	**21.8**	**23.7**	**23.3**	**22.2**	**22.3**
牲畜	Livestock Raising	14.4	11.5	13.3	12.6	14.8	14.3	13.4	13.6
家禽饲养	Poultry Raising	3.6	4.3	3.1	2.2	2.5	2.6	2.5	2.2
活的畜禽产品	Livestock Products	3.7	2.9	3.2	2.8	3.1	3.5	3.4	3.5
捕猎野兽野禽	Hunting Wild Beast and Wild Fowl	–	0.1	0.1	0.1	0.1	0.1	0.1	0.1
其他动物饲养	Other Animals Raising	2.8	2.9	2.9	4.1	3.2	2.8	2.8	2.9
四、渔业产值	**Fishery**	**5.1**	**10.1**	**12.3**	**9.1**	**9**	**11.3**	**11.2**	**11**

3－08 分地区农林牧

Gross Output Value of Farming, Forestry,

单位:万元

指　　标	Item	全　市 Whole Municipality	市　区 Urban District	#江干区 Jianggan	#拱墅区 Gongshu
合　　计	**Gross Output Value**	**3163392**	**1480179**	**15188**	**4519**
#一、农业产值	**Farming**	**1698775**	**776763**	**12285**	**4034**
(一)种植业产值	Planting	1673470	774721	12265	4034
#副产品产值	By－products	11274	4816	－	－
1.粮食作物	Grain	215990	97101	－	－
谷　　物	Cereal	159426	77072	－	－
豆　　类	Beans	28050	12464	－	－
薯　　类	Tubers	28514	7565	－	－
2.油　　料	Oil Plants	31137	8365	－	－
3.棉　　花	Cotton	1255	869	－	－
4.麻　　类	Fiber Crops	42	18	－	－
5.甘　　蔗	Sugarcane	18756	13885	－	－
6.烟　　叶	Tobacco	1	－	－	－
7.药 材 类	Crude Drugs	42927	1512	－	－
8.蔬　　菜	Vegetables	535623	289432	11132	420
9.茶、桑、果	Tea, Mulberry & Fruits	484261	110539	47	－
10.其　　他	Others	343478	253000	1086	3614
(二)其他农业产值	Other Farming	25305	2042	20	－
二、林业产值	**Forestry**	**329278**	**66659**	**18**	**8**
1.人造林木生长	Artificial Forestry	27964	6776	18	8
2.林产品	Forest Products	184740	40181	－	－
3.村及村以下竹木采伐	Lumbering	82063	16813	－	－
4.采集野生植物	Wild Plant collected	34511	2889	－	－
三、牧业产值	**Animal Husbandry**	**705596**	**316017**	**1169**	**1**
1.牲畜	Livestock	430193	236786	1003	－
2.家禽饲养	Poultry Raising	70201	39159	－	1
3.活的畜禽产品	Livestock Products	109625	25493	－	－
4.捕猎野兽野禽	Hunting Wild Beast and Wild Fowl	4455	798	－	－
5.其他动物饲养	Other Animals Raising	91122	13781	166	－
四、渔业产值	**Fishery**	**349011**	**263848**	**1601**	**476**

注:本表按当年价格计算。

渔业总产值(2010 年)

Animal Husbandry and Fishery by Region(2010)

(10000 yuan)

#西湖区 Xihu	#高新(滨江)区 Hi-Tech(Binjiang)	#萧山区 Xiaoshan	#余杭区 Yuhang	桐庐县 Tonglu	淳安县 Chun'an	建德市 Jiande	富阳市 Fuyang	临安市 Lin'an
57719	**26182**	**750777**	**601040**	**237577**	**310050**	**331956**	**413040**	**390590**
22572	**21383**	**420565**	**284080**	**143851**	**201011**	**178807**	**227621**	**170722**
22544	21383	420474	282177	143772	200622	170791	215358	168205
169	20	2763	1849	897	1370	1128	1721	1342
3050	357	44930	48456	24853	18301	19129	32440	24166
2355	311	36544	37554	15262	11122	14457	25049	16464
402	45	7263	4754	4877	2613	1990	3792	2314
293	1	1123	6148	4714	4566	2682	3599	5388
58	1	4704	3595	6170	3813	4455	5237	3097
–	1	669	199	–	124	259	–	3
–	–	7	11	–	24	–	–	–
271	211	10819	2584	1304	985	942	1502	138
–	–	–	–	–	1	–	–	–
101	–	14	1397	6323	18031	8877	3886	4298
7870	6337	172520	87185	37071	59228	42915	78801	28176
5800	1132	21269	74850	55357	92914	86226	53553	85672
5394	13344	165542	63900	12695	7201	7988	39939	22655
28	–	91	1903	78	389	8016	12263	2517
610	**18**	**9830**	**56107**	**20762**	**31383**	**15986**	**60164**	**134324**
395	–	1163	5124	336	6586	945	6209	7112
65	18	6446	33652	11851	8093	4503	35897	84215
150	–	1778	14885	4399	8871	8260	8457	35263
–	–	443	2446	4176	7833	2278	9601	7734
3299	**2095**	**214660**	**87080**	**52011**	**54814**	**112265**	**97115**	**73374**
1764	1982	178803	52151	21444	27382	33752	60276	50553
432	89	19370	19177	2893	978	10246	14468	2457
316	6	4432	14199	3162	2991	63827	7367	6785
–	–	514	284	707	93	394	2087	376
787	18	11541	1269	23805	23370	4046	12917	13203
30578	**2686**	**79605**	**143773**	**16326**	**20202**	**17398**	**25208**	**6029**

a) Data in this table are calculated at current prices.

3－09 农林牧渔业

Value－Added and Commodity Output Value of Farming,

单位:万元

指　　标	Item	全　市 Whole Municipality	市　区 Urban District	#江干区 Jianggan	#拱墅区 Gongshu
一、总产值	**Gross Output Value**	**3163392**	**1480179**	**15188**	**4519**
#农业产值	Farming	1698775	776763	12285	4034
林业产值	Forestry	329278	66659	18	8
牧业产值	Animal Husbandry	705596	316017	1169	1
渔业产值	Fishery	349011	263848	1601	476
二、中间消耗	**Intermediate Consume**	**1079248**	**538588**	**5632**	**1607**
1. 物质消耗	Material Consume	818900	394829	3964	1085
2. 劳务支出	Labor Services Expense	260348	143759	1668	522
#农业中间消耗	Agriculture Consume	479432	218036	4749	1491
林业中间消耗	Forestry Consume	68991	20759	2	3
牧业中间消耗	Animal Husbandry Consume	354102	163062	204	－
渔业中间消耗	Fishery Consume	122915	97942	617	113
三、增加值	**The Value－Added**	**2084144**	**941591**	**9556**	**2912**
1. 生产法	1. Production Approach	－	－	－	－
#农业增加值	Farming	1219343	558727	7536	2543
林业增加值	Forestry	260287	45900	16	5
牧业增加值	Husbandry	351494	152955	965	1
渔业增加值	Fishery	226096	165906	984	363
2. 收入法	2. Income Approach	－	－	－	－
#固定资产折旧	Depreciation of Fixed Assets	94377	47695	3166	187
劳动者报酬	Compensation of Laborers	2087800	929238	6390	2725

注:本表按当年价格计算。

产值及增加值(2010 年)

Forestry, Animal Husbandry and Fishery(2010)

(10000 yuan)

#西湖区 Xihu	#高新(滨江)区 Hi-Tech(Binjiang)	#萧山区 Xiaoshan	#余杭区 Yuhang	桐庐县 Tonglu	淳安县 Chun'an	建德市 Jiande	富阳市 Fuyang	临安市 Lin'an
57719	**26182**	**750777**	**601040**	**237577**	**310050**	**331956**	**413040**	**390590**
22572	21383	420565	284080	143851	201011	178807	227621	170722
610	18	9830	56107	20762	31383	15986	60164	134324
3299	2095	214660	87080	52011	54814	112265	97115	73374
30578	2686	79605	143773	16326	20202	17398	25208	6029
19033	**9237**	**278566**	**216522**	**77549**	**91618**	**124404**	**126379**	**120710**
15168	5047	202276	161586	49529	70806	104704	98145	100887
3865	4190	76290	54936	28020	20812	19700	28234	19823
7835	6840	117040	77157	43122	47813	51932	65878	52651
74	7	5824	14823	3694	7903	2957	6362	27316
1557	767	105619	51614	22956	27594	59234	46654	34602
9118	1623	32653	52078	4779	7066	5081	5727	2320
38686	**16945**	**472211**	**384518**	**160028**	**218432**	**207552**	**286661**	**269880**
–	–	–	–	–	–	–	–	–
14737	14543	303525	206923	100729	153198	126875	161743	118071
536	11	4006	41284	17068	23480	13029	53802	107008
1742	1328	109041	35466	29055	27220	53031	50461	38772
21460	1063	46952	91695	11547	13136	12317	19481	3709
–	–	–	–	–	–	–	–	–
2567	1303	23052	16223	9166	4328	13051	6701	13436
36119	15642	455854	396942	158634	218164	238274	280133	263357

a) Data in this table are calculated at current prices.

3－10 主要农作物播种面积及产量

Sown Areas and Yield of Major Farm Crops

指　标	Item	2010			2009		
		播种面积（千公顷）Sown Area（1000 hectares）	总产量（吨）Total Output（ton）	公顷产量（公斤）Yield per Hectare（kg/hectare）	播种面积（千公顷）Sown Area（1000 hectares）	总产量（吨）Total Output（ton）	公顷产量（公斤）Yield per Hectare（kg/hectare）
农作物总计	**Total Farm Crops**	**381.83**	**–**	**–**	**396.31**	**–**	**–**
一、粮食作物合计	**Grain Crops**	**174.65**	**1002517**	**5740**	**188.99**	**1072434**	**5675**
#春粮	#Spring Grain	26.15	95934	3669	26.38	96054	3642
秋粮	Autumn Grain	146.43	893895	6105	160.58	963692	6001
（一）谷　物	Cereals	118.49	792057	6685	127.49	848438	6655
1.稻谷	Rice	80.78	626331	7753	89.01	680616	7646
①早稻及早中稻	Early Rice & Semi－late Rice	2.08	11997	5765	2.04	12688	6220
②晚稻及迟中稻	Late Rice & Semi－late Rice	78.71	614334	7806	86.97	667928	7680
#单季稻	#Single－crop Rice	76.36	597765	7828	84.57	651294	7701
2.小麦	Wheat	16.41	65237	3976	16.38	65545	4001
3.大麦	Barley	0.51	1759	3449	0.69	2476	3588
4.玉米	Corn	19.39	93216	4807	20.06	94625	4718
5.其他谷物	Other Cereals	1.4	5514	3950	1.35	5176	3823
（二）豆　类	Beans	34.45	93164	2704	38.51	101128	2626
1.大豆	Soybeans	25.63	68389	2668	29.68	76412	2574
2.蚕（豌）豆	Broad Beans	4.63	12331	2663	4.47	11865	2657
3.杂豆	Other Beans	4.19	12444	2971	4.36	12851	2948
（三）蕃　薯	Yam	21.71	117296	5403	22.99	122868	5344

3－10 续表 continued

指 标	Item	2010 播种面积（千公顷）Sown Area (1000 hectares)	2010 总产量（吨）Total Output (ton)	2010 公顷产量（公斤）Yield per Hectare (kg/hectare)	2009 播种面积（千公顷）Sown Area (1000 hectares)	2009 总产量（吨）Total Output (ton)	2009 公顷产量（公斤）Yield per Hectare (kg/hectare)
二、油料合计	**Oil Plants**	**43.08**	**86556**	**2009**	**42.75**	**90065**	**2107**
1. 油菜籽	Rapeseeds	39.09	76676	1962	38.72	80081	2068
2. 花生	Peanuts	2.73	8052	2948	2.78	8170	2944
3. 芝麻	Sesame	1.26	1828	1445	1.25	1814	1455
三、棉花（皮棉）	**Cotton**	**0.66**	**929**	**1412**	**0.75**	**959**	**1279**
四、麻类合计	**Fiber Cropers**	**0.04**	**125**	**3571**	**0.03**	**189**	**5906**
五、糖料	**Sugar Crops**	**2.48**	**149231**	**60125**	**2.61**	**157432**	**60435**
六、烟叶	**Tobacco**	**－**	**1**	**333**	**－**	**2**	**667**
七、药材类	**Crude Drugs**	**4.07**	**23306**	**5731**	**3.65**	**26017**	**7122**
八、蔬菜	**Vegetables**	**98.06**	**3124381**	**31862**	**98.93**	**3133542**	**31674**
九、果用瓜	**Melon as Fruit**	**12.77**	**421277**	**32992**	**12.89**	**428884**	**33265**
#1. 西瓜	Watermelon	10.04	354309	35297	10.42	365190	35057
2. 草莓	Strawberry	0.83	26434	31887	0.74	24407	32805
十、花卉园艺	**Flower Gardening**	**31.94**	**－**	**－**	**30.78**	**－**	**－**
十一、其他作物	**Others**	**14.08**	**－**	**－**	**14.93**	**－**	**－**
#绿肥	Green Manure	1.99	－	－	2.27	－	－

3-11 分地区粮食
Sown Areas and Yield of

指 标		Item		全市 Whole Municipality	市区 Urban District	#江干区 Jianggan	#拱墅区 Gongshu	#西湖区 Xihu	#高新(滨江)区 Hi-Tech (Binjiang)
一、粮食播种面积总计	**(公顷)**	**Sown Area of Grain Crops**	**(hectare)**	**174651**	**75239**	**–**	**–**	**2592**	**290**
春粮	(公顷)	Spring Grain	(hectare)	26145	14260	–	–	161	120
早稻	(公顷)	Early Rice	(hectare)	2081	1136	–	–	–	–
晚稻	(公顷)	Late Rice	(hectare)	78705	40024	–	–	1509	92
薯类	(公顷)	Tubers	(hectare)	21710	3102	–	–	203	1
玉米	(公顷)	Corn	(hectare)	19390	3475	–	–	229	30
大豆	(公顷)	Soybeans	(hectare)	25633	12807	–	–	287	47
杂豆	(公顷)	Other Beans	(hectare)	4189	1175	–	–	158	–
其他谷物	(公顷)	Other Cereals	(hectare)	1396	240	–	–	86	–
二、粮食总产量	**(吨)**	**Yield of Grain Crops**	**(ton)**	**1002517**	**455970**	**–**	**–**	**17291**	**1285**
春粮	(吨)	Spring Grain	(ton)	95934	60796	–		417	336
早稻	(吨)	Early Rice	(ton)	11997	6961	–	–	–	–
晚稻	(吨)	Late Rice	(ton)	614334	319505	–	–	12700	694
薯类	(吨)	Tubers	(ton)	117296	17859	–	–	1162	3
玉米	(吨)	Corn	(ton)	93216	17573	–	–	1342	129
大豆	(吨)	Soybeans	(ton)	68389	32043	–	–	806	122
杂豆	(吨)	Other Beans	(ton)	12444	3780	–	–	420	–
其他谷物	(吨)	Other Cereals	(ton)	5514	1147	–	–	557	–
三、粮食平均每公顷产量		**Yield of Grain Crops per Hectare**		**5740**	**6060**	**–**	**–**	**6671**	**4431**
春粮	(公斤)	Spring Grain	(kg)	3669	4263	–	–	2594	2800
早稻	(公斤)	Early Rice	(kg)	5765	6128	–	–	–	–
晚稻	(公斤)	Late Rice	(kg)	7806	7983	–	–	8416	7543
薯类	(公斤)	Tubers	(kg)	5403	5757	–	–	5724	3000
玉米	(公斤)	Corn	(kg)	4807	5057	–	–	5860	4300
大豆	(公斤)	Soybeans	(kg)	2668	2502	–	–	2808	2596

备注:春粮包括薯类中的马铃薯。

播种面积及产量(2010年)
Grain Crops by Region(2010)

#萧山区 Xiaoshan	#余杭区 Yuhang	桐庐县 Tonglu	淳安县 Chun'an	建德市 Jiande	富阳市 Fuyang	临安市 Lin'an
44298	**27937**	**16171**	**24706**	**18249**	**24656**	**15630**
10727	3145	2010	1918	2599	2988	2370
63	1058	26	–	819	100	–
20286	18137	6938	3755	8490	12455	7043
987	1911	2786	6545	2993	3505	2779
1848	1368	1957	7295	1497	2930	2236
10195	2278	2282	5173	1805	2160	1406
350	667	581	457	435	970	571
67	87	270	327	189	277	93
244475	**191694**	**95059**	**102539**	**99336**	**157674**	**91939**
49597	10126	5465	5104	7779	9497	7293
365	6524	144	–	4319	573	–
156861	148416	52818	27332	63602	98169	52908
5894	10800	17632	28119	12987	22974	17725
8676	7426	9521	32755	7113	15613	10641
22735	8380	8489	10537	4403	8435	4482
1045	2315	1844	786	822	3537	1675
266	324	1197	834	651	1355	330
5519	**6862**	**5878**	**4150**	**5444**	**6395**	**5882**
4623	3220	2719	2660	2994	3178	3076
5794	6166	5538	–	5277	5730	–
7732	8183	7613	7279	7491	7882	7512
5972	5651	6329	4297	4340	6555	6378
4695	5428	4865	4490	4751	5329	4759
2230	3679	3720	2037	2439	3905	3188

a) Spring grain includes patato in tubers.

3－12 油、菜、茶、

Statistics on Rapeseeds, Vegetables, Tea,

指标		Item		全市 Whole Municipality	市区 Urban District	#江干区 Jianggan	#拱墅区 Gongshu	#西湖区 Xihu	#高新(滨江)区 Hi－Tech (Binjiang)
一、油菜籽		**Rapeseeds**							
播种面积	(公顷)	Sown Area	(hectare)	39086	9512	－	－	129	2
每公顷产量	(公斤)	Yield per Hectare	(kg)	1962	2136	－	－	2078	1500
总产量	(吨)	Total Output	(ton)	76676	20320	－	－	269	3
二、蔬菜		**Vegetables**							
播种面积	(公顷)	Sown Area	(hectare)	98060	58832	2477	143	2290	990
总产量	(吨)	Total Output	(ton)	3124381	1818779	61847	2237	52531	40894
三、茶叶		**Tea**							
(一)茶园面积	(公顷)	Tea Garden Area	(hectare)	32262	6013	29	－	640	57
(二)总产量	(吨)	Output of Tea	(ton)	30500	11334	13	－	529	65
春　茶	(吨)	Spring Tea	(ton)	19733	6531	13	－	169	20
夏　茶	(吨)	Summer Tea	(ton)	5483	2530	－	－	103	15
秋　茶	(吨)	Autumn Tea	(ton)	5284	2273	－	－	257	30
四、桑蚕		**Silkworm Cocoons & Mulberry**							
(一)桑园总面积	(公顷)	Mulberry Garden Area	(hectare)	16651	1734	1	－	1	－
(二)蚕茧总产量	(吨)	Output of Silkworm Cocoons	(ton)	15637	476	11	－	－	－
春　茧	(吨)	Spring Silkworm Cocoons	(ton)	6979	409	8	－	－	－
夏　茧	(吨)	Summer Silkworm Cocoons	(ton)	1303	8	－	－	－	－
秋　茧	(吨)	Autumn Silkworm Cocoons	(ton)	7355	59	3	－	－	－

蚕、果生产情况(2010 年)
Silkworm Cocoons and Fruits Production(2010)

#萧山区 Xiaoshan	#余杭区 Yuhang	桐庐县 Tonglu	淳安县 Chun'an	建德市 Jiande	富阳市 Fuyang	临安市 Lin'an
4754	4614	6331	6978	5971	7454	2840
2336	1934	1803	1731	1653	2282	2108
11104	8924	11412	12079	9871	17007	5987
29042	23063	6412	9028	7321	10452	6015
1113035	528395	205952	315042	208022	437786	138800
1287	3657	3485	12157	3541	3475	3591
890	9614	1651	6850	3681	5039	1945
741	5506	1268	4496	2930	3000	1508
30	2344	225	706	551	1163	308
119	1764	158	1648	200	876	129
98	1634	1964	8356	1371	1102	2124
6	459	3606	6151	840	1967	2597
6	395	1865	2371	328	845	1161
–	8	78	892	30	264	31
–	56	1663	2888	482	858	1405

指标	Item	全市 Whole Municipality	市区 Urban District	#江干区 Jianggan	#拱墅区 Gongshu	#西湖区 Xihu	#高新(滨江)区 Hi－Tech (Binjiang)
五、水果生产	**Fruits**						
(一)果园面积合计 (公顷)	Area of Orchards (hectare)	28059	6112	–	–	76	99
柑桔园 (公顷)	Citrus (hectare)	9859	113	–	–	11	10
梨　园 (公顷)	Pears (hectare)	4008	1179	–	–	11	35
桃　园 (公顷)	Peaches (hectare)	3173	622	–	–	7	1
杨梅园 (公顷)	Red Bayberry (hectare)	2812	985	–	–	7	49
枇杷园 (公顷)	Loquat (hectare)	2124	743	–	–	–	–
柿子园 (公顷)	Persimmons (hectare)	898	122	–	–	4	–
葡萄园 (公顷)	Grapes (hectare)	582	186	–	–	32	3
其他果园 (公顷)	Others (hectare)	4603	2162	–	–	4	1
(二)水果总产量 (吨)	Yield of Fruits (ton)	777113	233518	–	–	3390	3149
柑　桔 (吨)	Citrus (ton)	156346	1286	–	–	298	100
梨　头 (吨)	Pears (ton)	63020	16236	–	–	365	1655
桃　子 (吨)	Peaches (ton)	54510	9940	–	–	130	5
杨　梅 (吨)	Red Bayberry (ton)	11757	2842	–	–	15	49
枇　杷 (吨)	Loquat (ton)	12770	5729	–	–	–	–
柿　子 (吨)	Persimmons (ton)	9816	1963	–	–	57	–
葡　萄 (吨)	Grapes (ton)	11881	3426	–	–	895	10
果用瓜 (吨)	Melon as Fruit (ton)	421277	184213	–	–	1548	1325
其他水果 (吨)	Others (ton)	35736	7883	–	–	82	5

注:水果产量包括果用瓜和草莓产量。

continued

#萧山区 Xiaoshan	#余杭区 Yuhang	桐庐县 Tonglu	淳安县 Chun'an	建德市 Jiande	富阳市 Fuyang	临安市 Lin'an
2584	3350	3114	8408	6572	2431	1422
30	62	550	4578	4232	273	113
232	901	1170	549	299	558	253
212	402	469	740	354	696	292
726	203	329	371	530	413	184
1	742	125	660	507	80	9
84	34	50	455	139	93	39
74	77	114	50	20	123	89
1225	929	307	1005	491	195	443
121244	104385	97655	105771	173497	122170	44502
418	470	8365	54443	86632	4856	764
2537	11679	18444	4178	5478	14426	4258
2513	7292	8329	5378	4094	20842	5927
1826	952	1840	689	1148	4033	1205
34	5695	1344	2855	2028	697	117
1333	573	1078	3106	1319	1976	374
1344	1177	1622	615	186	4989	1043
105229	74811	52527	25028	68396	67498	23615
6010	1736	4106	9479	4216	2853	7199

a) Yield of fruits including melon as fruit and yield of strawberry.

3－13 分地区畜牧业
Statistics on Animal

指 标		Item		全市 Whole Municipality	市区 Urban District	#江干区 Jianggan	#拱墅区 Gongshu
一、生猪饲养		**Hogs**					
生猪年末存栏	（万头）	Being Raised at Year－end	（10000 heads）	192.53	105.01	0.2	－
#能繁殖的母猪	（万头）	#Reproducible	（10000 heads）	16.55	10.92	0.01	－
年内肥猪出栏	（万头）	Slaughtered Hogs of the Year	（10000 heads）	324.91	174.52	0.31	－
全年饲养量	（万头）	Number of Hogs Raised in the year	（10000 heads）	517.44	279.53	0.51	－
二、牛		**Cattle & Buffaloes**					
牛年末存栏	（头）	Being Raised at Year－end	（head）	22688	8130	－	－
#良种及改良种乳牛	（头）	#Improved Milk Cows	（head）	10482	7288	－	－
牛年内出栏	（头）	Slaughtered Cattle & Buffaloes of the Year	（head）	10631	1237	－	－
三、羊		**Sheep & Goats**					
羊年末存栏	（万只）	Being Raised at Year－end	（10000 heads）	17.5	10.04	3.36	－
羊年内出栏	（万只）	Slaughtered Sheep & Goats of the Year	（10000 heads）	21.7	12.04	2.27	－
四、家禽		**Poultry**					
家禽年末存栏	（万只）	Being Raised at Year－end	（10000 heads）	1985.35	755.37	－	0.3
家禽年内出栏	（万只）	Slaughtered Poultry of the Year	（10000 heads）	4493.69	2471.58	－	0.29
五、兔		**Rabbits**					
兔年末存栏	（万只）	Being Raised at Year－end	（10000 heads）	18.12	6.59	－	－
兔年内出栏	（万只）	Slaughtered Rabbits of the Year	（10000 heads）	33.71	14.01	－	－
六、年末养蜂箱数	**（箱）**	**Beehives**	**（case）**	**185023**	**37341**	**3500**	**－**
七、畜禽产品产量		**Output of Livestock Products**					
1. 肉类产量	（吨）	Output of Meat	（ton）	317872	168293	891	3
#猪　肉	（吨）	Pork	（ton）	242902	128480	120	－

渔业生产(2010年)
Husbanday and Fishery by Region(2010)

#西湖区 Xihu	#高新(滨江)区 Hi-Tech(Binjiang)	#萧山区 Xiaoshan	#余杭区 Yuhang	桐庐县 Tonglu	淳安县 Chun'an	建德市 Jiande	富阳市 Fuyang	临安市 Lin'an
1.68	0.35	85.22	17	13.26	17	18.4	19.57	19.29
0.02	0.03	9.69	1.11	0.73	0.75	1.7	1.02	1.43
1.98	1.53	135.45	34.59	20.82	20.86	25.1	46.31	37.3
3.66	1.88	220.67	51.59	34.08	37.86	43.5	65.88	56.59
8	-	2199	773	2867	2140	2426	3700	3425
-	-	1902	236	190	-	189	1415	1400
16	-	104	417	1259	870	1368	3050	2847
0.09	-	1.79	4.77	1.31	0.29	1	3.22	1.64
0.07	-	3.34	6.33	1.76	0.28	1	4.3	2.32
14.27	1.65	385.33	353.17	87.29	41.14	792	205.07	104.48
31.31	5.42	1232.03	1197.53	144.64	55.67	708	964.49	149.31
-	-	1.42	5.17	3.92	0.32	2	2.08	3.21
-	-	4.14	9.87	7.34	0.34	2	7.8	2.22
200	**100**	**31265**	**2276**	**82073**	**17842**	**10436**	**26097**	**11234**
1800	1243	115695	47986	18736	17160	29936	50721	33026
1318	1171	96655	28666	15711	16173	18728	34733	29077

3－13 续表

指 标	Item	全市 Whole Municipality	市区 Urban District	#江干区 Jianggan	#拱墅区 Gongshu	#西湖区 Xihu	#高新(滨江)区 Hi－Tech (Binjiang)
牛 肉 （吨）	Beef (ton)	1760	246	－	－	4	－
羊 肉 （吨）	Mutton (ton)	4232	2608	68	－	8	－
兔 肉 （吨）	Rabbit Meat (ton)	634	320	－	－	－	－
禽 肉 （吨）	Poultry Meat (ton)	67896	36639	－	3	470	72
2. 禽蛋产量 （吨）	Poultry Eggs (ton)	147663	27954	－	－	791	12
3. 蜂蜜产量 （吨）	Honey (ton)	22076	2321	200	－	－	15
4. 蜂皇浆产量 （公斤）	Honey Tonic (kg)	660208	137854	17000	－	－	400
5. 牛奶产量 （吨）	Milk (ton)	41374	29710	－	－	－	－
6. 兔毛产量 （吨）	Rabbit Wool (ton)	32	4	－	－	－	－
八、渔业生产	**Fishery**						
（一）淡水产品产量总计（吨）	Total Output of Freshwater Aquatic Products (ton)	208945	159568	620	319	30932	2214
其中：养殖产量（吨）	Artificially Cultured (ton)	188944	145927	540	319	20574	1334
1. 鱼 类 （吨）	Fish (ton)	111242	75554	320	270	14544	786
#鲫 鱼 （吨）	#Crucians (ton)	11836	5983	70	－	2537	280
鳊 鱼 （吨）	Breams (ton)	6262	3125	15	－	1081	50
黑 鱼 （吨）	Snake Heads (ton)	18351	18289	－	19	1357	22
2. 虾蟹类 （吨）	Shrimps, Prawns & Crabs (ton)	43142	42001	40	－	1763	506
3. 贝 类 （吨）	Shellfish (ton)	1330	201	－	－	201	－
4. 其 他 （吨）	Others (ton)	33230	28171	180	49	4066	42
#甲 鱼 （吨）	Turtles (ton)	30942	27072	－	49	4017	40
（二）淡水养殖面积合计 （公顷）	Freshwater Aquiculture Area (hectare)	61571	12249	151	16	2467	246

continued

#萧山区 Xiaoshan	#余杭区 Yuhang	桐庐县 Tonglu	淳安县 Chun'an	建德市 Jiande	富阳市 Fuyang	临安市 Lin'an
18	89	252	128	198	456	480
632	1282	362	44	142	645	431
62	258	121	5	35	118	35
18328	17691	2138	805	10823	14761	2730
3756	23395	5790	3826	93650	9613	6830
1794	312	9919	1893	497	6318	1128
118603	1851	400021	22278	21805	48782	29468
7370	540	350	–	534	6150	4630
3	1	–	–	–	–	28
59876	63461	7355	15278	12735	9910	4099
59236	61851	7062	12870	10076	9460	3549
18504	40757	3304	12735	8801	7680	3168
206	2820	742	1018	1254	2136	703
–	1958	75	732	1428	793	109
6756	10133	–	–	–	55	7
35997	1995	137	–	193	792	19
–	–	–	–	903	226	–
4735	19099	3621	135	179	762	362
4245	18721	3034	135	85	362	254
3895	4838	1440	41660	2011	1503	2708

3－14 分地区林业
Statistics on Forestry

指 标		Item		全市 Whole Municipality	市区 Urban District
一、营林情况		**Afforestation**			
1. 当年造林面积	(公顷)	Afforested Areas	(hectare)	1473	－
#用材林	(公顷)	#Timber Forest	(hectare)	461	－
经济林	(公顷)	Economic Forest	(hectare)	498	－
2. 迹地更新面积	(公顷)	Area of Forest Updating	(hectare)	2095	319
3. 封山育林面积	(公顷)	Area of Afforestation in Enclosed Mountain	(hectare)	61059	14604
4. 零星(四旁)植树	(万株)	Planting Trees	(10000 plant)	430.3	288.6
5. 幼林抚育作业面积	(公顷)	Area of Seedling Cultivated	(hectare)	11699	1706
6. 成林抚育面积	(公顷)	Area of Grown Forest Cultivated	(hectare)	24803	14960
二、林产品产量		**Output of Forest Products**			
1. 油桐籽	(吨)	Tung－oil Seeds	(ton)	－	－
2. 油茶籽	(吨)	Tea－oil Seeds	(ton)	7588	－
3. 竹笋干	(吨)	Dried Bamboo Shoots	(ton)	50748	10913
4. 核 桃	(吨)	Walnuts	(ton)	16100	40
5. 板 栗	(吨)	Chestnuts	(ton)	12349	886
三、竹木采伐量		**Lumbering**			
1. 木 材	(万立方米)	Timber Cut	(10000 cu. m)	36.87	1.09
2. 竹 材	(万支)	Bamboo Cut	(10000 pieces)	2233	839

生产(2010 年)
by Region(2010)

#萧山区 Xiaoshan	#余杭区 Yuhang	桐庐县 Tonglu	淳安县 Chun'an	建德市 Jiande	富阳市 Fuyang	临安市 Lin'an
–	–	51	266	200	454	502
–	–	–	201	53	121	86
–	–	51	65	13	86	283
7	12	639	32	473	130	502
13339	–	39333	2347	1127	2613	1035
31	252.3	48	32.7	15	31	15
–	1706	1867	3500	4126	500	–
–	14960	701	4867	2000	–	2275
–	–	–	–	–	–	–
–	–	1400	5187	910	–	91
1650	9263	397	4594	675	10159	24010
–	40	1002	5025	34	99	9900
642	244	2610	3738	2320	1702	1093
0.26	0.69	4.21	10.72	6.41	2.77	11.67
116	721	141	552	41	210	450

3-15 分地区灌溉和水利

Irrigation and Water Conservancy

指　　标		Item		全　市 Whole Municipality
一、乡、村办水电站		**Hydroelectric Station in Rural Areas**		
水电站个数	（个）	Number of Hydroelectric Station	(unit)	346
装机容量	（千瓦）	Installed Capacity	(kw)	370820
发电量	（万千瓦时）	Generating Capacity	(10000 kwh)	102301.88
二、灌溉面积		**Irrigated Area**		
1. 有效灌溉面积(农田面积)	（千公顷）	Irrigable Land	(1000 hectares)	162.88
2. 旱涝保收面积	（千公顷）	Area of Stable Yields Despite Drought or Excessive Rain	(1000 hectares)	130.89
3. 机电排灌面积	（千公顷）	Electrical Irrigation Area	(1000 hectares)	115.62
三、机电井		**Motor - pumped Well**		
已配套机电井	（眼）	Motor - pumped Well System	(unit)	122
装机容量	（千瓦）	Installed Capacity	(kw)	480

设施情况(2010年)
Facilities by Region(2010)

市 区 Urban District	#江干区 Jianggan	#拱墅区 Gongshu	#西湖区 Xihu	#萧山区 Xiaoshan	#余杭区 Yuhang	桐庐县 Tonglu	淳安县 Chun'an	建德市 Jiande	富阳市 Fuyang	临安市 Lin'an
5	-	-	-	-	5	72	100	49	24	96
2520	-	-	-	-	2520	79525	103620	20995	17950	146210
538.29	-	-	-	-	538.29	19221.23	31335.19	4341.41	4277.74	42588.02
89.5	0.83	-	2.83	53.08	32.24	11.85	8.85	14.31	20.5	17.87
79.48	0.83	-	2.07	44.88	31.18	9	6.33	11.25	13.71	11.12
87.86	0.83	-	2.83	53.08	30.6	5.14	1.8	4.51	13.24	3.07
122	-	-	-	-	122	-	-	-	-	-
480	-	-	-	-	480	-	-	-	-	-

3－16 分地区主要农
Possession of Major Agricultural

指　标		Item		全　市 Whole Municipality	
				2010 年	为上年(%) As Compared with the Preceding Year(%)
一、农业机械总动力	**(千瓦)**	**Total Power of Agricultural Machinery**	**(kw)**	**3307463**	**102.6**
耕作机械动力	(千瓦)	Cultivation Machinery	(kw)	208454	105.2
收获机械动力	(千瓦)	Harvest Machinery	(kw)	284466	96.8
植保机械动力	(千瓦)	Plant Protection Machinery	(kw)	33019	113.3
排灌机械动力	(千瓦)	Drainage & Irrigation Machinery	(kw)	420886	99.7
农副产品加工机械动力	(千瓦)	Processing Machinery of Agricultural Products	(kw)	183411	100.8
运输机械动力	(千瓦)	Transport Machinery	(kw)	919692	100.8
渔业机械动力	(千瓦)	Fishery Machinery	(kw)	108868	99.8
其他机械动力	(千瓦)	Other Machinery	(kw)	1148667	106.6
二、主要农机具		**Agricultural Machinery and Machinery For Processing Farm Products**			
大中型拖拉机	(台)	Large & Medium Tractors	(unit)	856	111.2
机引农具	(台)	Mechanized Farm Implement	(unit)	1549	106.8
农用小型拖拉机	(台)	Mini－tractors	(unit)	15903	99.8
联合收获机	(台)	Combine Harvesters	(unit)	972	101.4
机动割晒机	(台)	Motorized Harvesters	(unit)	15	57.7
机动脱粒机	(台)	Motorized Thresher	(unit)	180822	96.2
谷物烘干机	(台)	Cereal Dryer	(unit)	94	213.6
机动喷雾(粉)器	(架)	Motorized Sprayer	(unit)	20147	125.8
农用水泵	(台)	Water Pump for Agricultural Use	(unit)	147648	101.9
节水喷灌机械	(套)	Saving Water and Sprinkling Machinery	(set)	3779	99.5
粮食加工机械	(台)	Grain Processing Machinery	(unit)	19828	102.2
棉花加工机械	(台)	Cotton Processing Machinery	(unit)	242	55.5
油料加工机械	(台)	Oil Processing Machinery	(unit)	1619	106.7
农用运输机械	(台)	Vehicles for Agricultural Use	(unit)	41307	98.8
淡水机动渔船	(艘)	Motorized Fishing Boats	(unit)	2011	102.7

机具年末拥有量(2010 年)

Machinery at the Year - end by Region(2010)

市区 Urban District	#萧山区 Xiaoshan	#余杭区 Yuhang	桐庐县 Tonglu	淳安县 Chun'an	建德市 Jiande	富阳市 Fuyang	临安市 Lin'an
1637408	**765182**	**502897**	**249906**	**277526**	**277186.87**	**427830**	**437606**
103145	51846	46692	15697	13844	18964.87	28228	28576
136377	44165	85975	38407	7261	29608.43	54767	18046
6203	3636	2263	798	1687	4009.09	1894	18428
196222	83357	87800	36377	20364	51798.95	56325	59799
52746	30721	15274	11609	53724	21751.72	14198	29382
408381	264091	127622	91565	58944	77200.8	132825	150776
91608	71420	8927	970	12672	1860.86	1314	443
642727	215946	128344	54483	109030	71992.15	138279	132156
724	550	165	12	1	4	109	6
1454	1131	315	13	-	12	63	7
6282	2028	3831	1594	1500	1963	2492	2072
617	443	148	70	4	52	214	15
11	-	11	-	1	-	2	1
90572	25318	60841	25895	3259	18042	31643	11411
67	41	26	3	1	13	7	3
3973	2572	1246	362	866	1691	1202	12053
43223	16537	22700	15936	4618	24767	15138	43966
540	145	379	21	453	2725	6	34
2915	1602	1132	1362	7166	1748	1016	5621
86	70	16	16	62	14	47	17
227	158	48	260	612	258	88	174
17743	10910	5787	4096	2467	3449	7468	6084
363	141	89	23	1374	173	50	28

3－17 农业机械作业和
Agricultural Mechanization and

指　　标	Item	全　　市 Whole Municipality	
		2010 年	为上年(％) As Compared with the Preceding Year(％)
一、农业机械作业	**Agricultural Mechanization**		
当年机械收割面积　（千公顷）	Harvest Area by Tractors　(1000 hectares)	103.84	99.4
二、农村用电量　（万千瓦时）	**Electricity Consumed in Rural Area (10000 kwh)**	**1093715**	**110.5**
三、农业化肥用量	**Consumption of Chemical Fertilizer**		
（一）按实物量计算　（吨）	Physical Quantity Consumption　(ton)	590348	94.4
1. 氮　肥　（吨）	Nitrogenous Fertilizer　(ton)	271519	91.9
2. 磷　肥　（吨）	Phosphate Fertilizer　(ton)	92341	92.2
3. 钾　肥　（吨）	Potash Fertilizer　(ton)	45444	97.9
4. 复合肥　（吨）	Compound Fertilizer　(ton)	181044	98.7
（二）按折纯法计算　（吨）	Pure Consumption　(ton)	115140	96.8
1. 氮　肥　（吨）	Nitrogenous Fertilizer　(ton)	58478	97.2
2. 磷　肥　（吨）	Phosphate Fertilizer　(ton)	12996	93.9
3. 钾　肥　（吨）	Potash Fertilizer　(ton)	8645	97.1
4. 复合肥　（吨）	Compound Fertilizer　(ton)	35021	97.3
四、农用塑料薄膜使用量　（吨）	**Use of Plastic Film　(ton)**	**8010**	**104.4**
五、农用柴油使用量　（吨）	**Consumption of Diesel Oil　(ton)**	**27573**	**100.9**
六、农药使用量　（吨）	**Consumption of Pesticide　(ton)**	**8737**	**99.1**

物资消耗情况(2010 年)
Material Consumption(2010)

市　区 Urban District	#萧山区 Xiaoshan	#余杭区 Yuhang	桐庐县 Tonglu	淳安县 Chun'an	建德市 Jiande	富阳市 Fuyang	临安市 Lin'an
60.01	31.71	25.35	8.17	1.25	12.19	15.67	6.55
540503	**224821**	**211493**	**65648**	**9899**	**19288**	**362938**	**95439**
343369	264037	68039	39327	60080	55104	18433	74035
159128	119719	34790	18515	32834	25373	10489	25180
59604	48681	9469	8592	7026	7990	2158	6971
22761	16243	5631	4294	6566	4973	366	6484
101876	79394	18149	7926	13654	16768	5420	35400
52605	31487	16880	8204	7425	19679	7750	19477
25817	16977	7321	3798	3172	11534	4405	9752
6371	4382	1498	1481	809	2335	777	1223
3569	2030	1248	1012	410	1806	183	1665
16848	8098	6813	1913	3034	4004	2385	6837
3128	**2253**	**409**	**664**	**1620**	**1942**	**192**	**464**
10364	**7590**	**2445**	**4527**	**1538**	**3627**	**269**	**7248**
3930	**2574**	**1158**	**834**	**669**	**1130**	**924**	**1250**

3－18 农村经济

Rural Economic Income

单位:万元

指　　标	Item	全　市 Whole Municipality	
		2010年	为上年(%) As Compared with the Preceding Year(%)
一、农村经济总收入	**Total Rural Economic Income**	**129823320**	**116.3**
#出售产品收入	Sales Income	88397972	118.5
1.农林牧渔业收入	Income from Farming, Forestry, Animal Husbandry & Fishery	3302465	109.3
①农业收入	Income from Farming	1775134	108.0
#出售种植业产品收入	Income from Planting		
②林业收入	Income from Forestry	435197	117.5
③牧业收入	Income from Animal Husbandry	697769	107.8
④渔业收入	Income from Fishery	394365	109.5
2.工业收入	Income from Industry	92203776	116.6
3.建筑业收入	Income from Construction	7803896	111.9
4.运输业收入	Income from Transportation	2171471	155.8
5.商业、饮食业收入	Income from Trade & Catering Services	10220766	84.9
6.服务业收入	Income from Services	12143266	164.2
7.其他收入	Other Income	1977680	110.1
二、农村经济总费用	**Total Rural Economic Expenses**	**115695841**	**116.7**
#生产费用	Production Expenses	106606836	116.2
三、可分配净收入	**Disposable Net Income**	**15173241**	**114.1**
#国家税金	State Taxes	3233980	107.4
农民所得收入	Farmers' Earnings	5635492	115.0
每人平均所得(元)	Per Capita Income(yuan)	13775	－
为上年(%)	As Compared with the Preceding Year(%)	111.5	－

收入分配(2010年)
Distribution(2010)

(10000 yuan)

市 区 Urban District	#萧山区 Xiaoshan	#余杭区 Yuhang	桐庐县 Tonglu	淳安县 Chun'an	建德市 Jiande	富阳市 Fuyang	临安市 Lin'an
94364521	**48724665**	**18645297**	**5215030**	**1865759**	**3589563**	**16309320**	**8479127**
60787256	39558333	15660925	4774438	1174103	2748003	11961288	6952884
1362929	691148	520756	292744	417778	283529	622335	323150
770164	414029	251440	158401	241012	146041	330666	128850
48660	14174	33780	47622	89514	15267	110751	123383
246212	125227	115244	53041	75208	115747	140722	66839
297893	137718	120292	33680	12044	6474	40196	4078
64948866	43044066	15771340	4579597	1153179	2827387	11808237	6886510
6683783	2966598	512647	68146	62340	58667	519462	411498
1286329	668853	311463	76817	61421	49846	547180	149878
8021504	225079	774870	81396	82940	48672	1600395	385859
10805672	805062	364332	53766	60120	40596	1058630	124482
1255438	323859	389889	62564	27981	280866	153081	197750
85227360	**44228193**	**16196990**	**4419238**	**1601881**	**3167749**	**14009366**	**7270247**
80453752	42760084	14343115	4052361	1379282	2456334	11797030	6468077
9776707	**4886038**	**2604845**	**847405**	**323479**	**505126**	**2401491**	**1319033**
2391767	1403821	471667	134705	21177	68406	444361	173564
3355631	1606548	1074559	336812	271349	359354	773098	539248
–	16611	15884	10882	7169	9094	14857	12602
–	109.3	112.1	109.9	110.1	113.8	112.9	110.7

3－19 乡(镇)
Statistics on Towns

乡镇名称 Town		村民委员会(个) Number of Villagers' Committees (unit)	农村常住户数(户) Resident Households in Rural Areas (household)	农村常住人口数(人) Resident Population in Rural Areas (person)	农村从业人员数(人) Labor Force in Rural Areas (person)
江干区	**Jianggan District**				
丁桥镇	Dingqiao	2	3702	15025	8477
笕桥镇	Jianqiao	–	12247	47363	24995
彭埠镇	Pengbu	–	11767	47125	30515
九堡镇	Jiubao	4	9331	36226	18807
拱墅区	**Gongshu District**				
康桥街道	Kangqiao Subdistrict	9	4178	16758	11878
半山街道	Banshan Subdistrict	–	17633	47237	30750
祥符街道	Xiangfu Subdistrict	–	9277	30840	22744
西湖区	**Xihu District**				
留下街道	Liuxia Subdistrict	2	6647	77270	30494
转塘街道	Zhuantang Subdistrict	16	13930	74238	34043
双浦镇	Shuangpu	27	14694	56214	30227
三墩镇	Sandun	4	27368	117233	59788
高新(滨江)区	**Hi－Tech(Bingjiang) District**				
浦沿街道	Puyan Subdistrict	4	15195	63950	33799
长河街道	Changhe Subdistrict	6	16013	54401	24488
西兴街道	Xixing Subdistrict	5	17168	64158	26667
开发区	**Development Zone**				
下沙街道	Xiasha Subdistrict	–	9712	79852	46534
西湖风景名胜区	**The West Lake Scenic Zone**				
西湖街道	West Lake Subdistrict	9	3951	7459	4870

基本情况(2010 年)
and Townships(2010)

乡镇常用耕地面积(亩) (mu)	粮食播种面积(亩) Sown Area of Grain Crops (mu)	粮食总产量(吨) Yield of Grain Crops (ton)	农业总产值(当年价格)(万元) Gross Output Value of Agriculture (10000 yuan)	财政总收入(万元) Financial Revenue (10000 yuan)	农村经济总收入(万元) Total Income of Rural Economy (10000 yuan)	农民人均年纯收入(元) Per Capita Annual Net Income (yuan)
500	–	–	131	35103	770057	15330
4004	–	–	5096	120419	2214199	17891
4090	–	–	4382	51012	1907503	17165
5044	–	–	5221	62238	1010005	15368
3315	–	–	345	57540	3617425	16636
155	–	–	551	44061	1816551	16624
2206	–	–	–	50136	1101183	16513
325	–	–	96	76121	443912	17319
7191	3347	1320	5980	108178	570350	16635
24384	22050	10604	40245	8696	945918	15548
14522	13500	5373	8576	68192	591382	16491
3249	1148	410	6795	57518	1633322	15600
2251	663	223	11855	38005	1591814	16670
3368	3122	1041	7532	64123	1380003	15395
21460	4580	1603	18562	20214	384023	–
–	–	–	6192	5563	65013	–

3－19　续表1

乡镇名称 Town		村民委员会(个) Number of Villagers' Committees (unit)	农村常住户数(户) Resident Households in Rural Areas (household)	农村常住人口数(人) Resident Population in Rural Areas (person)	农村从业人员数(人) Labor Force in Rural Areas (person)
萧山区	**Xiaoshan District**				
河上镇	Heshang	15	10703	28507	19411
楼塔镇	Louta	12	9311	27557	17487
浦阳镇	Puyang	18	12735	37685	24461
戴村镇	Daicun	22	10833	37359	25306
临浦镇	Linpu	20	18660	56789	36271
进化镇	Jinhua	25	14925	51192	30688
义桥镇	Yiqiao	21	13883	45185	28834
衙前镇	Yaqian	11	6923	26234	16016
所前镇	Suoqian	19	13598	47043	24344
闻堰镇	Wenyan	6	7380	21006	19679
坎山镇	Kanshan	19	17807	51313	32309
新街镇	Xinjie	15	19796	60533	34006
宁围镇	Ningwei	15	19281	54231	39943
瓜沥镇	Guali	23	23958	63880	39866
义蓬街道	Yipeng Subdistrict	22	19441	58445	38427
南阳街道	Nanyang Subdistrict	13	12043	39766	23933
靖江街道	Jingjiang Subdistrict	10	11722	36333	23396
益农镇	Yinong	19	13998	42887	29563
党山镇	Dangshan	21	16438	51777	32702
新湾街道	Xinwan Subdistrict	12	8255	27309	13464
党湾镇	Dangwan	17	13001	41682	29890
河庄街道	Hezhuang Subdistrict	20	14488	49265	29642
城厢街道	Chengxiang Subdistrict	0	40598	159155	112186
北干街道	Beigan Subdistrict	6	27074	79002	45084
蜀山街道	Shushan Subdistrict	8	14822	48915	31487
新塘街道	Xintang Subdistrict	17	19783	70993	39336
前进街道	Qianjin Subdistrict	3	4229	12349	8497
临江街道	Linjiang Subdistrict	2	1183	4139	2747
余杭区	**Yuhang District**				
运河镇	Yunhe	14	10392	40880	34807

continued 1

乡镇常用耕地面积(亩) (mu)	粮食播种面积(亩) Sown Area of Grain Crops (mu)	粮食总产量(吨) Yield of Grain Crops (ton)	农业总产值(当年价格)(万元) Gross Output Value of Agriculture (10000 yuan)	财政总收入(万元) Financial Revenue (10000 yuan)	农村经济总收入(万元) Total Income of Rural Economy (10000 yuan)	农民人均年纯收入(元) Per Capita Annual Net Income (yuan)
13058	16054	6539.5	12897	21685	1088444	12786
12710	10670	4098.3	5838	19650	409175	11923
19796	23087	10225.6	18966	30514	555590	13700
18675	19793	7677.2	12248	27263	721995	13984
18161	14538	5848	19807	70492	1319181	14504
19019	19413	9229.4	22716	26174	623458	14303
21843	21565	9866	20521	53143	1194602	15977
8803	5711	1873.2	10903	95174	4534400	19720
17573	16390	7124.4	33035	46191	1220777	15162
4646	2256	812.3	14337	79640	1063556	17457
30643	18097	4600.1	27849	44739	1317674	17197
31652	11306	3326.9	69634	75087	2857766	18930
24622	8418	2559.2	38240	588840	12037744	23496
32176	36952	13438.3	28337	107045	3813200	17085
49775	67519	21480.4	60502	50379	981185	16438
28802	29384	12376	17402	39860	1138900	17098
23179	31358	10606.3	12874	47996	1225500	18398
43750	49309	19122.1	36282	53572	2936812	16530
40877	58871	23593.2	38345	43634	2992547	16418
21197	34938	11671.9	19216	18743	569989	15298
35238	56061	19439.1	34194	34502	1357973	17881
40200	65279	21344.1	39228	59307	860050	17309
2278	1238	437	1882	169392	514479	16021
4166	320	89	4550	142406	396513	21210
14633	3900	1187.9	11184	38587	926987	14775
12300	2555	881	16380	121421	1918048	15398
11494	14977	5129.5	10875	14287	50020	15139
6244	8700	2639.9	6696	54686	15550	13968
14714	11434	5116	35900	14438	713600	16052

3－19 续表2

乡镇名称 Town		村民委员会(个) Number of Villagers' Committees (unit)	农村常住户数(户) Resident Households in Rural Areas (household)	农村常住人口数(人) Resident Population in Rural Areas (person)	农村从业人员数(人) Labor Force in Rural Areas (person)
塘栖镇	Tangxi	27	28187	115129	73077
乔司镇	Qiaosi	11	13936	75656	41524
仁和镇	Renhe	18	18278	70066	42832
崇贤镇	Chongxian	11	11304	54863	40088
余杭镇	Yuhang	14	23278	71510	55850
闲林镇	Xianlin	8	9130	48260	34539
仓前镇	Cangqian	9	8650	47040	35702
良渚镇	Liangzhu	23	25247	152899	86250
中泰乡	Zhongtai	10	8476	28533	21013
瓶窑镇	Pingyao	13	19190	71637	40010
径山镇	Jingshan	13	11977	36805	23288
黄湖镇	Huanghu	5	4605	14302	9377
鸬鸟镇	Luniao	6	3762	12331	10085
百丈镇	Baizhang	6	3235	11492	7225
临平街道	Linping Subdistrict	–	20660	77700	61560
南苑街道	Nanyuan Subdistrict	–	24985	79713	48725
五常街道	Wuchang Subdistrict	–	12276	53654	31982
星桥街道	Xingqiao Subdistrict	–	9256	41085	23239
桐庐县	**Tonglu County**				
桐君街道	Tongjun Subdistrict	25	65552	152415	90257
旧县街道	Jiuxian Subdistrict	5	3117	8524	5544
富春江镇	Fuchunjiang	15	10411	25969	19164
江南镇	Jiangnan	20	14523	52025	33449
凤川镇	Fengchuan	8	6468	17517	13435
新合乡	Xinghe	5	1718	5114	4036
横村镇	Hengcun	24	14920	41238	26086
莪山畲族乡	Eshan	7	2966	8915	5926
钟山乡	Zhongshan	11	6270	17898	13268
分水镇	Fenshui	26	26779	71588	50201

continued 2

乡镇常用耕地面积(亩) (mu)	粮食播种面积(亩) Sown Area of Grain Crops (mu)	粮食总产量(吨) Yield of Grain Crops (ton)	农业总产值(当年价格)(万元) Gross Output Value of Agriculture (10000 yuan)	财政总收入(万元) Financial Revenue (10000 yuan)	农村经济总收入(万元) Total Income of Rural Economy (10000 yuan)	农民人均年纯收入(元) Per Capita Annual Net Income (yuan)
34862	37367	16745.7	52296	106586	2195800	17066
19441	7988	1960.4	23577	50790	1072801	16522
37851	40616	19831.2	40528	35299	1081774	15220
18193	15166	6795.5	22407	23973	1587260	16086
44166	53614	25717.8	39106	77110	1207150	16216
9270	12863	5387.3	16639	67647	1543052	17402
29560	44386	20510.1	27079	49184	553770	16566
47110	42518	21572	39359	161391	2069124	15031
19130	16564	7418.7	21592	30761	429218	16189
42293	35130	17303.3	48208	59097	1559786	14625
47862	43575	19507.5	67364	17670	601379	13776
14187	12507	5436	15957	8563	237836	14818
11665	9510	4860	32855	3377	197301	14958
2816	4816	2004.8	11302	4169	292914	16255
4153	1998	735	17554	17273	273511	15832
13825	10485	3398.9	30243	21394	554933	16247
5875	2285	849.6	4745	70223	959028	21794
5414	1405	489	12403	59202	417199	16998
17530	21592	9039	30219	32498	1304213	10356
7344	9014	3530	4576	3671	173626	12669
13056	19813	8187	28281	26157	468645	11680
25371	25361	10444	13884	17844	661369	11003
12032	11451	4852	12777	2858	190771	10530
3472	2759	1263	2671	926	41621	9709
41957	35640	14302	28816	13632	972503	12701
6894	9780	3913	5831	1467	96220	9708
17693	21291	7411	11571	10732	205562	10278
31253	32853	12785	39938	21469	730619	10854

3－19　续表3

乡镇名称 Town		村民委员会(个) Number of Villagers' Committees (unit)	农村常住户数(户) Resident Households in Rural Areas (household)	农村常住人口数(人) Resident Population in Rural Areas (person)	农村从业人员数(人) Labor Force in Rural Areas (person)
瑶琳镇	Yaolin	16	12877	35539	24966
百江镇	Baijiang	15	5567	15462	13008
合村乡	Hecun	6	2835	8787	6784
淳安县	**Chun'an County**				
千岛湖镇	Qiandaohu	22	26361	77959	61588
文昌镇	Wenchang	16	4139	12650	9698
石林镇	Shilin	8	1417	4557	3255
临岐镇	Linqi	17	6079	20136	15038
威坪镇	Weiping	44	17720	49618	39695
姜家镇	Jiangjia	28	8785	25475	19875
梓桐镇	Zitong	19	6322	18966	14854
汾口镇	Fenkou	51	16685	53492	39333
中洲镇	Zhongzhou	19	5866	19240	13852
大墅镇	Dashu	17	4570	13993	10844
枫树岭镇	Fengshuling	28	6079	18217	14421
里商乡	Lishang	16	3626	11603	8868
金峰乡	Jinfeng	11	2117	6350	4880
富文乡	Fuwen	10	2492	8165	5880
左口乡	Zuokou	11	3559	11230	8852
屏门乡	Pingmen	15	3926	12322	9619
瑶山乡	Yaoshan	11	2834	9324	7260
王阜乡	Wangfu	18	6358	18110	13504
宋村乡	Songcun	8	2225	6730	5306
鸠坑乡	Jiukeng	9	2757	7895	5869
浪川乡	Langchuan	19	6364	18878	14645

continued 3

乡镇常用耕地面积(亩) (mu)	粮食播种面积(亩) Sown Area of Grain Crops (mu)	粮食总产量(吨) Yield of Grain Crops (ton)	农业总产值(当年价格)(万元) Gross Output Value of Agriculture (10000 yuan)	财政总收入(万元) Financial Revenue (10000 yuan)	农村经济总收入(万元) Total Income of Rural Economy (10000 yuan)	农民人均年纯收入(元) Per Capita Annual Net Income (yuan)
26979	26509	9660	38435	5270	244475	10508
13756	14830	4768	11598	1004	74476	8926
7754	11672	4904	9457	721	34216	7828
7121	8964	2838	17419	9713	251171	8290
6497	12704	3660	11795	3636	125759	8210
2356	4814	1141	5330	1404	35544	8160
11450	15513	4396	16257	4288	51429	7927
18998	31836	8562	31353	9242	166346	6692
13392	23091	7190	18172	4110	111962	7280
10954	26946	6913	18368	2719	120220	7625
25936	43630	14178	30235	9164	284900	6649
9014	13854	4346	10697	3819	51333	6294
9426	10719	3583	9620	2663	168740	7858
13536	13207	4611	17568	3082	94824	7568
3355	10819	2600	9611	1887	41451	7787
3972	6932	2331	6081	1105	14600	6995
4351	7147	1909	6242	1887	28675	7278
5065	11074	2914	9559	1755	21155	6885
5326	17017	3963	12346	1861	45403	7290
4340	10584	2406	10506	1231	33987	7638
4161	13324	2864	12279	2159	37158	5875
1848	3432	649	2904	1562	12392	6006
1672	5339	1241	6732	1447	30376	6385
10652	17450	5630	12708	2570	67712	7461

3－19 续表4

乡镇名称 Town		村民委员会(个) Number of Villagers' Committees (unit)	农村常住户数(户) Resident Households in Rural Areas (household)	农村常住人口数(人) Resident Population in Rural Areas (person)	农村从业人员数(人) Labor Force in Rural Areas (person)
界首乡	Jieshou	13	3078	8909	6870
安阳乡	Anyang	15	3826	11600	8806
建德市	**Jiande City**				
新安江街道	Xin'anjiang Subdistrict	4	28687	76355	56404
洋溪街道	Yangxi Subdistrict	5	5328	14738	8814
更楼街道	Genglou Subdistrict	14	7486	22783	13570
莲花镇	Lianhua	6	3135	10547	6816
乾潭镇	Qiantan	24	14527	43044	40480
钦堂乡	Qintang	7	2701	8833	6131
梅城镇	Meicheng	13	19460	47939	33411
杨村桥镇	Yangcunqiao	13	6051	19500	11661
下涯镇	Xiaya	11	7905	25404	16181
大洋镇	Dayang	19	10551	32964	20923
三都镇	Sandu	19	9505	26999	16543
寿昌镇	Shouchang	23	15793	45399	35967
航头镇	Hangtou	18	9746	33065	21967
大慈岩镇	Daciyan	12	6270	20183	12754
大同镇	Datong	34	17538	55989	36811
李家镇	Lijia	10	6329	20156	15188

continued 4

乡镇常用耕地面积(亩) (mu)	粮食播种面积(亩) Sown Area of Grain Crops (mu)	粮食总产量(吨) Yield of Grain Crops (ton)	农业总产值(当年价格)(万元) Gross Output Value of Agriculture (10000 yuan)	财政总收入(万元) Financial Revenue (10000 yuan)	农村经济总收入(万元) Total Income of Rural Economy (10000 yuan)	农民人均年纯收入(元) Per Capita Annual Net Income (yuan)
5670	8497	1990	11205	1908	27420	7201
6814	13577	3870	12127	2000	43202	7480
3208	3110	1039	11993	34174	258780	11056
3084	3352	792	5025	6246	111600	9548
10991	17432	6599	11645	4652	109955	9436
5525	4453	1344	23633	1376	93973	11409
24800	27642	9046	18706	10020	831924	12550
7141	8576	3169	5104	2119	32020	11013
16996	16807	5461	24949	7086	478915	9209
14267	16897	6390	29578	2895	239035	11496
17329	15332	5048	37522	2731	168946	8495
21678	21694	7281	30980	6585	264342	8005
17846	13367	4789	41309	1962	176612	7362
21598	27791	10609	12192	10683	414005	8833
25656	25806	9829	23077	2032	115021	8138
15329	17080	6916	11527	2180	146356	7258
34832	38098	16062	28556	7309	148100	7458
10965	16286	5963	12666	3311	74137	8974

3－19　续表5

乡镇名称 Town		村民委员会(个) Number of Villagers´ Committees (unit)	农村常住户数(户) Resident Households in Rural Areas (household)	农村常住人口数(人) Resident Population in Rural Areas (person)	农村从业人员数(人) Labor Force in Rural Areas (person)
富阳市	**Fuyang City**				
万市镇	Wanshi	15	6581	21888	14372
洞桥镇	Dongqiao	11	5895	18642	11268
胥口镇	Xukou	13	5669	17309	9690
永昌镇	Yongchang	5	3328	10485	7341
渌渚镇	Luzhu	13	5173	15991	10034
新登镇	Xindeng	31	30609	91827	48395
上官乡	Shangguan	5	2711	8299	4604
常绿镇	Changlu	8	4643	13748	9355
大源镇	Dayuan	15	11068	34860	24064
灵桥镇	Lingqiao	13	7250	23936	14831
里山镇	Lishan	5	3217	10581	6054
渔山乡	Yushan	4	3710	13176	8888
场口镇	Changkou	24	12862	40298	24933
龙门镇	Longmen	4	2523	6879	4574
环山乡	Huanshan	7	3722	12012	7547
常安镇	Chang´an	16	7378	24434	15579
湖源乡	Huyuan	10	4157	13549	8646
高桥镇	Gaoqiao	16	9989	30317	23022
受降镇	Shouxiang	6	6804	19659	10487
春建乡	Chunjian	6	2912	8793	5257
新桐乡	Xintong	7	4489	12590	8081
鹿山街道	Lushan Subdistrict	9	7280	21216	14544
富春街道	Fuchun Subdistrict	17	50484	135422	62686
春江街道	Chunjiang Subdistrict	9	9116	28428	23607
东洲街道	Dongzhou Subdistrict	15	13098	45871	25800

continued 5

乡镇常用耕地面积(亩) (mu)	粮食播种面积(亩) Sown Area of Grain Crops (mu)	粮食总产量(吨) Yield of Grain Crops (ton)	农业总产值(当年价格)(万元) Gross Output Value of Agriculture (10000 yuan)	财政总收入(万元) Financial Revenue (10000 yuan)	农村经济总收入(万元) Total Income of Rural Economy (10000 yuan)	农民人均年纯收入(元) Per Capita Annual Net Income (yuan)
18279	27133	10524	37974	5951	347823	11824
16234	19335	7581	50211	6318	275169	12061
16680	15987	6797	24201	6011	144802	11413
8467	8757	4249	14448	4400	98364	14430
11153	16580	7290	20369	6889	136936	14194
38410	41211	17308	56196	23087	1017913	13448
2593	3380	1366	5940	2372	68670	14510
3899	5087	2261	5553	4183	103509	12134
8610	10876	4386	16475	20800	1447450	18609
8803	9604	3909	11783	34600	832008	16439
3816	6240	2588	6582	3549	283689	13927
4776	7507	3562	7625	4336	156460	13915
25890	39403	12465	31098	11100	281257	11000
4354	5823	2496	5008	2806	40024	11976
6327	6680	2851	4948	9436	571305	13549
13542	16945	7674	17326	4875	220686	11441
5915	6872	2758	10076	5066	33726	10257
18112	27549	11877	46982	29776	2292376	19797
6756	11465	4517	16749	13855	1251984	19789
8497	10130	4032	19300	3278	124110	14097
8584	11195	5260	7578	3703	80049	12227
13011	13404	6531	23215	30346	451180	17001
17565	21616	9266	18489	68178	2879897	18108
7184	11047	4351	12995	88000	2259210	19281
21726	24436	11061	39950	28396	730585	16835

3－19　续表6

乡镇名称 Town	村民委员会(个) Number of Villagers' Committees (unit)	农村常住户数(户) Resident Households in Rural Areas (household)	农村常住人口数(人) Resident Population in Rural Areas (person)	农村从业人员数(人) Labor Force in Rural Areas (person)
临安市　Lin'an City				
锦城街道　Jincheng Subdistrict	17	63000	163495	79001
玲珑街道　Linlong Subdistrict	16	9461	26301	17133
青山湖街道 Qingshanghu Subdistrict	9	7800	23000	11527
锦南街道　jinnan Subdistrict	9	8503	20038	8379
三口镇　Sankou	6	2799	8434	5128
横畈镇　Hengfan	10	4970	15160	8962
高虹镇　Gaohong	9	7596	22908	18937
太湖源镇　Taihuyuan	20	11922	36146	21143
板桥乡　Banqiao	9	6635	22040	12846
於潜镇　Yuqian	26	16707	49560	23992
藻溪镇　Zaoxi	12	7051	18578	13971
太阳镇　Taiyang	11	5253	15415	10800
潜川镇　Qianchuan	10	5251	15589	8829
西天目乡　Xitianmu	11	4793	12352	8954
千洪乡　Qianhong	4	2101	6345	4512
横路乡　Henglu	7	3024	7690	6339
乐平乡　Leping	6	3531	10495	7316
昌化镇　Changhua	14	8689	26796	12215
龙岗镇　Longgang	8	3684	10925	7040
河桥镇　Heqiao	11	5955	16509	11562
湍口镇　Tuankou	13	4027	13394	8761
清凉峰镇　Qingliangfeng	10	6723	18920	12637
马啸乡　Maxiao	7	3066	9419	5969
岛石镇　Daoshi	10	6697	18810	12154
大峡谷镇　Daxiagu	16	3841	11135	8073
新桥乡　Xinqiao	6	2332	6066	4478

continued 6

乡镇常用耕地面积(亩) (mu)	粮食播种面积(亩) Sown Area of Grain Crops (mu)	粮食总产量(吨) Yield of Grain Crops (ton)	农业总产值(当年价格)(万元) Gross Output Value of Agriculture (10000 yuan)	财政总收入(万元) Financial Revenue (10000 yuan)	农村经济总收入(万元) Total Income of Rural Economy (10000 yuan)	农民人均年纯收入(元) Per Capita Annual Net Income (yuan)
12063	13079	5163.8	26000	35681	1266611	13145
10507	8889	3937	17270	19633	1055819	13838
1993	4909	1992.4	6965	56500	1168193	17622
4316	4112	1588.9	5755	6178	70500	11768
3876	3535	1759.5	11300	2559	112410	12608
12497	7521	4005.6	15878	5905	148984	13368
10099	8544	4217.9	18225	6045	390149	13614
27943	16347	6207.2	40970	9208	922937	14145
9304	12962	4700.6	21530	7848	268562	12520
26142	11776	5484	34400	10178	816644	13054
15885	14605	7147.7	18120	3884	195556	12246
11935	10181	5105.2	14412	2592	441524	12983
6420	6332	2040.2	19460	1913	174599	11109
6982	5026	2243.9	25030	2427	135867	12828
8813	2559	1011.8	5588	1442	68172	14834
5737	3350	1020.3	10780	1491	68671	10715
2532	2469	989.9	14082	900	149000	13641
12914	13172	4400.7	14071	7980	277986	13208
7818	11252	4931.1	9995	3840	163920	12771
12216	12041	4641.7	12880	2806	72488	8736
6688	11673	3694.2	11735	2405	46522	10377
10053	16345	4471.4	15472	2005	73996	11305
5636	7908	2747.5	6253	759	41929	10973
4808	11229	3122.4	21170	1880	66831	10270
8746	9437	3254.2	15360	3093	76758	10128
4160	5203	2059.5	7098	1085	42052	9935

主要统计指标解释

农林牧渔业总产值　是以货币表现的农、林、牧、渔业全部产品的总量和对农林牧渔生产活动进行的各种支持性服务活动的价值。他反映一定时期内的农林牧渔业生产的总规模和总成果。

农林牧渔业的统计范围是：

(1)农业　包括农作物种植业和其他农业。

农作物种植业　包括谷类、豆类、薯类、棉花、麻类、烟叶、蔬菜、药材、瓜类和其他农作物的种植以及茶园、桑园、果园的生产经营。

其他农业　包括采集野生植物的果实、纤维、树脂、油料以及柴草、野生药材、菌类等。

(2)林业　包括林木的栽培(不包括茶园、桑园和果园的栽培、管理和收获等活动)、林产品的采集和村及村以下合作经济组织和农户的竹木砍伐。

(3)牧业　包括除渔业养殖以外的一切动物饲养和放牧以及野生动物的捕猎和饲养。

(4)渔业　包括水生动物和海藻类植物的养殖和捕捞。

(5)农林牧渔服务业　包括对农林牧渔生产活动进行的各种支持性服务活动。

粮食产量　指全社会的产量,包括国营农场等全民所有制经营、集体统一经营的和农民家庭经营的产量,还包括工矿企业家属办的农场和其他生产单位的产量。粮食除包括稻谷、小麦、大麦、玉米、高粱、谷子及其他杂粮外,还包括薯类和豆类。其产量计算方法,豆类按去豆荚后的干豆计算,薯类按5公斤鲜薯折1公斤粮食计算,其他粮食一律按脱粒后的原粮计算。

猪、牛、羊肉产量　指当年出栏并已屠宰的猪、牛、羊的肉产量,即屠宰后除去头蹄下水后带骨的(即胴体重)重量。

水产品产量　指人工养殖的水产品和天然生长的水产品的捕捞量。包括海水的鱼类、虾蟹类、贝类和藻类以及内陆水域的鱼类、虾蟹类和贝类,不包括淡水生植物。

有效灌溉面积　指具有一定的水源,地块比较平整、灌溉工程或设备已经配套,在一般年景下当年能够进行正常灌溉的耕地面积。

农业机械总动力　指主要用于农、林、牧、渔业的各种动力机械的动力总和。包括耕作机械、排灌机械、收获机械、农用运输机械、植物保护机械、牧业机械、林业机械和其他农业机械[内燃机按引擎马力折成瓦(特)计算,电动机按功率折成瓦(特)计算]。不包括专门用于乡、镇、村、组办工业、基本建设、非农业运输、科学试验和教学等非农业方面的动力机械与作业机械。

农村用电量　指本年度内扣除在农村中的全民所有制工业、交通、基建单位的用电量以后的农村生产上和生活上的全年用电总度数(全年累计数),包括国家电网的供电量,也包括农村自办电站的供电量。

农用化肥施用量　指本年内实际用于农业生产的化肥数量。包括氮肥、磷肥、钾肥及复合肥。化肥施用量要求按折纯量计算数量。折纯量是指氮肥、磷肥、钾肥分别按含氮、含五氧化二磷、含氧化钾的百分之一百成份进行折算后的数量。复合肥按其所含主要成份折算。

Explanatory Notes on Main Statistical Indicators

Gross Output Value of Farming, Forestry, Animal Husbandry and Fishery refers to the total volume of products of farming, forestry, animal husbandry and fishery in value terms and output value of all kinds of service activities that support farming, forestry, animal husbandry and fishery production. It reflects the total scale and total result of agricultural production during a given period of time.

The statistical scopes for Farming, Forestry, Animal Husbandry and Fishery are:

(1) **Farming** include crop cultivation and other farming crop cultivation, include planting of grain, beans, tubers, cotton, oil – bearing crops, sugar crops, fiber crops, tobacco, vegetables, medicinal materials, melons and others, as well as tea, mulberry and fruit plantation.

Other farming include gathering of wild plant fruits, fiber, gum, oil, firewood, wild medicinal materials, fungi and commodity industry run by rural household.

(2) **Forestry** include planting of trees (not including planting, management & harvest of tea, mulberry and fruit plantation), collection of forest products, cutting and felling of bamboo and trees by villages and other cooperative organizations under villages.

(3) **Animal Husbandry** include raising and grazing of any kind of animal and hunting and raising of wild animal, excluding fish breeding.

(4) **Fishery** include cultivation and catches of aquatic animals and seaweed.

(5) **Service Industry for Farming, Forestry, Animal Husbandry and Fishery** refers to all kinds of service activities that support farming, forestry, animal husbandry and fishery production.

Grain Yield refers to the total yield including grains produced by state farms, collective units, industrial enterprises and mines. Grain includes rice, wheat, corn, sorghum, millet and other miscellaneous grains as well as tubers and beans. Output of beans refers to dry beans without pods. The output of tubers was converted into that of grain at the ratio 5:1. Output of all other grains refers to husked grain.

Output of Pork, Beef, and Mutton refers to the meat of slaughtered hogs, cattle, sheep and goats with head, feet and offal taken away.

Output of Aquatic Products refers to catches of both artificially cultured and naturally grown aquatic products, including fish, shrimps, crabs and shellfish in sea and inland water as well as seaweed. Freshwater plants are not included.

Irrigated Area refers to areas that are effectively irrigated, i. e. level land which has water source and complete sets of irrigation facilities to lift and move adequate water for irrigation purpose under normal conditions.

Total Power of Farm Machinery refers to total mechanical power of machinery used in farming, forestry, animal husbandry, and fishery, including ploughing, irrigation and drainage, harvesting, transport, plant protection, stock breeding, forestry and fishery. The power of internal combustion engines is required to convert horsepower into watts and the power of electric motors is required to be converted into watts. Machinery employed for non – agricultural purposes, such as the machines used in township – run and village – run industry, construction, non – agricultural transport, scientific experiments and teaching, is excluded.

Electricity Consumption in Rural Areas refers to the total degree of electricity consumption in rural production and living (annual aggregate) after discounting the ownership by the whole people in the rural areas of industrial, transport and infrastructure unit of electricity consumption, including the national grid power supply, and also including the power supply in rural areas on their own power station.

Consumption of Chemical Fertilizers in Agriculture refers to the quantity of chemical fertilizers applied in agriculture in the year, including nitrogenous fertilizer, phosphate fertilizer, potash fertilizer, and compound fertilizer. The consumption of chemical fertilizers is required in calculation to convert the gross weight into weight into weight containing 100% effective component (e. g. 100% nitrogen content in nitrogenous fertilizer, 100% phosphorous pentoxide contents in phosphate fertilizer, 100% potassium oxide contents in potash fertilizer). Compound fertilizer is converted with its major component.

第四篇
CHAPTER-4

工业、能源

Industry And Energy

工 业 、 能 源
Industry and Energy

主 要 统 计 指 标
Major Statistical Indicators

规模以上工业企业单位数	Number of Industrial Enterprises above Designated Size	10370	个	(unit)
为上年	As Compared with the Preceding Year	103.4	%	(%)
规模以上工业销售产值	Sales Value of Industrial Enterprises above Designated Size	10951.31	亿元	(100 million yuan)
为上年	As Compared with the Preceding Year	124.2	%	(%)
规模以上工业总产值	Gross Output Value of Industrial Enterprises above Designated Size	11081.04	亿元	(100 million yuan)
为上年	As Compared with the Preceding Year	124.1	%	(%)
轻工业	Light Industry	4576.47	亿元	(100 million yuan)
为上年	As Compared with the Preceding Year	120.0	%	(%)
重工业	Heavy Industry	6504.57	亿元	(100 million yuan)
为上年	As Compared with the Preceding Year	127.0	%	(%)

4-01 主要年份工业企业单位数

Number of Industrial Enterprises in Main Years

单位:个 (unit)

年份 Year	合计 Total	国有经济 State-owned Enterprises	集体经济 Collective-owned Enterprises	其他各种经济类型 Enterprises of Other Types of Ownership	合计中:农村工业 of the Total: Rural Industry
全市 Whole Municipality					
1978	2868	680	2188	-	1241
1980	3519	691	-	-	-
1985	5800	823	-	-	-
1990	6183	921	4966	11	3130
1991	6234	933	5219	82	3361
1992	6235	941	5162	132	3274
1995	6744	1086	4722	936	2949
1996	6148	1011	4268	869	2719
1997	4980	760	3250	970	1729
1998	2559	464	815	1280	1366
1999	2474	396	689	1389	1313
2000	2715	282	598	1835	1536
2001	3580	237	252	3091	2051
2002	4015	172	232	3611	2398
2003	4689	144	219	4326	2622
2004	7738	185	192	7361	-
2005	7359	124	169	7066	-
2006	7826	110	162	7554	-
2007	8674	71	131	8472	-
2008	9907	73	101	9733	-
2009	10032	71	84	9877	-
2010	10370	74	68	10228	-
市区 Urban District					
1978	787	313	414	-	59
1980	894	315	579	-	95
1985	1250	345	859	7	184
1990	1360	361	971	28	209
1991	1411	382	990	39	209
1992	1490	395	1024	71	207
1995	1998	440	1102	456	200
1996	2043	458	1109	476	294
1997	1733	372	951	410	200
1998	1019	315	315	389	375
1999	959	255	284	420	349
2000	1005	182	253	570	393
2001	2645	195	200	2250	1369
2002	2838	140	178	2520	1399
2003	3230	115	158	2957	1308
2004	5527	156	122	5249	-
2005	4995	98	104	4793	-
2006	5195	85	91	5019	-
2007	5726	54	77	5595	-
2008	6530	55	64	6411	-
2009	6477	52	49	6376	-
2010	6478	51	37	6390	-

注:本表范围1998年开始为全部国有和年销售收入500万元及以上的非国有工业,1997年以前为乡及乡以上工业。

a) Data in this table refer to all state-owned enterprises and non-state-owned industrial enterprises with annual sales income of over 5 million yuan, before 1997, refer to enterprises at township and above level.

4－02 主要年份

Gross Industrial

单位:万元

年 份 Year	全部工业 All Industry	规模 以上工业 Industry above Designated Size	# 轻 工 业 Light Industry
全市 Whole Municipality			
1978		429624	
1980		617910	
1985		1285888	793766
1990		2922600	1848911
1991		3524900	2201757
1992		4527400	2735168
1995		10200259	5600664
1996		8831167	4606720
1997		9114651	4871887
1998		11099357	5726407
1999		12000796	6129963
2000		15435682	7623300
2001	28672833	19195133	9957027
2002	34655472	24002972	12435498
2003	43513526	32025226	15652463
2004	56941379	44865779	19761946
2005	65895071	54411271	24059690
2006	82582990	69754590	29093450
2007	98464729	83514029	35878400
2008	110162700	93795792	38735329
2009	108703234	93907334	40115956
2010	128105197	110810397	45764739
市区 Urban District			
1978		304242	
1980		433623	
1985		812246	512767
1990		1533000	1026764
1991		1814600	1140394
1992		2291300	1379154
1995		4760900	2507752
1996		4599778	2460319
1997		4997257	2889406
1998		6110192	3068600
1999		6280838	3178286
2000		7804302	3635578
2001	21008145	16156245	8377563
2002	25466884	20252484	10431428
2003	32010406	26945006	13080771
2004	42514768	37564968	16361706
2005	50045260	44775260	19601053
2006	62823653	57255453	23722868
2007	73882956	67565456	29452269
2008	81717903	74564803	31236743
2009	80383555	74059755	32178951
2010	94300085	86653885	36440816

注:本表规模以上工业范围 1998 年开始为全部国有和年销售收入 500 万元及以上的非国有工业,1997 年以前为乡及乡以上工业。2002 年起,市区数据为新口径。

工业总产值
Output Value in Main Years

(10000 yuan)

重工业 Heavy Industry	国有经济 State - owned	集体经济 Collective - owned	其他经济 Other Types of Ownership
	334799	94825	
	451349	166561	
492122	726172	546642	13074
1073689	1532900	1300900	88800
1323143	1779400	1601400	144200
1792232	2141000	2084000	302400
4599595	3585284	3999638	2615337
4224447	2905614	3320757	2604796
4242764	3185886	2971634	2957131
5372950	3422316	2824793	4852248
5870833	3164602	2543981	6292213
7812382	1860336	2698406	10876940
9238106	1788783	1911315	15495035
11567474	2147066	2151485	19704421
16372763	2484171	2444002	27097053
25103833	3419970	558890	40886919
30351581	6054280	603438	47753553
40661140	6776754	667615	62310221
47635629	7688908	517878	75307243
55060463	7440679	386111	85969002
53791378	7576482	354714	85976138
65045658	9050510	300262	101459625
	248534	55708	
	335789	97834	
301998	536498	267613	8135
599899	1067400	416500	49100
674072	1237600	496800	80200
917085	1497400	601200	192700
2753196	2252300	908900	1599700
2139459	2018768	951432	1629578
2609217	2537740	819984	1639533
3041592	2989467	1123013	1997712
3102552	2668519	979070	2633249
4168724	1498595	968509	5337198
7778681	1695132	1792228	12668885
9821056	2036097	2045450	16170937
13864235	2390424	2305431	22249151
21203262	3097656	419720	34047592
25174207	5592419	390555	38792286
33532585	6305071	347788	50602594
38113187	7123810	323842	60117804
43328060	6812616	219140	67533047
41880805	6880470	148937	67030348
50213069	8155395	156026	78342464

a) Data in the column of Industry Above Designated Size refer to all state - owned enterprises and non - state - owned industrial enterprises with annual sales income of over 5 million yuan, before 1997, refer to enterprises at township and above level.
b) From 2002, data of urban district belong to new administrative area.

4－03 分县(市)工业

Number of Industrial

单位:个

项　目	Item	全　市 Whole Municipality	市区 Urban District	#萧山区 Xiaoshan
规模以上工业合计	**Industrial above Designated Size**	**10370**	**6478**	**2509**
一、按轻重工业分	**Grouped by Light & Heavy Industry**			
轻工业	Light Industry	5275	3256	1443
重工业	Heavy Industry	5095	3222	1066
二、按所有制分	**Grouped by Ownership**			
国有企业	State－owned Enterprises	74	51	6
集体企业	Collective－owned Enterprises	68	37	8
股份合作企业	Cooperative Enterprises	48	43	4
联营企业	Joint Ownership Enterprises	7	4	－
股份制企业	Share－holding Corporations	7299	4674	1770
外商及港澳台投资企业	Enterprises with Investment from Foreign、Hong Kong、Macao and Taiwan	1646	1256	499
其他企业	Other Enterprises	1228	413	222
合计中:国有控股企业	Of the Total:Controlling Share Hold Enterprises	210	154	21
三、按企业规模分	**Grouped by Size of Enterprises**			
大型企业	Large	45	43	11
中型企业	Medium－sized	796	620	310
小型企业	Small	9529	5815	2188

企业单位数(2010 年)
Enterprises by Region(2010)

(unit)

#余杭区 Yuhang	桐庐县 Tonglu	淳安县 Chun'an	建德市 Jiande	富阳市 Fuyang	临安市 Lin'an
2116	**767**	**175**	**823**	**1120**	**1007**
1065	510	97	376	542	494
1051	257	78	447	578	513
7	4	4	6	4	5
8	7	6	10	3	5
22	–	–	1	3	1
1	1	–	2	–	–
1706	472	124	542	793	694
263	128	13	28	153	68
109	155	28	234	164	234
23	7	7	10	15	17
4	–	–	–	1	1
112	25	7	17	74	53
2000	742	168	806	1045	953

4－04 分县(市)工业

Gross Industrial

单位:万元

项　目	Item	全　市 Whole Municipality	市　区 Urban District	#萧山区 Xiaoshan
规模以上工业合计	**Industrial above Designated Size**	**110810397**	**86653885**	**39911504**
一、按轻重工业分	**Grouped by Light & Heavy Industry**			
轻工业	Light Industry	45764739	36440816	19902906
重工业	Heavy Industry	65045658	50213069	20008598
二、按所有制分	**Grouped by Ownership**			
国有企业	State－owned Enterprises	9050510	8155395	1153701
集体企业	Collective－owned Enterprises	300262	156026	37828
股份合作企业	Cooperative Enterprises	113654	106429	18418
联营企业	Joint Ownership Enterprises	39734	9839	－
股份制企业	Share－holding Corporations	64972315	47504105	28775182
外商及港澳台投资企业	Enterprises with Investment from Foreign、Hong Kong、Macao and Taiwan	33547643	29655898	9256805
其他企业	Other Enterprises	2786281	1066194	669570
合计中:国有控股企业	Of the Total:Controlling Share Hold Enterprises	15518121	13902988	2045129
三、按企业规模分	**Grouped by Size of Enterprises**			
大型企业	Large	23334149	23006848	9025494
中型企业	Medium－sized	40945613	32322167	17562930
小型企业	Small	46530635	31324870	13323080

总产值(2010年)
Output Value by Region(2010)

(10000 yuan)

#余杭区 Yuhang	桐庐县 Tonglu	淳安县 Chun'an	建德市 Jiande	富阳市 Fuyang	临安市 Lin'an
12913523	**3736364**	**1512038**	**3435984**	**10110473**	**5361653**
4659714	1753670	1130041	1138732	3312319	1989161
8253809	1982694	381997	2297252	6798154	3372492
400869	101623	46674	210293	314858	221666
22547	19832	17696	41264	53388	12056
40309	–	–	2010	4205	1010
6409	837	–	29058	–	–
9574819	2185496	1239708	2671642	7771682	3599682
2669078	1141001	133725	203998	1613630	799391
199491	287576	74235	277719	352710	727847
672217	157985	56009	275228	592696	533215
1472248	–	–	–	213681	113621
4163290	1227136	384992	869488	3868088	2273742
7277985	2509228	1127046	2566496	6028704	2974290

4－05 分县(市)工业
Gross Industrial

单位:万元

项　目	Item	全　市 Whole Municipality	市　区 Urban District	#萧山区 Xiaoshan
规模以上工业合计	**Industrial above Designated Size**	**109513119**	**85776560**	**39469569**
一、按轻重工业分	**Grouped by Light & Heavy Industry**			
轻工业	Light Industry	45102791	35955014	19614439
重工业	Heavy Industry	64410328	49821546	19855130
二、按所有制分	**Grouped by Ownership**			
国有企业	State－owned Enterprises	9054019	8163003	1153205
集体企业	Collective－owned Enterprises	292078	155216	37580
股份合作企业	Cooperative Enterprises	109831	102864	17864
联营企业	Joint Ownership Enterprises	39637	9867	－
股份制企业	Share－holding Corporations	64168593	46996052	28543545
外商及港澳台投资企业	Enterprises with Investment from Foreign、Hong Kong、Macao and Taiwan	33127923	29299201	9058601
其他企业	Other Enterprises	2721039	1050357	658773
合计中:国有控股企业	Of the Total:Controlling Share Hold Enterprises	15472482	13862266	1995181
三、按企业规模分	**Grouped by Size of Enterprises**			
大型企业	Large	23162228	22837462	8932579
中型企业	Medium－sized	40586322	32049976	17444551
小型企业	Small	45764569	30889122	13092439

销售产值(2010年)

Products Sales by Region(2010)

(10000 yuan)

#余杭区 Yuhang	桐庐县 Tonglu	淳安县 Chun'an	建德市 Jiande	富阳市 Fuyang	临安市 Lin'an
12636712	**3685616**	**1460740**	**3371141**	**9921773**	**5297290**
4592114	1725053	1090573	1108987	3273878	1949286
8044598	1960563	370166	2262154	6647894	3348004
400664	101623	46124	211102	313554	218612
22395	19802	17636	41706	45836	11882
40333	–	–	2005	4052	909
6357	742	–	29028	–	–
9371261	2163895	1194527	2615011	7629392	3569716
2598343	1118996	128880	200411	1586453	793982
197360	280558	73572	271879	342486	702188
640305	158233	55549	275716	591020	529697
1458505	–	–	–	211207	113559
4042185	1215401	353463	855511	3828038	2283933
7136022	2470215	1107277	2515630	5882528	2899799

4－06 全市规模以上工业

Main Economic Indicators of Industrial

单位:万元

项　目	Item	企业单位数(个) Number of Enterprises (unit)	#亏损企业(个) Loss Making Enterprises (unit)
总　　计	**Total**	**10370**	**1105**
按隶属关系分	**Grouped by Subordination**		
中　央　属	Central	28	2
省　　　属	Provincial	61	5
市　　　属	Municipal	6402	768
县(市)属	County and below	3879	330
按所有制分	**Grouped by Ownership**		
国有企业	State－owned Enterprises	74	14
集体企业	Collective－owned Enterprises	68	6
股份合作企业	Cooperative Enterprises	48	8
联营企业	Joint Ownership Enterprises	7	1
股份制企业	Share－holding Corporations	7299	727
外商及港澳台投资企业	Enterprises with Investment from Foreign、Hong Kong、Macao and Taiwan	1646	293
其他企业	Other Enterprises	1228	56
按企业规模分	**Grouped by Size of Enterprises**		
大型企业	Large	45	1
中型企业	Medium－sized	796	56
小型企业	Small	9529	1048
按轻重工业分	**Grouped by Light & Heavy Industry**		
轻工业	Light Industry	5275	597
重工业	Heavy Industry	5095	508

注:本表范围为年销售收入500万元及以上工业。

企业主要经济指标(一)
Enterprises Above Designated Size(Ⅰ)

(10000 yuan)

工业总产值(当年价格) Gross Industrial Output Value (current price)	工业销售产值 Value of Industrial Products Sales	全部从业人员年平均人数(人) Annual Average Number of Staff and Workers(person)
110810397	**109513119**	**1396482**
6546665	6552690	16183
4265304	4236937	29497
76581523	75726653	1008928
23416905	22996839	341874
9050510	9054019	34994
300262	292078	4932
113654	109831	2763
39734	39637	647
64972315	64168593	832603
33547643	33127923	462179
2786281	2721039	58364
23334149	23162228	189907
40945613	40586322	490985
46530635	45764569	715590
45764739	45102791	745678
65045658	64410328	650804

a) Data in this table refer to enterprises with annual sales income of over 5 million yuan.

单位:万元　　4－06　续表1

项　目	Item	企业单位数(个) Number of Enterprises (unit)	#亏损企业(个) Loss Making Enterprises (unit)
按市、县分	**Grouped by County**		
市　区	Urban District	6478	773
#萧山区	Xiaoshan	2509	172
余杭区	Yuhang	2116	312
桐庐县	Tonglu	767	45
淳安县	Chun'an	175	11
建德市	Jiande	823	42
富阳市	Fuyang	1120	118
临安市	Lin'an	1007	116
按国民经济行业分	**Grouped by Economic Sector**		
煤炭开采和洗选业	Coal Mining and Dressing	－	－
黑色金属矿采选业	Ferrous Metals Mining and Dressing	1	－
有色金属矿采选业	Nonferrous Metals Mining and Dressing	9	1
非金属矿采选业	Nonmetal Minerals Mining and Dressing	56	9
农副食品加工业	Agricultural Products Processing	205	17
食品制造业	Food Manufacturing	138	20
饮料制造业	Beverage Manufacturing	78	11
烟草制品业	Tobacco Processing	3	－
纺织业	Textile Industry	1516	134
纺织服装、鞋、帽制造业	Textile Products, Garments, Shoes and Caps Processing	567	110
皮革、毛皮、羽毛(绒)及其制品业	Leather, Furs, Down and Related Products	215	25
木材加工及木、竹、藤、棕、草制品业	Timber Processing, Bamboo, Cane, Palm Fiber and Straw Products	129	8
家具制造业	Furniture Manufacturing	157	20

continued 1 (10000 yuan)

工业总产值(当年价格) Gross Industrial Output Value (current price)	工业销售产值 Value of Industrial Products Sales	全部从业人员年平均人数(人) Annual Average Number of Staff and Workers(person)
86653885	85776560	1051759
39911504	39469569	444729
12913523	12636712	229542
3736364	3685616	61741
1512038	1460740	17234
3435984	3371141	48375
10110473	9921773	121200
5361653	5297290	96173
–	–	–
2427	1877	105
54566	54436	789
175123	173414	3552
1020475	1002918	12372
1939022	1867233	30099
2004886	1976511	20258
1815241	1815271	2302
10662693	10532277	195293
2559716	2570112	100441
1722717	1694178	38875
373984	364901	7931
1272873	1220483	34318

项　目	Item	企业单位数(个) Number of Enterprises (unit)	#亏损企业(个) Loss Making Enterprises (unit)
造纸及纸制品业	Paper Making and Paper Products	571	52
印刷业和记录媒介的复制	Printing and Record Media	180	23
文教体育用品制造业	Cultural, Educational and Sports Goods	182	20
石油加工、炼焦及核燃料加工业	Petroleum Processing, Coking and Nuclear Fuel Processing	24	2
化学原料及化学制品制造业	Raw Chemical Materials and Chemical Products	600	51
医药制造业	Medical and Pharmaceutical Products	107	14
化学纤维制造业	Chemical Fiber	80	8
橡胶制品业	Rubber Products	100	8
塑料制品业	Plastic Products	516	43
非金属矿物制品业	Nonmetal Minerals Products	456	57
黑色金属冶炼及压延加工业	Smelting and Processing of Ferrous Metals	111	13
有色金属冶炼及压延加工业	Smelting and Processing of Nonferrous Metals	103	10
金属制品业	Metals Products	656	66
通用设备制造业	Ordinary Machinery	1005	74
专用设备制造业	For Special Purpose Equipment Manufacturing	405	46
交通运输设备制造业	Transport Equipment Manufacturing	415	44
电气机械及器材制造业	Electric Equipment and Machinery	847	116
通信设备、计算机及其他电子设备制造业	Telecommunications Equipment, Computers and Other Electronic Equipment Manufacturing	372	50
仪器仪表及文化、办公用机械制造业	Instruments, Meters, Cultural and Office Machinery	241	21
工艺品及其他制造业	Craftworks and Other Manufacturing	204	13
废弃资源和废旧材料回收加工业	Waste Resouces and Waste or Old Material Recycled	25	1
电力、热力的生产和供应业	Production and Supply of Electric Power and Hot Water	59	6
燃气生产和供应业	Production and Supply of Gas	13	–
水的生产和供应业	Production and Supply of Tap Water	24	12

continued 2 (10000 yuan)

工业总产值(当年价格) Gross Industrial Output Value (current price)	工业销售产值 Value of Industrial Products Sales	全部从业人员年平均人数(人) Annual Average Number of Staff and Workers(person)
4076584	4023064	58478
755552	740888	13643
551061	542331	16668
552780	551053	1472
8343234	8296794	55253
1794809	1753985	26619
6036847	5973345	23755
2666481	2708394	32998
2806202	2774097	39348
4147581	4101237	56557
4068208	4047246	22906
2111499	2088614	7590
3604505	3567118	55566
8253446	8115272	115454
2197354	2150672	38261
9031681	8981546	72987
8978237	8858693	137985
6590543	6469842	90766
2338276	2271854	36801
1248527	1192738	23038
408654	411124	1605
5620108	5605086	15594
788983	788540	1958
235527	225975	4845

4－07 全市规模以上工业

Main Economic Indicators of Industrial

单位:万元

项　目	Item	资产总计 Total Assets	#产成品 Finished Products
总　计	**Total**	**99374132**	**5220142**
按隶属关系分	**Grouped by Subordination**		
中　央　属	Central	4280192	86538
省　　属	Provincial	4893557	118946
市　　属	Municipal	70341174	3993180
县(市)属	County and below	19859209	1021478
按所有制分	**Grouped by Ownership**		
国有企业	State－owned Enterprises	7836288	100986
集体企业	Collective－owned Enterprises	274999	11194
股份合作企业	Cooperative Enterprises	155218	9171
联营企业	Joint Ownership Enterprises	42099	1076
股份制企业	Share－holding Corporations	59961159	3259186
外商及港澳台投资企业	Enterprises with Investment from Foreign、Hong Kong、Macao and Taiwan	29483431	1732975
其他企业	Other Enterprises	1620938	105554
按企业规模分	**Grouped by Size of Enterprises**		
大型企业	Large	18537381	998821
中型企业	Medium－sized	39232168	1929969
小型企业	Small	41604583	2291352
按轻重工业分	**Grouped by Light & Heavy Industry**		
轻工业	Light Industry	42328986	2285953
重工业	Heavy Industry	57045146	2934189

企业主要经济指标(二)

Enterprises Above Designated Size(Ⅱ)

(10000 yuan)

流动资产合计 Total Circulating Funds	#本年折旧 Depreciation of the year	固定资产净值 Net Value of Fixed Assets	年末负债合计 Total Liabilities	所有者权益合计 Creditors´Equity
60116766	**2629621**	**23120810**	**57979673**	**41394459**
1625410	248140	1943659	2367854	1912338
2158212	156794	1654209	2653854	2239703
44319907	1740713	14910948	41038919	29302255
12013238	483974	4611994	11919047	7940163
3120175	384238	3102720	4084170	3752117
189195	6595	42779	164046	110953
99554	2673	24085	82885	72334
25881	345	5533	9239	32860
36013534	1410569	12850768	36808109	23153049
19609281	778666	6686486	15765639	13717792
1059146	46534	408438	1065585	555353
12103465	369200	2869415	9796715	8740666
23082260	1070243	9455712	22613448	16618720
24931041	1190179	10795683	25569510	16035073
25779113	1122004	10014868	23931825	18397161
34337653	1507617	13105941	34047848	22997298

项　目	Item	资产总计 Total Assets	#产成品 Finished Products
按市、县分	**Grouped by County**		
市　区	Urban District	79095603	4196749
#萧山区	Xiaoshan	35138617	1834165
余杭区	Yuhang	11665607	746378
桐庐县	Tonglu	2806855	121757
淳安县	Chun'an	854232	38055
建德市	Jiande	2842100	152716
富阳市	Fuyang	9142725	452145
临安市	Lin'an	4632618	258721
按国民经济行业分	**Grouped by Economic Sector**		
煤炭开采和洗选业	Coal Mining and Dressing	-	-
黑色金属矿采选业	Ferrous Metals Mining and Dressing	1022	155
有色金属矿采选业	Nonferrous Metals Mining and Dressing	70467	3500
非金属矿采选业	Nonmetal Minerals Mining and Dressing	218319	3887
农副食品加工业	Agricultural Products Processing	698436	50054
食品制造业	Food Manufacturing	1457313	75191
饮料制造业	Beverage Manufacturing	1737713	52867
烟草制品业	Tobacco Processing	1598237	70340
纺织业	Textile Industry	9811853	614678
纺织服装、鞋、帽制造业	Textile Products, Garments, Shoes and Caps Processing	2571451	146859
皮革、毛皮、羽毛(绒)及其制品业	Leather, Furs, Down and Related Products	1521609	79506
木材加工及木、竹、藤、棕、草制品业	Timber Processing, Bamboo, Cane, Palm Fiber and Straw Products	283696	18799
家具制造业	Furniture Manufacturing	1182726	63057

continued 1 (10000 yuan)

流动资产合计 Total Circulating Funds	#本年折旧 Depreciation of the year	固定资产净值 Net Value of Fixed Assets	年末负债合计 Total Liabilities	所有者权益合计 Creditors´Equity
48040809	2112870	18189873	45822832	33272771
21197288	893500	8013229	21739086	13399531
7303625	323698	2827690	7185941	4479666
1558850	86499	737450	1718273	1088582
427123	38577	291321	443191	411041
1574759	67423	759466	1643841	1198258
5632628	207844	1986675	5615003	3527722
2882597	116408	1156025	2736532	1896086
–	–	–	–	–
672	50	350	86	936
41211	860	5961	39638	30829
93048	7488	48816	149210	69109
411716	17033	159550	444582	253853
947914	31001	338854	693758	763555
906690	62898	570376	905966	831747
1169420	24257	163434	156791	1441445
5821329	313060	2617308	6161206	3650647
1644693	54493	571567	1524031	1047421
1077588	20107	181999	1084414	437195
160702	7911	83302	155047	128649
806805	19222	224508	679844	502882

单位:万元　　　　4－07　续表2

项　目	Item	资产总计 Total Assets	#产成品 Finished Products
造纸及纸制品业	Paper Making and Paper Products	4109390	180831
印刷业和记录媒介的复制	Printing and Record Media	907069	34020
文教体育用品制造业	Cultural, Educational and Sports Goods	424381	19355
石油加工、炼焦及核燃料加工业	Petroleum Processing, Coking and Nuclear Fuel Processing	127275	7625
化学原料及化学制品制造业	Raw Chemical Materials and Chemical Products	6419252	345521
医药制造业	Medical and Pharmaceutical Products	2098673	148336
化学纤维制造业	Chemical Fiber	4784508	215157
橡胶制品业	Rubber Products	1714761	200405
塑料制品业	Plastic Products	2460120	139391
非金属矿物制品业	Nonmetal Mineral Products	4696385	297325
黑色金属冶炼及压延加工业	Smelting and Processing of Ferrous Metals	4132802	144425
有色金属冶炼及压延加工业	Smelting and Processing of Nonferrous Metals	936496	60726
金属制品业	Metal Products	2801155	201543
通用设备制造业	Ordinary Machinery	8298490	553061
专用设备制造业	For Special Purpose Equipment Manufacturing	2235874	132820
交通运输设备制造业	Transport Equipment Manufacturing	7466626	296191
电气机械及器材制造业	Electric Equipment and Machinery	8433498	487852
通信设备、计算机及其他电子设备制造业	Telecommunications Equipment, Computers and Other Electronic Equipment Manufacturing	6543221	375413
仪器仪表及文化、办公用机械制造业	Instruments, Meters, Cultural and Office Machinery	2253885	102779
工艺品及其他制造业	Craftworks and Other Manufacturing	830170	74574
废弃资源和废旧材料回收加工业	Waste Resouces and Waste or Old Material Recycled	240080	18689
电力、热力的生产和供应业	Production and Supply of Electric Power and Hot Water	4152395	1012
燃气生产和供应业	Production and Supply of Gas	663833	3701
水的生产和供应业	Production and Supply of Tap Water	1490955	496

continued 2

(10000 yuan)

流动资产合计 Total Circulating Funds	#本年折旧 Depreciation of the year	固定资产净值 Net Value of Fixed Assets	年末负债合计 Total Liabilities	所有者权益合计 Creditors´Equity
2638166	107863	950217	2651633	1457757
510938	40404	311722	551304	355764
244692	12736	131697	204369	220011
80403	5448	35508	127206	69
3795598	168949	1422771	3599609	2819642
1245571	43523	395900	953901	1144772
2588704	130689	1285524	2922280	1862228
916530	81232	529427	1078058	636703
1489816	71805	628545	1413414	1046707
2806567	136309	1188314	3042500	1653885
2599809	81572	667864	2647884	1484917
727008	12348	122352	637137	299359
1854335	60301	590309	1796143	1005012
5314415	172789	1625421	4580562	3717928
1512279	46963	420876	1238572	997302
4542081	118186	999982	5089152	2377474
5752454	167641	1506441	4747605	3685892
4770454	105305	819053	2936883	3606338
1600249	42953	368855	1226925	1026960
519199	27950	206340	449908	380262
184895	2787	22133	164561	75519
809680	341975	2865721	2862900	1289495
145093	25333	408228	350087	313746
386047	66183	651587	712507	778449

4－08 全市规模以上工业

Main Economic Indicators of Industrial

单位:万元

项 目	Item	主营业务收入 Revenues in Main Business	营业费用 Expenses of Business	主营业务税金及附加 Sales Taxes and Extra Charges in Main Business
总 计	**Total**	**108432436**	**3655946**	**1540228**
按隶属关系分	**Grouped by Subordination**			
中 央 属	Central	4128349	68332	1161840
省 属	Provincial	4386446	43272	15163
市 属	Municipal	77312093	3023360	279743
县(市)属	County and Below	22605549	520983	83482
按所有制分	**Grouped by Ownership**			
国有企业	State－owned Enterprises	6612356	65496	1169220
集体企业	Collective－owned Enterprises	275194	6662	2423
股份合作企业	Cooperative Enterprises	104990	2000	473
联营企业	Joint Ownership Enterprises	40558	315	54
股份制企业	Share－holding Corporations	65358557	1464875	277481
外商及港澳台投资企业	Enterprises with Investment from Foreign、Hong Kong、Macao and Taiwan	33350448	2070579	76437
其他企业	Other Enterprises	2690333	46019	14141
按企业规模分	**Grouped by Size of Enterprises**			
大型企业	Large	23575218	1174483	1168916
中型企业	Medium－sized	41699058	1548575	194289
小型企业	Small	43158160	932889	177024
按轻重工业分	**Grouped by Light & Heavy Industry**			
轻工业	Light Industry	45840862	2126543	1288574
重工业	Heavy Industry	62591575	1529404	251654

企业主要经济指标(三)
Enterprises Above Designated Size(Ⅲ)

(10000 yuan)

管理费用 Management Expenses	利息支出 Interest Expenditure	利润总额 Total Profits	利税总额 Total Pre－tax Profits	本年应交增值税 Value Added Tax Payable
4631454	**1174958**	**7644672**	**12244758**	**3059858**
143352	21187	223912	1730770	345018
232519	34577	176940	303272	111170
3358095	835546	5664416	7934445	1990286
897488	283649	1579404	2276271	613385
311586	24688	351485	1938317	417612
19294	2302	22919	38693	13352
7435	1563	2705	6352	3174
1236	6	3711	4179	413
2470415	882518	3992781	5767751	1497489
1730041	243541	3143477	4280795	1060881
91448	20341	127594	208671	66936
866470	170830	1881042	3729382	679425
1796336	474084	3283232	4734681	1257161
1968648	530043	2480398	3780695	1123272
1897498	492545	3400538	6292797	1603685
2733957	682413	4244133	5951960	1456173

单位:万元　　　　　　　　　　　　　　4－08　续表1

项　目	Item	主营业务收　入 Revenues in Main Business	营业费用 Expenses of Business	主营业务税金及附加 Sales Taxes and Extra Charges in Main Business
按市、县分	**Grouped by County**			
市　区	Urban District	85106331	3133252	1453257
#萧山区	Xiaoshan	39712969	534920	158206
余杭区	Yuhang	12784640	437575	46777
桐庐县	Tonglu	3615725	62645	16112
淳安县	Chun'an	1425495	70524	7923
建德市	Jiande	3346587	82654	15068
富阳市	Fuyang	9782136	165745	30690
临安市	Lin'an	5156162	141125	17179
按国民经济行业分	**Grouped by Economic Sector**			
煤炭开采和洗选业	Coal Mining and Dressing	-	-	-
黑色金属矿采选业	Ferrous Metals Mining and Dressing	2065	134	19
有色金属矿采选业	Nonferrous Metals Mining and Dressing	53387	1029	540
非金属矿采选业	Nonmetal Minerals Mining and Dressing	170418	6994	4313
农副食品加工业	Agricultural Products Processing	1034481	31154	3195
食品制造业	Food Manufacturing	1887937	317918	8044
饮料制造业	Beverage Manufacturing	2635204	330769	26240
烟草制品业	Tobacco Processing	1805373	49100	1100682
纺织业	Textile Industry	10503196	123090	50829
纺织服装、鞋、帽制造业	Textile Products, Garments, Shoes and Caps Processing	2566328	80246	12443
皮革、毛皮、羽毛(绒)及其制品业	Leather, Furs, Down and Related Products	1682790	38660	4385
木材加工及木、竹、藤、棕、草制品业	Timber Processing, Bamboo, Cane, Palm Fiber and Straw Products	357117	8885	2786
家具制造业	Furniture Manufacturing	1225148	46789	3922

continued 1 (10000 yuan)

管理费用 Management Expenses	利息支出 Interest Expenditure	利润总额 Total Profits	利税总额 Total Pre - tax Profits	本年应交增值税 Value Added Tax Payable
3682004	884559	6051851	9923215	2418107
1060490	570639	2494577	3529556	876773
639507	146320	751074	1116896	319045
142481	27321	288145	436977	132720
39175	9475	89885	132632	34824
152593	30507	290184	388323	83071
336649	171351	595503	863924	237731
278553	51745	329103	499687	153405
–	–	–	–	–
300	–	211	415	185
6198	894	11032	15927	4354
12078	3460	9181	22251	8757
28790	12128	48986	73867	21686
79309	7049	171919	283979	104017
70865	5862	196289	327178	104649
95109	-7590	126362	1446362	219318
306536	150418	561633	847338	234877
161900	32879	139946	240124	87735
49790	23968	83833	147894	59675
14077	4698	18612	33141	11743
48523	12195	95032	138690	39736

项　目	Item	主营业务收入 Revenues in Main Business	营业费用 Expenses of Business	主营业务税金及附加 Sales Taxes and Extra Charges in Main Business
造纸及纸制品业	Paper Making and Paper Products	4001978	66060	13754
印刷业和记录媒介的复制	Printing and Record Media	749036	16290	2398
文教体育用品制造业	Cultural, Educational and Sports Goods	540702	14776	1576
石油加工、炼焦及核燃料加工业	Petroleum Processing, Coking and Nuclear Fuel Processing	551232	3080	54310
化学原料及化学制品制造业	Raw Chemical Materials and Chemical Products	8362932	362183	23485
医药制造业	Medical and Pharmaceutical Products	1744788	465988	7619
化学纤维制造业	Chemical Fiber	6084411	39075	18461
橡胶制品业	Rubber Products	2717826	79112	10016
塑料制品业	Plastic Products	2739628	58301	8844
非金属矿物制品业	Nonmetal Mineral Products	4143289	160116	16982
黑色金属冶炼及压延加工业	Smelting and Processing of Ferrous Metals	4164417	33557	10143
有色金属冶炼及压延加工业	Smelting and Processing of Nonferrous Metals	2054378	4815	3735
金属制品业	Metal Products	3502700	56981	12232
通用设备制造业	Ordinary Machinery	8356814	236980	24268
专用设备制造业	For Special Purpose Equipment Manufacturing	2158293	54828	8113
交通运输设备制造业	Transport Equipment Manufacturing	9191848	136584	27498
电气机械及器材制造业	Electric Equipment and Machinery	8770990	349549	23188
通信设备、计算机及其他电子设备制造业	Telecommunications Equipment, Computers and Other Electronic Equipment Manufacturing	6672953	307590	20869
仪器仪表及文化、办公用机械制造业	Instruments, Meters, Cultural and Office Machinery	2253807	116931	11068
工艺品及其他制造业	Craftworks and Other Manufacturing	1202371	14780	6661
废弃资源和废旧材料回收加工业	Waste Resouces and Waste or Old Material Recycled	403168	1236	3346
电力、热力的生产和供应业	Production and Supply of Electric Power and Hot Water	3095967	988	9273
燃气生产和供应业	Production and Supply of Gas	809963	29964	3398
水的生产和供应业	Production and Supply of Tap Water	235503	11416	1595

continued 2 (10000 yuan)

管理费用 Management Expenses	利息支出 Interest Expenditure	利润总额 Total Profits	利税总额 Total Pre - tax Profits	本年应交增值税 Value Added Tax Payable
134843	79006	261610	396694	121330
44636	8301	46564	70534	21572
27915	3102	23586	38751	13589
8195	3965	18962	121098	47826
412903	86450	730245	979722	225992
193908	9851	283298	435111	144194
73234	80208	549776	713769	145533
49780	24390	108886	166185	47283
102697	34357	189083	259783	61857
152961	66054	289432	447944	141529
113786	36161	159784	256078	86151
24394	17842	126661	166174	35778
145469	36862	177910	262510	72368
485777	65950	734074	986315	227974
156018	20387	195565	249511	45833
270159	134988	441641	579197	110057
469357	87493	494163	718240	200890
505622	24954	786880	960846	153097
191835	26718	214844	300778	74867
41905	10363	58063	90248	25524
5030	3290	26610	54146	24191
100318	46085	126740	261671	125658
18992	9325	47252	52630	1980
28247	12899	90010	99659	8054

4-09 市区规模以上工业
Main Economic Indicators of Industrial Enterprises

单位:万元

项 目	Item	企业单位数(个) Number of Enterprises (unit)	#亏损企业(个) Loss Making Enterprises (unit)
总 计	**Total**	**6478**	**773**
按隶属关系分	**Grouped by Subordination**		
中 央 属	Central	24	2
省 属	Provincial	52	3
市 属	Municipal	6402	768
按所有制分	**Grouped by Ownership**		
国有企业	State - owned Enterprises	51	7
集体企业	Collective - owned Enterprises	37	6
股份合作企业	Cooperative Enterprises	43	6
联营企业	Joint Ownership Enterprises	4	1
股份制企业	Share - holding Corporations	4674	489
外商及港澳台投资企业	Enterprises with Investment from Foreign、Hong Kong、Macao and Taiwan	1256	242
其他企业	Other Enterprises	413	22
按企业规模分	**Grouped by Size of Enterprises**		
大型企业	Large	43	1
中型企业	Medium - sized	620	47
小型企业	Small	5815	725
按轻重工业分	**Grouped by Light & Heavy Industry**		
轻工业	Light Industry	3256	421
重工业	Heavy Industry	3222	352

企业主要经济指标(一)

Above Designated Size in Urban District(Ⅰ)

(10000 yuan)

工业总产值(当年价格) Gross Industrial Output Value (current price)	工业销售产值 Value of Industrial Products Sales	全部从业人员年平均人数(人) Annual Average Number of Staff and Workers(person)
86653885	**85776560**	**1051759**
6465621	6471645	15159
3606742	3578262	27672
76581523	75726653	1008928
8155395	8163003	30032
156026	155216	3214
106429	102864	2575
9839	9867	305
47504105	46996052	592312
29655898	29299201	397801
1066194	1050357	25520
23006848	22837462	184241
32322167	32049976	391198
31324870	30889122	476320
36440816	35955014	557055
50213069	49821546	494704

项 目	Item	企业单位数(个) Number of Enterprises (unit)	#亏损企业(个) Loss Making Enterprises (unit)
按国民经济行业分	**Grouped by Economic Sector**		
煤炭开采和洗选业	Coal Mining and Dressing	–	–
黑色金属矿采选业	Ferrous Metals Mining and Dressing	–	–
有色金属矿采选业	Nonferrous Metals Mining and Dressing	–	–
非金属矿采选业	Nonmetal Minerals Mining and Dressing	14	1
农副食品加工业	Agricultural Products Processing	83	11
食品制造业	Food Manufacturing	90	13
饮料制造业	Beverage Manufacturing	38	6
烟草制品业	Tobacco Processing	3	–
纺织业	Textile Industry	1061	104
纺织服装、鞋、帽制造业	Textile Products, Garments, Shoes and Caps Processing	478	100
皮革、毛皮、羽毛(绒)及其制品业	Leather, Furs, Down and Related Products	135	16
木材加工及木、竹、藤、棕、草制品业	Timber Processing, Bamboo, Cane, Palm Fiber and Straw Products	62	5
家具制造业	Furniture Manufacturing	105	15
造纸及纸制品业	Paper Making and Paper Products	153	19
印刷业和记录媒介的复制	Printing and Record Media	146	21
文教体育用品制造业	Cultural, Educational and Sports Goods	54	10
石油加工、炼焦及核燃料加工业	Petroleum Processing, Coking and Nuclear Fuel Processing	19	2

continued 1 (10000 yuan)

工业总产值(当年价格) Gross Industrial Output Value (current price)	工业销售产值 Value of Industrial Products Sales	全部从业人员年平均人数(人) Annual Average Number of Staff and Workers(person)
–	–	–
–	–	–
–	–	–
55603	55356	1315
658233	651038	8071
1745043	1679243	25694
1546957	1547491	16115
1815241	1815271	2302
8775021	8668991	158324
2219380	2231918	90710
1264930	1241729	26171
230442	225452	4785
1030758	983959	28273
1284541	1254384	17677
696174	682585	11708
330051	327251	9016
534523	533663	1312

单位:万元　　4－09　续表2

项　目	Item	企业单位数(个) Number of Enterprises (unit)	#亏损企业(个) Loss Making Enterprises (unit)
化学原料及化学制品制造业	Raw Chemical Materials and Chemical Products	358	40
医药制造业	Medical and Pharmaceutical Products	76	11
化学纤维制造业	Chemical Fiber	65	5
橡胶制品业	Rubber Products	48	6
塑料制品业	Plastic Products	341	34
非金属矿物制品业	Nonmetal Mineral Products	248	32
黑色金属冶炼及压延加工业	Smelting and Processing of Ferrous Metals	73	7
有色金属冶炼及压延加工业	Smelting and Processing of Nonferrous Metals	31	6
金属制品业	Metal Products	377	47
通用设备制造业	Ordinary Machinery	726	50
专用设备制造业	For Special Purpose Equipment Manufacturing	275	32
交通运输设备制造业	Transport Equipment Manufacturing	319	39
电气机械及器材制造业	Electric Equipment and Machinery	415	65
通信设备、计算机及其他电子设备制造业	Telecommunications Equipment, Computers and Other Electronic Equipment Manufacturing	287	42
仪器仪表及文化、办公用机械制造业	Instruments, Meters, Cultural and Office Machinery	196	18
工艺品及其他制造业	Craftworks and Other Manufacturing	150	10
废弃资源和废旧材料回收加工业	Waste Resouces and Waste or Old Material Recycled	6	-
电力、热力的生产和供应业	Production and Supply of Electric Power and Hot Water	27	2
燃气生产和供应业	Production and Supply of Gas	9	-
水的生产和供应业	Production and Supply of Tap Water	10	4

continued 2

(10000 yuan)

工业总产值(当年价格) Gross Industrial Output Value (current price)	工业销售产值 Value of Industrial Products Sales	全部从业人员年平均人数(人) Annual Average Number of Staff and Workers(person)
6364766	6350599	38752
1620600	1586532	22241
5895614	5834043	22162
2300356	2350836	24901
2291184	2279388	30252
2759028	2727590	37580
3402818	3406187	19726
371435	368732	2764
2268662	2266034	37100
6482278	6375262	91486
1764353	1731672	29036
8643025	8605240	63502
5390662	5319517	82447
6090415	5989591	79366
2218175	2154679	33168
1077204	1024470	19707
16239	15535	284
4542409	4533199	10336
776454	775940	1755
191314	183186	3721

4-10 市区规模以上工业

Main Economic Indicators of Industrial

单位:万元

项　目	Item	资产总计 Total Assets	#产成品 Finished Products
总　　计	**Total**	**79095603**	**4196749**
按隶属关系分	**Grouped by Subordination**		
中　央　属	Central	4205351	86501
省　　　属	Provincial	4549078	117068
市　　　属	Municipal	70341174	3993180
按所有制分	**Grouped by Ownership**		
国有企业	State - owned Enterprises	7169859	98367
集体企业	Collective - owned Enterprises	179026	6861
股份合作企业	Cooperative Enterprises	141004	8822
联营企业	Joint Ownership Enterprises	8013	368
股份制企业	Share - holding Corporations	45099493	2487053
外商及港澳台投资企业	Enterprises with Investment from Foreign、Hong Kong、Macao and Taiwan	25743362	1559409
其他企业	Other Enterprises	754845	35870
按企业规模分	**Grouped by Size of Enterprises**		
大型企业	Large	18330627	969511
中型企业	Medium - sized	31026205	1565528
小型企业	Small	29738771	1661710
按轻重工业分	**Grouped by Light & Heavy Industry**		
轻工业	Light Industry	33950394	1886703
重工业	Heavy Industry	45145209	2310046

企业主要经济指标(二)

Enterprises Above Designated Size in Urban District(Ⅱ)

(10000 yuan)

流动资产合计 Total Circulating Funds	#本年折旧 Depreciation of the year	固定资产净值 Net Value of Fixed Assets	年末负债合计 Total Liabilities	所有者权益合计 Creditors´Equity
48040809	**2112870**	**18189873**	**45822832**	**33272771**
1614652	240778	1881953	2325822	1879529
2106250	131379	1396972	2458091	2090987
44319907	1740713	14910948	41038919	29302255
2935328	335392	2678844	3713985	3455875
122107	3978	25980	103736	75291
92753	2505	19623	79354	61650
6519	213	1191	6734	1280
27172111	1061308	9429771	27884977	17214516
17209471	685437	5836175	13525185	12218177
502521	24037	198288	508863	245983
11961079	366417	2826797	9649355	8681272
18379232	858944	7519892	18027649	12998556
17700498	887509	7843184	18145828	11592943
20721291	904826	8065756	18699296	15251098
27319518	1208045	10124117	27123536	18021672

项　目	Item	资产总计 Total Assets	#产成品 Finished Products
按国民经济行业分	**Grouped by Economic Sector**		
煤炭开采和洗选业	Coal Mining and Dressing	-	-
黑色金属矿采选业	Ferrous Metals Mining and Dressing	-	-
有色金属矿采选业	Nonferrous Metals Mining and Dressing	-	-
非金属矿采选业	Nonmetal Minerals Mining and Dressing	36693	924
农副食品加工业	Agricultural Products Processing	489652	38552
食品制造业	Food Manufacturing	1269925	60307
饮料制造业	Beverage Manufacturing	1343691	40888
烟草制品业	Tobacco Processing	1598237	70340
纺织业	Textile Industry	8657194	546379
纺织服装、鞋、帽制造业	Textile Products, Garments, Shoes and Caps Processing	2210841	126081
皮革、毛皮、羽毛(绒)及其制品业	Leather, Furs, Down and Related Products	1249045	67086
木材加工及木、竹、藤、棕、草制品业	Timber Processing, Bamboo, Cane, Palm Fiber and Straw Products	186892	12484
家具制造业	Furniture Manufacturing	990441	55458
造纸及纸制品业	Paper Making and Paper Products	1096087	48335
印刷业和记录媒介的复制	Printing and Record Media	816403	30347
文教体育用品制造业	Cultural, Educational and Sports Goods	282280	12472
石油加工、炼焦及核燃料加工业	Petroleum Processing, Coking and Nuclear Fuel Processing	114039	6306

continued 1 (10000 yuan)

流动资产合计 Total Circulating Funds	#本年折旧 Depreciation of the year	固定资产净值 Net Value of Fixed Assets	年末负债合计 Total Liabilities	所有者权益合计 Creditors´Equity
–	–	–	–	–
–	–	–	–	–
–	–	–	–	–
18686	2310	10087	22141	14552
282103	12467	111653	320860	168792
834858	26393	294065	590576	679348
740233	47405	399385	645074	698616
1169420	24257	163434	156791	1441445
5201322	271436	2313282	5463461	3193733
1425849	47553	512793	1329909	880931
901740	13617	137361	888597	360448
102387	5884	58334	105171	81721
690460	15567	183303	558748	431693
686601	32626	277972	682450	413638
457171	36561	285999	493042	323360
156160	8789	99375	125292	156988
71260	5149	32415	121139	-7100

单位:万元　　4－10　续表2

项　目	Item	资产总计 Total Assets	#产成品 Finished Products
化学原料及化学制品制造业	Raw Chemical Materials and Chemical Products	4611402	268625
医药制造业	Medical and Pharmaceutical Products	1628619	129286
化学纤维制造业	Chemical Fiber	4691327	208181
橡胶制品业	Rubber Products	1506313	190130
塑料制品业	Plastic Products	1994821	110470
非金属矿物制品业	Nonmetal Mineral Products	3240078	246430
黑色金属冶炼及压延加工业	Smelting and Processing of Ferrous Metals	3719232	88627
有色金属冶炼及压延加工业	Smelting and Processing of Nonferrous Metals	255141	10688
金属制品业	Metal Products	2000464	131824
通用设备制造业	Ordinary Machinery	6809812	456966
专用设备制造业	For Special Purpose Equipment Manufacturing	1835025	106543
交通运输设备制造业	Transport Equipment Manufacturing	7113254	280561
电气机械及器材制造业	Electric Equipment and Machinery	5341535	332212
通信设备、计算机及其他电子设备制造业	Telecommunications Equipment, Computers and Other Electronic Equipment Manufacturing	6113459	349012
仪器仪表及文化、办公用机械制造业	Instruments, Meters, Cultural and Office Machinery	2122493	97296
工艺品及其他制造业	Craftworks and Other Manufacturing	696692	68908
废弃资源和废旧材料回收加工业	Waste Resouces and Waste or Old Material Recycled	55552	1172
电力、热力的生产和供应业	Production and Supply of Electric Power and Hot Water	3198014	316
燃气生产和供应业	Production and Supply of Gas	640808	3546
水的生产和供应业	Production and Supply of Tap Water	1180148	-

continued 2 (10000 yuan)

流动资产合计 Total Circulating Funds	#本年折旧 Depreciation of the year	固定资产净值 Net Value of Fixed Assets	年末负债合计 Total Liabilities	所有者权益合计 Creditors´Equity
2756315	131286	1100850	2669584	1941817
1075029	34957	294828	680971	947648
2522213	128219	1265463	2850628	1840699
812971	73820	466653	988141	518172
1179988	63162	541477	1117426	877395
2126645	86305	623934	2094582	1145496
2297492	76915	604248	2347689	1371543
169526	5061	51516	167830	87311
1316819	44123	434530	1287784	712680
4366306	144911	1304705	3743033	3066779
1237002	39071	346714	1015331	819694
4294838	110741	927406	4911106	2202148
3678532	106703	926106	2925706	2415829
4485687	97634	725705	2672951	3440508
1518607	39961	341154	1153967	968526
444004	23644	173334	378986	317706
30645	1042	6072	26312	29240
588062	277861	2259575	2420052	777962
136126	24769	397260	343801	297007
265753	52673	518887	523703	656445

4－11 市区规模以上工业

Main Economic Indicators of Industrial

单位:万元

项 目	Item	主营业务收入 Revenues in Main Business	营业费用 Expenses of Business	主营业务税金及附加 Sales Taxes and Extra Charges in Main Business
总 计	**Total**	**85106331**	**3133252**	**1453257**
按隶属关系分	**Grouped by Subordination**			
中 央 属	Central	4059738	68332	1161259
省 属	Provincial	3734500	41561	12255
市 属	Municipal	77312093	3023360	279743
按所有制分	**Grouped by Ownership**			
国有企业	State－owned Enterprises	5743656	63653	1165427
集体企业	Collective－owned Enterprises	142039	3652	1417
股份合作企业	Cooperative Enterprises	98143	1764	445
联营企业	Joint Ownership Enterprises	10801	294	51
股份制企业	Share－holding Corporations	48502798	1071379	211184
外商及港澳台投资企业	Enterprises with Investment from Foreign、Hong Kong、Macao and Taiwan	29571107	1981032	67892
其他企业	Other Enterprises	1037788	11478	6841
按企业规模分	**Grouped by Size of Enterprises**			
大型企业	Large	23259894	1169514	1168425
中型企业	Medium－sized	33307181	1331866	161593
小型企业	Small	28539256	631871	123239
按轻重工业分	**Grouped by Light & Heavy Industry**			
轻工业	Light Industry	36835817	1898600	1250798
重工业	Heavy Industry	48270514	1234651	202458

企业主要经济指标(三)

Enterprises Above Designated Size in Urban District(Ⅲ)

(10000 yuan)

管理费用 Management Expenses	利息支出 Interest Expenditure	利润总额 Total Profits	利税总额 Total Pre - tax Profits	本年应交增值税 Value Added Tax Payable
3682004	**884559**	**6051851**	**9923215**	**2418107**
140133	20647	220521	1723071	341291
183777	28367	166914	265700	86531
3358095	835546	5664416	7934445	1990286
233230	15275	328761	1878267	384079
11716	902	5026	11944	5501
6851	1534	2790	6165	2929
895	6	125	575	400
1833323	664143	2854568	4123724	1057972
1560924	190998	2822293	3831952	941768
35065	11702	38289	70588	25458
860510	166302	1868661	3711058	673971
1413308	363042	2676166	3858890	1021132
1408186	355215	1507024	2353267	723004
1547131	369165	2811476	5404124	1341849
2134873	515395	3240375	4519091	1076258

单位:万元　　　　4－11　续表1

项　目	Item	主营业务收　入 Revenues in Main Business	营业费用 Expenses of Business	主营业务税金及附加 Sales Taxes and Extra Charges in Main Business
按国民经济行业分	**Grouped by Economic Sector**			
煤炭开采和洗选业	Coal Mining and Dressing	-	-	-
黑色金属矿采选业	Ferrous Metals Mining and Dressing	-	-	-
有色金属矿采选业	Nonferrous Metals Mining and Dressing	-	-	-
非金属矿采选业	Nonmetal Minerals Mining and Dressing	53115	2263	1614
农副食品加工业	Agricultural Products Processing	685358	25996	2110
食品制造业	Food Manufacturing	1701457	309843	6846
饮料制造业	Beverage Manufacturing	2231381	263420	20730
烟草制品业	Tobacco Processing	1805373	49100	1100682
纺织业	Textile Industry	8664047	97136	43455
纺织服装、鞋、帽制造业	Textile Products, Garments, Shoes and Caps Processing	2232883	73741	9921
皮革、毛皮、羽毛(绒)及其制品业	Leather, Furs, Down and Related Products	1231601	25576	3272
木材加工及木、竹、藤、棕、草制品业	Timber Processing, Bamboo, Cane, Palm Fiber and Straw Products	219004	6245	2212
家具制造业	Furniture Manufacturing	987435	39081	2976
造纸及纸制品业	Paper Making and Paper Products	1278093	30915	4430
印刷业和记录媒介的复制	Printing and Record Media	692203	15224	1945
文教体育用品制造业	Cultural, Educational and Sports Goods	326641	9272	909
石油加工、炼焦及核燃料加工业	Petroleum Processing, Coking and Nuclear Fuel Processing	533879	2153	54235

continued 1 (10000 yuan)

管理费用 Management Expenses	利息支出 Interest Expenditure	利润总额 Total Profits	利税总额 Total Pre - tax Profits	本年应交增值税 Value Added Tax Payable
–	–	–	–	–
–	–	–	–	–
–	–	–	–	–
3635	456	3554	8355	3186
19383	8455	30938	46370	13322
69064	5050	159962	265489	98682
58928	2771	160483	269984	88771
95109	-7590	126362	1446362	219318
250116	133391	443117	675567	188995
146216	27625	119020	208021	79080
34245	20622	52647	100269	44351
9769	3379	9464	18482	6805
39439	9948	82549	119231	33706
45714	17420	74687	119184	40068
40901	7072	42428	63972	19599
18320	1599	13032	20837	6896
7108	3737	17209	118711	47267

单位:万元　　4－11　续表2

项　目	Item	主营业务收　入 Revenues in Main Business	营业费用 Expenses of Business	主营业务税金及附加 Sales Taxes and Extra Charges in Main Business
化学原料及化学制品制造业	Raw Chemical Materials and Chemical Products	6430156	308874	17866
医药制造业	Medical and Pharmaceutical Products	1576839	459362	7048
化学纤维制造业	Chemical Fiber	5952587	36436	18191
橡胶制品业	Rubber Products	2367992	76087	9295
塑料制品业	Plastic Products	2251035	44155	7064
非金属矿物制品业	Nonmetal Mineral Products	2791270	123550	9571
黑色金属冶炼及压延加工业	Smelting and Processing of Ferrous Metals	3542119	29874	9029
有色金属冶炼及压延加工业	Smelting and Processing of Nonferrous Metals	350156	2093	481
金属制品业	Metal Products	2224771	35358	7843
通用设备制造业	Ordinary Machinery	6636100	191039	19489
专用设备制造业	For Special Purpose Equipment Manufacturing	1754911	41391	6289
交通运输设备制造业	Transport Equipment Manufacturing	8822300	123376	26269
电气机械及器材制造业	Electric Equipment and Machinery	5331033	259545	14393
通信设备、计算机及其他电子设备制造业	Telecommunications Equipment, Computers and Other Electronic Equipment Manufacturing	6216097	290582	19508
仪器仪表及文化、办公用机械制造业	Instruments, Meters, Cultural and Office Machinery	2137748	112013	10211
工艺品及其他制造业	Craftworks and Other Manufacturing	1032571	11521	5598
废弃资源和废旧材料回收加工业	Waste Resouces and Waste or Old Material Recycled	15120	263	61
电力、热力的生产和供应业	Production and Supply of Electric Power and Hot Water	2041262	374	4922
燃气生产和供应业	Production and Supply of Gas	797348	28784	3375
水的生产和供应业	Production and Supply of Tap Water	192447	8610	1416

continued 2 (10000 yuan)

管理费用 Management Expenses	利息支出 Interest Expenditure	利润总额 Total Profits	利税总额 Total Pre - tax Profits	本年应交增值税 Value Added Tax Payable
312411	71949	536549	735166	180751
172944	7616	271497	414650	136104
69984	77631	541620	701981	142170
41861	21267	99044	149490	41152
78769	26951	160357	216741	49320
103108	39763	152771	252453	90111
106714	30589	119744	194697	65924
7996	4061	19357	23693	3855
100814	25913	97081	157799	52875
389128	55201	613424	824151	191238
125589	15809	160643	198750	31818
246204	130942	413997	538928	98662
331933	41675	311472	440145	114280
476892	18931	751058	912818	142252
182989	25271	207354	288475	70910
35056	8460	42302	68506	20605
1929	118	1749	2804	995
20724	29458	77333	168277	86022
17770	9305	46135	51326	1816
21243	9715	92912	101532	7204

4－12 全市规模以上工业企业

Main Economic Indicators of Industrial Enterprises

单位:万元

项 目	Item	企业单位数(个) Number of Enterprises (unit)	#亏损企业(个) Loss Making Enterprises (unit)	工业总产值(当年价格) Gross Industrial Output Value (current price)	工业销售产值 Value of Industrial Products Sales
按登记注册类型分组	**Grouped by Status of Registration**				
内资企业	Domestic－funded Enterprises	8724	812	77262754	76385196
国有企业	State－owned Enterprises	74	14	9050510	9054019
集体企业	Collective－owned Enterprises	68	6	300262	292078
股份合作企业	Cooperative Enterprises	48	8	113654	109831
联营企业	Joint Ownership Enterprises	7	1	39734	39637
国有联营企业	State Joint Ownership Enterprises	－	－	－	－
集体联营企业	Collective Joint Ownership Enterprises	3	－	31080	31050
国有与集体联营企业	Joint State－collective Enterprises	1	1	1092	1154
其他联营企业	Other Joint Ownership Enterprises	3	－	7562	7433
有限责任公司	Limited Liability Corporations	1054	132	15899281	15752234
国有独资公司	State－funded Corporations	12	2	205010	197047
其他有限责任公司	Other Limited Liability Corporations	1042	130	15694271	15555187
股份有限公司	Share－holding Corporations Ltd.	110	12	7042228	7004293
私营企业	Private Enterprises	7361	639	44806643	44123182
私营独资企业	Private－funded Enterprises	1118	49	2531658	2472459
私营合伙企业	Private Partnership Enterprises	108	7	244178	238656
私营有限责任公司	Private Limited Liability Corporations	6042	573	34850312	34248865
私营股份有限公司	Private Share－holding Corporations Ltd.	93	10	7180495	7163201
其他企业	Other Enterprises	2	－	10445	9923
港、澳、台商投资	Enterprises with Investment from Hong Kong, Macao and Taiwan	727	134	13285812	13072992
内地与港澳台合资经营企业	Joint－venture Enterprises with funds from Hong Kong, Macao and Taiwan	460	62	7676434	7528071
内地与港澳台合作经营企业	Cooperative Enterprises with funds from Hong Kong, Macao and Taiwan	12	－	124805	125049
港澳台商独资经营企业	Enterprises with Sole Investment from Hong Kong, Macao and Taiwan	248	70	5095822	5027827
港澳台商投资股份有限公司	Share－holding Corporations Ltd. with Investment from Hong Kong, Macao and Taiwan	7	2	388751	392045
外商投资企业	Enterprises with Foreign Investment	919	159	20261831	20054930
中外合资经营企业	Joint－venture Enterprises	516	68	10857228	10781853
中外合作经营企业	Cooperation Enterprises	15	2	360737	351319
外商独资经营企业	Enterprises with Sole Foreign Investment	378	87	8078718	8001038
外商投资股份有限公司	Share－holding Corporations Ltd. with Foreign Investment	10	2	965148	920720

主要经济指标按登记注册类型分(2010 年)

Above Designated Size by Status of Registration(2010)

(10000 yuan)

全部从业人员年平均人数(人) Annual Average Number of Staff and Workers(person)	资产总计 Total Assets	#产成品 Finished Products	流动资产合计 Total Circulating Funds	#本年折旧 Depreciation of the year
934303	69890700	3487167	40507485	1850955
34994	7836288	100986	3120175	384238
4932	274999	11194	189195	6595
2763	155218	9171	99554	2673
647	42099	1076	25881	345
–	–	–	–	–
380	32277	151	18900	67
66	1888	217	1842	14
201	7933	709	5139	265
187152	16487423	793087	9184884	440808
6081	784383	7160	311236	38408
181071	15703040	785927	8873648	402400
62258	9252117	441330	5160266	149730
641326	35835862	2129927	22723820	866282
51335	1442867	95908	947576	40895
6798	171377	9251	107860	5356
549726	28842317	1814652	18517570	758073
33467	5379302	210116	3150814	61958
231	6695	395	3711	283
201455	13183693	745547	8999092	291928
111704	7307195	419488	4772350	174048
1255	95324	6958	70788	1357
83083	4846891	275433	3374487	109235
5413	934282	43669	781467	7289
260724	16299738	987429	10610189	486738
138276	8865463	545927	5927888	244282
6178	258844	10008	140790	9546
102666	6259882	375932	3924651	213919
13604	915549	55561	616860	18992

项 目	Item	固定资产净值 Net Value of Fixed Assets	年末负债合计 Total Liabilities	年末所有者权益合计 Creditors′ Equity	主营业务收入 Revenues in Main Business
按登记注册类型分组	**Grouped by Status of Registration**				
内资企业	Domestic－funded Enterprises	16434324	42214034	27676666	75081988
国有企业	State－owned Enterprises	3102720	4084170	3752117	6612356
集体企业	Collective－owned Enterprises	42779	164046	110953	275194
股份合作企业	Cooperative Enterprises	24085	82885	72334	104990
联营企业	Joint Ownership Enterprises	5533	9239	32860	40558
国有联营企业	State Joint Ownership Enterprises	－	－	－	－
集体联营企业	Collective Joint Ownership Enterprises	2995	1873	30405	31061
国有与集体联营企业	Joint State－collective Enterprises	47	2444	－556	1662
其他联营企业	Other Joint Ownership Enterprises	2491	4922	3012	7836
有限责任公司	Limited Liability Corporations	4354317	10221799	6265624	16602138
国有独资公司	State－funded Corporations	282854	417527	366856	222634
其他有限责任公司	Other Limited Liability Corporations	4071463	9804272	5898768	16379504
股份有限公司	Share－holding Corporations Ltd.	1538293	4057802	5194316	7315709
私营企业	Private Enterprises	7363967	23590118	12245744	44120904
私营独资企业	Private－funded Enterprises	358422	949048	493818	2441071
私营合伙企业	Private Partnership Enterprises	47387	112561	58816	239123
私营有限责任公司	Private Limited Liability Corporations	6382167	18827387	10014930	34113484
私营股份有限公司	Private Share－holding Corporations Ltd.	575991	3701122	1678180	7327225
其他企业	Other Enterprises	2629	3976	2719	10138
港、澳、台商投资	Enterprises with Investment from Hong Kong, Macao and Taiwan	2732066	7175354	6008339	13139569
内地与港澳台合资经营企业	Joint－venture Enterprises with funds from Hong Kong, Macao and Taiwan	1660131	4320783	2986412	7661161
内地与港澳台合作经营企业	Cooperative Enterprises with funds from Hong Kong, Macao and Taiwan	14019	43274	52051	122349
港澳台商独资经营企业	Enterprises with Sole Investment from Hong Kong, Macao and Taiwan	1002330	2452850	2394041	4899281
港澳台商投资股份有限公司	Share－holding Corporations Ltd. with Investment from Hong Kong, Macao and Taiwan	55586	358447	575835	456779
外商投资企业	Enterprises with Foreign Investment	3954421	8590285	7709453	20210880
中外合资经营企业	Joint－venture Enterprises	2033929	5003331	3862132	10879462
中外合作经营企业	Cooperation Enterprises	96198	156237	102607	338126
外商独资经营企业	Enterprises with Sole Foreign Investment	1668072	2981932	3277950	8033323
外商投资股份有限公司	Share－holding Corporations Ltd. with Foreign Investment	156222	448784	466765	959969

continued (10000 yuan)

营业费用 Expenses of Business	主营业务税金及附加 Sales Taxes and Extra Charges in Main Business	管理费用 Management Expenses	利息支出 Interest Expenditure	利润总额 Total Profits	利税总额 Total Pre - tax Profits	本年应交增值税 Value Added Tax Payable
1585368	1463791	2901414	931417	4501194	7963963	1998977
65496	1169220	311586	24688	351485	1938317	417612
6662	2423	19294	2302	22919	38693	13352
2000	473	7435	1563	2705	6352	3174
315	54	1236	6	3711	4179	413
–	–	–	–	–	–	–
7	13	337	–	3591	3698	94
293	3	296	– 70	– 199	– 167	29
14	38	603	75	319	647	290
405213	63443	701186	235266	1056645	1539207	419120
33875	1329	32830	579	5210	14590	8052
371337	62114	668356	234686	1051435	1524617	411069
255934	30402	363605	72538	762538	979582	186642
849072	197690	1496186	595055	2301013	3456975	958272
41266	12586	80414	18063	118409	190331	59336
4077	1468	10148	2278	9005	17682	7209
740118	163577	1268239	458112	1809475	2795263	822211
63611	20060	137385	116602	364123	453698	69516
676	87	886	–	179	658	391
717280	23933	640564	127296	1224410	1662812	414469
275779	11358	273963	101879	527719	752855	213778
1434	141	5499	370	13886	17912	3885
385044	11388	288423	24938	622844	811106	176874
55023	1045	72678	108	59962	80939	19933
1353299	52504	1089477	116245	1919067	2617983	646411
551494	26316	507270	78434	1031879	1383513	325318
4758	283	11875	2541	25211	34734	9241
586830	9673	492171	32989	744219	1009283	255391
210216	16233	78161	2282	117759	190453	56462

4－13 全市规模以上工业企业

Main Economic Indicators of Industrial

单位:万元

项 目	Item	企业单位数(个) Number of Enterprises (unit)	#亏损企业(个) Loss Making Enterprises (unit)	工业总产值(当年价格) Gross Industrial Output Value (current price)	工业销售产值 Value of Industrial Products Sales
按经济组织类型分组	**Grouped by Type of Ownership**				
独资企业	Solely－owned Enterprises	1886	226	25056969	24847421
国有企业	State－owned	74	14	9050510	9054019
集体企业	Collective－owned	68	6	300262	292078
私营独资企业	Private－owned	1118	49	2531658	2472459
港澳台商独资经营企业	Enterprises with Sole Investment from Hong Kong, Macao and Taiwan	248	70	5095822	5027827
外商独资经营企业	Enterprises with Sole Foreign Investment	378	87	8078718	8001038
合作、合伙企业	Cooperation and Partnership Enterprises	192	18	893552	874415
股份合作企业	Share－holding Cooperative	48	8	113654	109831
国有联营企业	State Joint Ownership	－	－	－	－
集体联营企业	Collective Joint Ownership	3	－	31080	31050
国有与集体联营企业	Joint State－collective Ownership	1	1	1092	1154
其他联营企业	Other Joint Ownership	3	－	7562	7433
私营合伙企业	Private Partnership	108	7	244178	238656
内地与港澳台合作经营企业	Cooperative Enterprises with funds from Hong Kong, Macao and Taiwan	12	－	124805	125049
中外合作经营企业	Sino－foreign Cooperation Enterprises	15	2	360737	351319
其他企业	Other Enterprises (Domestic Investment)	2	－	10445	9923
股份有限公司	Share－holding Corporations Ltd.	220	26	15576621	15480259
股份有限公司(内资)	Share－holding Corporations Ltd. (Domestic Investment)	110	12	7042228	7004293
私营股份有限公司	Private Share－holding Corporations Ltd.	93	10	7180495	7163201
港澳台商投资股份有限公司	Share－holding Corporations Ltd. with Investment from Hong Kong, Macao and Taiwan	7	2	388751	392045
外商投资股份有限公司	Share－holding Corporations Ltd. with Foreign Investment	10	2	965148	920720
有限责任公司	Limited Liability Corporations	8072	835	69283254	68311023
国有独资公司	State－owned	12	2	205010	197047
私营有限责任公司	Private	6042	573	34850312	34248865
内地与港澳台合资经营企业	Joint Venture Enterprises with funds from Hong Kong, Macao and Taiwan	460	62	7676434	7528071
中外合资经营企业	Sino－foreign Joint Venture	516	68	10857228	10781853
其他有限责任公司	Others	1042	130	15694271	15555187

主要经济指标按经济组织类型分(2010 年)

Enterprises Above Designated Size by the Type of Ownership(2010)

(10000 yuan)

全部从业人员年平均人数(人) Annual Average Number of Staff and Workers(person)	资产总计 Total Assets	#产成品 Finished Products	流动资产合计 Total Circulating Funds	#本年折旧 Depreciation of the year
277010	20660927	859453	11556084	754882
34994	7836288	100986	3120175	384238
4932	274999	11194	189195	6595
51335	1442867	95908	947576	40895
83083	4846891	275433	3374487	109235
102666	6259882	375932	3924651	213919
17872	729556	36859	448583	19560
2763	155218	9171	99554	2673
-	-	-	-	-
380	32277	151	18900	67
66	1888	217	1842	14
201	7933	709	5139	265
6798	171377	9251	107860	5356
1255	95324	6958	70788	1357
6178	258844	10008	140790	9546
231	6695	395	3711	283
114742	16481251	750676	9709407	237968
62258	9252117	441330	5160266	149730
33467	5379302	210116	3150814	61958
5413	934282	43669	781467	7289
13604	915549	55561	616860	18992
986858	61502398	3573154	38402692	1617211
6081	784383	7160	311236	38408
549726	28842317	1814652	18517570	758073
111704	7307195	419488	4772350	174048
138276	8865463	545927	5927888	244282
181071	15703040	785927	8873648	402400

项　目	Item	固定资产净值 Net Value of Fixed Assets	年末负债合计 Total Liabilities	所有者权益合计 Creditors´ Equity	主营业务收入 Revenues in Main Business
按经济组织类型分组	**Grouped by Type of Ownership**				
独资企业	Solely－owned Enterprises	6174324	10632048	10028879	22261226
国有企业	State－owned	3102720	4084170	3752117	6612356
集体企业	Collective－owned	42779	164046	110953	275194
私营独资企业	Private－owned	358422	949048	493818	2441071
港澳台商独资经营企业	Enterprises with Sole Investment from Hong Kong, Macao and Taiwan	1002330	2452850	2394041	4899281
外商独资经营企业	Enterprises with Sole Foreign Investment	1668072	2981932	3277950	8033323
合作、合伙企业	Cooperation and Partnership Enterprises	189851	408171	321386	855284
股份合作企业	Share－holding Cooperative	24085	82885	72334	104990
国有联营企业	State Joint Ownership	－	－	－	－
集体联营企业	Collective Joint Ownership	2995	1873	30405	31061
国有与集体联营企业	Joint State－collective Ownership	47	2444	－556	1662
其他联营企业	Other Joint Ownership	2491	4922	3012	7836
私营合伙企业	Private Partnership	47387	112561	58816	239123
内地与港澳台合作经营企业	Cooperative Enterprises with funds from Hong Kong, Macao and Taiwan	14019	43274	52051	122349
中外合作经营企业	Sino－foreign Cooperation Enterprises	96198	156237	102607	338126
其他企业	Other Enterprises (Domestic Investment)	2629	3976	2719	10138
股份有限公司	Share－holding Corporations Ltd.	2326092	8566155	7915096	16059682
股份有限公司(内资)	Share－holding Corporations Ltd. (Domestic Investment)	1538293	4057802	5194316	7315709
私营股份有限公司	Private Share－holding Corporations Ltd.	575991	3701122	1678180	7327225
港澳台商投资股份有限公司	Share－holding Corporations Ltd. with Investment from Hong Kong, Macao and Taiwan	55586	358447	575835	456779
外商投资股份有限公司	Share－holding Corporations Ltd. with Foreign Investment	156222	448784	466765	959969
有限责任公司	Limited Liability Corporations	14430544	38373300	23129098	69256245
国有独资公司	State－owned	282854	417527	366856	222634
私营有限责任公司	Private	6382167	18827387	10014930	34113484
内地与港澳台合资经营企业	Joint Venture Enterprises with funds from Hong Kong, Macao and Taiwan	1660131	4320783	2986412	7661161
中外合资经营企业	Sino－foreign Joint Venture	2033929	5003331	3862132	10879462
其他有限责任公司	Others	4071463	9804272	5898768	16379504

continued (10000 yuan)

营业费用 Expenses of Business	主营业务税金及附加 Sales Taxes and Extra Charges in Main Business	管理费用 Management Expenses	利息支出 Interest Expenditure	利润总额 Total Profits	利税总额 Total Pre - tax Profits	本年应交增值税 Value Added Tax Payable
1085300	1205289	1191889	102980	1859876	3987730	922565
65496	1169220	311586	24688	351485	1938317	417612
6662	2423	19294	2302	22919	38693	13352
41266	12586	80414	18063	118409	190331	59336
385044	11388	288423	24938	622844	811106	176874
586830	9673	492171	32989	744219	1009283	255391
13260	2506	37079	6757	54697	81517	24314
2000	473	7435	1563	2705	6352	3174
-	-	-	-	-	-	-
7	13	337	-	3591	3698	94
293	3	296	-70	-199	-167	29
14	38	603	75	319	647	290
4077	1468	10148	2278	9005	17682	7209
1434	141	5499	370	13886	17912	3885
4758	283	11875	2541	25211	34734	9241
676	87	886	-	179	658	391
584784	67740	651829	191531	1304381	1704673	332552
255934	30402	363605	72538	762538	979582	186642
63611	20060	137385	116602	364123	453698	69516
55023	1045	72678	108	59962	80939	19933
210216	16233	78161	2282	117759	190453	56462
1972603	264693	2750658	873690	4425717	6470838	1780427
33875	1329	32830	579	5210	14590	8052
740118	163577	1268239	458112	1809475	2795263	822211
275779	11358	273963	101879	527719	752855	213778
551494	26316	507270	78434	1031879	1383513	325318
371337	62114	668356	234686	1051435	1524617	411069

4-14　全市1998-2010年规模以上工业企业主要经济效益指标

Main Economic Indicators of Industrial Enterprises Above Designated Size(1998-2010)

单位:亿元　　(100 million yuan)

年份 Year	规模以上工业总产值 Output Value of Industrial Enterprises Above Designated Size	规模以上工业增加值 Added Value of Industrial Enterprises Above Designated Size	资产总计 Total Assets	流动资产合计 Total Current Assets	主营业务收入 Revenne from Principal Business	利润总额 Total Profits	利税总额 Total Profits and Tax
1998	1109.94	274.70	1486.02	732.72	1036.09	38.44	101.36
1999	1200.07	298.90	1620.93	800.60	1132.80	54.47	127.89
2000	1543.57	360.97	1828.35	946.32	1465.49	76.20	161.61
2001	1919.51	444.91	2148.96	1122.07	1828.28	107.56	208.54
2002	2400.30	597.01	2514.19	1313.92	2288.21	145.48	274.98
2003	3202.52	783.51	3258.93	1783.5	3117.46	194.16	359.54
2004	4486.58	1019.47	4118.31	2300.84	4363.27	226.74	427.23
2005	5441.13	1126.54	4781.34	2692.73	5282.8	234.99	450.68
2006	6975.46	1363.17	5564.68	3215.19	6807.64	314.49	576.51
2007	8351.40	1717.65	6573.12	3880.23	8057.03	414.55	730.50
2008	9379.58	1743.20	7506.26	4437.50	8976.46	453.92	802.13
2009	9390.73	1792.00	8405.62	4968.21	9026.32	510.97	882.62
2010	11081.04	2153.83	9937.41	6011.68	10843.24	764.47	1224.48

4-14　续表　continued

年份 Year	工业增加值率(%) Rate of Industrial Added Valne (%)	资产负债率(%) Rate of Assets and Liabilites	流动资产周转次数(计量单位为次) the Number of Current Assets Turnover	成本费用利润率(%) Profit Rate of Costs	全员劳动生产率(元/人) All-personnel Labor Productivity (Yuan/Ren)	产品销售率(%) Prodnct Sales Rate(%)
1998	24.75	57.02	1.47	3.86	37976	95.91
1999	24.91	55.69	1.46	5.06	44307	98.07
2000	23.39	58.59	1.62	5.49	52713	97.19
2001	23.18	57.20	1.70	6.26	59518	97.40
2002	24.87	56.82	1.82	6.84	76402	97.76
2003	24.47	58.70	1.87	6.69	91284	97.68
2004	22.72	59.80	2.00	5.50	98809	98.10
2005	20.70	60.12	2.06	4.69	105786	98.25
2006	19.54	59.83	2.23	4.87	120289	98.36
2007	20.57	60.43	2.21	5.44	138016	98.17
2008	18.59	60.42	2.10	5.34	152070	98.14
2009	19.08	59.07	1.86	5.86	151002	98.63
2010	19.44	58.34	1.96	7.60	166516	98.83

4－15　主要工业产品生产量(2010 年)

Output of Major Industrial Products(2010)

产品名称	Item	全市 Whole Municipality 2010 年	为上年(%) As Compared with the Preceding Year(%)	市区 Urban District
铁矿石原矿量 (万吨)	The volume of iron ore (10000 tons)	2.59	–	–
原油加工量 (万吨)	Crude oil processing volume (10000 tons)	75.14	127.8	75.14
发电量 (亿千瓦小时)	Electricity (100 million kwh)	176.22	115.4	111.04
罐头 (万吨)	Canned Food (10000 tons)	8.15	51.6	2.84
乳制品 (吨)	Dairy Products (ton)	154296	89.2	139206
啤酒 (千升)	Beer (1000 litres)	931371	93.4	745819
软饮料 (万吨)	Soft Drinks (10000 tons)	536.13	96.2	373.96
精制茶 (吨)	Tea (ton)	49686.59	125.2	9119.46
卷烟 (亿支)	Cigarettes (100 million)	491.70	102.1	491.70
方便面 (吨)	Instant Noodle (ton)	299089	122.4	298693
味精 (吨)	Monosodium Glutamate (ton)	18973.80	86.8	16729.00
化学纤维 (吨)	Chemical Fiber (ton)	5307522	128.6	5164068
其中:合成纤维 (吨)	Synthetic Fibre (ton)	5144444	129.6	5000990
纱 (万吨)	Yarn (10000 tons)	53.63	106.0	44.51
布 (万米)	Cloth (10000 m)	384663	110.3	332291
印染布 (万米)	Printed Fabric (10000 m)	512441	107.3	487217
生丝 (吨)	Raw Silk (ton)	3172.06	83.5	995.92
蚕丝及交织机织物(含蚕丝≥50%) (万米)	Silk and Woven Fabrics (Containing Greater than or Equal 50% silk) (10000 m)	9524.72	106.8	8033.61
服装 (万件)	Garment (10000 units)	60672.40	122.6	53085.16

4-15 续表1 continued 1

产品名称	Item	全市 Whole Municipality 2010年	为上年(%) As Compared with the Preceding Year(%)	市区 Urban District
皮革鞋靴 (万双)	Leather Footwear (10000 units)	1446.61	99.5	549.02
家具 (万件)	Furniture (10000 units)	4146.36	121.2	3758.76
塑料制品 (吨)	Plastic Membrane (ton)	1736596	104.9	1375809
机制纸及纸板 (万吨)	Machine Made Paper and Paperboard (10000 tons)	719.41	103.8	22.82
焦炭 (万吨)	Coke (10000 tons)	52.24	109.3	52.24
盐酸(含量31%以上)(吨)	Mariatic Acid(above 31% percent) (ton)	97808	88.9	97808
氢氧化钠(烧碱)(折100%) (吨)	Caustic Soda (ton)	140000	112.9	140000
碳酸钠(纯碱) (吨)	Soda ash (ton)	119167	80.1	119167
初级形态的塑料(塑料树脂及共聚物)(吨)	Plastics in Primary Form(Plastic Resins and Copolymers) (ton)	190884	96.9	140062
合成氨 (吨)	Synthetic Ammonia (ton)	89850	92.3	68129
农用氮、磷、钾化学肥料总计(折纯) (吨)	Chemical Fertilizer (ton)	59118	94.5	47590
化学农药原药(折有效成分100%) (吨)	Chemical Pesticide (ton)	120418	114.1	17137
涂料(油漆) (吨)	Paint (ton)	155870	111.8	119779
油墨 (吨)	Printing Ink (ton)	31719	94.6	30257
合成洗涤剂 (吨)	Synthetic Detergent (ton)	124902	114.0	100515
化学药品原药(化学原料药) (吨)	Original Drug Chemicals (ton)	9467.19	114.4	6948.18
中成药 (吨)	Traditional Chinese Medicine (ton)	8942.65	92.3	6521.12
橡胶轮胎外胎(轮胎外胎) (万条)	Rubber Tires (10000 units)	3685.24	117.9	3486.79
水泥 (万吨)	Cement (10000 tons)	2021.01	110.5	1000.65

4－15　续表2　continued 2

产品名称	Item	全市 Whole Municipality 2010年	为上年(%) As Compared with the Preceding Year(%)	市区 Urban District
平板玻璃　(万重量箱)	Plate Glass　(10000 weight cases)	437.52	103.2	437.52
粗钢　(万吨)	Crude Steel　(10000 tons)	354.6	101.3	354.63
生铁　(万吨)	Pig Iron　(10000 tons)	267.75	102.4	267.57
铁合金　(万吨)	Iron Alloy　(10000 tons)	8.92	82.6	1.61
钢材　(万吨)	Steel Products　(10000 tons)	888.60	111.2	811.14
精炼铜(电解铜)　(吨)	Refined Copper　(ton)	148637	92.2	10655
搪瓷制品　(吨)	Enamelware　(ton)	34821	116.8	34821
工业锅炉　(蒸发量吨)	Industry Boiler　(ton)	10143	115.4	10143
金属切削机床　(台)	Metal－cutting Machine Tools　(unit)	31495	183.3	17450
金属成形机床(锻压设备)　(台)	Metal Forming Machine(Forge Equipment)　(Tai)	19230	146.4	19230
泵(液体泵)　(万台)	Pump　(10000 sets)	61.49	139.1	60.21
滚动轴承(轴承)　(万套)	Bearings　(10000 units)	32367.55	127.7	29840.15
汽车　(辆)	Motor Vehicles　(unit)	3477	264.4	3477
叉车　(台)	Forklift　(unit)	65699	273.4	1965.00
两轮自行车(自行车)　(万辆)	Bicycles　(10000 units)	639.61	121.7	635.90

4－15 续表3 continued 3

产品名称	Item	全市 Whole Municipality 2010年	为上年(%) As Compared with the Preceding Year(%)	市区 Urban District
交流电动机 （万千瓦）	AC Motor (10000 kw)	49.33	117.1	39.86
钢绞线 （吨）	Strand (ton)	46991	85.5	43276
通信及电子网络用电缆 （万对千米）	Communication Cable (10000 km)	802.29	80.9	50.05
光缆(光纤通讯电缆)（万芯千米）	Electric Power Cable (10000 km)	1532.43	120.3	90.38
家用电冰箱 （万台）	Household Refrigerators (10000 units)	107.63	114.8	107.63
家用洗衣机 （万台）	Household Washing Machines (10000 units)	328.48	116.7	328.48
吸排油烟机 （万台）	Smoke Absorbers (10000 units)	115.50	113.4	115.50
移动通信手持机(手机)（万部）	Mobile Telephone Sets (10000 units)	1129.93	90.0	1129.93
电工仪器仪表 （万台）	Electric Instrument and Apparatus (10000 units)	2686.96	98.8	2077.07
工业自动调节仪表与控制系统 （万台）	Industrial Automatic Adjustment Meter and Control System (10000 units)	153.28	112.7	153.28
电光源(灯泡) （亿只）	Light Bulbs (100 million units)	19.62	107.2	3.82
彩色电视机 （万部）	Color－Television Sets (10000 units)	21.56	91.2	21.56
微型计算机设备 （万台）	Micro－computer Equipment (10000 units)	157.01	176.0	157.01
肥(香)皂 （吨）	Soaps (ton)	27114	106.3	27114

4-16 单位GDP能耗降低情况(2010年)

Increase or Decrease of Energy Consumption Per Unit of GDP(2010)

地 区	Region	单位GDP能耗(吨标准煤/万元) Energy Consumption Per Unit of GDP (tons of SCE/10000 yuan)		单位GDP电耗(千瓦时/万元) Electricity Consumption Per Unit of GDP (kwh/10000 yuan)		单位工业增加值能耗(吨标准煤/万元) Energy Consumption Per Unit of Industriul Value-Added (tons of SCE/10000 yuan)	
		2010年	降低率 Increase or Decrease Rate (±%)	2010年	降低率 Increase or Decrease Rate (±%)	2010年	降低率 Increase or Decrease Rate (±%)
杭州市	Hangzhou	0.68	3.08	990	-1.36	0.93	8.52
#上城区	Shangcheng					0.18	6.83
下城区	Xiacheng					0.17	5.78
江干区	Jianggan					0.29	10.31
拱墅区	Gongshu					2.49	8.67
西湖区	Xihu					0.26	6.18
高新(滨江)区	Hi-Tech(Binjiang)					0.18	5.33
下沙经济技术开发区	HEDA					0.43	4.04
萧山区	Xiaoshan	0.89	3.01	1498	-1.08	1.04	6.02
余杭区	Yuhang	0.69	5.31	1116	0.53	0.80	12.52
桐庐县	Tonglu	0.68	2.13	795	-3.03	0.70	6.30
淳安县	Chun'an	0.41	1.20	668	1.07	0.68	8.33
建德市	Jiande	1.28	3.40	1345	-7.12	2.71	8.57
富阳市	Fuyang	1.33	4.17	1591	0.45	2.09	8.50
临安市	Lin'an	0.68	3.06	1056	-2.48	1.09	11.23

注:江干区不含杭州经济技术开发区。

a) HEDA is not included in Jianggan district in this table.

4－17 全市工业企业主要能源

Energy Consumption of Industrial

行 业 Sector	原煤(吨) Raw Coal(Ton)	洗精煤(吨) Washing Coal(Ton)	焦炭(吨) Coke(Ton)	汽油(吨) Gasoline(Ton)	煤油(吨) Kerosene(Ton)
总 计 Total	**14019911**	**751010**	**1398514**	**67039**	**2366**
煤炭开采和洗选业 Coal Mining and Dressing	-	-	-	-	-
黑色金属矿采选业 Ferrous Metals Mining and Dressing	-	-	-	-	-
有色金属矿采选业 Nonferrous Minerals Mining and Dressing	-	-	-	23	-
非金属矿采选业 Nonmetal Minerals Mining and Dressing	25605	-	-	45	-
农副食品加工业 Agricultural Products Processing	33256	-	18	398	-
食品制造业 Food Manufacturing	32767	-	27	867	-
饮料制造业 Beverage Manufacturing	27352	-	-	822	-
烟草制品业 Tobacco Processing	-	-	-	55	-
纺织业 Textile Processing	1293092	7	274	7586	134
纺织服装、鞋、帽制造业 Textile Products, Garments, Shoes and Caps Processing	11771	188	219	3385	9
皮革、毛皮、羽毛(绒)及其制品业 Leather, Furs, Down and Related Products	46463	-	-	1000	-
木材加工及木、竹、藤、棕、草制品业 Timber Processing, Bamboo, Cane, Plam Fiber and Straw Products	2154	-	-	341	-
家具制造业 Furniture Manufacturing	5524	140	798	1080	-
造纸及纸制品业 Paper Making and Paper Products	586197	-	-	1892	-
印刷业和记录媒介的复制 Printing	2043	-	-	1785	13
文教体育用品制造业 Cultural, Educational and Sports Goods	672	-	-	613	-
石油加工、炼焦及核燃料加工业 Petroleum Processing, Coking and Nuclear Fuel Processing	1914	-	-	185	56

消费量按行业分(2010 年)
Enterprises by Sector(2010)

柴油(吨) Diesel oil(Ton)	燃料油(吨) Fuel Oil(Ton)	液化石油气(吨) Liquefied Petroleum Gas(Ton)	天然气(万立方米) Natural Gas (10000 cu. m)	其他石油制品(吨) Other Petroleum Products(Ton)	热力(百万千焦) Heat(Million kilo - joule)	电力(万千瓦时) Electricity (10000 kwh)
201633	**94309**	**36421**	**128425**	**321435**	**88364620**	**3306346**
-	-	-	-	-	-	-
-	-	-	-	-	-	220
13	-	-	-	-	-	2421
9742	-	-	-	67	-	11986
1751	-	35	-	67	86100	12228
2822	111	1247	694	-	1616972	20532
2900	2687	26	8	2	2049996	56846
5544	-	-	-	-	145707	4836
6894	2101	714	983	392	24203193	520903
3001	-	18	32	-	666229	27853
1102	-	-	-	-	115721	14183
544	-	373	-	-	179994	10389
4689	209	-	267	14	85899	13114
4136	426	25	162	7	29041556	293946
1523	-	88	114	14	32836	15993
819	-	93	-	6	134088	9080
436	6816	-	-	196332	1575	6058

4－17 续表

行 业 Sector	原煤(吨) Raw Coal(Ton)	洗精煤(吨) Washing Coal(Ton)	焦炭(吨) Coke(Ton)	汽油(吨) Gasoline(Ton)	煤油(吨) Kerosene(Ton)
化学原料及化学制品制造业 Raw Chemical Materials and Chemical Products	944875	10	290	6216	372
医药制造业 Medical and Pharmaceutical Products	47418	–	–	1029	2
化学纤维制造业 Chemical Fiber	277834	–	–	817	6
橡胶制品业 Rubber Products	258634	–	158	3158	12
塑料制品业 Plastic Products	30828	–	–	2068	54
非金属矿物制品业 Nonmetal Minerals Products	2819895	115	13204	2938	–
黑色金属冶炼及压延加工业 Smelting and Processing of Ferrous Metals	489527	750525	1335519	586	–
有色金属冶炼及压延加工业 Smelting and Processing of Nonferrous Metals	37720	–	16610	354	24
金属制品业 Metal Products	56714	25	58	4527	87
通用设备制造业 Ordinary Machinery	81640	–	28221	6292	925
专用设备制造业 Special Purpose Equipment	6733	–	817	2447	9
交通运输设备制造业 Transportation Equtpment	16417	–	1127	3427	646
电气机械及器材制造业 Electric Equipment and Machinery	10636	–	138	4147	5
通信设备、计算机及其他电子设备制造业 Telecommunications Equipment, Computers and Other Electronic Equipment	3883	–	138	2822	4
仪器仪表及文化、办公用机械制造业 Instruments, Meters, Cultural and Office Machinery	14148	–	–	2344	1
工艺品及其他制造业 Craftworks and Other Manufacturing	1268	–	–	1345	4
废弃资源和废旧材料回收加工业 Waste Resouces and Waste or Old Material Recycled	6106	–	897	28	–
电力、热力的生产和供应业 Production and Supply of Electric Power and Hot Water	6846826	–	–	1893	–
燃气生产和供应业 Production and Supply of Gas	–	–	–	201	–
水的生产和供应业 Production and Supply of Tap Water	–	–	–	324	–

continued

柴油(吨) Diesel oil(Ton)	燃料油(吨) Fuel Oil(Ton)	液化石油气(吨) Liquefied Petroleum Gas(Ton)	天然气(万立方米) Natural Gas (10000 cu. m)	其他石油制品(吨) Other Petroleum Products(Ton)	热力(百万千焦) Heat(Million kilo - joule)	电力(万千瓦时) Electricity (10000 kwh)
10753	6701	18	1306	119841	7025077	244292
2199	–	29	1313	16	519806	27718
1202	34949	48	27	611	6415473	274976
1860	1	–	1358	555	3070408	90961
3915	2588	1142	286	565	415790	92507
78797	12957	13297	13080	250	7752910	267032
4150	996	1451	1537	9	1816904	324444
1819	13992	148	172	66	54044	38527
9263	5383	375	1770	149	248070	82489
17428	2586	1342	1264	1210	229299	155157
2340	15	520	130	230	59885	28161
7083	–	579	198	881	172596	76666
6391	–	14385	471	87	264690	117953
2344	50	337	115	–	457939	74111
1719	–	12	203	36	12217	18927
1672	–	105	91	20	61395	15195
323	1741	–	–	–	–	6279
2068	–	–	102816	10	1428254	297562
278	–	–	24	–	–	514
114	–	13	3	–	–	52287

4-18 电力消费量(2010年)
Electricity Consumption(2010)

单位:万千瓦时 (10000 kwh)

项 目	Item	总计 Total 2010年	为上年(%) As Compared with the Preceding Year(%)	杭州市电力局 Hangzhou Electricity Bureau	建德市电力局 Jiande Electricity Bureau	淳安县电力局 Chun'an Electricity Bureau
总 计	**Total**	**5219258**	**113.5**	**4921642**	**228095**	**69521**
#线路损失电量	#Losses in Transmission	181112	102.9	170363	7356	3393
农林牧渔业	Farming,Forestry,Animal Husbandry and Fishery Conservancy	42872	110.4	41198	1167	507
工业	Industry	3642820	112.9	3404624	193429	44767
轻工业	Light Industry	1764617	111.1	1715935	18656	30026
重工业	Heavy Industry	1878203	114.7	1688689	174773	14741
#采矿业	#Mining and Quarrying	38531	108.3	34334	3001	1196
制造业	Manufacturing Industry	3272665	113.7	3056580	177022	39064
电力、燃气及水的生产和供应业	Produotion and supply of electricity,gas & water	331624	106.4	313710	13407	4507
建筑业	Construction	93805	126.4	90807	1199	1799
交通运输、仓储及邮政业	Transportation,Storage,Post & Telecommunications	55235	108.7	53708	973	554
信息传输、计算机服务和软件业	Information Transmission,Computer Services and Software	66882	135.7	64640	1277	965
商业、住宿和餐饮业	Commerce,Catering and lodging	242998	112.1	231935	4755	6308
金融、房地产、商务及居民服务业	Finance,Real Estate Commerce and Service for the Residents	167346	120.7	164023	1794	1529
公共管理和社会组织	Public Management and Social Organizations	272769	114.3	265844	4223	2702
城乡居民生活用电	Residential Consumption	634529	112.4	604861	19278	10390
城市	Cities	388942	111.5	373938	9980	5023
#乡村	#Rural Areas	245588	114.0	230923	9298	5367

4－19　2001－2010年水资源量和总用水量

Total Water Resources and Water Consumption(2001－2010)

单位:亿立方米　　　　(100 million Cubic Meters)

		全市 Whole City	市区 Urban District	桐庐 Tonglu	淳安 Chan'an	建德 Jiangde	富阳 Fuyang	临安 Lin'an
2001年	水资源量 Water Resources	156.37	18.87	14.28	41.14	18.54	14.23	26.76
	用水量 Water Consumption	40.29	28.05	2.01	1.03	2.11	4.17	2.92
2002年	水资源量 Water Resources	213	30.21	24.3	65.46	31.59	23.54	37.9
	用水量 Water Consumption	39.92	27.51	2.01	1.05	2.18	4.35	2.82
2003年	水资源量 Water Resources	102.65	9.31	10.32	41.43	15.57	8.13	17.9
	用水量 Water Consumption	44.72	29.13	1.98	1.38	2.3	7.12	2.81
2004年	水资源量 Water Resources	85.28	12.04	10.35	27.82	11.34	9.15	14.58
	用水量 Water Consumption	48.9	32.89	2.21	1.09	2.35	7.17	3.19
2005年	水资源量 Water Resources	90.65	14.32	9.46	26.66	10.36	10.31	19.54
	用水量 Water Consumption	49.58	32.95	2.25	1.24	2.38	7.16	3.61
2006年	水资源量 Water Resources	109.8	15.14	11.7	38.42	13.41	10.36	20.75
	用水量 Water Consumption	48.73	31.39	2.39	1.42	2.68	7.13	3.72
2007年	水资源量 Water Resources	104.13	20.28	10.12	29.88	11.72	11.76	20.36
	用水量 Water Consumption	49.56	32.57	2.53	1.53	3.09	6.45	3.39
2008年	水资源量 Water Resources	154.38	24.58	14.95	49.22	18.52	14.2	32.92
	用水量 Water Consumption	56.7	39.57	2.9	1.32	2.69	6.49	3.7
2009年	水资源量 Water Resources	141.5	23.38	16.67	37.46	15.63	16.33	32.03
	用水量 Water Consumption	54.28	39.24	2.52	1.46	2.81	5.18	3.07
2010年	水资源量 Water Resources	190.4	29.58	19.03	63.61	30.36	17.92	29.91
	用水量 Water Consumption	54.95	39.00	2.79	1.61	2.88	4.80	3.87

主要统计指标解释

工业总产值 是以货币表现的工业企业在报告期内生产的已出售或可供出售工业产品总量，它反映一定时间内工业生产的总规模和总水平，它包括：在本企业内不再进行加工，经检验、包装入库（规定不需包装的产品除外）的成品价值，对外加工费收入，自制半成品，在产品期末初差额价值。工业总产值采用“工厂法”计算，即以工业企业作为一个整体，按企业工业生产活动的最终成果来计算，企业内部不允许重复计算，不能把企业内部各个车间（分厂）生产的成果相加。

工业销售产值 是以货币表现的工业企业在一定时期内销售的本企业生产的工业产品总量。包括已销售的成品、半成品价值，对外提供的工业性作业和对本单位基本建设部门、生活福利部门等提供的产品和工业性作业及自制设备的价值。已销售的成品、半成品不论是本期生产的、还是上期生产的，只要是本期销售出去的均包括在内。对外提供的工业性作业是指企业按合同对外提供的工业性劳务。企业为本单位基本建设部门、生活福利部门等提供的产品和工业性作业及自制设备也应视同销售，这部分也作为销售统计。工业销售产值的计算范围、计算价格和计算方法与工业总产值一致，但两者计算的基础不同；工业销售产值计算的基础是产品销售总量，工业总产值计算的基础是工业产品生产总量。

工业增加值 是指工业行业在报告期内以货币表现的工业生产活动的最终成果。

固定资产原价 固定资产原值指企业在建造、购置、安装、改建、扩建、技术改造某项固定资产时所支出的全部货币总额。它一般包括买价、包装费、运杂费和安装费等。

固定资产净值 是指固定资产原价减去历年已提折旧额后的净额。

利税总额 指企业利润总额、产品销售税金及附加和应交增值税之和。

产品销售收入 指企业销售产品的销售收入和提供劳务等主要经营业务取得的收入总额。

产品销售成本 指企业销售产品和提供劳务等主要经营业务的实际成本。

产品销售税金及附加 指企业销售产品和提供工业性劳务等主要经营业务应负担的城市维护建设税、消费税、资源税和教育费附加。

产品销售利润 指企业销售产品和提供工业性劳务等主要经营业务收入和除其成本、费用、税金后的利润。

利润总额 指企业实现的利润。

应交增值税 指企业在报告期内应交纳的增值税额。

总资产 指企业拥有或控制的全部资产。包括流动资产、长期投资、固定资产、无形及递延资产、其他长期资产、递延税项等，即为企业资产负债表的资产总计项。

（1）流动资产指企业可以在一年内或者超过一年的一个生产周期内变现或耗用的资产合计。包括现金及各种存款、短期投资、应收及预付款项、存货等。

（2）固定资产指企业固定资产净值、固定资产清理、在建工程、待处理固定资产损失所占用的资金合计。

（3）无形资产指企业长期使用而没有实物形态的资产。包括专利权、非专利技术、商标权、著作权、土地使用权、商誉等。

总负债 指企业承担并需要偿还的全部债务。包括流动负债和长期负债、递延税项等，即为企业资产负债表的负债合计项。

（1）流动负债指企业在一年内或者超过一年的一个营业周期内需要偿还的债务合计，其中包括短期借款、应付及预收款项、应付工资、应交税金和应交利润等。

（2）长期负债指企业在一年以上或者超过一年的一个生产周期以上需要偿还的债务合计，其中包括长期借款、应付债务、长期应付款项等。

所有者权益 指企业投资人对企业净资产的所有权。企业净资产等于企业全部资产减去全部负债后的余额。其中包括投资者对企业的最初投入，以及资本公积金、盈余公积金和未分配利润，对股份制企业即为股东权益。

Explanatory Notes on Main Statistical Indicators

Gross Industrial Output Value is the total volume of industrial products sold or available for sale in value terms which reflects the total achievements and overall scale of industrial production during a given period. It includes the value of the finished products, which are not to be further processed in the enterprises and have been inspected, packed and put in storage, the value of industrial services rendered to other units, and the changes in the value of the semi – finished products and products in process between the beginning and closing of the period. The gross industrial output value is calculated with "factory method". No double calculations are to be made within the same enterprise. However, double counting does occur among different enterprises.

Industrial Sales Output Value is the total volume of industrial products sold in value term of an industrial enterprise during a given period. It includes the value of finished products, semi – finished products, industrial operations rendered to other units, products industrial operations & self – made equipment provided to the basic construction department, welfare department, etc. of the enterprise. For finished products & semi – finished products, whether produced in this calculation period or the previous one, if they are sold in this calculation period, they should be included. Industrial operations are industrial services rendered to other units according to contracts. Products, industrial operations & self – made equipment provided to basic construction department, welfare department, etc. of the enterprise should be regarded as act of sale, and included in sales statistics.

The scope , price and method of calculation of industrial sales output value are the same as those for gross industrial output value. But the calculation bases are different: the base for sales output value is the total volume of products sold; the base for gross industrial output value is total volume of production of industrial products.

Value – added of Industry refers to the final results of industrial production of the industrial trade in money terms during the reference period.

Original Value of Fixed Assets refers to the original value of all assets owned by industrial enterprises, calculated at the cost paid at the time of purchase, installation, reconstruction, expansion, and technical innovation and transformation of the said assets, which includes expenses on purchase, package, transportation, and installation, etc.

Net Value of Fixed Assets is obtained by deducting depreciation over years from the original value of fixed assets.

Total Pre – tax Profits refers to the sum of sales tax and extra charges adding total profits.

Sales Revenue of Industrial Products refers to the revenue from the sales of products by industrial enterprises and the revenue from services provided and etc.

Sales Cost of Industrial Products refers to the actual cost of products of industrial enterprises and industrial services provided, etc.

Tax and Extra Charges on Sales of Products refer to the tax on city maintenance and construction, consumption tax, resources tax and extra charges for education , which should be borne by the enterprises in selling products and providing industrial services.

Sales Profit of Products refers to the profit gained by the enterprises by deducting cost, charges and taxes from the business income of the enterprises obtained in selling products and providing industrial services.

Total Profits refer to the profits gained by the enterprises.

Value – added Tax Payable refers to the amount of the value added tax which should be paid by the enterprises in the reporting period.

Total Assets refer to all assets which are owned or controlled by enterprises, including circulating assets, long term investment, fixed assets, intangible assets and deferred assets, other long term assets, and deferred taxes, etc. The summation of above items is equal to total assets shown in the balance sheets of the enterprises.

(1) Circulating assets (working capital) refer to assets which can be cashed in or spent or consumed in an operating cycle of one year or over one year, including cash, all kinds of deposits, short term investment, receivables, advance payment, stock, etc.

(2) Fixed assets refer to the net value of fixed assets, clearance of fixed assets, project under construction, fixed assets losses in suspense. These are corporations' fund holdings.

(3) Intangible assets refer to assets without material form used by enterprises over a lone time, such as patents, non – patent technologies, trade marks, copyright, land use right, business reputation, etc.

Total Liabilities refer to the debts that enterprises are responsible for repayment, including liquid liabilities, long – term liabilities and deferred taxes, etc. Total liabilities correspond to the summation item of liabilities shown in the balance sheets of the enterprises.

(1) Liquid liabilities (also called quick liabilities or immediate liabilities) refer to enterprises' total debt payable within an operating cycle of one year or over one year, including short term loans, payables and advance payments, wages payable, taxes payable and profit payable, etc.

(2) Long term liabilities refers to total debt payable within an operating cycle of one year or over one year, including long – term loans, payable liabilities, long – term payables, etc.

Creditors' Equity refers to investors' ownership of net assets of the enterprise. It is equal to the total assets of the enterprise minus its total liabilities, including the primary input from investors, capital accumulation fund, surplus accumulation fund and undistributed profit. It is the shareholder's equity in share – holding companies.

第五篇
CHAPTER-5

建筑业

Construction

5

建筑业
Construction

主要统计指标
Major Statistical Indicators

建筑业总产值	Gross Output Value of Construction	2663.83	亿元	(100 million yuan)
为上年	As Compared with the Preceding Year	126.2	%	(%)
房屋建筑施工面积	Floor Space of Buildings Under Construction	22650	万平方米	(10000 sq.m)
为上年	As Compared with the Preceding Year	116.5	%	(%)
房屋建筑竣工面积	Floor Space of Buildings Completed	8220	万平方米	(10000 sq.m)
为上年	As Compared with the Preceding Year	124.4	%	(%)

5－01 建筑业总产值(2010年)

Gross Output Value of Construction(2010)

单位:万元 (10000 yuan)

地 区	Region	建筑企业单位数(个) Number of Construction Enterprises (unit)	建筑企业年末从业人员数(人) Number of Employed Persons at the end of the Year (Person)	建筑业总产值 Gross Output Value of Construction	其中: 建筑工程产值 Output Value of Construction Projects	安装工程产值 Output value of Installation Projects	其他产值 Other Output Values
全 市	**Total**	**1331**	**1117287**	**26638312**	**23307310**	**2557314**	**773688**
市 区	Urban District	1079	1002633	24416231	21374235	2316442	725555
上城区	Shangcheng	87	69704	1791418	1266497	475896	49025
下城区	Xiacheng	100	43826	1318361	1162323	141447	14591
江干区	Jianggan	155	102153	2121524	1905744	209870	5910
拱墅区	Gongshu	147	83711	1789606	1348292	379957	61357
西湖区	Xihu	154	249272	5673906	5037275	459326	177305
高新(滨江)区	Hi－Tech (Binjiang)	41	50060	2030366	1897385	27384	105597
萧山区	Xiaoshan	255	332119	8267509	7465273	521006	281230
余杭区	Yuhang	140	71788	1423542	1291446	101556	30540
桐庐县	Tonglu	44	17634	289051	244579	37411	7061
淳安县	Chun'an	36	10741	178936	133341	35907	9688
建德市	Jiande	36	11575	177683	136844	40298	541
富阳市	Fuyang	84	41756	986988	872106	88578	26304
临安市	Lin'an	52	32948	589422	546205	38678	4539

5-02 各种分组总专包

Financial Conditions

单位:万元

指标名称	Item	二、年末资产 Asset and Liabilities		
		流动资产合计 Circulating Funds	固定资产合计 Fixed Assets	资产合计 Total Assets
总 计	**Total**	**13758468**	**1896442**	**17450148**
其中:特、一、二级企业	of Which: Special Grade, First Grade, Second Grade	11295075	1454186	14368014
其中:国有及国有控股企业	of Which: State - owned and State Holding Enterprises	1614386	150253	2020206
一、按登记注册类型分组	**Grouped by Registration Status**			
内资企业	Domestic Funded	13633761	1878611	17296499
国有企业	State - owned	389615	62968	467580
集体企业	Collective - owned	96209	3681	102082
股份合作企业	Share - holding Cooperative Enterprises	35	95	129
联营企业	Joint Venture	6593	4062	11720
有限责任公司	Limited Liability Corporations	6222948	673880	7863788
股份有限公司	Share - holding Corporations Ltd.	848261	160133	1192019
私营企业	Private Enterprises	6070100	973791	7659181
港、澳、台商投资企业	Funded from Hong Kong, Macao and Taiwan	110181	15583	135573
外商投资企业	Foreign Funded	14526	2248	18076
二、按国民经济行业分组	**Grouped by Sector**			
房屋和土木工程建筑业	Housing and Civil Engineering Construction	12205010	1674722	15566538
建筑安装业	Installation of Lines, Pipelines and Equipment	742274	93600	895570
建筑装饰业	Fitting and Decoration of Buildings	588695	86202	713253
其他建筑业	Others Construction	222489	41918	274787

企业财务汇总表(2010年)
of Construction Enterprises(2010)

(10000 yuan)

负债 at Year - end				
流动负债合计 Liquid Liabilities	负债合计 Total Liabilities	所有者权益合计 Owners´Equity	其中:实收资本 of Which: Paid - in Capitals	其中:国家资本 of Which: State Capital
11294749	**11760309**	**5689839**	**3472567**	**242640**
9574217	9995708	4372306	2498344	227273
1492511	1615124	405082	270011	227709
11175419	11640969	5655530	3450487	242640
342681	342684	124896	64412	64412
76062	77071	25011	8700	-
52	52	77	116	-
6341	6341	5379	3010	3010
5422196	5679094	2184694	1215848	175218
870332	911770	280249	124878	-
4457755	4623957	3035224	2033524	-
111004	111004	24568	16248	-
8326	8336	9741	5832	-
10112745	10557239	5009299	3017872	224780
585043	599369	296201	201446	11627
434616	440182	273071	176238	3208
162345	163519	111268	77011	3025

单位:万元　　5－02　续表

指标名称	Item	三、损益 Expenditure, Income	
		工程结算收入 Revenue of Project Settlement Accounts	工程结算成本 Costs of Project Settlement Accounts
总　计	**Total**	**23987860**	**21768815**
其中:特、一、二级企业	of Which: Special Grade, First Grade, Second Grade	20536819	18810578
其中:国有及国有控股企业	of Which: State－owned and State Holding Enterprises	2774037	2503447
一、按登记注册类型分组	**Grouped by Registration Status**		
内资企业	Domestic Funded	23824567	21631049
国有企业	State－owned	673160	566820
集体企业	Collective－owned	59513	48657
股份合作企业	Share－holding Cooperative Enterprises	31	18
联营企业	Joint Venture	19325	16987
有限责任公司	Limited Liability Corporations	11498269	10584259
股份有限公司	Share－holding Corporations Ltd.	1287341	1156623
私营企业	Private Enterprises	10286928	9257685
港、澳、台商投资企业	Funded from Hong Kong, Macao and Taiwan	124033	104044
外商投资企业	Foreign Funded	39260	33722
二、按国民经济行业分组	**Grouped by Sector**		
房屋和土木工程建筑业	Housing and Civil Engineering Construction	21527245	19610665
建筑安装业	Installation of Lines, Pipelines and Equipment	1085485	936548
建筑装饰业	Fitting and Decoration of Buildings	1060670	942026
其他建筑业	Others Construction	314459	279576

continued (10000 yuan)

及分配 and Distribution						六、全部从业人员年平均人数（人） Annual Average Number of Employed Persons (person)
工程结算税金及附加 Taxes and Extra Charges Project Settlement Accounts	经营费用 Operating Cost	管理费用 Management Expenditure	财务费用 Financial Expenditure	利润总额 Total Profits	应交所得税 Income Taxes Payable	
757611	**57302**	**651233**	**178931**	**676599**	**144331**	**1161335**
645420	32913	485889	155597	487245	102009	968167
86248	852	134581	4111	53479	12604	120619
755723	55135	642021	175425	667127	142580	1157288
18575	245	72680	242	18716	4256	18839
1402	218	6948	-25	2601	742	2095
1	-	20	-	-8	1	10
621	-	1654	-12	188	16	1848
372830	10927	244745	77357	269119	58098	556504
26565	9487	49751	11131	32050	5803	51316
335730	34258	266223	86732	344463	73664	526676
1248	1932	7508	3316	6465	1122	2935
640	236	1704	189	3006	629	1112
680277	43659	525901	165474	598646	126797	1047526
31325	9104	72551	3466	35193	7947	42573
35144	3541	41035	7609	33101	7364	55360
10865	998	11746	2382	9659	2223	15876

5－03 建筑业企业生产情况

Statistics on Production of Construction Enterprises

指标名称	Item	2006	2007	2008	2009	2010
一、建筑业合同情况	**Contract of Construction**					
签订的合同额（万元）	Total Value of Contracts (10000 yuan)	20010853	24696898	30088537	36623552	46427916
上年结转合同额（万元）	Value from Contracts Signed in 2009 (10000 yuan)	7548539	9290912	11210961	14824477	17396267
本年新签合同额（万元）	Value from New Contracts Signed in 2010 (10000 yuan)	12462314	15405986	18877576	21799075	29031649
二、承包工程完成情况	**Completion of Contracted Projects**					
直接从建设单位承揽工程完成的产值（万元）	Complete Output Value of Projects Contacted Directly from Investors (10000 yuan)	12662433	14853868	17871119	20791153	26259274
自行完成施工产值（万元）	Own－completed Output Value (10000 yuan)	12326935	14495495	17427692	20424041	25689110
分包出去工程的产值（万元）	Output Value of Out－sourced Projects (10000 yuan)	335498	358373	443427	367112	570163
从建设单位以外承揽工程完成的产值（万元）	Completed Output Value of Projects Contacted from Non－investors (10000 yuan)	345587	349254	576832	677632	949202
建筑业总产值（万元）	Gross Output Value (10000 yuan)	12672522	14844749	18004524	21101673	26638312
其中:装饰装修产值（万元）	of Which: Output Value of Fitting and Decoration of Buildings (10000 yuan)	882969	1149597	1404589	1641467	2177414
其中:在外省完成的产值（万元）	of Which: Completed Output Value outside of Zhejiang Province (10000 yuan)	2686936	3489987	4971040	5828938	8882553
按构成分	by Structure					
建筑工程产值（万元）	Output Value of Construction Projects (10000 yuan)	10749915	12768968	15351303	18280567	23307310
安装工程产值（万元）	Output value of Installation Projects (10000 yuan)	1497416	1729043	2083405	2193971	2557314
其他产值（万元）	Other Output Values (10000 yuan)	425191	346738	569816	627135	773688
竣工产值（万元）	Output Value of Buildings Completed (10000 yuan)	8828029	9344723	10976179	12919145	16373795
房屋建筑施工面积（万平方米）	Floor Space of Buildings Under Construction (10000 sq. m)	13612.35	15108.93	16059.15	19433.82	22650.40
其中:本年新开工面积（万平方米）	of Which: Beginning Projects in this Year (10000 sq. m)	7165.20	7516.70	7281.49	7839.32	11063.95
其中:实行投标承包面积（万平方米）	of Which: Floor Space of Biding System (10000 sq. m)	12421.93	13865.27	14725.56	18133.40	19792.30
其中:本年新开工（万平方米）	of Which: Beginning Projects in this Year (10000 sq. m)	6695.82	7064.70	6646.09	7390.40	9705.96
房屋建筑竣工面积（万平方米）		5030.65	5380.57	5799.98	6610.35	8219.87
三、年末自有施工机械设备	**Machinery and Equipment Owned (year－end)**					
年末自有施工机械设备净值（万元）	Net Value of Machinery and Equipment Owned (10000 yuan)	439174	462157	559442	683528	798573
年末自有施工机械设备总台数（台）	Number of Machinery and Equipment Owned (set)	144384	148722	157385	178586	205574
年末自有施工机械设备总功率（千瓦）	Total Power of Machinery and Equipment Owned (10000 kw)	1845585	1958612	2435575	2748357	3261216
四、从业人员情况	**Number of Employed Persons**					
计算劳动生产率的平均人数（人）	Average Employed Persons Overall Labor Productivity (person)	695674	775498	863862	966098	1149924
年末从业人员数（人）	Employed Persons (year－end) (person)	671610	758171	801246	923046	1117287

主要统计指标解释

建筑业总产值 建筑业总产值是以货币表现的建筑业企业在一定时期内生产的建筑业产品和服务的总和。建筑业总产值包括建筑工程产值、安装工程产值和其他产值三部分内容。

房屋建筑施工面积 指报告期内施过工的全部房屋建筑面积,它包括本期新开工的面积、上期跨入本期继续施工的房屋面积、上期停缓建在本期恢复施工的房屋面积、本期竣工的房屋面积以及本期施工后又停缓建的房屋面积。

房屋建筑竣工面积 指在报告期内房屋建筑按照设计要求已全部完工,达到了使用条件,经检查验收鉴定合格的房屋建筑面积。

工程结算收入(主营业务收入) 指本企业承包工程实现的工程价款结算收入以及向发包单位收取的除工程价款以外按规定列作营业收入的各种款项,如临时设施费、劳动保险费、施工机构调迁费等以及向发包单位收取的各种索赔款。

工程结算成本(主营业务成本) 指在报告期内与发包单位办理工程价款结算的已完工程实际成本。

Explanatory Notes on Main Statistical Indicators

Gross Output Value of Construction refers to total of construction products and services, expressed in money terms, produced or rendered by construction and installation enterprises during a given period of time. It includes: output value of construction projects, output value of installation projects and other output values.

Floor Space of Buildings Under Construction refers to floor space of buildings under construction during the reference period, including the floor space of buildings for which construction has newly started; buildings for which construction has started earlier and is continuing during the reference period; and buildings for which construction has been suspended earlier but has restarted during the reference period; buildings completed during the reference period; and buildings under construction but construction has subsequently been during the reference period.

Floor Space of Buildings Completed refers to the floor space of buildings that are completed in the reference period in accordance with the requirements of the design, up to the standard for being put into use, and having been checked and accepted by departments concerned as qualified ones.

Income from Settlement of Projects refers to the income received by the construction enterprise from the contracted project through settlement procedures, and other charges to the contractor as operational costs in addition to the value of the project, such as temporary facility fee, labor insurance premium, moving cost of construction equipment, as well as various types of claims to the contractor.

Project Settlement Costs refers to the contracting process works price of the actual settlement costs of projects have been completed during the reporting period.

第六篇
CHAPTER-6

交通运输、邮电

Transportation, Post And Telecommunications

交通运输、邮电
Transportation, Post and Telecommunications

主要统计指标
Major Statistical Indicators

客运量	Passenger Traffic	33772	万人次	(10000 person-times)
为上年	As Compared with the Preceding Year	112.1	%	(%)
货运量	Freight Traffic	25915	万吨	(10000 tons)
为上年	As Compared with the Preceding Year	115.8	%	(%)
邮电业务收入	Business Income of Post & Telecommunication Service	144.06	亿元	(100 million yuan)
为上年	As Compared with the Preceding Year	106.3	%	(%)
年末固定电话用户数	Number of Local Telephone Subscribers(year-end)	368.57	万户	(10000 subscribers)
为上年	As Compared with the Preceding Year	94.4	%	(%)
年末移动电话用户数	Number of Mobile Telephone Subscribers(year-end)	1061.8	万户	(10000 subscribers)
为上年	As Compared with the Preceding Year	104.9	%	(%)

6－01　全市主要年份客运量

Total Passenger Traffic in Main Years

单位:万人次　　(10000 person－times)

年　份 Year	合　计 Total	铁　路 Railways	公　路 Highways	水　路 Waterways	民　航 Civil Aviation
1978	2878	485	－	－	3
1979	3122	560	1829	729	4
1980	3905	672	2358	870	5
1981	4484	769	2857	850	8
1982	5263	813	3377	1064	9
1983	5451	878	3530	1035	8
1984	6056	983	3912	1151	10
1985	6724	1004	4595	1111	14
1986	6765	1034	4768	941	22
1987	6905	1127	4852	896	30
1988	6593	1237	4445	877	34
1989	7493	1182	5488	801	22
1990	8119	1056	6350	691	22
1991	10701	1062	8876	710	53
1992	13358	1083	11538	670	67
1993	13070	1139	11403	454	74
1994	13373	1230	11669	390	84
1995	16620	1242	14921	339	118
1996	16714	1112	15184	273	145
1997	17034	1040	15623	260	111
1998	17395	1120	15925	235	115
1999	17882	1168	16369	235	110
2000	18607	1202	17102	179	124
2001	20342	1342	18707	148	145
2002	21089	1574	19213	108	194
2003	21348	1534	19510	89	215
2004	22833	1908	20372	237	316
2005	24124	2011	21431	304	378
2006	25810	2124	22961	267	458
2007	28026	2255	24836	306	629
2008	29084	2498	25630	277	679
2009	30116	2494	26454	372	796
2010	33772	2741	29671	456	904

注:客运量全市数自1990年起为全社会数,1990年以前为交通系统数。

a) Since 1990 the data in this table include non－transportation system, while data for previous years only included transportation system.

6-02 全市主要年份货运量

Total Freight Traffic in Main Years

单位:万吨 (10000 tons)

年份 Year	合计 Total	铁路 Railways	公路 Highways	水路 Waterways	民航 Civil Aviation
1978	1706	418	633	655	-
1979	1983	440	771	772	-
1980	2070	444	762	864	-
1981	1972	449	886	637	-
1982	2261	485	795	981	-
1983	2299	488	838	973	-
1984	2385	510	888	987	-
1985	2488	524	890	1074	-
1986	2558	551	874	1133	-
1987	2515	574	899	1041	1
1988	2416	555	823	1037	1
1989	7377	539	5095	1743	…
1990	6522	449	4479	1594	…
1991	7017	451	4891	1675	…
1992	8434	534	6063	1836	1
1993	9082	580	6353	2148	1
1994	8962	491	6563	1907	1
1995	10347	482	7021	2842	2
1996	10962	445	7735	2780	2
1997	11015	406	7932	2676	1
1998	11329	418	8196	2713	2
1999	11684	403	8037	3241	3
2000	11459	417	7865	3173	4
2001	12443	452	8588	3398	5
2002	14347	446	10391	3504	6
2003	16815	438	12118	4253	6
2004	18895	480	13117	5289	9
2005	19909	525	13539	5833	12
2006	20924	569	14588	5754	13
2007	22569	573	16484	5500	12
2008	22550	483	16822	5232	13
2009	22372	427	16536	5396	13
2010	25915	379	19148	6371	17

注:货运量全市数自1990年起为全社会数,1990年以前为交通系统数。

a) Since 1990 the data in this table include non-transportation system, while data for previous years only included transportation system.

6-03 全社会客货运输量(2010年)
Total Passenger and Freight Traffic(2010)

项 目	Item	全市 Whole Municipality	为上年(%) As Compared with the Preceding Year(%)
一、客运量合计(万人次)	**Passenger Traffic(10000 person-times)**	**33772**	**112.1**
铁路客运量	Passenger Railways	2741	109.9
民航客运量	Passenger Civil Aviation	904	113.6
公路客运量	Passenger Highways	29671	112.2
水路客运量	Passenger Waterways	456	122.6
二、旅客周转量合计(万人公里)	**Total Passenger-kilometers(10000 passenger-km)**	**1422280**	**107.6**
公路旅客周转量	Passenger-kilometers Highways	1416057	107.6
水路旅客周转量	Passenger-kilometers Waterways	6223.00	115.8
三、货运量合计(万吨)	**Total Freight Traffic(10000 tons)**	**25915**	**115.8**
铁路货运量	Freight Railways	379	88.9
民航货运量	Freight Civil Aviation	17	123.9
公路货运量	Freight Highways	19148	113.4
水路货运量	Freight Waterways	6371	130.2
四、货运周转量合计(万吨公里)	**Total Freight Ton-kilometers(10000 ton-km)**	**3733634**	**152.2**
公路货物周转量	Freight Ton-kilometers Highways	2153961	155.0
水路货物周转量	Freight Ton-kilometers Waterways	1579673	148.5

6-04 社会机动车辆年末拥有量(2010年)
Total Number of Motor Vehicles End of the Year(2010)

单位:辆 (unit)

项 目	Item	全市 Whole Municipality	为上年(%) As Compared with the Preceding Year(%)	市区 Urban District
总计	**Total**	**1832496**	**116.1**	**1379822**
民用汽车拥有量	**Possession of Civilian Vehicles**	**1243087**	**125.2**	**1055666**
#私人汽车	Private Vehicles	942427	131.1	790298
载客汽车	**Passenger Vehicles**	**1076983**	**127.8**	**919251**
大型载客汽车	Large	14427	109.5	12433
中型载客汽车	Medium	19214	95.8	14675
小型载客汽车	Small	1009298	130.2	866716
微型载客汽车	Minicar	34044	100.6	25427
载货汽车	**Trucks**	**155546**	**110.6**	**128762**
重型载货汽车	Heavy	22867	133.7	19726
中型载货汽车	Light - heavy	27672	95.1	24358
轻型载货汽车	Light	103807	112.1	83813
微型载货汽车	Mini	1200	66.5	865
其他汽车	**Else**	**10558**	**105.5**	**7653**
摩 托 车	**Motorcycles**	**584440**	**100.5**	**319863**
普通摩托车	Genera Motorcycles	520932	100.6	277876
轻便摩托车	Light Motorcycles	63508	99.8	41987

6－05　邮政、电信主要指标(2010 年)

Post and Telecommunications(2010)

项　目	Item	全市 Whole Municipality	为上年(%) As Compared with the Preceding Year(%)	市区 Urban District
邮电业务总收入　(万元)	Total Business Income of Post & Telecommunications Service (10000 yuan)	1440636	106.3	1213991
函件　(万件)	Number of Letters (10000 pcs)	20037	193.3	18150
包件　(万件)	Number of Parcels (10000 pcs)	113	85.0	100
汇票　(万张)	Number of Bill of Exchange (10000 pcs)	311	89.9	263
订销报刊累计量　(万份)	Number of Newspapers & Magazines Circulation (10000 copies)	28419	104.7	22673
集邮　(万枚)	Philutely (10000 pcs)	1138	121.3	941
邮储期末余额　(万元)	Balance of Postal Deposits (10000 yuan)	1563792	93.0	1202075
年末固定电话用户数　(万户)	Number of Local Telephone Subscribers (year－end) (10000 subscribers)	368.57	94.4	293.49
年末移动电话用户数　(万户)	Number of Subscribers of Mobile Telephone(year－end) (10000 subscribers)	1061.8	104.9	858.31
年末国际互联网用户数　(万户)	Number of Internet Subscribers(year－end) (10000 subscribers)	218.41	122.5	177.59
#宽带业务户数　(万户)	Number of Wide Band Subscribers (10000 subscribers)	217.89	134.2	177.13

主要统计指标解释

货(客)运量　指在一定时期内,各种运输工具实际运送的货物(旅客)数量。是反映运输业为国民经济和人民生活服务的数量指标,也是制定和检查运输生产计划、研究运输发展规模和速度的重要指标。货运按吨计算,客运按人计算。货物不论运输距离长短、货物类别,均按实际重量统计。旅客不论行程远近或票价多少,均按一人一次作为客运量统计;半价票、小孩票也按一人统计。

货物(旅客)周转量　指在一定时期内,由各种运输工具运送的货物(旅客)数量与其相应运输距离的乘积之总和。是反映运输业生产总成果的重要指标,也是编制和检查运输生产计划,计算运输效率、劳动生产率以及核算运输单位成本的主要基础资料。通常以吨公里和人公里为计算单位。计算货物周转量通常按发出站与到达站之间的最短距离,也就是计费距离计算。

移动电话用户　指在邮电部门登记,通过移动电话交换机进入移动电话网,占有移动电话号码的电话用户。用户数量以实际办理登记手续进入邮电部门移动电话网的户数进行计算,一部或一台移动电话统计为一户。

Explanatory Notes on Main Statistical Indicators

Freight(passenger)Traffic refers to the volume of freight (passenger) transported with various means. Freight transport is calculated in tons and passenger traffic is calculated in the number of persons. Despite the type of freight and traveling distance, the freight transport is calculated in the actual weight of the goods; and despite the traveling distance and ticket price, the passenger traffic is calculated by the principle that one person can be counted only once in one travel. The passenger who travel with a half – price ticket or a child ticket is also calculated as one person. The freight (passenger) traffic provides a quantitative measure to show how the transport industry serves the national economy and people, and is also an important indicator for plan the transport industry and for studying the development scale and speed of the transport industry.

Freight Ton – kilometers(Passenger – kilometers) refers to the sum of the products of the volume of transported cargo (passengers) multiplying by the transport distance, usually using ton – kilometer and passenger – kilometer as units for measurement . Normally, the shortest distance between the departure station and the destination station (i. e. , the payable distance) is the basis to calculate the freight ton – kilometers. This is an important indicator to show the total results of the transport industry, to prepare and examine the transport plan and to measure the efficiency, the labour productivity and the unit cost of transport.

Mobile Telephone Subscribers refer to the persons who own mobile telephone number connected with the mobile telephone communication network and registered by post and telecommunications organization. The number of subscribers is calculated only when the subscribers who have gone through all the register formalities and entered into the mobile telephone network. One mobile telephone is treated as a subscriber.

第七篇
CHAPTER-7

固定资产投资
Investment In Fixed Assets

固定资产投资
Investment in Fixed Assets

主要统计指标
Major Statistical Indicators

全市限额以上固定资产投资	Investment of Super-scale projects	2651.88	亿元	(100 million yuan)
为上年	As Compared with the Preceding Year	120.8	%	(%)
第一产业	Primary Industry	4.20	亿元	(100 million yuan)
为上年	As Compared with the Preceding Year	133.9	%	(%)
第二产业	Secondary Industry	687.58	亿元	(100 million yuan)
为上年	As Compared with the Preceding Year	112.4	%	(%)
第三产业	Tertiary Industry	1960.10	亿元	(100 million yuan)
为上年	As Compared with the Preceding Year	124.0	%	(%)

7－01　主要年份全市全社会固定资产投资总额

Total Investment in Fixed Assets in Main Years

单位:万元　　　　(10000 yuan)

年　份 Year	合　计 Total	基本建设 Capital Construction	更新改造 Innovation	房地产开发 Real Estate Development	其他投资 Others	农村集体 Rural collective－owned Units	农村私人投资 Rural Individuals
1978	48307	23941	5316		765	10242	8043
1979	55828	25008	8327		1072	11380	10041
1980	70936	33257	9190		3305	12645	12539
1981	79791	23772	21423		6343	14050	14203
1982	97895	32518	25596		8009	15611	16161
1983	102413	35269	22181		1056	13350	20757
1984	148601	52313	27269		13662	25922	2945
1985	229746	85718	33219		22952	48611	39246
1986	284936	95102	52701		34595	48352	54223
1987	350033	93113	70399		34304	61848	87669
1988	370954	80939	77481		47547	55456	109531
1989	345548	87320	72994		41817	42340	101077
1990	366296	99805	73933	20409	35067	38442	98640
1991	418845	96589	92103	25247	41757	64433	98716
1992	654537	119216	136850	41886	86204	140783	129618
1993	1310914	273991	204412	218006	128973	342267	143265
1994	1620301	397651	205109	320532	136145	358581	202283
1995	2323355	541890	279388	527985	217017	453746	303329
1996	2611772	688794	254507	572749	302283	453720	339719
1997	3033904	906554	323091	572686	335681	538980	355912
1998	3636607	1240740	492814	666244	281942	590911	363956
1999	4354770	1535925	625617	848441	223626	711076	410085
2000	5154923	1704012	770229	1015347	276885	997463	390987
2001	6309723	1938875	996305	1409132	290617	1308500	366294
2002	7697578	2424601	1011054	1982517	205194	1758436	315776
2003	10067440	3260181	945777	2588452	375214	2577280	320536
2004	12022243	–	–	3285409	–	–	–
2005	13866833	–	–	4105706	–	–	–
2006	14607422	–	–	4426534	–	–	–
2007	16841298	–	–	5187904	–	–	–
2008	19805018	–	–	6154060	–	–	–
2009	22916543	–	–	7046752	–	–	–
2010	27531348	–	–	9561970	–	–	–

注:2006 年起全市固定资产投资口径不含 50 万元以下农村非农户投资(下同)。

a) From 2006, the data of investment of non－farmers in village bellow 500000 yuan are excluded in the total investment in fixed assets. The same as in the following tables.

7－02 主要年份市区全社会固定资产投资总额

Total Investment in Fixed Assets of Urban District in Main Years

单位：万元 （10000 yuan）

年 份 Year	合 计 Total	基本建设 Capital Construction	更新改造 Innovation	房地产开发 Real Estate Development	其他投资 Others	农村集体 Rural collective－owned Units	农村私人投资 Rural Individuals
1978	22468	16451	3403		557	1087	970
1979	26793	18085	5499		820	1207	1182
1980	35925	24385	6904		1850	1342	1444
1981	41729	19478	15248		3744	1491	1768
1982	52541	26703	17174		4878	1657	2129
1983	57191	29654	15431		4616	3220	4270
1984	88074	45993	20494		6133	8242	7212
1985	125927	70527	22495		10579	14776	7550
1986	154417	81678	36880		17252	6788	11819
1987	163067	80067	46885		13163	8636	14316
1988	159599	63482	46636		22657	9633	17191
1989	150113	65322	44310		20422	7972	12087
1990	170878	79792	48131	12750	12470	6045	11690
1991	176914	66724	56497	16509	14664	12096	10424
1992	231616	62271	84548	29784	22568	20070	12375
1993	499373	140113	119235	115116	37049	70355	17505
1994	717285	227983	129824	189357	46645	100385	23091
1995	1148688	339016	162799	375816	129480	105247	36330
1996	1485008	523573	165631	439245	140633	148576	67350
1997	1821969	731925	245759	445316	176948	147506	74515
1998	2260918	939373	407351	538499	124538	166389	84768
1999	2672757	1195699	466289	636705	98869	193173	82022
2000	3009630	1233350	515716	737950	214280	216928	91406
2001	5381284	1768151	868561	1255605	25330	996347	237290
2002	6388204	2168121	811362	1724128	196471	1301262	186860
2003	7971044	2814796	725643	2176433	334528	1746610	173034
2004	9648206	－	－	3088508	－	－	－
2005	10787387	－	－	3485810	－	－	－
2006	11169155	－	－	3653393	－	－	－
2007	13150724	－	－	4298687	－	－	－
2008	15634404	－	－	5269947	－	－	－
2009	18172403	－	－	6261562	－	－	－
2010	21827468	－	－	8486495	－	－	－

注：2001 年起市区数据含萧山、余杭区。

a) Since 2001, data in the table include Xiaoshan district and Yuhang district.

7-03 主要年份全市固定资产投资按三次产业分

Investment in Fixed Assets Grouped by Three Industries in Main Years

单位:万元 (10000 yuan)

年份 Year	绝对数(万元) Absolute Figure(10000 yuan)				比重(以投资总额为100) Proportion(%)		
	合计 Total	第一产业 Primary Industry	第二产业 Secondary Industry	第三产业 Tertiary Industry	第一产业 Primary Industry	第二产业 Secondary Industry	第三产业 Tertiary Industry
1978	23941	2174	14455	7312	9.1	60.4	30.5
1979	34407	2454	19927	12026	7.1	57.9	35.0
1980	45752	1608	26211	17933	3.5	57.3	39.2
1981	51538	850	29176	21512	1.6	56.6	41.8
1982	66123	1352	37648	27123	2.0	57.0	41.0
1983	68306	1297	37823	29186	1.9	55.4	42.7
1984	93244	2831	46619	43794	3.0	50.0	47.0
1985	141889	3207	71608	67074	2.3	50.5	47.2
1986	182398	2265	94394	85739	1.2	51.8	47.0
1987	200516	2994	106600	90922	1.5	53.2	45.3
1988	205967	4746	118736	82485	2.3	57.6	40.1
1989	202131	3038	117651	81442	1.5	58.2	40.3
1990	229214	2181	126263	100770	1.0	55.1	43.9
1991	255696	3204	132303	120189	1.3	51.7	47.0
1992	384136	4424	206659	173053	1.2	53.8	45.0
1993	825382	5650	346416	473316	0.7	42.0	57.3
1994	1059437	3905	354672	700860	0.4	33.5	66.1
1995	1566280	5821	534687	1025772	0.4	34.1	65.5
1996	1819333	3100	640273	1175960	0.2	35.2	64.6
1997	2139012	1712	595966	1541334	-	27.9	72.1
1998	2681740	4053	706948	1970739	0.2	26.4	73.4
1999	3233609	23546	764309	2445754	0.7	23.6	75.7
2000	3766473	774	844334	2921365	0.2	22.4	77.4
2001	4634929	595	953494	3680840	-	20.6	79.4
2002	5623366	6514	1104212	4512640	0.1	19.6	80.3
2003	8952090	10489	3208885	5732716	0.1	35.9	64.0
2004	11081993	15992	4369015	6696986	0.1	39.4	60.5
2005	12777972	13982	4451936	8312054	0.1	34.8	65.1
2006	13734482	17892	4651420	9065170	0.1	33.9	66.0
2007	15837775	23278	5286340	10528157	0.1	33.4	66.5
2008	18822936	30810	5705736	13086390	0.2	30.3	69.5
2009	21951706	31335	6115482	15804889	0.1	27.9	72.0
2010	26518839	41959	6875840	19601040	0.2	25.9	73.9

注:2002年以前为全部城镇及以上投资,不包括农村集体及私人投资。从2003年开始为全部限额以上投资口径。

a) Before year 2002, data in this table refer to urban investments and the rural investments are excluded. From 2003, refer to investment of super-scale projects.

7-04 主要年份全市固定资产投资房屋建筑面积及造价

Floor Space of Buildings and Their Cost in Main Years

年份 Year	施工面积（万平方米） Floor Space of Buildings Under Construction (10000sq. m)	#住宅 Residential Buildings	竣工面积（万平方米） Floor Space of Buildings Completed (10000 sq. m)	#住宅 Residential Buildings	竣工房屋价值（万元） Value of Buildings Completed (10000 yuan)	#住宅 Residential Buildings	每平方米造价（元） Cost Per Square (yuan)	#住宅 Residential Buildings
1978			101.95	39.58	8869	2810	87	71
1979			150.26	68.01	13223	4965	88	73
1980	456.54		202.58	104.44	19448	8564	96	82
1981	507.94		232.25	120.35	26709	12396	115	103
1982	554.89	258.09	281.63	148.66	34095	16470	121	111
1983	531.79	244.36	247.07	125.86	33938	15494	137	123
1984	620.71	293.21	267.85	138.71	42740	18398	160	133
1985	741.47	333.72	327.75	157.85	56561	22825	173	145
1986	674.58	278.19	338.19	160.19	50561	27338	238	170
1987	544.64	149.07	254.73	73.16	68801	14944	270	204
1988	526.70	156.92	230.21	75.44	68407	17820	297	236
1989	420.81	116.12	202.15	64.15	69750	18200	345	284
1990	472.59	209.50	236.44	112.77	93557	34266	396	304
1991	459.00	205.41	226.84	92.72	93158	28599	411	308
1992	604.85	301.21	262.11	114.97	116169	39834	452	350
1993	958.91	533.01	380.29	199.96	224251	105107	589	525
1994	1069.68	613.62	460.20	274.19	375211	212705	815	776
1995	1320.68	737.79	524.58	319.41	491705	274314	937	859
1996	1399.70	758.00	582.70	354.50	688569	370485	1182	1045
1997	1363.80	660.70	642.10	338.00	871361	449235	1357	1329
1998	1456.02	743.59	515.16	271.91	709730	390624	1378	1437
1999	1681.71	956.15	709.10	411.44	1119141	641717	1578	1560
2000	1721.58	949.32	744.42	419.80	1207767	709044	1622	1689
2001	2318.95	1251.92	830.05	402.46	1310380	679449	1579	1688
2002	2713.02	1586.28	890.05	492.95	1623662	956643	1820	1941
2003	4392.79	2083.58	1618.01	651.58	2732763	1353422	1689	2077
2004	5731.48	2909.03	1865.83	717.46	2791115	1313596	1496	1831
2005	6671.39	3628.34	1856.34	801.34	3265491	1865538	1759	2328
2006	7260.08	3747.6	1737.51	706.13	2900836	1580689	1670	2239
2007	7942.07	4040.54	1849.24	858.99	3750264	2329184	2028	2712
2008	9471.42	4160.27	2057.86	846.34	4113211	2171525	1999	2566
2009	10308.45	4441.84	2009.90	700.63	3626421	1684092	1804	2404
2010	12971.81	5534.10	2695.90	902.57	5274936	2285285	1957	2532

注：2002 年以前为全部城镇及以上投资，不包括农村集体及私人投资。从 2003 年开始为全部限额以上投资口径。

a) Before year 2002, data in this table refer to urban investments and the rural investments are excluded. From 2003, refer to investment of super-scale projects.

7-05 主要年份市区固定资产投资房屋建筑面积及造价

Urban District Floor Space of Buildings and Their Cost in Main Years

年份 Year	施工面积（万平方米）Floor Space of Buildings Under Construction (10000 sq. m)	#住宅 Residential Buildings	竣工面积（万平方米）Floor Space of Buildings Completed (10000sq. m)	#住宅 Residential Buildings	竣工房屋价值（万元）Value of Buildings Completed (10000 yuan)	#住宅 Residential Buildings	每平方米造价（元）Cost Per Square (yuan)	#住宅 Residential Buildings
1978			71.56	29.06	6941	2237	97	77
1979			109.23	53.37	10267	4056	94	76
1980			137.11	76.73	14396	6752	105	88
1981			160.36	90.12	20093	9643	123	107
1982	378.88	172.11	189.92	100.07	25200	11980	133	120
1983	376.32	169.17	157.14	81.68	24029	11045	153	135
1984	465.27	221.72	191.13	104.55	33863	14658	177	140
1985	532.66	258.19	219.79	114.26	40344	17489	184	153
1986	465.75	203.22	219.33	116.70	58619	21149	267	181
1987	336.85	86.05	150.59	41.72	46530	9513	309	228
1988	315.80	90.98	117.71	37.63	38501	10117	330	269
1989	253.41	56.39	99.86	28.89	38680	9087	387	315
1990	301.82	128.50	137.88	62.47	60551	20361	439	326
1991	265.61	118.99	114.19	42.31	53819	12892	471	305
1992	329.16	190.55	115.59	57.36	55758	19706	483	344
1993	500.08	266.80	175.22	104.83	101528	53540	579	511
1994	618.91	352.16	212.06	123.74	182730	102924	862	832
1995	821.03	463.98	244.94	152.10	250073	139666	1021	918
1996	969.10	538.50	350.10	229.00	437239	274244	1249	1196
1997	1017.30	485.20	442.00	232.70	675762	357624	1529	1537
1998	1055.24	541.41	321.17	184.18	516400	317402	1608	1723
1999	1204.30	656.07	489.23	294.85	908844	533675	1858	1810
2000	1176.29	617.80	497.64	269.94	916212	528385	1841	1957
2001	2053.02	1085.30	698.29	325.64	1193818	615802	1710	1891
2002	2330.97	1335.78	744.48	404.35	1483862	869969	1993	2152
2003	3637.82	1699.61	1325.48	516.33	2395039	1174735	1807	2275
2004	4740.42	2453.87	1389.30	528.26	2257386	1068708	1625	2023
2005	5533.58	3039.08	1478.07	661.56	2804402	1626514	1897	2459
2006	5898.15	3114.45	1327.37	580.22	2365342	1357671	1782	2340
2007	6496.01	3357.18	1355.43	674.97	3063585	1992874	2260	2953
2008	7812.71	3466.88	1537.69	668.13	3372465	1827426	2193	2735
2009	8558.17	3807.67	1398.49	537.39	2725150	1321357	1949	2459
2010	10738.49	4759.75	1983.33	732.55	4255543	1927150	2146	2631

注：2002 年以前为全部城镇及以上投资，不包括农村集体及私人投资。从 2003 年开始为全部限额以上投资口径。

a) Before year 2002, data in this table refer to urban investments and the rural investments are excluded. From 2003, refer to investment of super-scale projects.

7－06 分县(市)固定资产
Investment in Fixed Assets

单位:万元

指　　标	Item	全市 Total 2010年	全市 Total 上年 Preceding Year	全市 Total 为上年(%) As Compared with the Preceding Year(%)	市区 Urban District 2010年
全社会固定资产投资	**Total Investment in Fixed Assets**	**27531348**	**22916543**	**120.1**	**21827468**
限额以上固定资产投资额	**Investment of Super－scale Projects**	**26518839**	**21951706**	**120.8**	**21437496**
#住宅	#Residential Buildings	7838596	5795988	135.2	6872400
#工业投资	Industrial Investment	6855587	6091653	112.5	4293707
#基础设施投资	Infrastructural Investment	6452236	6018416	107.2	5438685
一、按投资、房地产分	**Grouped by Sector**				
投资项目完成额	Investment Projects	16956869	14904954	113.8	12951001
房地产开发完成额	Real Estate	9561970	7046752	135.7	8486495
二、按登记注册类型分	**Grouped by Status of Registration**				
内资	Domestic－funded	23940232	19729856	121.3	19316267
国有	State－owned	7940680	6772964	117.2	6953730
集体	Collective－owned	516448	504752	102.3	420874
股份合作	Cooperative	24938	72460	34.4	24938
国有联营	Joint State Ownership	－	4707	－	－
集体联营	Collective Joint Ownership	－	4850	－	－
国有与集体联营	Joint State－collective Ownership	3045	379	803.4	－
其他联营	Other Joint Ownership	－	－	－	－
国有独资公司	State－owned Corporations	603038	528685	114.1	446729
其他有限责任公司	Other Limited Liability Corporations	9846163	7475964	131.7	8364921
股份有限公司	Share－holding Corporations Ltd.	695742	947213	73.5	492945
私营	Private	4154997	3188840	130.3	2545259
其他	Other	155181	229042	67.8	66871
港、澳、台商投资	Investment from Hong Kong, Macao and Taiwan	1324916	1139267	116.3	1039898
外商投资	Foreign Investment	1236253	1059272	116.7	1081331

投资完成额(2010 年)

by Region(2010)

(10000 yuan)

上　年 Preceding Year	为上年(%) As Compared with the Preceding Year(%)	#萧山区 Xiaoshan	#余杭区 Yuhang	桐庐县 Tonglu	淳安县 Chun'an	建德市 Jiande	富阳市 Fuyang	临安市 Lin'an
18172403	**120.1**	**4765557**	**3616691**	**1172860**	**746572**	**782507**	**1918161**	**1083780**
17797778	**120.5**	**4515095**	**3480147**	**1001737**	**668168**	**658530**	**1796500**	**956408**
5113183	134.4	570238	1063798	204725	191945	105751	290973	172802
3821313	112.4	2034365	903621	451857	204914	359676	998889	546544
5070500	107.3	1208242	893844	150885	146257	104434	455930	156045
11536216	112.3	3768261	2271723	750909	454187	558161	1505581	737030
6261562	135.5	746834	1208424	250828	213981	100369	290919	219378
16124285	119.8	3932418	3183040	856225	603620	653059	1569410	941651
5844629	119.0	1353454	1093415	136096	198677	204677	271346	176154
414631	101.5	80900	17385	11645	850	-	74192	8887
72460	34.4	2300	11594	-	-	-	-	-
-	-	-	-	-	-	-	-	-
4850	-	-	-	-	-	-	-	-
-	-	-	-	-	3040	-	5	-
-	-	-	-	-	-	-	-	-
419912	106.4	146058	98555	20077	12415	-	118685	5132
6544114	127.8	1224202	954040	269339	288989	120798	220568	581548
755601	65.2	221251	33799	27790	20707	39106	77456	37738
1932782	131.7	893181	960102	384526	33892	259983	800645	130692
135306	49.4	11072	14150	6752	45050	28495	6513	1500
913309	113.9	353121	159012	114082	14390	4051	151495	1000
895104	120.8	229556	138095	22291	50158	860	67856	13757

指　　标	Item	全　市 Total 2010年	全　市 Total 上年 Preceding Year	全　市 Total 为上年(%) As Compared with the Preceding Year(%)	市　区 Urban District 2010年
三、按行业分	**Grouped by Sector**				
农林牧渔业	Farming, Forestry, Animal Husbandry and Fishery	41959	31335	133.9	12988
采矿业	Mining & Quarrying	48177	35088	137.3	8012
制造业	Manufacturing	6124928	5319748	115.1	3723042
电力、燃气及水的生产和供应业	Production and Supply of Electricity, Gas and Water	682482	736817	92.6	562653
建筑业	Construction	20253	22936	88.3	20253
交通运输、仓储及邮政业	Transportation, Storage, Post & Telecommunications	2415265	1726152	139.9	2024617
信息传输、计算机服务和软件业	Information Transmission, Computer Services and Software	291493	362142	80.5	288767
批发和零售业	Wholesale & Retail Trade	700713	616104	113.7	643860
住宿和餐饮业	Lodging and Catering	412265	316649	130.2	255085
金融业	Banking and Insurance	4449	41245	10.8	4449
房地产业	Real Estate	11872598	8746206	135.7	10603157
租赁和商务服务业	Renting and Business Service	437254	416630	105.0	391108
科学研究、技术服务和地质勘查业	Scientific Research, Technical Service and Geological Prospecting	94091	66362	141.8	94091
水利、环境和公共设施管理业	Water Conservancy, Environment and Public Utility	2593603	2639993	98.2	2178374
居民服务和其他服务业	Service for the Residents and Other	19362	9991	193.8	14015
教育	Education	339381	335848	101.1	279940
卫生、社会保障和社会福利业	Health Care, Sports & Social Welfare	188622	187735	100.5	159491
文化、体育和娱乐业	Culture, Sports and Entertainment	163703	269450	60.8	138424
公共管理和社会组织	Public Management and Social Organizations	68241	71275	95.7	35170
国际组织	International Organizations	－	－	－	－

continued (10000 yuan)

上　年 Preceding Year	为上年(%) As Compared with the Preceding Year(%)	#萧山区 Xiaoshan	#余杭区 Yuhang	桐庐县 Tonglu	淳安县 Chun'an	建德市 Jiande	富阳市 Fuyang	临安市 Lin'an
6714	193.4	9180	3808	3931	–	3631	17719	3690
		7259	753	4510	3681	1290	28587	2097
3254453	114.4	1943206	820368	432135	181169	338432	909708	540442
566860	99.3	83900	82500	15212	20064	19954	60594	4005
21469	94.3	5586	–	–	–	–	–	–
1455671	139.1	520613	270463	19776	37335	46349	231361	55827
361842	79.8	6569	47683	1310	–	–	360	1056
558287	115.3	44192	115335	11535	18384	4951	12314	9669
237451	107.4	48555	38042	97714	23400	15947	6024	14095
41245	10.8	2300	–	–	–	–	–	–
7878044	134.6	1099348	1509880	254358	264190	177427	353588	219878
370317	105.6	73372	18298	24721	21425	–	–	–
65447	143.8	27783	30958	–	–	–	–	–
2244755	97.0	523724	417218	99805	68678	28387	130831	87528
8656	161.9	3970	–	736	–	935	–	3676
244516	114.5	56489	98834	13478	8328	8814	23366	5455
168873	94.4	9573	19617	1304	9840	930	13827	3230
257059	53.8	42562	597	12986	2012	751	6530	3000
56119	62.7	6914	5793	8226	9662	10732	1691	2760
–	–	–	–	–	–	–	–	–

7-07 分县(市)限额以上工业

Super-Scale Investment

单位:万元

指标	Item	全市 Total 2010年	全市 Total 上年 Preceding Year	全市 Total 为上年(%) As Compared with the Preceding Year(%)	市区 Urban District 2010年
总计	**Total**	**6855587**	**6091653**	**112.5**	**4293707**
一、按登记注册类型分	**Total Investment**				
内资	Domestic-funded	5463470	4904821	111.4	3197971
国有	State-owned	788307	779694	101.1	705006
集体	Collective-owned	47580	63203	75.3	20140
股份合作	Cooperative	7317	14242	51.4	7317
集体联营	Collective Joint Ownership	-	-		-
国有独资公司	State-funded Corporations	74408	112461	66.2	63558
其他有限责任公司	Other Limited Liability Corporations	1983722	1861383	106.6	1101069
股份有限公司	Share-holding Corporations Ltd.	396983	435855	91.1	229582
私营	Private	2126400	1616682	131.5	1061976
其他	Other	38753	21301	181.9	9323
港、澳、台商投资	Investment from Hong Kong, Macao and Taiwan	699889	493640	141.8	506815
外商投资	Foreign Investment	678392	676050	100.3	588921
二、按行业分	**Grouped by Sector**		-		
采矿业	Mining & Quarrying	48177	35088	137.3	8012
制造业	Manufacturing	6124928	5319748	115.1	3723042
农副食品加工业	Agricultural Products Processing	81431	98252	82.9	46596
食品制造业	Food Manufacturing	66420	103558	64.1	48945
饮料制造业	Beverage Manufacturing	97377	85002	114.6	9686
烟草制品业	Tobacco Processing	96754	31983	302.5	96754
纺织业	Textile Processing	621674	544187	114.2	471008
纺织服装、鞋、帽制造业	Textile Products, Garments, Shoes and Caps Processing	80001	133380	60.0	60705

投资完成额(2010 年)

in Industrial Sector by Region(2010)

(10000 yuan)

上 年 Preceding Year	为上年(%) As Compared with the Preceding Year(%)	#萧山区 Xiaoshan	#余杭区 Yuhang	桐庐县 Tonglu	淳安县 Chun'an	建德市 Jiande	富阳市 Fuyang	临安市 Lin'an
3821313	**112.4**	**2034365**	**903621**	**451857**	**204914**	**359676**	**998889**	**546544**
2917862	109.6	1522279	725882	385663	192680	357331	786368	543457
557170	126.5	60411	94397	12949	10344	23410	18437	18161
16447	122.5	1857	6225	925	–	–	26235	280
14242	51.4	–	7317	–	–	–	–	–
–		–	–	–	–	–	–	–
109716	57.9	13898	1256	2943	2775	–	–	5132
1209280	91.1	720422	132143	83870	137225	116331	147749	397478
257703	89.1	174252	24004	24237	18885	39106	50285	34888
753304	141.0	542116	460540	259804	23451	149989	543662	87518
–		9323	–	935	–	28495	–	–
327173	154.9	322758	58613	45005	6608	925	139536	1000
569738	103.4	189328	119126	13042	5626	860	67856	2087
–								
		7259	753	4510	3681	1290	28587	2097
3254453	114.4	1943206	820368	432135	181169	338432	909708	540442
58536	79.6	12505	31887	6844	11058	5230	–	11703
72052	67.9	7205	14559	2569	–	1000	5348	8558
31777	30.5	3607	3391	2111	47091	38489	–	–
31983	302.5	–	–	–	–	–	–	–
408696	115.2	399441	66165	52683	42812	12199	22677	20295
95258	63.7	22210	22810	9102	5462	1885	1847	1000

单位:万元　　7－07　续表

指标	Item	全市 Total 2010年	上年 Preceding Year	为上年(%) As Compared with the Preceding Year(%)	市区 Urban District 2010年
皮革、毛皮、羽毛(绒)及其制造业	Leather, Furs, Down and Related Products	51096	37821	135.1	30874
木材加工及木、竹、藤、棕、草制品业	Timber Processing, Bamboo, Cane, Palm Fiber and Straw Products	25461	25988	98.0	13618
家具制造业	Furniture Manufacturing	67055	47022	142.6	40453
造纸及纸制品业	Paper Making and Paper Products	293914	238202	123.4	58262
印刷业和记录媒介的复制	Printing and Record Media	85694	52862	162.1	55770
文教体育用品制造业	Cultural, Educational and Sports Goods	75046	66786	112.4	29787
石油加工、炼焦及核燃料加工业	Petroleum and Nuclear Fuel Processing	3531	1458	242.2	2896
化学原料及化学制品制造业	Raw Chemical Material and Chemical Products	339126	427115	79.4	154960
医药制造业	Medical and Pharmaceutical Products	194954	120027	162.4	78911
化学纤维制造业	Chemical Fiber	127883	64385	198.6	126673
橡胶制造业	Rubber Products	160395	89963	178.3	103916
塑料制品业	Plastic Products	195727	133386	146.7	143573
非金属矿物制品业	Nonmetal Mineral Products	293948	286732	102.5	143332
黑色金属冶炼及压延加工业	Smelting and Pressing of Ferrous Metals	90710	77720	116.7	66563
有色金属冶炼及压延加工业	Smelting and Pressing of Nonferrous Metal	119646	70865	168.8	39787
金属制品业	Metal Products	326856	360505	90.7	177360
通用设备制造业	Ordinary Machinery	536877	601509	89.3	334220
专业设备制造业	Special Purpose Equipment	199812	272257	73.4	167172
交通运输设备制造业	Transportation Equipment	742097	351460	211.1	520519
电气机械及器材制造业	Electric Equipment and Machinery	688746	600350	114.7	367532
通信设备、计算机及其他电子设备制造业	Telecommunications Equipment, Computers and Other Electornic Equipment	264010	256233	103.0	215913
仪器仪表及文化、办公用机械制造业	Instruments, Meters, Cultural and Office Machinery	54134	58856	92.0	41753
工艺品及其他制造业	Craftworks and Other Manufacturing	122714	73201	167.6	75004
废弃资源和废旧材料回收加工业	Scrap Recycle and Processing	21839	8683	251.5	500
电力、燃气及水的生产和供应业	Production and Supply of Electricity, Gas and Water	430870	466029	92.5	365255

continued (10000 yuan)

上　年 Preceding Year	为上年(%) As Compared with the Preceding Year(%)	#萧山区 Xiaoshan	#余杭区 Yuhang	桐庐县 Tonglu	淳安县 Chun'an	建德市 Jiande	富阳市 Fuyang	临安市 Lin'an
21050	146.7	23870	7004	46	–	8750	4526	6900
19009	71.6	6284	7334	5302	–	2325	991	3225
32654	123.9	19352	19400	9626	–	6720	10206	50
61858	94.2	23017	23067	17984	–	850	143431	73387
37606	148.3	17441	14628	16675	–	1860	8855	2534
28302	105.2	10915	2500	21379	–	800	23080	–
358	808.9	896	2000	–	–	–	635	–
277943	55.8	112449	29359	22791	1256	69696	59163	31260
47778	165.2	13617	23843	740	10540	10754	78717	15292
57736	219.4	126204	–	–	–	–	1210	–
51247	202.8	–	7639	–	–	38358	15877	2244
82971	173.0	68889	67750	6311	5299	8207	24728	7609
128928	111.2	63243	65693	35867	13210	47753	42925	10861
37804	176.1	36926	10985	2676	–	5045	13008	3418
14203	280.1	36202	3585	11714	–	1650	60456	6039
198750	89.2	101453	51087	28129	1148	21643	82956	15620
305138	109.5	195781	80515	96297	2429	18360	39177	46394
222441	75.2	64189	57558	9683	4803	1621	11048	5485
305703	170.3	401373	41554	20115	8248	9251	52982	130982
353295	104.0	116725	80060	41342	19876	3316	142481	114199
187821	115.0	21944	34003	5343	1648	6250	18994	15862
40024	104.3	3651	25462	–	5200	690	6491	–
42832	175.1	33817	26030	6806	1089	15730	18160	5925
700	71.4	–	500	–	–	–	19739	1600
374701	97.5	34637	8725	11968	6945	9444	36238	1020

7－08 分县(市)房地产开发
Real Estate Development

指标	Item	全市 Total			市区 Urban District
		2010年	上年 Preceding Year	为上年(%) As Compared with the Preceding Year(%)	2010年
房地产开发投资额 (万元)	**Investment in Real Estate Development (10000 yuan)**	**9561970**	**7046752**	**135.7**	**8486495**
住宅 (万元)	Residential Buildings (10000 yuan)	6762737	5096425	132.7	5929013
办公楼 (万元)	Office Buildings (10000 yuan)	808391	722468	111.9	789234
商业营业用房 (万元)	Buildings for Commercial Business (10000 yuan)	692440	499939	138.5	579908
其他 (万元)	Others (10000 yuan)	1298402	727920	178.4	1188340
房屋建筑面积	**Floor space of Buildings**				
施工面积 (万平方米)	Under Construction (10000 sq. m)	6227.05	5151.62	120.9	5342.90
其中:住宅 (万平方米)	#Residential Buildings (10000 sq. m)	4249.18	3676.04	115.6	3571.80
新开工面积(万平方米)	Beginning to Construction Floor Space (10000 sq. m)	1929.08	1092.00	176.7	1562.10
其中:住宅 (万平方米)	#Residential Buildings (10000 sq. m)	1267.43	769.95	164.6	979.39
竣工面积 (万平方米)	Construction Completed (10000 sq. m)	1100.18	836.95	131.5	915.28
其中:住宅 (万平方米)	#Residential Buildings (10000 sq. m)	802.29	626.64	128.0	661.53
商品房销售情况	**Selling of Buildings**				
销售金额 (万元)	Total Sales of Buildings (10000 yuan)	13967706	15372226	90.9	12220188
其中:住宅 (万元)	#Residential Buildings (10000 yuan)	11372940	13949554	81.5	9814582
现房销售额 (万元)	Selling of Completed Buildings (10000 yuan)	1054803	1383771	76.2	862126
其中:住宅 (万元)	#Residential Buildings (10000 yuan)	458537	959299	47.8	329562
期房销售金额 (万元)	Selling of Futures Buildings (10000 yuan)	12912903	13988455	92.3	11358062
其中:住宅 (万元)	#Residential Buildings (10000 yuan)	10914403	12990255	84.0	9485020
销售面积 (万平方米)	Floor Space of Buildings Sold (10000 sq. m)	988.34	1456.38	67.9	758.93
其中:住宅 (万平方米)	#Residential Buildings (10000 sq. m)	797.59	1314.38	60.7	593.05
现房销售面积(万平方米)	Floor Space of Completed Buildings Sold (10000 sq. m)	118.34	166.02	71.3	82.59
其中:住宅 (万平方米)	#Residential Buildings (10000 sq. m)	64.47	121.05	53.3	39.37
期房销售面积(万平方米)	Floor Space of Futures Buildings Sold (10000 sq. m)	870.00	1290.37	67.4	676.33
其中:住宅 (万平方米)	#Residential Buildings (10000 sq. m)	733.12	1193.33	61.4	553.67

投资情况(2010年)
by Region(2010)

上年 Preceding Year	为上年(%) As Compared with the Preceding Year(%)	#萧山区 Xiaoshan	#余杭区 Yuhang	桐庐县 Tonglu	淳安县 Chun'an	建德市 Jiande	富阳市 Fuyang	临安市 Lin'an
6261562	**135.5**	**746834**	**1208424**	**250828**	**213981**	**100369**	**290919**	**219378**
4458247	133.0	489054	992485	204615	152972	73351	229984	172802
716222	110.2	88366	26656	11063	170	–	4289	3635
429310	135.1	69919	54227	30289	25311	14467	30361	12104
657783	180.7	99495	135056	4861	35528	12551	26285	30837
4445.05	120.2	707.16	1341.51	199.58	135.26	99.03	238.30	211.98
3134.50	114.0	441.58	1074.34	160.93	83.60	74.65	187.90	170.30
948.59	164.7	230.56	447.24	101.65	39.32	29.55	79.76	116.70
653.53	149.9	116.40	318.00	85.03	23.21	25.30	61.63	92.87
634.33	144.3	110.17	167.73	57.63	16.45	21.20	48.80	40.82
474.13	139.5	79.50	141.96	45.30	16.14	11.70	37.35	30.27
13814248	88.5	1158856	2576979	309412	254667	189106	592825	401508
12539126	78.3	901860	2284518	277436	250297	151745	530243	348637
1116894	77.2	113816	157289	81128	5224	19470	38545	48310
747121	44.1	93734	101244	65531	5012	10266	21306	26860
12697354	89.5	1045040	2419690	228284	249443	169636	554280	353198
11792005	80.4	808126	2183274	211905	245285	141479	508937	321777
1207.09	62.9	110.74	227.24	56.30	21.30	31.84	55.95	64.02
1088.94	54.5	86.09	192.36	50.02	20.83	27.88	49.86	55.95
104.96	78.7	20.97	19.96	15.57	0.41	3.34	4.89	11.54
69.52	56.6	17.25	13.01	12.14	0.40	2.43	3.15	6.98
1102.13	61.4	89.76	207.28	40.74	20.89	28.50	51.06	52.48
1019.43	54.3	68.83	179.35	37.88	20.43	25.45	46.72	48.97

7－09 分县(市)限额以上农村

Super－Scale Rural Investment

单位:万元

指标	Item	全市 Total 2010年	全市 Total 上年 Preceding Year	全市 Total 为上年(%) As Compared with the Preceding Year(%)	市区 Urban District 2010年
本年完成投资额	**Total Investment of the Year**	**5157149**	**3870719**	**133.2**	**3029808**
按行业分	**Grouped by Sector**				
农林牧渔业	Farming, Forestry, Animal Husbandry and Fishery	41959	29346	143.0	12988
采矿业	Mining & Quarrying	46887	32838	142.8	8012
制造业	Manufacturing	3345482	2822284	118.5	1740658
电力、燃气及水的生产和供应业	Production and Supply of Electricity, Gas and Water	219132	166768	131.4	137982
建筑业	Construction	5586	680	821.5	5586
交通运输、仓储及邮政业	Transportation, Storage, Post & Telecommunications	273556	134185	203.9	194772
信息传输、计算机服务和软件业	Information Transmission, Computer Services and Software	11857			9491
批发和零售业	Wholesale & Retail Trade	62175	42628	145.9	49057
住宿和餐饮业	Lodging and Catering	68104	69525	98.0	40829
金融业	Banking and Insurance	1300	200	650.0	1300
房地产业	Real Estate	418392	205587	203.5	327703
租赁和商务服务业	Renting and Busyness Service	26523	8962	295.9	21689
科学研究、技术服务和地质勘查业	Scientific Research, Technical Service and Geological Prospecting	19876	5839	340.4	19876
水利、环境和公共设施管理业	Water Conservancy, Enviroment and Public Utility	470097	283267	166.0	345943
居民服务和其他服务业	Service for the Residents and Other Service Sector	8581	6931	123.8	3970
教育	Education	99146	35986	275.5	94897
卫生、社会保障和社会福利业	Health Care, Sports & Social Welfare	5048	5821	86.7	5048
文化、体育和娱乐业	Culture, Sports and Entertainment	19998	10786	185.4	1300
公共管理和社会组织	Public Management and Social Organizations	13450	9086	148.0	3088
国际组织	International Organizations				
房屋建筑施工面积(万平方米)	**Floor Space of Buildings Under Construction (10000sq. m)**	**2063.45**	**1470.99**	**140.3**	**1350.75**
其中:住宅	Residential Buildings	211.41	163.97	128.9	145.25
房屋建筑竣工面积(万平方米)	**Floor Space of Buildings Completed (10000sq. m)**	**669.47**	**519.39**	**128.9**	**375.61**
其中:住宅	Residential Buildings	13.66	12.17	112.2	9.87

固定资产投资完成额(2010 年)
by Region(2010)

(10000 yuan)

上 年 Preceding Year	为上年(%) As Compared with the Preceding Year(%)	#萧山区 Xiaoshan	#余杭区 Yuhang	桐庐县 Tonglu	淳安县 Chun'an	建德市 Jiande	富阳市 Fuyang	临安市 Lin'an
2329787	**130.0**	**1986942**	**928068**	**304244**	**108813**	**303897**	**838642**	**571745**
6714	193.4	9180	3808	3931		3631	17719	3690
–		7259	753	4510	3681		28587	2097
1650134	105.5	1294779	445879	236324	58150	229848	610612	469890
93675	147.3	55143	10996	8983	14865	15694	38722	2886
680	821.5	5586						
76675	254.0	74900	119872	5072	22850	9946	10935	29981
			9491	1310				1056
33083	148.3	21873	8464	1660			3289	8169
55318	73.8	35729	5100	5832			4769	11055
200	650.0	1300						
174700	187.6	237056	72031	1845	1180	29152	58012	500
5411	400.8	8935	12754	4834				
5204	381.9	6349	13527					
188543	183.5	191781	154162	14656	3654	12152	62057	31635
6030	65.8	3970				935		3676
23116	410.5	25134	69763			650	2249	1350
2495	202.3	4330	718					
2605	49.9	1300		12986	2012	700		3000
6410	48.2	300			2012			
		2338	750	2301	2421	1189	1691	2760
965.2	**139.9**	**769.45**	**542.42**	**111.86**	**16.67**	**125.98**	**311.87**	**146.32**
89.55	162.2	109.62	1.49	0.14	0.43	2.31	63.33	–
281.08	**133.6**	**263.52**	**107.35**	**49.68**	**6.66**	**83.30**	**89.68**	**64.54**
1.44	685.1	9.87	–	0.14	0.07	–	3.58	–

7-10 房屋建筑面积及造价(2010 年)
Floor Space of Buildings and Their Cost(2010)

指　　标	Item	施工面积(万平方米) Floor Space of Buildings Under Construction (10000 sq. m)	竣工面积(万平方米) Floor Space of Buildings Completed (10000 sq. m)	竣工房屋的价值(万元) Value of Buildings Completed (10000 yuan)	每平方米造价(元) Cost Per Square Meter (yuan)
全　　市	**Total**				
房屋建筑面积合计	**Floor Space of Buildings**	**12971.81**	**2695.90**	**5274936**	**1957**
#住宅	#Residential Buildings	5534.10	902.57	2285285	2532
房地产开发	Real Estate Development	6227.05	1100.18	2966946	2697
#住宅	#Residential Buildings	4249.18	802.29	2128177	2653
市　　区	**Urban District**				
房屋建筑面积合计	**Floor Space of Buildings**	**10738.49**	**1983.33**	**4255543**	**2146**
#住宅	#Residential Buildings	4759.75	732.55	1927150	2631
房地产开发	Real Estate Development	5342.91	915.27	2546314	2782
#住宅	#Residential Buildings	3571.79	661.52	1813056	2741
#萧 山 区	**Xiaoshan**				
房屋建筑面积合计	**Total Floor Space of Buildings**	**2034.47**	**515.54**	**717532**	**1392**
#住宅	#Residential Buildings	609.32	92.65	267396	2886
房地产开发	Real Estate Development	707.16	110.17	336648	3056
#住宅	#Residential Buildings	441.58	79.50	253216	3185
余 杭 区	**Yuhang**				
房屋建筑面积合计	**Total Floor Space of Buildings**	**2460.43**	**349.69**	**510843**	**1461**
#住宅	#Residential Buildings	1161.80	146.09	262444	1796
房地产开发	Real Estate Development	1341.51	167.73	306762	1829
#住宅	#Residential Buildings	1074.34	141.96	257286	1812

注:本表为限额以上口径。

a) Data in this table refer to super-scale investments.

7－10 续表 continued

指 标	Item	施工面积（万平方米）Floor Space of Buildings Under Construction (10000 sq. m)	竣工面积（万平方米）Floor Space of Buildings Completed (10000 sq. m)	竣工房屋的价值（万元）Value of Buildings Completed (10000 yuan)	每平方米造价（元）Cost Per Square Meter (yuan)
桐庐县	**Tonglu**				
房屋建筑面积合计	**Total Floor Space of Buildings**	**496.58**	**184.86**	**252877**	**1368**
#住宅	#Residential Buildings	161.14	45.51	69398	1525
房地产开发	Real Estate Development	199.58	57.63	90827	1576
#住宅	#Residential Buildings	160.93	45.30	69103	1525
淳安县	**Chunán**				
房屋建筑面积合计	**Total Floor Space of Buildings**	**241.94**	**60.78**	**101413**	**1668**
#住宅	#Residential Buildings	96.09	24.25	62775	2589
房地产开发	Real Estate Development	135.26	16.45	52710	3204
#住宅	#Residential Buildings	83.60	16.14	51893	3215
建德市	**Jiande**				
房屋建筑面积合计	**Total Floor Space of Buildings**	**325.81**	**163.96**	**178628**	**1089**
#住宅	#Residential Buildings	90.03	24.77	44089	1780
房地产开发	Real Estate Development	99.03	21.20	53534	2525
#住宅	#Residential Buildings	74.65	11.70	23453	2004
富阳市	**Fuyang**				
房屋建筑面积合计	**Total Floor Space of Buildings**	**738.93**	**182.92**	**250234**	**1368**
#住宅	#Residential Buildings	256.79	45.22	95535	2112
房地产开发	Real Estate Development	238.30	48.80	108221	2218
#住宅	#Residential Buildings	187.90	37.35	84334	2258
临安市	**Linán**				
房屋建筑面积合计	**Total Floor Space of Buildings**	**430.07**	**120.04**	**236241**	**1968**
#住宅	#Residential Buildings	170.30	30.27	86338	2852
房地产开发	Real Estate Development	211.98	40.82	115340	2825
#住宅	#Residential Buildings	170.30	30.27	86338	2852

7-11 固定资产投资新增生产能力(或效益)(2010年)

The New Productive Capacity or Facilities Created by Investment in Fixed Assets(2010)

指　　标	Item	全　市 Total	市　区 Urban District
水泥 (万吨/年)	Cement (10000tons/year)	361.6	150
化学农药原药 (吨/年)	Chemical Pesticide(TC) (tons/year)	3000	-
塑料树脂及共聚物 (吨/年)	Plastic Resins and Copolymers (tons/year)	53000	47000
化学纤维 (万吨/年)	Chemical Fiber (10000tons/year)	406735	406725
其中:合成纤维 (万吨/年)	Of Which:Synthetic fiber (10000tons/year)	400225	400225
棉纺锭 (锭)	Cotton Spindles (spindles)	49480	49280
火力发电 (万千瓦)	Thermal Power Generation (10000kilowatt)	1.8	-
水力发电 (万千瓦)	Hydroelectric Power Generation (10000kilowatt)	0.31	-
输电线路长度(11万伏及以上) (千米)	Length of Electricity Transmission Line (110000volts and above) (km)	226.1	226.1
新建公路 (公里)	New Highway (km)	47.94	47.94
改建公路 (公里)	Revamped Highway (km)	209.19	44.42
城市污水处理能力 (万吨/每日)	Urban Sewage Treatment Capacity (10000tons/day)	2.4	-

注:本表为城镇50万元以上固定资产投资项目和农村非农户50万元以上建设项目。
a) Data in this table refer to cities and towns more than 500,000 yuan in fixed assets investment projects and rural non-farm households more than 500,000 yuan construcion projects.

主要统计指标解释

固定资产投资完成额 固定资产投资完成额是以货币表现的建造和购置固定资产的工作量以及与此有关的费用的总称。它是反映固定资产投资规模、速度、比例关系和使用方向的综合性指标。

房地产开发投资 包括各种经济类型的房地产开发公司、商品房建设公司及其他房地产开发单位统一开发的包括统代建、拆迁还建的住宅、厂房、仓库、饭店、宾馆、度假村、写字楼、办公楼等房屋建筑物和配套的服务设施、土地开发工程,如道路、给水、排水、供电、供热、通讯、平整场地等基础设施工程的投资。包括非房地产企业实际从事房地产开发或经济活动,不包括单纯的土地交易活动。

施工和竣工房屋建筑面积 房屋建筑面积是从房屋外墙线算起的各层平面面积的总和,包括房屋结构(如柱、墙)占用的面积和地下室面积。多层建筑按各自然层面积总和计算,包括房屋内的楼隔层,突出墙面的眺望间、门斗、有柱雨罩的面积。不包括突出墙面结构的构件、艺术装饰等所占的面积,如台阶等。凹阳台、挑阳台按其水平投影面积一半计算建筑面积。

房屋新开工面积 指在报告期内新开工建设的房屋面积。不包括上期跨入报告期继续施工的房屋面积和上期停缓建而在本期恢复施工的房屋面积。房屋的开工应以房屋正式开始破土刨槽(地基处理或打永久桩)的日期为准。

商品房销售面积 指报告期内出售商品房屋的合同总面积(即双方签署的正式买卖合同中所确定的建筑面积)。由现房销售建筑面积和期房销售建筑面积两部分组成。

(1)现房销售面积:是指在报告期内正式签订买卖合同、已经竣工达到入住条件的商品房屋建筑面积。包括以一次性付款方式和分期付款方式销售的现房建筑面积。

(2)期房销售面积:是指在报告期内正式签订买卖合同、正在建设尚未竣工交付使用的商品房屋建筑面积。包括以一次性付款方式和分期付款方式销售的商品房屋建筑面积。期房销售建筑面积竣工后不再转为现房销售建筑面积。

新增固定资产 指通过投资活动所形成的新的固定资产价值。包括已经建成投入生产或交付使用的工程价值和达到固定资产标准的设备、工具、器具的价值及有关应摊入的费用。它是以价值形式表示的固定资产投资成果的综合性指标,可以综合反映不同时期、不同部门、不同地区的固定资产投资成果。

Explanatory Notes on Main Statistical Indicators

Total Investment in Fixed Assets refer to the volume of activities in construction and purchases of fixed assets in monetary terms and other relative expenses. It is a comprehensive indicator which shows the size, pace, proportional relations and use orientation of investment in fixed assets.

Investment in Real Estate Development include the investment by the real estate development companies, commercial buildings construction companies and other real estate development units of various types of ownership in the construction of house buildings, such as residential buildings, factory buildings, warehouses, hotels, guesthouses, holiday supply, water drainage, power supply, heating, telecommunications, land leveling and other projects of infrastructure, it excludes the activities in simple land transaction.

Floor space of Building Under Construction and Completed refer to total floor space in each story of buildings calculate from the outside line of building walls, including the space occupied by construction like pillars or walls and basements. The floor space of multi – story building includes the total floor space of each story, including area occupied by separating walls, watching rooms, door – ways, and pillars, but excluding protruding wall structures, artistic decoration, etc. (for example, flight of steps). The space of balcony is counted by half of the projection area.

Beginning to Construction Floor Space of Building refer to the area space which constructed in report period, not including the floor whose construction lasted to report period and which stopped in the last period to continue construction in the report period. And the beginning of construction of floor space should base on the date of breaking the earth(disposal the basement or piling).

Selling of the Commercial Building refer to the total area that sold by contract(which reflected in the contract), which include completed and future buildings.

(1) Floor Space of Completed Building: refer to the area which formal contract has been signed and which has been completed and reached the condition of living, including payment in one time and installment payment.

(2) Floor Space of Future Building: refer to the area which signed by formal contract and under constructing, including payment in one time and installment payment. Which can not be turned into completed building's sale when they completed.

Newly Increased Fixed Assets refer to the newly increased value of fixed assets through investment, including the value of projects completed and put into production, the value of equipment, tools, and vessels considered as fixed assets, as well as the relevant expenses as investment in fixed assets. This is a comprehensive indicator of investment in fixed assets, reflecting the achievements of investment in fixed assets in different periods, different sectors, and different regions.

第八篇
CHAPTER-8

国内商业

Domestic Trade

国 内 商 业
Domestic Trade

主 要 统 计 指 标
Major Statistical Indicators

社会消费品零售总额	Total Retail Sales of Consumer Goods	2146.08	亿元	(100 million yuan)
为上年	As Compared with the Preceding Year	119.9	%	(%)
批发和零售贸易业	Wholesale and Retail Trade	1917.12	亿元	(100 million yuan)
为上年	As Compared with the Preceding Year	120.1	%	(%)
住宿和餐饮业	Lodging and Catering	228.96	亿元	(100 million yuan)
为上年	As Compared with the Preceding Year	118.4	%	(%)

8－01 主要年份社会消费品零售总额

Total Retail Sale of Consumer Goods in Main Years

单位:万元 （10,000 yuan）

年 份 Year	全 市 Total	市 区 Urban District	县(市)合计 All Counties
1978	119509	73653	45856
1979	150462	93342	57120
1980	205381	128440	76941
1981	236188	148152	88036
1982	251068	154582	96486
1983	273664	169508	104156
1984	343722	215901	127821
1985	478117	308901	169216
1986	557963	360479	197484
1987	657838	426745	231093
1988	866373	557374	308999
1989	927019	600816	326203
1990	981713	650278	331435
1991	1155476	777559	377917
1992	1408525	928586	479939
1993	1901509	1300037	601472
1994	2616477	1733572	882905
1995	2993250	1930140	1063110
1996	3478156	2310619	1167537
1997	3815537	2537537	1278000
1998	4178013	2794171	1383842
1999	4574924	3053983	1520941
2000	5146789	3436536	1710253
2001	5790138	4993078	797060
2002	6606548	5701707	904841
2003	7425760	6401970	1023790
2004	8554476	7385662	1168814
2005	9784275	8440559	1343716
2006	11191900	9630210	1561690
2007	13082930	11247539	1835391
2008	15775872	13542665	2233207
2009	18049303	15498990	2550313
2010	21460790	18432319	3028471

注:1. 从2001年起市区数据包括萧山区和余杭区。

2. 2010年零售额口径范围有调整,增幅按同口径计算。

a) Data of urban district include Xiaoshan and Yuhang district since 2001.

b) The statistical coverage of total retail sale in 2010 has been adjusted, but the increase was calculated at the same statistical coverage.

8－02 主要年份分县(市)

Total Retail Sale of Consumer Goods

单位:万元

年 份 Year	全 市 Whole Municipality		市 区 Urban District		
	合 计 Total	为上年(%) As Compared with the Preceding Year(%)	合 计 Total	为上年(%) As Compared with the Preceding Year(%)	#萧山区 Xiaoshan
1978	119509	112.5	73653	115.8	12985
1979	150462	125.9	93342	127.2	16270
1980	205381	136.5	128440	138.1	22292
1981	236188	115.0	148152	115.6	25297
1982	251068	106.3	154582	103.3	29007
1983	273664	109.0	169508	110.1	32136
1984	343722	125.6	215901	128.4	41210
1985	478117	139.1	308901	145.2	51879
1986	557963	116.7	360479	116.8	61421
1987	657838	117.9	426745	118.6	73159
1988	866373	131.7	557374	130.1	101227
1989	927019	107.0	600816	108.3	103419
1990	981713	105.9	650278	109.5	111757
1991	1155476	117.7	777559	120.4	123753
1992	1408525	121.9	928586	118.3	153254
1993	1901509	135.0	1300037	134.4	195472
1994	2616477	137.6	1733572	132.2	299072
1995	2993250	114.4	1930140	118.2	339447
1996	3478156	116.2	2310619	120.9	390364
1997	3815537	109.7	2537537	109.9	431742
1998	4178013	109.5	2794171	110.5	470599
1999	4574924	109.5	3053983	109.3	520482
2000	5146789	112.5	3436536	112.8	602198
2001	5790138	113.6	4993078	113.9	690721
2002	6606548	114.1	5701707	114.2	795711
2003	7425760	112.4	6401970	112.3	929390
2004	8554476	115.2	7385662	115.4	1069728
2005	9784275	114.4	8440559	114.3	1234568
2006	11191900	114.4	9630210	114.1	1462157
2007	13082930	116.9	11247539	116.8	1721511
2008	15775872	120.6	13542665	120.4	2059811
2009	18049303	114.4	15498990	114.4	2376949
2010	21460790	119.9	18432319	120.1	2839433

注:1. 从2001年起市区数据包括萧山区和余杭区。
2. 2010年零售额口径范围有调整,增幅按同口径计算。

社会消费品零售总额
by Region in Main Years

(10000 yuan)

#余杭区 Yuhang	桐庐县 Tonglu	淳安县 Chun'an	建德市 Jiande	富阳市 Fuyang	临安市 Lin'an
11472	3536	3507	4390	5209	4757
14439	4283	4274	5300	6435	6119
19917	5501	5225	7119	8661	8226
22172	6456	6201	7970	10226	9714
23435	7101	6663	8562	11016	10702
23496	7694	7168	9380	12307	11975
29292	9235	8331	10770	14972	14011
39798	11826	11081	14687	21013	18932
47499	13217	12525	15832	23400	23590
53005	17394	14449	18076	27939	27071
64653	24390	18944	23545	42601	33639
74044	23029	19014	23138	48836	34723
69360	23141	18764	23820	45364	39229
84399	26350	20950	25107	52807	44551
110075	34110	23983	30770	74865	52882
149128	44909	28038	40237	76162	67526
212955	69025	34179	54562	101829	111283
255972	93736	42143	70570	127592	133650
266467	104234	51794	77620	146348	130710
294446	114032	58994	83837	163324	131625
321241	123154	67136	93169	171654	136889
352723	135223	74293	103417	185730	149073
397166	148745	81054	115062	198917	167111
446812	166892	90133	128754	223782	187499
508919	188087	101581	144849	254887	215437
584748	209153	114990	163244	289297	247106
674799	237598	130974	185772	331534	282936
778848	272394	149456	212138	382960	326768
906960	317484	173272	247425	450365	373144
1064956	371057	201769	288873	526750	446942
1302135	451356	244069	350854	643169	543759
1499377	516037	278356	400157	734925	620838
1767194	608722	328351	484678	871296	735424

a) Data of urban district include Xiaoshan and Yuhang district since 2001.

b) The statistical coverage of total retail sale in 2010 has been adjusted, but the increase was calculated at the same statistical coverage.

8－03 社会消费品

Total Retail Sale of

单位:万元

地　区	Region	合　计 Total
全　市	**Total**	**21460790**
市　区	Urban District	18432319
上城区	Shangcheng	1820811
下城区	Xiacheng	4537447
江干区	Jianggan	1882775
拱墅区	Gongshu	2350069
西湖区	Xihu	2356288
高新(滨江)区	Hi－Tech(Binjiang)	399629
萧山区	Xiaoshan	2839433
余杭区	Yuhang	1767194
桐庐县	Tonglu	608722
淳安县	Chun′an	328351
建德市	Jiande	484678
富阳市	Fuyang	871296
临安市	Lin′an	735424

零售总额(2010年)
Consumer Goods(2010)

(10000 yuan)

按销售分 By Location		按行业分 By sector	
城镇零售额 City	乡村零售额 County	批发和零售贸易业 Wholesale and Retail Trades	住宿和餐饮业 Hotels and Catering Services
20742366	**718424**	**19171194**	**2289596**
18432319	–	16548341	1883977
1820811	–	1532946	287865
4537447	–	4332563	204884
1882775	–	1751038	131738
2350069	–	2228813	121256
2356288	–	2016075	340213
399629	–	363988	35641
2839433	–	2494784	344649
1767194	–	1525004	242191
435398	173324	534236	74486
226207	102145	277111	51241
442384	42294	430520	54158
751089	120207	750009	121287
454970	280454	630976	104448

8-04 全市限额以上批发零售贸易企业商品销售总额按登记注册类型分(2010年)

Sales of Wholesale and Retail Trade Above Designated Size by Status of Registration(2010)

单位:万元 (10000 yuan)

项目	Item	法人企业(个) Number of Enterprises (unit)	销售总额 Total Sales	批发额 Wholesale	零售额 Retail
总计	**Total**	**3135**	**102672522**	**88484379**	**14188143**
1.内资企业	**Domestic - funded Enterprises**	**3061**	**99668671**	**87460180**	**12208491**
国有企业	State - owned Enterprises	84	9073412	8624961	448451
集体企业	Collective - owned Enterprises	29	775936	699455	76481
股份合作企业	Cooperative Enterprises	5	46485	42921	3564
联营企业	Joint Ownership Enterprises	16	284638	75509	209129
国有联营企业	State Joint Ownership Enterprises	3	37686	11877	25809
集体联营企业	Collective Joint Ownership Enterprises	2	49810	46247	3563
国有与集体联营企业	Joint State - collective Enterprises	10	194774	15017	179757
其他联营企业	Other Joint Ownership Enterprises	1	2369	2369	-
有限责任公司	Limited Liability Corporations	846	43279165	36550811	6728354
国有独资公司	State - funded Corporations	7	105163	87909	17253
其他有限责任公司	Other Limited Liability Corporations	839	43174002	36462902	6711100
股份有限公司	Share - holding Corporations Ltd.	98	11887627	9195733	2691894
私营企业	Private Enterprises	1975	34220634	32170016	2050619
私营独资企业	Private - funded Enterprises	63	693766	620900	72866
私营合伙企业	Private Partnership Enterprises	11	146462	118992	27470
私营有限责任公司	Private Limited Liability Corporations	1841	32419670	30564987	1854683
私营股份有限公司	Private Share - holding Corporations Ltd.	60	960737	865136	95601
其他企业	Other Enterprises	8	100774	100774	-
2.港、澳、台商投资企业	**Enterprises With Investment from Hong Kong, Macao and Taiwan**	**27**	**944434**	**482555**	**461879**
合资经营企业(港或澳、台资)	Joint - venture Enterprises (With Funds from Hong Kong, Macao and Taiwan)	12	311700	93757	217943
合作经营企业(港或澳、台资)	Coorperative Enterprises (With Funds from Hong Kong, Macao and Taiwan)	1	64941	-	64941
港、澳、台商独资经营企业	Enterprises With Sole Investment from Hong Kong, Macao and Taiwan	13	561588	388799	172790
港、澳、台商投资股份有限公司	Share - holding Corporations Ltd. With Investment from Hong Kong, Macao and Taiwan	1	6205	-	6205
3.外商投资企业	**Enterprises With Foreign Investment**	**47**	**2059417**	**541644**	**1517773**
中外合资经营企业	Joint - venture Enterprises	14	774247	315342	458905
中外合作经营企业	Cooperation Enterprises	2	14042	-	14042
外资企业	Enterprises With Sole Foreign Investment	29	1260218	216989	1043228
外商投资股份有限公司	Share - holding Corporations Ltd. With Foreign Investment	2	10911	9313	1598

8-05 全市限额以上批发零售贸易企业商品销售总额按国民经济行业分(2010年)
Sales of Wholesale and Retail Trade Above Designated Size by Sector(2010)

单位:万元 (10000 yuan)

项目	Item	法人企业(个) Number of Enterprises (unit)	销售总额 Total Sales	批发额 Wholesale	零售额 Retail
总计	**Total**	**3135**	**102672522**	**88484379**	**14188143**
一、批发业	**Wholesale**	**2523**	**90194245**	**87101520**	**3092725**
农畜产品批发业	Wholesale of Farm and Animal Products	33	696683	692508	4175
食品、饮料及烟草制品批发	Wholesale of Food, Beverages and Tobaccos	127	7609441	7572666	36774
纺织品、服装和鞋、帽批发业	Wholesale of Textile Products, Garments, Shoes and Caps	474	8900205	8811783	88422
文化、体育用品及器材批发	Wholesale of Cultural and Sports Goods	68	1431958	1415368	16590
医药及医疗器材批发	Wholesale of Medicines and Medical Appliances	89	4011809	2490802	1521007
矿产品、建材及化工产品批发	Wholesale of Mineral Products, Building and Chemical Materials	1228	54013657	52797732	1215925
机械设备、五金交电及电子产品批发	Wholesale of Machinery, Hardware and Electronic Products	441	11411011	11201180	209831
其中:汽车、摩托车及零配件批发	Wholesale of Automobiles, Motorcycle and Parts	54	3124758	3029659	95099
其他批发	Other	60	2100047	2100047	-
二、零售业	**Retail Trade**	**612**	**12478278**	**1382859**	**11095418**
综合零售	Comprehensive Retail Trade	86	3214518	371718	2842800
食品、饮料及烟草制品专门零售	Specialism Retail of Food, Beverages and Tobaccos	19	125286	10242	115044
纺织品、服装和鞋、帽专门零售	Specialism Retail of Textile Products, Garments, Shoes and Caps	32	195724	29885	165839
文化、体育用品及器材专门零售	Specialism Retail of Cultural and Sports Goods	32	284896	79334	205561
医药及医疗器材专门零售	Specialism Retail of Medicines and Medical Appliances	38	258158	11131	247027
汽车、摩托车、燃料及零配件专门零售	Specialism Retail of Automobiles, Motorcycle, Fuels and Parts	318	7200992	711019	6489973
其中:汽车零售	Specialism Retail of Automobiles	190	5977578	581004	5396573
家用电器及电子产品专门零售	Specialism Retail of Household Electric Applianes, and Electronic Products	67	1020286	115208	905078
五金家具及室内装修材料专门零售	Specialism Retail of Hardware and Upholstery Materials	10	30691	-	30691
无店铺及其他零售	Other Retail Trade	10	147727	54322	93405

8－06 全市限额以上批发零售贸易企业

Main Financial Indicators of Enterprises Above Designated Size in

单位:万元

项　目	Item	企业数(个) Number of Enterprises (unit)	年末资产负债 Assets and Liabilities		
			流动资产合计 Circulating Funds	# 存　货 Inventory	固定资产原价 Orginal Value of Fixed Assets
批发、零售贸易企业总计	**Total**	**3135**	**34145031**	**5287127**	**3043500**
1.内资企业	**Domestic－funded Enterprises**	**3061**	**33108227**	**5116562**	**2783689**
国有企业	State－owned Enterprises	84	2650485	470894	276989
集体企业	Collective－owned Enterprises	29	402551	62969	28678
股份合作企业	Cooperative Enterprises	5	31545	1311	1465
联营企业	Joint Ownership Enterprises	16	62449	10201	8642
国有联营企业	State Joint Ownership Enterprises	3	6988	353	992
集体联营企业	Collective Joint Enterprises	2	32215	1460	346
国有与集体联营企业	Joint State－collective Enterprises	10	22772	8143	7282
其他联营企业	Other Joint Ownership Enterprises	1	474	245	22
有限责任公司	Limited Liability Corporations	846	13758241	2271490	1046219
国有独资公司	State－funded Corporations	7	157103	81016	17295
其他有限责任公司	Other Limited Liability Corporations	839	13601137	2190474	1028924
股份有限公司	Share－holding Corporations Ltd.	98	3551408	807140	653437
私营企业	Private Enterprises	1975	12594866	1488054	766079
私营独资企业	Private－funded Enterprises	63	361636	36241	24947
私营合伙企业	Private Partnership Enterprises	11	42199	5268	5420
私营有限责任公司	Private Limited Liability Corporations	1841	11619641	1374892	700751
私营股份有限公司	Private Share－holding Corporations Ltd.	60	571391	71654	34961
其他企业	Other Enterprises	8	56682	4503	2180
2.港、澳、台商投资企业	**Enterprises With Investment from Hong Kong, Macao and Taiwan**	**27**	**239420**	**48262**	**81076**
合资经营企业(港或澳、台资)	Joint－venture Enterprises (With Funds from Hong Kong, Macao and Taiwan)	12	98518	18755	31420
合作经营企业(港或澳、台资)	Coorperative Enterprises (With Funds from Hong Kong, Macao and Taiwan)	1	14803	631	12049
港、澳、台商独资经营企业	Enterprises With Sole Investment from Hong Kong, Macao and Taiwan	13	124533	28350	36569
港、澳、台商投资股份有限公司	Share－holding Corporations Ltd. With Investment from Hong Kong, Macao and Taiwan	1	1565	526	1038
3.外商投资企业	**Enterprises With Foreign Investment**	**47**	**797383**	**122303**	**178735**
中外合资经营企业	Joint－venture Enterprises	14	118430	41143	65537
中外合作经营企业	Cooperation Enterprises	2	4344	1087	8155
外资企业	Enterprises With Sole Foreign Investment	29	669376	79204	104856
外商投资股份有限公司	Share－holding Corporations Ltd. With Foreign Investment	2	5233	870	188

财务状况按登记注册类型分(2010 年)

Wholesale and Retail Sale Trade by Status of Registration(2010)

(10000 yuan)

累计折旧 Accumulated Depreciation	#本年折旧 Depreciation	资产合计 Total Assets	负债合计 Total Liabilities	所有者权益 Creditors' Equity	实收资本 Capital Hold	#国家资本 State Capital
954048	**185579**	**44091381**	**33390948**	**10700432**	**6023545**	**1017923**
871268	**167293**	**42696385**	**32473113**	**10223271**	**5652078**	**1008267**
101785	13003	3431364	2000265	1431099	365790	316852
12236	1266	565709	373198	192511	86634	–
788	30	34815	32289	2526	1493	–
4272	1076	72391	49285	23107	8313	1727
437	57	7621	3347	4275	1278	1278
287	5	33790	29167	4623	3500	–
3538	1007	30494	16496	13998	3335	449
11	7	486	276	210	200	–
342102	67677	17515448	13748574	3766873	2045776	268757
5382	2676	248341	143749	104591	31305	31305
336719	65001	17267107	13604825	3662282	2014471	237452
179466	25980	5830478	3917434	1913043	994594	419431
230143	58122	15182485	12302651	2879834	2137382	1500
4425	1187	496493	344066	152427	58060	–
1460	317	48713	43732	4981	6283	–
215671	54778	13927342	11353496	2573846	1981406	1500
8587	1840	709938	561358	148580	91634	–
477	139	63696	49418	14278	12095	–
21311	**8076**	**360176**	**177725**	**182451**	**131731**	**4250**
7719	3916	164954	73723	91232	46599	4250
7773	1113	27278	3256	24022	18975	–
5349	2578	165808	99606	66202	65220	–
470	470	2137	1141	995	937	–
61469	**10210**	**1034820**	**740110**	**294710**	**239735**	**5407**
22565	1952	191735	175277	16458	40491	5407
3554	410	12820	4562	8258	13416	–
35279	7820	824909	559309	265601	181659	–
71	29	5355	962	4394	4170	–

单位:万元　　　　8－06　续表

项　　目	Item	营业收入 Revenue of Business	其中:主营业务收入 Main Revenue of Business	主营业务成　本 Main Cost of Business	主营业务税金及附加 Main Sales Tax and Extra Charges
总　　计	**Total**	**91040440**	**89864622**	**85294180**	**175177**
1. 内资企业	**Domestic－funded Enterprises**	**88288677**	**87170442**	**82878431**	**170055**
国有企业	State－owned Enterprises	7977353	7944060	7414188	68311
集体企业	Collective－owned Enterprises	715246	708434	690933	1388
股份合作企业	Cooperative Enterprises	43616	43480	41390	24
联营企业	Joint Ownership Enterprises	244607	243984	229304	301
国有联营企业	State Joint Ownership Enterprises	32569	32569	29109	52
集体联营企业	Collective Joint Enterprises	42685	42573	41267	－
国有与集体联营企业	Joint State－collective Enterprises	166984	166473	156664	249
其他联营企业	Other Joint Ownership Enterprises	2369	2369	2264	－
有限责任公司	Limited Liability Corporations	38271785	37974492	36080778	48945
国有独资公司	State－funded Corporations	100408	99451	96217	30
其他有限责任公司	Other Limited Liability Corporations	38171377	37875041	35984560	48915
股份有限公司	Share－holding Corporations Ltd.	10866318	10178855	9585286	11996
私营企业	Private Enterprises	30077727	29985128	28748662	39047
私营独资企业	Private－funded Enterprises	616147	612228	574727	751
私营合伙企业	Private Partnership Enterprises	127181	127116	120300	67
私营有限责任公司	Private Limited Liability Corporations	28486499	28401613	27262401	36141
私营股份有限公司	Private Share－holding Corporations Ltd.	847901	844171	791234	2088
其他企业	Other Enterprises	92027	92009	87890	42
2. 港、澳、台商投资企业	**Enterprises With Investment from Hong Kong, Macao and Taiwan**	**867939**	**863082**	**787644**	**832**
合资经营企业(港或澳、台资)	Joint－venture Enterprises (With Funds from Hong Kong, Macao and Taiwan)	305300	303599	277340	359
合作经营企业(港或澳、台资)	Coorperative Enterprises (With Funds from Hong Kong, Macao and Taiwan)	59137	59137	49328	－
港、澳、台商独资经营企业	Enterprises With Sole Investment from Hong Kong, Macao and Taiwan	498193	495043	457581	461
港、澳、台商投资股份有限公司	Share－holding Corporations Ltd. With Investment from Hong Kong, Macao and Taiwan	5309	5303	3395	11
3. 外商投资企业	**Enterprises With Foreign Investment**	**1883824**	**1831097**	**1628106**	**4291**
中外合资经营企业	Joint－venture Enterprises	712818	690051	638199	1258
中外合作经营企业	Cooperation Enterprises	13187	12002	9022	27
外资企业	Enterprises With Sole Foreign Investment	1147111	1118366	971025	3006
外商投资股份有限公司	Share－holding Corporations Ltd. With Foreign Investment	10708	10679	9859	－

continued (10000 yuan)

主营业务利润 Main Profits of Business	营业费用 Expenses of Business	管理费用 Administration Cost	财务费用 Financil Cost	营业利润 Management Profits	利润总额 Total Profits	本年应付工资总额 Total Wages Payable	本年应付福利费总额 Total Welfare Expenses Payable	本年应交所得税 Income Tax
4395265	**2169340**	**1176277**	**483267**	**1240958**	**1625102**	**724713**	**40337**	**348365**
4121957	**2002456**	**1086311**	**471534**	**1178140**	**1561649**	**676103**	**37035**	**329227**
461560	76812	112249	3910	283387	300247	60136	5865	65629
16112	13700	5143	5366	763	29420	3328	204	2113
2067	1491	568	-29	172	256	370	9	60
14379	4486	1708	805	8021	9140	2595	124	2030
3408	521	208	-113	2811	2774	114	4	701
1306	158	45	768	530	681	45	4	131
9560	3746	1403	147	4692	5681	2407	116	1198
104	62	52	3	-12	5	30	-	1
1844769	994334	399010	146543	627856	744028	350810	17460	158821
3203	2087	4802	2332	-5084	2668	1837	205	16
1841566	992247	394208	144212	632940	741360	348973	17255	158804
581573	300642	199583	126763	136056	306270	109435	5976	49428
1197418	609413	366732	187421	121354	171940	148930	7338	51091
36750	21998	7915	9768	-95	285	3949	284	1555
6749	4470	1873	491	-26	-55	636	66	66
1103071	557485	342349	171436	113067	162598	136935	6618	47371
50849	25460	14595	5726	8408	9113	7411	371	2101
4077	1579	1316	753	533	349	499	60	56
74607	**37671**	**24603**	**2727**	**14364**	**15685**	**16082**	**690**	**3184**
25900	15915	6711	-223	5685	6609	6652	124	1014
9809	1810	3998	90	3567	3637	1961	274	855
37001	19509	12573	2822	5005	5329	7301	235	1290
1898	438	1321	38	107	110	169	58	26
198701	**129213**	**65364**	**9006**	**48453**	**47769**	**32528**	**2612**	**15954**
50594	48603	19431	1346	6543	6447	11187	1123	1832
2953	2948	157	31	743	262	490	63	-
144335	77296	45324	7628	41131	41048	20616	1418	14115
819	367	451	2	36	12	234	9	7

8-07 全市限额以上批发零售贸易企业

Main Financial Indicators of Enterprises Above Designated

单位:万元

项 目	Item	企业数(个) Number of Enterprises (unit)	年末资产负债 Assets and Liabilities		
			流动资产合计 Circulating Funds	# 存 货 Inventory	固定资产原价 Orginal Value of Fixed Assets
总 计	**Total**	**3135**	**34145031**	**5287127**	**3043500**
一、批发业	**Wholesale**	**2523**	**29791794**	**4153441**	**1962521**
农畜产品批发业	Wholesale of Farm and Animal Products	33	409227	52004	25445
食品、饮料、烟草制品批发	Wholesale of Food, Beverages and Tobaccos	127	2818717	317749	317586
纺织品、服装和鞋、帽批发业	Wholesale of Textile Products, Garments, Shoes and Caps	474	3401844	487484	249651
文化、体育用品及器材批发	Wholesale of Cultural and Sports Goods	68	645537	183828	82818
医药及医疗器材批发	Wholesale of Medicines and Medical Appliances	89	1261028	297739	87557
矿产品、建材及化工产品批发	Wholesale of Mineral Products, Building and Chemical Materials	1228	17038898	2249295	947613
机械设备、五金交电及电子产品批发	Wholesale of Machinery, Hardware and Electronic Products	441	3859606	548887	243579
其中:汽车、摩托车及零配件批发	Wholesale of Automobiles, Motorcycle and Parts	54	542040	80740	23191
其他批发	Other	60	314166	16157	7888
二、零售业	**Retail Trade**	**612**	**4353236**	**1133686**	**1080979**
综合零售	Comprehensive Retail Trade	86	1934358	443885	531029
食品、饮料及烟草制品专门零售	Specialism Retail of Food, Beverages and Tobaccos	19	44703	14218	7284
纺织品、服装和鞋、帽专门零售	Specialism Retail of Textile Products, Garments, Shoes and Caps	32	97477	49645	112844
文化、体育用品及器材专门零售	Specialism Retail of Cultural and Sports Goods	32	155935	69396	94282
医药及医疗器材专门零售	Specialism Retail of Medicines and Medical Appliances	38	112367	33314	14100
汽车、摩托车、燃料及零配件专门零售	Specialism Retail of Automobiles, Motorcycle, Fuels and Parts	318	1503149	417358	255354
其中:汽车零售	Specialism Retail of Automobiles	190	1356870	394617	194381
家用电器及电子产品专门零售	Specialism Retail of Household Electric Applianes, and Electronic Products	67	455008	98835	33908
五金家具及室内装修材料专门零售	Specialism Retail of Hardware and Upholstery Materials	10	16184	3538	8952
无店铺及其他零售	Other Retail Trade	10	34057	3497	23227

财务状况按国民经济行业分(2010 年)
Size in Wholesale and Retail Sale Trade by Sector(2010)

(10000 yuan)

累计折旧 Accumulated Depreciation	#本年折旧 Depreciation	资产合计 Total Assets	负债合计 Total Liabilities	所有者权益 Creditors' Equity	实收资本 Capital Hold	#国家资本 State Capital
954048	**185579**	**44091381**	**33390948**	**10700432**	**6023545**	**1017923**
648745	**127016**	**38334433**	**28982413**	**9352020**	**5118638**	**960102**
7880	3455	473513	370280	103234	50581	3305
99650	19430	3522656	2248772	1273883	422819	68313
97549	20353	4230835	3196984	1033851	578831	25862
28087	3696	962157	583376	378780	136705	76630
34398	5809	1434323	1109367	324956	184679	37341
294283	56778	22275796	17411879	4863917	2984221	706232
83422	16600	5045658	3737446	1308213	710122	37519
7933	1739	1026471	721346	305124	220710	3700
3363	853	346265	294997	51267	49181	4900
305303	**58563**	**5756947**	**4408535**	**1348412**	**904906**	**57821**
162046	26155	2584528	2035621	548907	338409	13241
3266	768	56550	34429	22122	17121	571
11788	3172	216084	190719	25364	37495	–
16350	2921	288644	202771	85873	52246	4540
5524	974	128569	101704	26865	19200	2346
83742	19329	1859370	1404377	454994	291237	29623
59912	15794	1633611	1270215	363396	229761	13004
10333	2712	540471	389390	151081	108233	–
3902	847	25545	14400	11146	17990	–
8353	1686	57186	35126	22060	22976	7500

项　目	Item	营业收入 Revenue of Business	其中:主营业务收入 Main Revenue of Business	主营业务成本 Main Cost of Business	主营业务税金及附加 Main Sales Tax and Extra Charges
总　计	**Total**	**91040440**	**89864622**	**85294180**	**175177**
一、批发业	**Wholesale**	**79897006**	**78976139**	**75405573**	**145246**
农畜产品批发业	Wholesale of Farm and Animal Products	625608	623848	592989	337
食品、饮料、烟草制品批发	Wholesale of Food, Beverages and Tobaccos	6709594	6639458	5798899	74002
纺织品、服装和鞋、帽批发业	Wholesale of Textile Products, Garments, Shoes and Caps	8386155	8361853	7799157	5626
文化、体育用品及器材批发	Wholesale of Cultural and Sports Goods	1270160	1261714	1195093	1774
医药及医疗器材批发	Wholesale of Medicines and Medical Appliances	3502291	3490686	3253089	5124
矿产品、建材及化工产品批发	Wholesale of Mineral Products, Building and Chemical Materials	47367122	46612570	45373342	24975
机械设备、五金交电及电子产品批发	Wholesale of Machinery, Hardware and Electronic Products	10156623	10107585	9503944	12883
其中:汽车、摩托车及零配件批发	Wholesale of Automobiles, Motorcycle and Parts	2692537	2689867	2558892	2537
其他批发	Other	1843641	1842616	1869607	19572
二、零售业	**Retail Trade**	**11143434**	**10888483**	**9888607**	**29932**
综合零售	Comprehensive Retail Trade	2907723	2743570	2358550	14785
食品、饮料及烟草制品专门零售	Specialism Retail of Food, Beverages and Tobaccos	109566	108129	79790	387
纺织品、服装和鞋、帽专门零售	Specialism Retail of Textile Products, Garments, Shoes and Caps	180423	171403	128121	760
文化、体育用品及器材专门零售	Specialism Retail of Cultural and Sports Goods	255334	251946	210097	3327
医药及医疗器材专门零售	Specialism Retail of Medicines and Medical Appliances	228408	225661	171356	993
汽车、摩托车、燃料及零配件专门零售	Specialism Retail of Automobiles, Motorcycle, Fuels and Parts	6396388	6366452	6022548	6664
其中:汽车零售	Specialism Retail of Automobiles	5315364	5289182	5003374	5617
家用电器及电子产品专门零售	Specialism Retail of Household Electric Appliances, and Electronic Products	906790	864494	788330	2496
五金家具及室内装修材料专门零售	Specialism Retail of Hardware and Upholstery Materials	28203	26604	19179	118
无店铺及其他零售	Other Retail Trade	130599	130224	110636	403

continued (10000 yuan)

主营业务利润 Main Profits of Business	营业费用 Expenses of Business	管理费用 Administration Cost	财务费用 Financial Cost	营业利润 Management Profits	利润总额 Total Profits	本年应付工资总额 Total Wages Payable	本年应付福利费总额 Total Welfare Expenses Payable	本年应交所得税 Income Tax
4395265	**2169340**	**1176277**	**483267**	**1240958**	**1625102**	**724713**	**40337**	**348365**
3425321	**1542871**	**899596**	**431938**	**999594**	**1352452**	**497457**	**27550**	**276902**
30522	11501	9611	4856	6022	10599	2558	246	1081
766557	304344	126009	24377	390404	483198	129309	6043	103564
557070	252487	163578	48882	125532	160322	98427	4326	30796
64847	25768	22338	204	21265	30021	10415	761	3209
232473	119110	56838	15438	78466	75093	35395	2228	16364
1214254	518331	356551	291742	198584	416237	123665	8316	84468
590759	305782	153242	36954	235287	162833	94538	5406	35444
128439	107999	14466	6910	98290	16681	11828	457	1888
-46563	5203	8001	9376	-67485	2609	2741	187	1886
969944	**626469**	**276681**	**51329**	**241363**	**272651**	**227256**	**12788**	**71463**
370235	293895	108772	9464	103506	130789	90611	5895	32796
27952	18506	5331	530	4701	4615	6108	303	1349
42522	25744	12155	6665	2161	1679	10555	398	1899
38523	23127	15149	5796	-2857	-2189	10786	945	317
53312	30782	12033	675	12485	12471	13415	666	3271
337241	147525	93385	25020	102419	105889	70781	3818	25768
280192	116158	84854	22423	85530	90115	61138	2999	21418
73668	68778	23308	2661	16044	17435	21652	484	5612
7307	5221	2189	144	568	81	935	80	31
19185	12892	4359	375	2336	1880	2414	198	420

8－08 全市限额以上住宿业和餐饮业

Main Financial Indicators of Lodging and Catering Services

单位：万元

项　　目	Item	企业数(个) Number of Enterprises (unit)	年末资产负债 Assets and Liabilities 流动资产合计 Circulating Funds	#存　货 Inventory	固定资产原价 Orginal Value of Fixed Assets
总　　计	**Total**	**761**	**1490706**	**95741**	**2040457**
(一)按登记注册类型分组	**Grouped By Registered Type**				
1. 内资企业	**Domestic－funded Enterprises**	**725**	**1057138**	**41647**	**1529613**
国有企业	State－owned Enterprises	63	109980	3829	283195
集体企业	Collective－owned Enterprises	26	17608	755	89960
股份合作企业	Cooperative Enterprises	2	893	131	1524
联营企业	Joint Ownership Enterprises	2	5584	163	6065
国有联营企业	State Joint Ownership Enterprises	－	－	－	－
集体联营企业	Collective Joint Enterprises	1	2157	81	－
国有与集体联营企业	Joint State－collective Enterprises	1	3427	82	6065
其他联营企业	Other Joint Ownership Enterprises	－	－	－	－
有限责任公司	Limited Liability Corporations	191	400827	16810	575935
国有独资公司	State－funded Corporations	4	25143	779	18786
其他有限责任公司	Other Limited Liability Corporations	187	375685	16031	557148
股份有限公司	Share－holding Corporations Ltd.	18	79855	2320	105791
私营企业	Private Enterprises	423	442392	17639	467144
私营独资企业	Private－funded Enterprises	31	9396	1050	12237
私营合伙企业	Private Partnership Enterprises	11	7034	74	9876
私营有限责任公司	Private Limited Liability Corporations	363	348125	15799	409769
私营股份有限公司	Private Share－holding Corporations Ltd.	18	77837	717	35262
其他企业	Other Enterprises	－	－	－	－
2. 港、澳、台商投资企业	**Enterprises With Investment from Hong Kong, Macao and Taiwan**	**20**	**359771**	**39088**	**410618**
合资经营企业(港或澳、台资)	Joint－venture Enterprises (With Funds from Hong Kong, Macao and Taiwan)	13	348653	38671	376633
合作经营企业(港或澳、台资)	Coorperative Enterprises (With Funds from Hong Kong, Macao and Taiwan)	－	－	－	－
港、澳、台商独资经营企业	Enterprises With Sole Investment from Hong Kong, Macao and Taiwan	7	11118	417	33985
港、澳、台商投资股份有限公司	Share－holding Corporations Ltd. With Investment from Hong Kong, Macao and Taiwan	－	－	－	－
3. 外商投资企业	**Enterprises With Foreign Investment**	**16**	**73797**	**15007**	**100226**
中外合资经营企业	Joint－venture Enterprises	6	43309	13481	54884
中外合作经营企业	Cooperation Enterprises	2	14685	248	24202
外资企业	Enterprises With Sole Foreign Investment	7	15090	1246	20966
外商投资股份有限公司	Share－holding Corporations Ltd. With Foreign Investment	1	714	31	174
(二)按国民经济行业分组	**Grouped By Sector**				
正餐	Dinner	331	336848	20966	215090
快餐	Short Order	20	38140	13153	65247
饮料及冷饮服务	Beverages and Services	16	3878	600	1619
其他餐饮业	Others	11	10516	405	4999

财务状况按注册类型、行业分(2010 年)

Enterprises Above Designated Size by Status of Registration and Sector(2010)

(10000 yuan)

累计折旧 Accumulated Depreciation	#本年折旧 Depreciation	资产合计 Total Assets	负债合计 Total Liabilities	所有者权益 Creditors' Equity	实收资本 Capital Hold	#国家资本 State Capital
790148	**118183**	**3574544**	**2489090**	**1085454**	**956033**	**267699**
588841	**85898**	**2678305**	**1845619**	**832686**	**771545**	**247493**
122365	11702	310240	162195	148044	121148	104200
38435	3712	85586	54639	30946	34936	50
465	218	2952	1833	1097	1050	–
3602	329	8186	1982	6204	6791	5691
–	–	–	–	–	–	–
–	–	2157	845	1312	1100	–
3602	329	6029	1137	4892	5691	5691
–	–	–	–	–	–	–
234778	35526	1181846	837529	344317	319237	91148
6937	1697	155626	128524	27103	35600	11600
227842	33829	1026220	709006	317214	283637	79548
48654	5078	168229	52900	115329	70818	46383
140543	29333	921268	734519	186749	217565	21
4290	816	19892	11171	8721	7742	–
2880	429	14206	13588	619	2455	–
123304	24914	769283	624547	144736	185840	21
10069	3174	117886	85214	32673	21528	–
–	–	–	–	–	–	–
159442	**17383**	**646792**	**461290**	**185502**	**112569**	**20205**
150708	15702	607877	423726	184151	98068	20205
–	–	–	–	–	–	–
8734	1681	38915	37564	1351	14502	–
–	–	–	–	–	–	–
41865	**14903**	**249447**	**182181**	**67266**	**71919**	**–**
29507	13131	115928	51240	64688	26234	–
4211	569	35486	22105	13381	18850	–
8007	1197	96930	108541	11611	25874	–
141	6	1104	295	808	960	–
69941	13245	594487	435361	159127	122505	8262
32587	13533	126664	94609	32054	25022	100
1106	145	4977	2551	2426	2375	245
2546	251	14394	6531	7864	3200	21

单位:万元　　　　8－08　续表

项　　目	Item	营业收入 Revenue of Business	主营业务收入 Main Revenue of Business	主营业务税金及附加 Business Tax and Extra Charges
总　　计	**Total**	**2476998**	**2450719**	**112642**
(一)按登记注册类型分组	**Grouped By Registered Type**			
1. 内资企业	**Domestic－funded Enterprises**	**1520964**	**1505871**	**81434**
国有企业	State－owned Enterprises	168435	165858	8382
集体企业	Collective－owned Enterprises	39344	39015	2229
股份合作企业	Cooperative Enterprises	2025	2025	116
联营企业	Joint Ownership Enterprises	8864	8864	500
国有联营企业	State Joint Ownership Enterprises	－	－	－
集体联营企业	Collective Joint Enterprises	5354	5354	305
国有与集体联营企业	Joint State－collective Enterprises	3510	3510	195
其他联营企业	Other Joint Ownership Enterprises	－	－	－
有限责任公司	Limited Liability Corporations	488756	483796	26924
国有独资公司	State－funded Corporations	18715	18480	1025
其他有限责任公司	Other Limited Liability Corporations	470041	465316	25899
股份有限公司	Share－holding Corporations Ltd.	82266	80584	3944
私营企业	Private Enterprises	731274	725730	39339
私营独资企业	Private－funded Enterprises	23798	23642	1382
私营合伙企业	Private Partnership Enterprises	6052	6041	348
私营有限责任公司	Private Limited Liability Corporations	515932	510753	29029
私营股份有限公司	Private Share－holding Corporations Ltd.	185492	185293	8581
其他企业	Other Enterprises	－	－	－
2. 港、澳、台商投资企业	**Enterprises With Investment from Hong Kong, Macao and Taiwan**	**554334**	**545526**	**10532**
合资经营企业(港或澳、台资)	Joint－venture Enterprises (With Funds from Hong Kong, Macao and Taiwan)	539367	530684	9756
合作经营企业(港或澳、台资)	Coorperative Enterprises (With Funds from Hong Kong, Macao and Taiwan)	－	－	－
港、澳、台商独资经营企业	Enterprises With Sole Investment from Hong Kong, Macao and Taiwan	14967	14842	776
港、澳、台商投资股份有限公司	Share－holding Corporations Ltd. With Investment from Hong Kong, Macao and Taiwan	－	－	－
3. 外商投资企业	**Enterprises With Foreign Investment**	**401700**	**399322**	**20677**
中外合资经营企业	Joint－venture Enterprises	339262	338148	17526
中外合作经营企业	Cooperation Enterprises	3625	3611	228
外资企业	Enterprises With Sole Foreign Investment	57452	56202	2855
外商投资股份有限公司	Share－holding Corporations Ltd. With Foreign Investment	1361	1361	68
(二)按国民经济行业分组	**Grouped By Sector**			
正餐	Dinner	721967	720037	38433
快餐	Short Order	366448	364118	18938
饮料及冷饮服务	Beverages and Services	11358	11230	615
其他餐饮业	Others	22065	21171	986

continued (10000 yuan)

主营业务利润 Main Profits of Business	营业费用 Expenses of Business	管理费用 Administration Cost	财务费用 Financial Cost	营业利润 Management Profits	利润总额 Total Profits	本年应付工资总额 Total Wages Payable	本年应付福利费总额 Total Welfare Expenses Payable	本年应交所得税 Income Tax
1202578	**651250**	**395723**	**59331**	**120247**	**148346**	**255569**	**16414**	**39028**
774373	**414035**	**316813**	**41382**	**18064**	**46975**	**179461**	**11077**	**14233**
110309	52738	50090	2144	7099	8158	28638	1778	2239
25590	13170	11908	794	57	2	5250	305	150
651	375	195	12	70	59	282	15	21
7204	2287	3323	60	1535	1545	1354	42	3
–	–	–	–	–	–	–	–	–
4652	1229	1834	53	1537	1537	1018	–	–
2553	1058	1489	8	2	8	337	42	3
–	–	–	–	–	–	–	–	–
284602	142014	126032	16553	5349	7813	67543	5915	4964
12122	6924	7842	245	2771	2781	4349	351	15
272480	135090	118190	16308	8120	10594	63194	5564	4949
42626	26046	16967	223	2264	17821	13354	782	1173
303390	177406	108298	22042	1804	11582	63040	2240	5682
9384	6267	2432	376	464	501	2469	60	135
2430	1427	882	265	133	109	554	11	51
241058	138962	96334	19496	8045	1526	47020	2101	2694
50517	30751	8649	1905	9518	9663	12997	68	2802
–	–	–	–	–	–	–	–	–
184664	**57592**	**60099**	**11966**	**62536**	**63043**	**29902**	**2632**	**13180**
175465	52979	55501	11403	63000	57602	28077	2561	13180
–	–	–	–	–	–	–	–	–
9200	4612	4598	564	465	5441	1826	71	–
–	–	–	–	–	–	–	–	–
243541	**179624**	**18812**	**5982**	**39647**	**38328**	**46205**	**2705**	**11616**
205606	149462	10326	187	45489	45232	36011	2225	11550
2724	975	2164	1174	1581	1578	926	–	–
35376	29187	6146	4600	3899	5005	8985	480	65
165	–	176	22	362	320	283	–	–
256272	168261	69999	10537	9629	27012	68282	2497	5926
219626	166041	9268	1813	43369	41744	37370	1692	11724
5682	2946	2488	112	257	298	1231	106	71
6357	2015	2378	68	2925	2888	2489	173	804

8-09 全市限额以上住宿业和餐饮业经营按登记注册类型分(2010年)

Management Conditions of Lodging and Catering Services Enterprises Above Designated Size by Status of Registration(2010)

单位:万元 (10000 yuan)

项目	Item	法人企业(个) Number of Enterprises (unit)	营业收入 Revenue of Business	#客房收入 Revenue of Guest Rooms	#餐饮收入 Revenue of Catering Services	#商品销售收入 Revenue of Goods Sales
总计	**Total**	**761**	**2060310**	**493797**	**1449526**	**18222**
1.内资企业	**Domestic-funded Enterprises**	**725**	**1504161**	**415981**	**992418**	**14878**
国有企业	State-owned Enterprises	63	168076	74592	71327	1924
集体企业	Collective-owned Enterprises	26	39323	22835	11185	541
股份合作企业	Cooperative Enterprises	2	2025	557	1467	-
联营企业	Joint Ownership Enterprises	2	8864	4727	2738	-
国有联营企业	State Joint Ownership Enterprises	-	-	-	-	-
集体联营企业	Collective Joint Enterprises	1	5354	3074	1279	-
国有与集体联营企业	Joint State-collective Enterprises	1	3510	1653	1459	-
其他联营企业	Other Joint Ownership Enterprises	-	-	-	-	-
有限责任公司	Limited Liability Corporations	191	474553	170756	261042	7739
国有独资公司	State-funded Corporations	4	18715	6750	10788	55
其他有限责任公司	Other Limited Liability Corporations	187	455838	164007	250254	7684
股份有限公司	Share-holding Corporations Ltd.	18	78862	16638	57240	1591
私营企业	Private Enterprises	423	732458	125876	587419	3083
私营独资企业	Private-funded Enterprises	31	23814	2534	20381	15
私营合伙企业	Private Partnership Enterprises	11	6174	1030	4798	95
私营有限责任公司	Private Limited Liability Corporations	363	517119	113162	387262	2940
私营股份有限公司	Private Share-holding Corporations Ltd.	18	185351	9151	174978	33
其他企业	Other Enterprises	-	-	-	-	-
2.港、澳、台商投资企业	**Enterprises With Investment from Hong Kong, Macao and Taiwan**	**20**	**154301**	**64472**	**75655**	**325**
合资经营企业(港或澳、台资)	Joint-venture Enterprises (With Funds from Hong Kong, Macao and Taiwan)	13	139334	60202	65573	256
合作经营企业(港或澳、台资)	Cooperative Enterprises (With Funds from Hong Kong, Macao and Taiwan)	-	-	-	-	-
港、澳、台商独资经营企业	Enterprises With Sole Investment from Hong Kong, Macao and Taiwan	7	14967	4270	10082	69
港、澳、台商投资股份有限公司	Share-holding Corporations Ltd. With Investment from Hong Kong, Macao and Taiwan	-	-	-	-	-
3.外商投资企业	**Enterprises With Foreign Investment**	**16**	**401849**	**13344**	**381453**	**3019**
中外合资经营企业	Joint-venture Enterprises	6	339262	4511	329514	2864
中外合作经营企业	Cooperation Enterprises	2	3625	2475	655	109
外资企业	Enterprises With Sole Foreign Investment	7	57600	6359	49924	47
外商投资股份有限公司	Share-holding Corporations Ltd. With Foreign Investment	1	1361	-	1361	-

8-10 全市限额以上住宿业和餐饮业经营按国民经济行业分(2010年)

Management Conditions of Lodging and Catering Services Enterprises Above Designated Size by Sector(2010)

单位:万元 (10000 yuan)

项 目	Item	法人企业(个) Number of Enterprises (unit)	营业收入 Revenue of Business	#客房收入 Revenue of Guest Rooms	#餐饮收入 Revenue of Catering Services	#商品销售收入 Revenue of Goods Sales
总 计	**Total**	**761**	**2060310**	**493797**	**1449526**	**18222**
住宿业	**Lodging**	**383**	**939704**	**470986**	**369522**	**11723**
旅游饭店	Restaurants for Junketing	269	834907	397078	346551	11468
一般旅馆	General Hotel	114	104797	73908	22970	256
其他住宿服务	Other Lodging	-	-	-	-	-
餐饮业	**Catering Services**	**378**	**1120606**	**22811**	**1080005**	**6499**
正餐	Dinner	331	720388	22779	682932	5813
快餐	Short Order	20	366505	-	365379	-
饮料及冷饮服务	Beverages and Services	16	11280	-	10976	166
其他餐饮业	Others Catering Services	11	22434	32	20718	520

8－11 个体工商业登记注册情况(2010 年末)

Statistics of Individual Owned Business(End of 2010)

项目	Item	全市 Whole Municipality		市区 Urban District	
		合计 Total	#城镇 Urban	合计 Total	#城镇 Urban
户数(户)	**Number of Households(household)**	**298787**	**219985**	**208184**	**172663**
农、林、牧、渔业	Farming, Forestry, Animal Husbandry and Fishery	3911	1606	2730	1330
采矿业	Mining and Quarrying	122	40	17	7
制造业	Manufacturing	21082	7760	11328	4590
电力、燃气及水的生产和供应业	Production and Supply of Electricity, Gas and Water	117	76	57	47
建筑业	Construction	834	426	496	313
交通运输、仓储和邮政业	Transportation, Storage and Post	6138	3378	3343	2143
信息传输、计算机服务和软件业	Information Transmission, Computer Services and Software	542	430	379	347
批发和零售业	Wholesale and Retail Trade & Catering Services	206734	160380	150514	129667
住宿和餐饮业	Lodging and Catering	23114	17519	14081	12320
房地产业	Real Estate	285	267	247	236
租赁和商务服务业	Renting and Business Service	2018	1637	1545	1265
居民服务和其他服务业	Service for the Residents and Other Service Sector	32005	24898	22239	19317
卫生、社会保障和社会福利业	Health Care, Sports & Social Welfare	304	222	138	120
文化、体育和娱乐业	Culture, Sports and Entertainment	1322	1120	856	772
其他行业	Others	259	226	214	189
从业人员(人)	**Employed Persons(person)**	**653057**	**463360**	**419651**	**359756**
农、林、牧、渔业	Farming, Forestry, Animal Husbandry and Fishery	9696	3459	5315	2449
采矿业	Mining and Quarrying	606	183	37	12
制造业	Manufacturing	70375	22551	26346	9825
电力、燃气及水的生产和供应业	Production and Supply of Electricity, Gas and Water	203	127	68	54
建筑业	Construction	2961	1138	1421	624
交通运输、仓储和邮政业	Transportation, Storage and Post	9008	5130	4388	2934
信息传输、计算机服务和软件业	Information Transmission, Computer Services and Software	1146	895	752	698

8-11 续表 continued

项目	Item	全市 Whole Municipality 合计 Total	全市 Whole Municipality #城镇 Urban	市区 Urban District 合计 Total	市区 Urban District #城镇 Urban
批发和零售业	Wholesale and Retail Trade & Catering Services	382299	280973	258134	228656
住宿和餐饮业	Lodging and Catering	64190	51732	38586	35067
房地产业	Real Estate	472	439	406	386
租赁和商务服务业	Renting and Business Service	36396	35625	35331	34774
居民服务和其他服务业	Service for the Residents and Other Service Sector	70287	56484	45618	41270
卫生、社会保障和社会福利业	Health Care, Sports & Social Welfare	825	647	431	400
文化、体育和娱乐业	Culture, Sports and Entertainment	3875	3364	2265	2119
其他行业	Others	718	613	553	488
注册资金(万元)	**Capital Registered(10000 yuan)**	**1632822**	**1212742**	**995630**	**833040**
农、林、牧、渔业	Farming, Forestry, Animal Husbandry and Fishery	88934	34197	52453	25535
采矿业	Mining and Quarrying	6269	1599	165	100
制造业	Manufacturing	173164	66054	80503	37237
电力、燃气及水的生产和供应业	Production and Supply of Electricity, Gas and Water	650	351	216	161
建筑业	Construction	29375	15078	16671	12491
交通运输、仓储和邮政业	Transportation, Storage and Post	56547	35156	30497	23638
信息传输、计算机服务和软件业	Information Transmission, Computer Services and Software	2848	2139	1496	1403
批发和零售业	Wholesale and Retail Trade & Catering Services	863005	719955	587826	528015
住宿和餐饮业	Lodging and Catering	178617	151345	104748	97631
房地产业	Real Estate	1035	841	945	766
租赁和商务服务业	Renting and Business Service	17476	13269	12421	9531
居民服务和其他服务业	Service for the Residents and Other Service Sector	187394	148004	93533	83141
卫生、社会保障和社会福利业	Health Care, Sports & Social Welfare	3318	2653	1484	1354
文化、体育和娱乐业	Culture, Sports and Entertainment	22806	20943	11608	11161
其他行业	Others	1384	1158	1064	876

8-12 私营企业登记注册情况(2010年末)
Statistics of Private Owned Business(End of 2010)

项目	Item	全市 Whole Municipality		市区 Urban District	
		合计 Total	#城镇 Urban	合计 Total	#城镇 Urban
户数(户)	**Number of Households(household)**	**161653**	**114987**	**134876**	**105757**
农、林、牧、渔业	Farming, Forestry, Animal Husbandry and Fishery	2121	725	1299	560
采矿业	Mining and Quarrying	193	36	32	14
制造业	Manufacturing	39947	13763	26343	10940
电力、燃气及水的生产和供应业	Production and Supply of Electricity, Gas and Water	353	76	98	39
建筑业	Construction	7778	6104	6805	5578
交通运输、仓储和邮政业	Transportation, Storage and Post	2955	2017	2603	1855
信息传输、计算机服务和软件业	Information Transmission, Computer Services and Software	9080	8532	8673	8289
批发和零售业	Wholesale and Retail Trade & Catering Services	53977	43561	47734	40916
住宿和餐饮业	Lodging and Catering	2318	1890	1914	1651
房地产业	Real Estate	4619	3574	3707	2972
租赁和商务服务业	Renting and Business Service	19797	18400	18626	17537
居民服务和其他服务业	Service for the Residents and Other Service Sector	7517	6154	6711	5663
卫生、社会保障和社会福利业	Health Care, Sports & Social Welfare	282	226	246	197
文化、体育和娱乐业	Culture, Sports and Entertainment	922	849	825	786
其他行业	Others	9794	9080	9260	8760
从业人员(人)	**Employed Persons(person)**	**1455901**	**1049141**	**1125412**	**952906**
农、林、牧、渔业	Farming, Forestry, Animal Husbandry and Fishery	13360	4862	6714	3232
采矿业	Mining and Quarrying	3118	631	693	193
制造业	Manufacturing	438769	150605	210211	114449
电力、燃气及水的生产和供应业	Production and Supply of Electricity, Gas and Water	2816	817	626	434
建筑业	Construction	75648	63265	63007	55571
交通运输、仓储和邮政业	Transportation, Storage and Post	24710	18434	19352	15108
信息传输、计算机服务和软件业	Information Transmission, Computer Services and Software	79551	76346	77767	75100

8－12 续表 continued

项 目	Item	全市 Whole Municipality 合计 Total	全市 Whole Municipality #城镇 Urban	市区 Urban District 合计 Total	市区 Urban District #城镇 Urban
批发和零售业	Wholesale and Retail Trade & Catering Services	426095	369720	386990	348101
住宿和餐饮业	Lodging and Catering	25436	22867	21189	19658
房地产业	Real Estate	37527	32506	30167	26718
租赁和商务服务业	Renting and Business Service	174306	167245	165606	160203
居民服务和其他服务业	Service for the Residents and Other Service Sector	55931	48992	50360	45278
卫生、社会保障和社会福利业	Health Care, Sports & Social Welfare	2369	1966	2008	1667
文化、体育和娱乐业	Culture, Sports and Entertainment	8476	7837	7503	7229
其他行业	Others	87789	83048	83219	79965
注册资金(万元)	**Capital Registered(10000 yuan)**	**42666019**	**31788882**	**35538401**	**28398408**
农、林、牧、渔业	Farming, Forestry, Animal Husbandry and Fishery	407094	137945	254868	101359
采矿业	Mining and Quarrying	83922	26979	16001	10807
制造业	Manufacturing	10273703	3852522	6937585	2949956
电力、燃气及水的生产和供应业	Production and Supply of Electricity, Gas and Water	89840	22920	24089	10119
建筑业	Construction	3117940	2413117	2705352	2127148
交通运输、仓储和邮政业	Transportation, Storage and Post	580788	399227	487010	363382
信息传输、计算机服务和软件业	Information Transmission, Computer Services and Software	1459819	1421967	1435248	1404431
批发和零售业	Wholesale and Retail Trade & Catering Services	9160188	7933255	8238467	7432826
住宿和餐饮业	Lodging and Catering	451813	354463	318208	263894
房地产业	Real Estate	4453080	3705243	3556887	3004250
租赁和商务服务业	Renting and Business Service	8117293	7443564	7684890	7100131
居民服务和其他服务业	Service for the Residents and Other Service Sector	1045962	882719	906378	798905
卫生、社会保障和社会福利业	Health Care, Sports & Social Welfare	44087	43091	34819	34183
文化、体育和娱乐业	Culture, Sports and Entertainment	196878	185529	176781	175188
其他行业	Others	3183612	2966341	2761818	2621829

主要统计指标解释

社会消费品零售额 指各种经济类型的批发零售贸易业、住宿餐饮业对城乡居民和社会集团的消费品零售额总和。这个指标反映通过各种商品流通渠道向居民和社会集团供应的生活消费品来满足他们生活需要，是研究人民生活，社会消费品购买力、货币流通等问题的重要指标。社会消费品零售额包括:(1)售给城乡居民作为生活用的商品和修建房屋用的建筑材料;(2)售给机关、团体、学校、部队、企业、事业单位的职工食堂各种食品、燃料;(3)售给部队干部、战士生活用的粮食、副食品、衣着品、日用品、燃料;(4)售给来华的外国人、华侨、港澳台同胞的消费品;(5)售给社会集团的办公用品、纸张、帐册、文印用品、计算工具、书刊杂志和奖品;公共用品和纺织品、针织品;学校用的教学用具;文体用品;非专用的劳动保护用品，如工作服、套袖、围裙、手套、毛巾、肥皂等;日用百货和杂品，包括职工食堂用的餐具、炊具、设备和清洁卫生工具等;家具、设备、日用电器、电讯设备、电影器材和照相器材等;取暖用的设备和燃料、防暑、降温的饮料;非生产经营用的交通工具如小轿车、面包车、工具车、卡车和油料;零星修理的各种零配件、材料、工具、建筑材料等;举办各种招待会、茶话会、宴会用的烟酒茶和各种食品及馈赠的礼品;从公费医疗经费中开支的中、西药品、中药材和医疗器材以及其他非生产性设备和用品。

限额以上批发零售贸易业 指批发贸易业主营业务收入在2000万元及以上，零售贸易业主营业务收入在500万元及以上的各种经济类型商贸企业。

商品销售总额 指对本企业(单位)以外的单位和个人出售(包括对国(境)外直接出口)的商品金额。这个指标反映批发零售贸易业在国内市场上销售商品以及出口商品的总量。商品销售总额包括:(1)售给城乡居民和社会集体团消费用的商品;(2)售给工业、农业、建筑业、运输邮电业、批发零售贸易业、餐饮业、服务业等作为生产、经营使用的商品;(3)售给批发零售贸易业作为转卖或加工后转卖的商品;(4)对国(境)外直接出口的商品，不包括:出售本企业(单位)自用的废旧包装用品，未通过买卖行为付出的商品，经本单位介绍，由买卖双方直接结算，本单位只收取手续费的业务，购货退出的商品以及商品损耗和损失等。

Explanatory Notes on Main Statistical Indicators

Total Retail Sales of Consumer Goods referring to the sum of retail sales of consumer goods sold by wholesale and retail, catering and lodging to urban and rural residents and social groups. This indicator is used to show the supply of consumer goods through various channels to households and institutions, and is very important for the study on people's livelihood, on the purchasing power of consumer goods and on the circulation of money. The retail sales of consumer goods include: (1) commodities sold to urban and rural residents for their daily use and building materials sold to them for the construction or repair of houses; (2)food and fuels sold to canteens of institutions, enterprises, schools and military units;(3) grains and non – staple food, clothing, daily articles and fuels sold to military personnel; (4)consumer goods sold to foreigners, overseas Chinese, and Chinese compatriots form Taiwan, Hong Kong and Macao during their stay in the mainland of China; (5)commodities sold to social groups. included under this heading are : office appliances, paper, account books, printing articles, calculaters, newspapers, magazines and prizes; public articles, textiles and knitgoods; realias for schools; cultural and sports articles; working articles for unspecial use i. e. working clothes, raglan sleeves, gloves, towels and soaps; commidities and miscellaneous goods for daily use i. e. dishwares, cookers and cleaning articles for canteens of institutions, enterprises, schools; furnishings, appliances, communications facilities , film and photograph equipments and materials; heating facilities, fuels and beverages; vehicles (exclude for business use) such as cars, microbuses, trucks and oils; parts , fittings, instruments and building materials, tobaccoes, alcohols, teas, foods for all kinds of reception meetings and banquets and prizes for presenting; Chinese and Western medicines, herbs and medical facilities expenditured by medical insurance fund and other non – production goods and equipments.

Wholesale And Retail Trade Above Designated Size wholesale trade,with main business revenue over 20 million yuan of different status of registration;retail sale trade,with main business revenue over 5 million yuan of different status of registration.

Total Sales of Commodities refer to selling of commodities by the establishments to other establishments and individuals (including direct export). This indictor is used to show the total value of sales of commodities at domestic markets and export. The total sales include: (1) commodities sold to urban and rural residents and social groups for their consumption; (2) commodities sold to establishments in industry, agriculture, construction, transportation, post and telecommunications, wholesale and retail trades, catering trade and public utility for their production and operation; (3) commodities sold to wholesale and retail establishment for re – selling, with or without further processing; and (4) commodities for direct export to other countries. Excluded are selling of waste packaging materials used by the establishments(units) themselves, commodities transferred without buying or selling procedures, commission income from brokerage in transactions whose settlement is directly handled by buyers and sellers, rejected commodities in the purchase, loss in commodities, etc.

对外经济、旅游

Foreign Trade And Tourism

对外经济、旅游
Foreign Trade and Tourism

主要统计指标
Major Statistical Indicators

协议利用外资金额	Total Contracted Foreign Investments	77.09	亿美元	(USD 100 million)
为上年	As Compared with the Preceding Year	110.7	%	(%)
实际利用外资金额	Foreign Investments Actually Used	43.56	亿美元	(USD 100 million)
为上年	As Compared with the Preceding Year	108.5	%	(%)
进出口总额	Total Imports and Exports	523.55	亿美元	(USD 100 million)
为上年	As Compared with the Preceding Year	129.5	%	(%)
#出口总额	Total Exports	353.37	亿美元	(USD 100 million)
为上年	As Compared with the Preceding Year	130.0	%	(%)
接待境外旅游	Number of Foreign Tourists	275.71	万人次	(10000 person-times)
为上年	As Compared with the Preceding Year	119.7	%	(%)
旅游外汇收入	Total Foreign Exchange Earnings from International Tourism	16.9	亿美元	(USD 100 million)
为上年	As Compared with the Preceding Year	122.5	%	(%)

9-01 主要年份外商直接投资情况
Foreign Direct Investment in Main Years

单位:万美元 (USD 10000)

年份 Year	项目个数(个) Number of Projects (unit)	协议总投资额 Total Investments of Agreements	协议利用外资金额 Foreign Investments of Agreements	实际利用外资金额 Foreign Investments Actually Used
1978				
1979				
1980	3	153	128	
1981				
1982				
1983	2	356	100	
1984	9	6932	2697	
1985	21	6638	1731	907
1986	9	5722	2017	683
1987	10	2685	1256	1470
1988	23	6781	2734	696
1989	34	3897	1569	1860
1990	68	7817	3951	751
1991	121	11107	5551	2129
1992	583	125224	60915	9678
1993	1078	222325	121947	35713
1994	624	174406	110541	41098
1995	427	136662	90207	42659
1996	221	108150	70982	53651
1997	174	51682	27888	41187
1998	216	98219	51400	38425
1999	212	83416	56742	42025
2000	315	89781	64548	43093
2001	483	154447	103023	50324
2002	587	247888	96720	52186
2003	869	432660	200104	100850
2004	802	629727	307746	140982
2005	756	770941	400503	171274
2006	747	1080602	537986	225536
2007	574	854907	558059	280181
2008	483	862523	622788	331154
2009	554	948323	696486	401370
2010	545	1188055	770911	435627

9－02 外商直接投资分行业情况(2010年)

Foreign Direct Investment by Sector(2010)

单位:万美元 (USD 10,000)

行业 Sector	项目数(个) Projects (unit)	占总数% Proportion (%)	合同外资 Total Contracted Foreign Investments	占总数% Proportion (%)	实际引资 Foreign Investments Actually Used	占总数(%) Proportion (%)
合计 Total	**545**	**100.0**	**770911**	**100.0**	**435627**	**100.0**
第一产业 Primary Industry	**5**	**0.92**	**4392**	**0.57**	**3874**	**0.89**
农业 Agriculture	4	0.73	2741	0.36	1700	0.39
第二产业 Secondary Industry	**247**	**45.32**	**321876**	**41.75**	**169366**	**38.88**
采矿业 Mining & Quarrying	2	0.37	6322	0.82		
制造业 Manufacturing	239	43.85	307615	39.90	165845	38.07
电子 Electronics	4	0.73	4546	0.59	1500	0.34
建筑业 Construction	2	0.37	3393	0.44	2021	0.46
第三产业 Tertiary Industry	**293**	**53.76**	**444643**	**57.68**	**262387**	**60.23**
交通运输、仓储、邮电通信业 Transportation, Storage and Post	1	0.18	5155	0.67	1146	0.26
信息传输、计算机服务和软件业 Information Transmission, Computer Service and Software	49	8.99	67128	8.71	29657	6.81
批发和零售贸易、餐饮业 Whole sale and Retail Tvade. Catering Services	90	16.51	39972	5.19	20930	4.80
房地产业 Real Estate	13	2.39	181125	23.49	168164	38.60
租赁及商务服务业 Renting and Business Service	70	12.84	78854	10.23	21550	4.95
科学研究和综合技术服务业 Scientific research and comprehensive technology Services	57	10.46	62887	8.16	17954	4.12
其他行业 Others	13	2.39	9522	1.24	2986	0.69

9－03　外商投资企业分国别(地区)情况(2010 年)

Foreign－Funded Enterprises by Region or Territory(2010)

单位:万美元　　　　(USD 10000)

国　别(地区)	Country (territory)	历年累计 Accumulated			2010 年 In Year 2010			
		项目(个) Projects (unit)	总投资额 Total Investments	协议外资金额 Total Contracted Foreign Investments	项目(个) Projects (unit)	总投资额 Total Investments	协议外资金额 Total Contracted Foreign Investments	实际引资 Foreign Investments Actually Used
合　计	**Total**	**10581**	**8318537**	**4974495**	**545**	**1188055**	**770911**	**435627**
#香港	#Hong Kong	4348	4322328	2675004	289	801688	538088	316511
澳门	Macao	66	59267	34422	2	20870	8670	719
台湾	Taiwan	1534	301591	164034	36	11410	6855	3941
日本	Japan	670	359475	182489	22	23991	13045	9263
美国	U. S. A	1395	782022	442655	57	92825	48447	20115
新加坡	Singapore	267	278601	163677	11	18327	25150	11025
澳大利亚	Australia	167	73562	42006	5	－332	－4050	675
泰国	Thailand	36	12799	3483				20
意大利	Italy	188	104346	54644	2	3094	1400	2019
荷兰	Netherlands	76	64567	20635	1	1480	－5206	2440
西班牙	Spain	61	57382	22435	2	4875	2695	318
马来西亚	Malaysia	70	28272	15650	3	573	52	81
韩国	Republic of Korea	266	77302	42762	10	9430	5621	1653
法国	France	109	64526	33812	8	2759	2636	1073
玻利维亚	Bolivia	12	1770	1262				
加拿大	Canada	174	74057	46425	9	11509	9070	4723
英国	Britain	162	159883	84846	19	24119	15889	4518
奥地利	Austria	20	13094	6612	1	3808	1284	1240
波兰	Poland	4	240	147				
洪都拉斯	Honduras	6	1118	563				
德国	Germany	176	89014	44227	5	2210	996	970
英属维尔京群岛	The British Virgin Islands	495	928176	512608	24	87328	39350	24822

9-04 外商直接投资分区县(市)情况
Foreign Direct Investment by Region

单位:万美元 (USD 10000)

区域	Region	批准项目数(个) Number of Projects(unit)		协议利用外资金额 Total Contracted Foreign Investments		实际利用外资金额 Foreign Investments Actually Used	
		2010年 In Year 2010	历年累计 Accumulated Until the End of 2010	2010年 In Year 2010	历年累计 Accumulated Until the End of 2010	2010年 In Year 2010	历年累计 Accumulated Until the End of 2010
全市	**Total**	**545**	**10581**	**770911**	**4974495**	**435627**	**2545770**
市区	Urban District	470	8759	652359	4276873	377610	2229315
上城	Shangcheng	31	544	42134	270594	13224	127375
下城	Xiacheng	36	635	43977	246730	21602	111413
江干	Jianggan	23	561	43645	278397	20152	104567
拱墅	Gongshu	22	760	57071	305732	52785	158633
西湖	Xihu	61	755	44941	279711	27232	154504
高新(滨江)区	Hi-Tech(Binjiang)	38	837	91503	522893	54817	327022
萧山	Xiaoshan	90	1264	89365	469605	47301	245683
余杭	Yuhang	75	1215	71526	420131	36880	195791
桐庐	Tonglu	19	438	21911	123555	10622	57538
淳安	Chun'an	8	158	19271	118770	9294	52656
建德	Jiande	17	200	19559	84571	2327	24796
富阳	Fuyang	23	644	34709	227780	19395	111087
临安	Lin'an	8	382	23102	142946	16379	70378

9－05 国内招商引资分区县(市)情况

Domestic Attract Investment by Region

单位:亿元 (100 million yuan)

区域	Region	批准项目数(个) Number of Projects(unit)		协议引进资金 Total Contracted Foreign Investments		实际引进资金 Foreign Investments Actually Used	
		2010 年 In Year 2010	2009 年 In Year 2009	2010 年 In Year 2010	2009 年 In Year 2009	2010 年 In Year 2010	2009 年 In Year 2009
全　市	**Total**	**5847**	**5451**	**1490.66**	**1287.02**	**650.27**	**560.55**
市　区	Urban District	5621	5133	1256.74	1090.05	552.27	475.32
上　城	Shangcheng	381	471	174.01	143.29	71.51	61.23
下　城	Xiacheng	905	876	189.04	167.78	84.73	71.71
江　干	Jianggan	351	490	157.65	139.28	73.87	62.76
拱　墅	Gongshu	2083	1796	185.84	165.03	83.21	70.54
西　湖	Xihu	990	832	144.79	124.12	71.43	64.62
高新(滨江)区	Hi－Tech(Binjiang)	276	238	139.73	121.01	66.98	57.16
萧　山	Xiaoshan	240	257	96.33	83.77	43.17	37.47
余　杭	Yuhang	148	41	84.22	74.21	32.08	28.44
桐　庐	Tonglu	69	117	46.62	39.91	19.47	16.96
淳　安	Chun'an	48	59	46.32	38.95	19.47	16.96
建　德	Jiande	50	37	46.63	39.25	19.36	16.58
富　阳	Fuyang	32	72	46.97	39.51	20.02	17.67
临　安	Lin'an	27	33	47.38	39.35	19.68	17.06

9-06 国家级开发区建设发展情况(2010年末)

The Construction of National - Class Development Zones(End of 2010)

项　目	Item	合计 Total	杭州经济技术开发区 Hangzhou Economic and Technological Development Zone	杭州高新技术开发区 Hangzhou High - tech Development Zone	杭州之江国家旅游度假区 Hangzhou Zhijiang National Tourism and Holiday Resort	萧山经济技术开发区 Xiaoshan Economic and Technological Development Zone
规划面积(平方公里)	Area of planning (sq. km)	224.74	34	12.64	156	22.1
已开发面积(平方公里)	Area of Development (sq. km)	83.48	39.93	12.64	11.15	19.76
有偿出让土地面积(平方公里)	Area of Being Sold (sq. km)	52.56	17.75	6.99	8.64	19.18
累计由开发区投入基础设施款 (亿元)	Investments in Infrastructure (100 million yuan)	439.64	205.74	131.62	36.38	65.9
年末批准进区企业(个)	Number of Enterprises Approved (unit)	8503	3764	3439	441	859
其中:三资企业 (个)	Foreign Investments Enter - prises (unit)	1682	608	480	82	512
累计协议利用外资(亿美元)	Foreign Investments of Agree-ments (USD 100 million)	183.74	78.73	53.31	13.8	37.9
累计实际利用外资(亿美元)	Foreign Investments Actually Used (USD 100 million)	103.61	41.79	31.72	8.5	21.6
年末投产企业个数(个)	Number of Enterprises in Pro-duction or Operation (unit)	5450	2100	1645	31	1674
当年销售收入(亿元)	Sales Revenue (100 million yuan)	4252.76	1515.76	1810	6	921
当年工业总产值(现价) (亿元)	Gross Industrial Output Value (100 million yuan)	3068.86	1328.62	1109.24	50	581
当年实现利税(亿元)	Fulfilled Profits and Tax (100 million yuan)	340.23	171.95	107.28		61
当年出口创汇(亿美元)	Foreign Exchange Earmings of Export (USD 100 million)	88.21	47.79	23.42		17
当年财政收入(亿元)	Financial Revenue (100 million yuan)	210.82	80.21	84.08	10.92	35.61

9-07 主要年份进出口情况
Imports and Exports in Main Years

单位:亿美元 (USD 100 million)

年 份 Year	进出口 Exports And Imports 总值 Total Value	进出口 为上年% As Compared with the Preceding Year(%)	出口 Exports 总值 Total Value	出口 为上年% As Compared with the Preceding Year(%)	进口 Imports 总值 Total Value	进口 为上年% As Compared with the Preceding Year(%)
1978						
1979						
1980						
1981						
1982						
1983						
1984						
1985						
1986						
1987						
1988						
1989	0.84		0.50		0.34	
1990	1.45	172.6	0.99	198.0	0.46	135.3
1991	2.18	150.3	1.48	149.5	0.70	152.2
1992	3.42	156.9	2.16	146.0	1.26	180.0
1993	8.73	255.3	4.92	227.8	3.81	302.4
1994	34.96	400.5	26.11	530.7	8.85	232.3
1995	45.18	129.2	33.18	127.1	12.00	135.6
1996	43.52	96.3	31.11	93.8	12.41	103.4
1997	48.83	112.2	37.43	120.3	11.40	91.8
1998	59.73	122.3	44.16	118.0	15.57	136.6
1999	73.40	122.9	50.79	115.0	22.61	145.3
2000	104.76	142.7	69.65	137.1	35.11	155.3
2001	112.98	107.9	72.84	104.6	40.14	114.3
2002	131.07	116.0	84.81	116.4	46.26	115.3
2003	182.38	139.2	109.55	129.2	72.83	157.4
2004	244.96	134.3	151.75	138.6	93.21	128.0
2005	298.70	121.9	198.04	130.5	100.66	108.0
2006	389.09	130.3	262.28	132.4	126.81	126.0
2007	434.26	111.7	299.66	114.3	134.60	106.2
2008	480.65	110.7	336.14	112.2	144.51	107.4
2009	404.20	84.1	271.80	80.9	132.40	91.6
2010	523.55	129.5	353.37	130.0	170.18	128.6

9-08 进 出 口 情 况(2010 年)
Imports and Exports(2010)

单位:亿美元 (USD 100 million)

项　目	Item	2010 年 In Year 2010	2009 年 In Year 2009	为上年(%) As Compared with year 2009 (%)
全市进出口总值(海关口径)	Total Exports And Imports	523.55	404.20	129.5
一、出口总额	Exports	353.37	271.80	130
1. 国有企业	State - owned Enterprises	79.14	67.63	117
2. 三资企业	Foreign Investment Enterprises	121.03	94.20	128.5
(1)中外合作企业	Cooperation Enterprises	0.97	0.80	122
(2)中外合资企业	Joint - Venture Enterprises	56.15	46.19	121.6
(3)外商独资企业	Enterprises With Sole Foreign Investment	63.91	47.22	135.4
3. 集体企业	Collective - owned Enterprises	15.30	13.10	116.8
4. 私营企业	Private Enterprises	137.43	96.49	142.4
二、进口总额	Imports	170.18	132.40	128.6

9-09 外贸出口分区县(市)情况(2010年)

Export of Foreign Trade by Region(2010)

单位:万美元　　　　(USD 10000)

区　域	Region	出口总值 Exports of This Year	为上年(%) As Compared with the Preceding Year(%)	进口总值 Imports of This Year	为上年(%) As Compared with the Preceding Year(%)
全市合计	**Total**	**3533741**	**130.0**	**1701808**	**128.6**
#不含省属	#Non-provincial	2856954	133.6	1381161	139.0
上　城	Shangcheng	104454	132.0	90641	143.9
下　城	Xiacheng	121308	130.4	113827	164.2
江　干	Jianggan	116665	122.6	16073	115.3
拱　墅	Gongshu	64320	122.8	29745	118.5
西　湖	Xihu	145691	124.1	54323	177.7
高新(滨江)区	Hi-Tech(Binjiang)	234230	142.1	71751	107.1
萧　山	Xiaoshan	741521	132.0	393805	146.9
余　杭	Yuhang	347637	135.2	38099	134.6
桐　庐	Tonglu	66139	125.2	7780	107.5
淳　安	Chun'an	11977	134.3	5206	166.8
建　德	Jiande	76487	138.9	20163	110.9
富　阳	Fuyang	78654	140.0	87998	147.2
临　安	Lin'an	85151	140.0	16236	171.0

9－10　出口企业自营出口前20位排名(2010年)
The List of First Twenty Export Enterprises(2010)

单位:万美元　　(USD 10000)

企业名称	Name of Enterprises	位次 Ranks	出口额 Export Value
东芝信息机器(杭州)有限公司	Toshiba Information Equipment (Hangzhou) Co., Ltd.	1	134763
杭州中策橡胶有限公司	Hangzhou Zhongce Rubber Co. Ltd.	2	83307
杭州华三通信技术有限公司	H3C	3	36664
杭州市轻工工艺纺织品进出口有限公司	Hangzhou Hardicrafts and Textiles Import and Export Corporation	4	30960
杭州巨星科技有限公司	Hangzhou Greatstar Indnserial Co.,Ltd.	5	28073
杭州市矢崎配件有限公司	HZ YAZAKI	6	24804
杭州正泰太阳能科技有限公司	Hangzhou Astronergy Solar energy Technology Co.,Ltd.	7	24408
博世电动工具(中国)有限公司	Bosch Power Tools(China) Co.,Ltd	8	22035
杭州热联进出口有限公司	Hangzhou Cogeneration Import and Export Co., Ltd.	9	20707
万向进出口有限公司	Wanxiang Import and Export Co.,Ltd	10	20156
杭州余杭国际贸易有限公司	Hangzhou Yuhang International Trade Co.,Ltd.	11	19289
杭州松下家用电器有限公司	Hangzhou Panasonic Home Appliances Washing Machine Co.,Ltd.	12	18217
浙江新安化工集团股份有限公司	Zhejiang Wynca Chemical Group Co., Ltd.	13	16598
杭州余杭对外贸易有限公司	Hangzhou Yuhang Foreign Trade Co.,Ltd.	14	16145
汉帛(中国)有限公司	Hempel (China) Co. Ltd.	15	14479
浙江舒奇蒙光伏科技有限公司	Zhejiang Shuqimeng Photovoltaic Technology Co., Ltd.	16	14140
杭州中艺实业有限公司	Hangzhou China Arts Industrial Co.,Ltd.	17	13880
西子奥的斯电梯有限公司	XiZi Otis Elevator Co.,Ltd.	18	13049
杭州松下住宅电器设备有限公司	Hangzhou Panasonic Home Appliances Co.,Ltd.	19	12930
浙江恒逸石化股份有限公司	Zhejiang HengYi Petroleum &Chemical Co.,Ltd.	20	12193

9－11 外贸出口主要国别(地区)情况

Export of Foreign Trade by Main Country or Territory

单位:万美元 (USD 10000)

国 别 (地区)	Country (territory)	2010 年 In Year 2010	2009 年 In Year 2009	为上年(%) As Compared with the Preceding Year(%)
合 计	**Total**	**3533740**	**2717961**	**130.0**
#香港	#Hong Kong	105078	96597	108.8
台湾	Taiwan	39472	28897	136.6
德国	Germany	229663	171904	133.6
日本	Japan	314672	248159	126.8
美国	U.S.A	714107	577419	123.7
新加坡	Singapore	38629	26237	147.2
澳大利亚	Australia	82154	62193	132.1
泰国	Thailand	35377	27684	127.6
意大利	Italy	127546	89900	141.9
荷兰	Netherlands	105981	85084	124.5
西班牙	Spain	68243	58407	116.8
马来西亚	Malaysia	31966	24850	128.7
韩国	Republic of Korea	69125	58721	117.8
法国	France	88559	69533	127.4
比利时	Belgium	44027	37556	117.3
加拿大	Canada	70324	56509	124.4
英国	Britain	133192	107030	124.4
印度尼西亚	Indonesia	44838	31339	143.0
丹麦	Denmark	26606	22797	116.7
俄罗斯	Russia	71042	37108	191.4

9-12 主要年份旅游事业发展情况
Development of Tourism in Main Years

年 份 Year	旅游总收入（亿元） Total Tourism Revenue (100 million yuan)	国内旅游收入（亿元） Domestic Earnings (100 million yuan)	旅游外汇收入（亿美元） Foreign Exchange Earnings from International Tourism (USD 100 million)	旅游总人数（万人次） Total Tourists (10000 person-times)	国内游客人数（万人次） Domestic Tourists (10000 person-times)
1978			0.07		
1979			0.10		
1980			0.11		
1981			0.13		
1982			0.13		
1983			0.14		
1984			0.15		
1985			0.23		
1986			0.36		
1987			0.38		
1988			0.47		
1989			0.23		
1990			0.48		
1991			0.66		
1992			0.86		
1993			0.80		
1994			1.01		
1995	106.0	94.3	1.45	2148	2104
1996	136.5	122.6	1.67	2055	2009
1997	158.8	142.1	2.01	2150	2100
1998	163.4	146.0	2.10	2172	2121
1999	186.0	166.7	2.37	2266	2207
2000	214.3	190.0	2.92	2376	2305
2001	249.7	218.9	3.37	2592	2510
2002	294.4	254.8	4.77	2758	2652
2003	325.9	290.9	4.22	2862	2776
2004	410.1	361.2	5.97	3139	3016
2005	465.1	403.6	7.58	3417	3266
2006	543.7	471.2	9.09	3864	3682
2007	630.1	548.6	11.19	4320	4112
2008	707.2	617.2	12.96	4773	4552
2009	803.1	708.9	13.80	5324	5094
2010	1025.7	910.9	16.90	6581	6305

9－13 主要年份境外旅游者人数
Number of International Tourists in Main Years

单位:人次 (person－times)

年份 Year	合计 Total	外国人 Foreigners	华侨 Overseas Chinese	港澳台同胞 Compatriots from Hong Kong,Macao and Taiwan	平均逗留天数 Average days of Staying
1978	53475	728	728	26648	
1979	84914	44714	1069	39131	2.59
1980	124960	61710	1868	61382	2.70
1981	154745	87727	2004	65014	2.71
1982	152897	89100	2483	61314	2.49
1983	160564	97803	3136	59625	2.18
1984	179200	105771	2514	70915	2.12
1985	238385	156311	7011	75063	2.18
1986	266370	170960	8318	87092	2.38
1987	300603	183477	17048	100078	2.38
1988	349246	149512	39989	159745	2.08
1989	248502	66094	18819	163589	2.08
1990	388345	86621	33593	268131	2.09
1991	390197	136809	23698	229690	2.00
1992	489578	183781	38541	267256	2.03
1993	459620	199796	25184	234640	2.06
1994	337362	201692	11324	124346	2.10
1995	441262	249418	14608	177236	2.06
1996	462313	273477	9991	178845	2.07
1997	504276	288949	10060	205267	2.20
1998	507243	261353	14281	231609	2.20
1999	591853	324625	9250	257978	2.09
2000	707148	400906	－	306242	2.15
2001	819438	447689	－	371749	2.41
2002	1056266	631576	－	424690	2.50
2003	861163	482073	－	379090	2.72
2004	1234063	791616	－	442447	2.59
2005	1513585	1020840	－	492745	2.63
2006	1820171	1236792	－	583379	2.57
2007	2085997	1453650	－	632347	2.67
2008	2213329	1543665	－	669654	2.73
2009	2304045	1572838	－	731207	2.87
2010	2757147	1878528	－	878619	2.94

注:从1995年起为全市数。

a) Data in this table has included the tourists of whole municipality since 1995.

9-14 接待境外游客及旅游外汇收入情况

Number of International Tourists and Foreign Exchange Earnings

项　目	Item	2010年 In Year 2010	2009年 In Year 2009	为上年(%) As Compared with year(%)
全年接待人数总计(人)	**Number of Foreign Tourists(person)**	**2757147**	**2304045**	**119.7**
#外国人	#Foreigners	1878528	1572838	119.4
港澳台同胞	Compatriots From Hong Kong, Macao and Taiwan	878619	731207	120.2
全年接待人天数(人天)	**Total Person-days (person-days)**	**8106012**	**6617700**	**122.5**
#外国人	#Foreigners	5297569	4381824	120.9
港澳台同胞	Compatriots From Hong Kong, Macao and Taiwan	2802212	2235876	125.3
平均逗留天数(天)	**Average Days of Staying (days)**	**2.94**	**2.87**	**102.4**
#外国人	#Foreigners	2.82	2.79	101.1
港澳台同胞	Compatriots From Hong Kong, Macao and Taiwan	3.19	3.06	104.2
旅游外汇总收入(万美元)	**Total Foreign Exchange Earnings From International Tourism (USD 10000)**	**169008**	**137995**	**122.5**

9－15 接待境外游客分国别(地区)情况

Number of International Tourists by Country or Territory

单位:人次 (person－times)

国 别(地区)	Country (territory)	2010 年 In Year 2010	2009 年 In Year 2009	为上年(%) As Compared with the Preceding Year(%)
合 计	**Total**	**2757147**	**2304045**	**119.7**
#香港	#Hong Kong	332626	278358	119.5
澳门	Macao	22095	17106	129.2
台湾	Taiwan	523898	435743	120.3
日本	Japan	334880	293732	114.0
美国	U.S.A	163485	126360	129.3
新加坡	Singapore	62777	48472	129.2
澳大利亚	Australia	34189	28340	120.7
泰国	Thailand	64023	58284	109.9
意大利	Italy	27690	22635	122.3
荷兰	Netherlands	15831	13124	120.6
西班牙	Spain	24271	21824	111.2
马来西亚	Malaysia	94393	80939	116.6
韩国	Republic of Korea	478999	418922	114.3
法国	France	41533	34561	120.2
德国	Germany	56168	49787	112.8
加拿大	Canada	33884	26807	126.3
英国	Britain	41898	32789	127.8
印度尼西亚	Indonesia	31633	22821	138.6
印度	India	20782	17795	116.7
菲律宾	Filipine	11303	11631	97.2

主要统计指标解释

外商直接投资 是指外国企业和经济组织或个人(包括华侨、港澳台胞以及我国在境外注册的企业)按我国有关政策、法规,用现汇、实物、技术等在我国境内开办外商独资企业、与我国境内的企业或经济组织共同举办中外合资经营企业、合作经营企业或者合作开发资源的投资(包括外商投资收益的再投资)以及经政府有关部门批准的项目投资总额内,企业从境外借入的资金。

进出口总额 海关进出口总额指实际进出我国国境的货物总金额。包括对外贸易实际进出口货物,来料加工装配进出口货物,国家间、联合国及国际组织无偿援助物资和赠送品,华侨、港澳台同胞和外籍华人捐赠品,租赁期满归承租人所有的租赁货物,进料加工进出口货物,边境地方贸易及边境地区小额贸易进出口货物(边民互市贸易除外),中外合资经营企业、中外合作经营企业、外商独资经营企业进出口货物和公用物品,到、离岸价格在规定限额以上的进出口货样和广告品(无商业价值、无使用价值和免费提供出口的除外),从保税仓库提取在中国境内销售的进口货物,以及其他进出口货物。进出口总额以观察一个国家在对外贸易方面的总规模。我国规定出口货物按离岸价格统计,进口货物按到岸价格统计。

境外旅游人数 指来我国参观、访问、旅行、探亲、访友、休养、考察、参加会议和从事经济、科技、文化、教育、体育、宗教等活动的外国人、华侨、港澳和台湾同胞的人数。不包括外国在我国的常驻机构,如使领馆、通讯社、企业办事处的工作人员;来我国常住的外国专家、留学生以及在岸逗留不过夜人员。

境外旅游(外汇)收入 指入境旅游的外国人、华侨、港澳台同胞在中国大陆旅游过程中发生的一切旅游支出,对国家来说就是境外旅游(外汇)收入。

Explanatory Notes on Main Statistical Indicators

Direct Investment by Foreign Entrepreneurs refers to the investments inside China by foreign enterprises and economic organizations or individuals (including overseas Chinese, compatriots from Hong Kong, Macao and Taiwan, and Chinese enterprises registered abroad), following the relevant policies and laws of China, for the establishment of ventures exclusively with foreign own investment, Sino - foreign joint ventures and cooperative enterprises or for co - operative exploration of resources with enterprises or economic organizations in China. It includes the re - investment of the foreign entrepreneurs with the profits gained from the investment and the funds that enterprises borrow from abroad in the total investment of projects which are approved by the relevant department of the government.

Total Imports and Exports at Customs refer to the value of commodities imported into and exported from the boundary of China. They include the actual imports and exports through foreign trade, imported and exported goods under the processing and assembling trades and materials, supplies and gifts as aid given gratis between governments and by the United Nations and other international organizations, and contributions donated by overseas Chinese, compatriots in Hong Kong, Macao and Chinese foreign citizenship, leasing commodities owned by tenant at the expiration of leasing period, the imported and exported commodities processed with imported materials, commodities trading in border areas (excluding mutual exchange goods), the imported and exported commodities and articles for public use of the Sino - foreign joint ventures, cooperative enterprises and ventures exclusively with foreign own investment. Also included are import or export of samples and advertising goods for whose CIF or FOB value are beyond the permitted ceiling (excluding goods of no trading or use value and free commodities for export), imported goods sold in China from bonded warehouses and other imported or exported goods. The indicator of the total imports and exports at customs can be used to observe the total size of external trade in a country. In accordance with the stipulation of Chinese government, imports are calculated at CIF, while exports are calculated at FOB.

International Tourists refer to foreigners, overseas Chinese compatriots from Hong Kong, Macao and Taiwan coming to China for sightseeing, visits, tours, family reunions, vacations, study tours, conferences and other activities of a business, scientific and technological, cultural, educational and religious nature. It does not include representatives and employees of resident institutions of foreign countries in China such as embassies, consulates, news agencies and offices of foreign companies and organizations, nor does it include long - term foreign experts or students residing in China, or persons in transition without spending a night in China.

Foreign Exchange Earnings from International Tourism refer to the total expenditures of foreigners, overseas Chinese, Chinese compatriots from Hong Kong, Macao and Taiwan during their stay in the mainland of China, which are earnings of foreign exchange form international tourism from the point of vies from China.

第十篇
CHAPTER-10

财政、金融、保险

Finance, Banking And Insurance

财政、金融、保险
Finance, Banking and Insurance

主要统计指标
Major Statistical Indicators

全市财政总收入	Total Financial Revenue	1245.43	亿元	(100 million yuan)
为上年	As Compared with the Preceding Year	122.2	%	(%)
地方财政收入	Financial Revenue of Local Government	671.34	亿元	(100 million yuan)
为上年	As Compared with the Preceding Year	128.9	%	(%)
地方财政支出	Financial Expenditure of Local Government	616.58	亿元	(100 million yuan)
为上年	As Compared with the Preceding Year	123.8	%	(%)
年末金融机构各项存款余额	Balance of Deposits of Financial Institutions at Year-end	17084.35	亿元	(100 million yuan)
为上年	As Compared with the Preceding Year	119.6	%	(%)
#城乡居民储蓄存款余额	Balance of Savings Deposits of Rural and Urban Residents at Year-end	4990.97	亿元	(100 million yuan)
为上年	As Compared with the Preceding Year	116.4	%	(%)
年末金融机构各项贷款余额	Balance of Loans of Financial Institutions at Year-end	15078.73	亿元	(100 million yuan)
为上年	As Compared with the Preceding Year	115.0	%	(%)

10－01 主要年份财政收入及支出
Financial Revenue and Expenditure in Main Years

单位:万元 (10000 yuan)

年 份 Year	财政收入 Financial Revenue		财政支出 Financial Expenditure	
	全 市 Total	市 区 Urban District	全 市 Total	市 区 Urban District
1978	94102	73396	16170	7779
1979	103259	81885	20334	11289
1980	118529	94015	21726	11867
1981	128564	100645	23964	13891
1982	140510	107298	24945	13687
1983	153941	116559	32765	17822
1984	172996	130757	46937	28710
1985	186472	131923	57710	35435
1986	205952	141943	73213	43959
1987	226262	152268	70717	41011
1988	246961	161208	95655	53031
1989	255003	156649	113571	61534
1990	252503	149904	118167	62587
1991	267597	158130	123134	62403
1992	286394	168341	132814	65984
1993	394946	233670	185168	90545
1994	484597	300014	215415	102430
1995	551262	339828	249050	120084
1996	635334	414557	302390	151016
1997	740725	485650	363834	197054
1998	869824	585615	424478	237221
1999	1026577	689394	563524	335243
2000	1428519	970937	734328	445698
2001	1884608	1612225	1049330	849479
2002	2571408	2235021	1410199	1166298
2003	3297091	2861459	1635948	1340463
2004	3957516	3488744	1956282	1602303
2005	5207930	4584112	2383344	1957619
2006	6244906	5484645	2754809	2254347
2007	7884237	6929667	3357153	2747060
2008	9105489	7991043	4196674	3454599
2009	10194264	8965758	4903983	4000324
2010	12454323	10988265	6165836	4988197

注:从2001年起市区数据包括萧山区和余杭区。

a) Data of urban district include Xiaoshan and Yuhang district since 2001.

10－02 分县(市)

Local Financial

单位:万元

指标 Item \ 年份 year	全市 Total		市区 Urban District	
	2010	为上年(%) As Compared with Year 2009(%)	2010	为上年(%) As Compared with Year 2009(%)
合计 Total	**12454323**	**122.2**	**10988265**	**122.6**
一、地方财政收入 Local Financial Revenue	6713413	128.9	5894415	130.0
(一)税收收入 Tax Revenue	6520916	129.3	5746967	130.1
1.增值税 Value added Tax	892292	104.2	745667	103.1
2.营业税 Business Tax	2213139	125.4	1982486	125.6
3.企业所得税 Enterprises´Income Tax	992319	132.8	900435	132.4
4.企业所得税退税 Company Income Tax Rebates				
5.个人所得税 Individual Income Tax	392018	122.1	348658	121.9
6.城市维护建设税 City Construction and Maintenance Tax	393580	128.5	347683	129.3
7.耕地占用税 Tax on the Use of Arable Land	136115	203.1	115940	234.5
8.契税 Contract Tax	718207	148.7	646832	151.4
9.房产税 Real Estate Tax	152443	94.1	132487	92.6
10.其他税收 Others Tax	630803	187.8	526779	202.6
(二)非税收入 Non－tax Revenue	192497	117.0	147448	124.1
1.专项收入 Special Revenue	166645	123.5	135176	121.6
其中:教育费附加 Revenue from Extra－Charges for Education	152036	126.2	126614	124.7
排污费 Revenue for Permitting Pollution	13889	96.9	8519	88.2
2.行政事业性收费收入 Income from Administrative Fees	11876	127.4	9798	130.2
3.罚没收入 Penalty and Confiscatory Income	108275	90.7	83049	95.9
4.国有资本经营收入 Seate－owned Assets Profits	－105338	99.7	－89828	97.7
其中:国有计划亏损补贴 Subsides to Loss－making of state－owned Enterprises	－105338	99.7	－89828	97.7
5.国有资源(资产)有偿使用收入 Compensation for the Use of Seate－owned Assets Income	11009	168.9	9223	170.2
6.其他收入 Others Revenue	30	47.6	30	88.2
二、上划中央二税 Revenue of Central Government	3664398	108.3	3220206	108.0
1.消费税 Consumption Tax	987525	121.2	983207	121.3
2.国内增值税 Value－added Tax	2676873	104.2	2236999	103.1
三、中央所得税 Central Government Income Tax	2076512	129.6	1873644	129.3
1.企业所得税 Enterprises Income Tax	1488482	132.8	1350655	132.4
2.个人所得税 Individual Income Tax	588030	122.1	522989	121.9

财政收入(2010 年)
Revenue by Region(2010)

(10000 yuan)

#萧山区 Xiaoshan	#余杭区 Yuhang	桐庐县 Tonglu	淳安县 Chun'an	建德市 Jiande	富阳市 Fuyang	临安市 Lin'an
1822983	**1208196**	**233007**	**119170**	**210158**	**602537**	**301186**
981659	760010	130775	71987	120060	326503	169673
946391	738082	121587	66846	115015	303910	166591
184237	87503	23768	7010	18613	67055	30179
269990	297788	39473	27744	33790	82662	46984
138290	90677	13250	11739	13820	35759	17316
44450	29958	7313	3753	8489	13862	9943
54004	39419	6666	2768	7405	18091	10967
71134	13702	2316	1063	3412	12088	1296
101199	96338	14668	4118	8953	26563	17073
8088	8272	2234	2124	3739	6914	4945
74999	74425	11899	6527	16794	40916	27888
35268	21928	9188	5141	5045	22593	3082
22831	15970	4588	1821	4439	15010	5611
21242	14470	4039	1554	3268	11910	4651
1589	1500	549	176	776	2909	960
	380	94	1044	940		
16678	10222	4153	1955	4136	10037	4945
-6428	-7000			-4700	-3000	-7810
-6428	-7000			-4700	-3000	-7810
2157	2356	353	321	230	546	336
30						
567215	267233	71388	23944	56634	201602	90624
14505	4725	84	2915	795	437	87
552710	262508	71304	21029	55839	201165	90537
274109	180953	30844	23239	33464	74432	40889
207434	136016	19875	17609	20730	53639	25974
66675	44937	10969	5630	12734	20793	14915

单位:万元

指　标 Item	全　市 Total		市　区 Urban District	
	2010	为上年(%) As Compared with Year 2009(%)	2010	为上年(%) As Compared with Year 2009(%)
合　计 Total	**6165836**	**123.8**	**4988197**	**122.3**
一、一般公共服务 Expenditure for General Public Services	763576	110.5	602084	108.1
二、国防 Expenditure for National Defense	9498	140.3	7718	138.5
三、公共安全 Expenditure for Public Security	415879	121.6	343986	122.1
四、教育 Expenditure for Education	1058828	122.7	772252	121.9
其中:教育费附加支出 Expenditure on Extra－Charges for Educations	108083	121.6	91920	118.6
五、科学技术 Expenditure for Science and Technology	288559	130.7	244478	130.9
六、文化体育与传媒 Expenditure for Culture, Sports and Media	153937	126.2	134711	127.7
七、社会保障和就业 Expenditure for Social Safety Net and Employment Effort	639154	131.7	530978	129.8
八、医疗卫生 Expenditure for Medical and Health Care	417085	128.9	324010	130.9
九、环境保护 Expenditure for Environmental Protection	138627	142.2	81168	129.5
其中:排污费支出 Sewage Expenses	15704	109.8	9088	129.4
十、城乡社区事务 Expenditure for Urban and Rural Community Affairs	982965	129.0	936946	130.0
十一、农林水事务 Expenditure for Agriculture, Forestry and water Conservancy	319655	125.6	174275	122.5
十二、交通运输 Expenditure for Trassportation	174339	65.5	119315	50.7
十三、资源勘探电力信息等事务 Resources exploration eletricity information, etc	320812	121.5	292412	119.6
十四、商业服务业等事务 Cornmercial and service business, etc	159164	205.9	130326	196.2
十五、金融监管支出 Expenditure for Financial Supervision	18347		18022	
十六、地震灾后恢复重建支出 Expenditure for Post－earthquake Recorery and Reconstruction	33541	133.3	29380	135.8
十七、国土资源气象等事务 Land resources, meteorological services, etc	28593	147.0	23647	147.7
十八、住房保障支出 Expenditure on housing support	31935	87.7	18567	60.1
十九、粮油物资储备等管理事务 Expenditure for Grrain and Ovl Reservation, and Other Materials Management Services	10718	421.1	8533	1099.6
二十、债务付息支出 Interest payment of debt	711	3742.1	681	3584.2
二十一、其他支出 Other Expenditure	199913	163.9	194708	176.5

财政支出(2010 年)
Expenditure by Region(2010)

(10000 yuan)

		桐庐县 Tonglu	淳安县 Chun'an	建德市 Jiande	富阳市 Fuyang	临安市 Lin'an
#萧山区 Xiaoshan	#余杭区 Yuhang					
811509	**738656**	**178385**	**191411**	**186581**	**362254**	**259008**
95731	97797	23781	29721	25001	43914	39075
2932	1501	492	398	430	33	427
47499	42686	12643	11536	11112	21361	15241
178967	150814	36804	43158	43011	108158	55445
19375	14157	3737	2505	3106	1295	5520
24397	23470	6551	3885	8184	14912	10549
16227	14932	3898	3087	3034	5116	4091
64639	70889	16149	15217	18931	38032	19847
58422	59389	14926	20722	15156	24000	18271
17304	19536	7770	6246	7674	13601	22168
3325	1305	565	1178	926	3071	876
125623	71691	8907	5922	7518	15854	7818
54486	54917	20181	26552	26357	46369	25921
31249	22392	8676	12346	8059	7329	18614
59402	24324	5748	4501	2501	6703	8947
13446	21399	6604	2894	3385	6310	9645
	20	65		25	25	210
6953					2757	1404
1488	3986	448	773	1356	1671	698
10408	2870	3912	913	3244	5060	239
604	1787	730	1083	92	140	140
	681		25			5
1732	53575	100	2432	1511	909	253

10-04 主要年份全市金融机构存、贷款余额

Balance of Deposits and Loans of Financial Institutions in Main Years

单位:万元　　　　(10000 yuan)

年份 Year \ 项目 Item	各项存款 Deposits	#城乡储蓄存款 Savings Deposits Of Urban and Rural Residents	#城镇储蓄存款 Savings Deposits of Urban Residents	各项贷款 Loans
1978	86824	20714	17056	136759
1979	108998	28937	22640	135713
1980	180707	40447	30896	174153
1981	226949	51440	38889	236678
1982	262156	67192	50113	216040
1983	303130	86635	64736	236203
1984	388305	115766	85439	329195
1985	484999	159596	115592	580180
1986	635514	222110	153572	769841
1987	776105	302762	207505	967477
1988	839680	351943	241839	1145989
1989	1017087	501592	346318	1338984
1990	1646165	697515	479031	1803266
1991	2036334	904490	616308	2136903
1992	2652966	1144737	763309	2651983
1993	3469954	1563328	1048413	3415527
1994	5061345	2394370	1642498	4450932
1995	7079650	3423379	2448787	5672105
1996	9619291	4638458	3459439	7434243
1997	12251840	5583306	4229591	9388500
1998	14948225	6701158	5155548	11620537
1999	17886717	7425967	5760527	14937506
2000	20884723	7885579	6151084	16866431
2001	26215100	9418400	7396800	20877000
2002	33731500	11834000	9492300	27523800
2003	46527300	15899600	13079600	38187000
2004	57072000	18351700	15016100	48000400
2005	67487200	21916600	17960100	55453000
2006	78555500	25552400	20789600	66038600
2007	93109600	26348300	21154300	84306800
2008	113333500	34765900	27584600	100690500
2009	142842104	42869189	34027871	131133023
2010	170843548	49909744	39352353	150787269

注:1989 年以前数据均为银行机构存贷款,1990 年及以后年份数据为调整后金融机构存贷款。2003 年起金融机构存贷款为本外币合并数据。

a) Data before 1989 was belonged to banking system, data after 1990 adjusted for deposits and loans of financial institutions, data of 2003 included both RMB and foreign currency.

10－05 主要年份市区金融机构存、贷款余额

Balance of Deposits and Loans of Financial Institutions of Urban District in Main Years

单位：万元 (10000 yuan)

项目 Item / 年份 Year	各项存款 Deposits	#城乡储蓄存款 Savings Deposits of Urban and Rural Residents	#城镇储蓄存款 Savings Deposits of Urban Residents	各项贷款 Loans
1978	58372	13774	13246	101144
1979	73720	18055	17241	98792
1980	134275	24702	23282	121231
1981	172721	31358	29345	170539
1982	198350	39756	37047	142091
1983	226160	50439	46833	155297
1984	293145	66108	61934	194977
1985	359825	89114	82868	418214
1986	458142	115818	106703	557763
1987	565429	156704	142642	714313
1988	610601	180341	163466	846998
1989	737388	256238	229518	1000731
1990	1062574	354316	297390	1271779
1991	1309462	451756	397322	1469671
1992	1695011	572660	479248	1774158
1993	2263969	762234	662234	2298124
1994	3383877	1242379	1085363	3033010
1995	4851774	1853512	1639875	3907199
1996	6828786	2734904	2371657	5350499
1997	8831147	3287475	2873638	6772221
1998	10785066	3905602	3440607	8615412
1999	13051806	4336058	3835542	11462505
2000	15436286	4620235	4101716	13105849
2001	23765400	7976400	6460200	19237800
2002	30638400	10139800	8370100	25476700
2003	42522000	13834200	11693000	30297500
2004	52542100	16014700	13479900	44517600
2005	62249500	19231800	16208400	51455900
2006	72269600	22391800	18737800	61190700
2007	86197300	23124600	19132300	78456200
2008	104930100	30665200	24996500	93838100
2009	131800234	37837816	30801878	121473548
2010	156776515	43676938	35370599	138671334

注：1989 年以前数据均为银行机构存贷款，1990 年及以后年份数据为调整后金融机构存贷款。2003 年起金融机构存贷款为本外币合并数据。

a) Data before 1989 was belonged to banking system, data after 1990 adjusted for deposits and loans of financial institutions. data of 2003 included both RMB and foreign currency.

10－06 金融机构

Balance of Deposits and

单位:万元

指 标	Item	全 市 Total 2010年末 At the End of Year 2010	全 市 Total 为上年(%) As Compared with the Preceding Year(%)	市 区 Urban District 2010年末 At the End of Year 2010	市 区 Urban District 为上年(%) As Compared with the Preceding Year(%)
一、各项存款	**Deposits**	**170843548**	**119.6**	**156776515**	**119.0**
1. 企事业单位存款	Deposits of Enterprises	81102044	117.9	76445813	117.3
(1)活期存款	Current Deposits	38908826	115.7	36077881	115.0
(2)定期存款	Fixed Deposits	42193219	120.1	40367933	119.5
2. 储蓄存款	Savings Deposits	49909744	116.4	43676938	115.4
(1)活期储蓄	Current Deposits	18032044	122.3	15256314	121.6
(2)定期储蓄	Fixed Deposits	31877700	113.3	28420624	112.4
3. 信托存款	Trust Deposits	–	–	–	–
4. 委托存款	Entrusting Deposits	2675599	151.8	2666968	152.1
5. 其他存款	Other Deposits	37156162	126.2	33986795	125.6
二、各项贷款	**Loans**	**150787269**	**115.0**	**138712722**	**114.2**
1. 短期贷款	Short－term Loans	65007839	114.2	58348480	112.9
2. 中长期贷款	Medium and Long term Loans	76098390	119.8	70977343	119.3
3. 信托贷款	Trust Loans	–	–	–	–
4. 委托贷款	Entrusting Loans	1707642	150.3	1707642	150.3
5. 其他贷款	Other Loans	5165677	133.2	5117329	133.6
6. 票据融资	Note Financing	2675217	51.0	2432201	46.3
7. 各项垫款	Advance Money	132504	20.9	129727	79.9

本外币存、贷款余额(2010 年末)
Loans of Financial Institutions(End of 2010)

(10000 yuan)

#萧山区 Xiaoshan	#余杭区 Yuhang	桐庐县 Tonglu	淳安县 Chun'an	建德市 Jiande	富阳市 Fuyang	临安市 Lin'an
23131969	**12183517**	**2143807**	**1651915**	**2110731**	**5263736**	**2896845**
9097461	4883643	602830	531344	590014	1963211	968833
4344162	2733965	367395	353234	448521	1054156	607639
4753299	2149678	235435	178110	141493	909055	361194
8362016	4601888	1011736	665690	1139613	2118338	1297428
2555411	1509012	403013	296824	437550	968198	670146
5806605	3092876	608723	368867	702063	1150141	627282
62621	48305			95	8536	
5609871	2649681	529242	454880	381010	1173651	630584
19344144	**9107196**	**1631248**	**1186661**	**1721890**	**4990140**	**2544609**
13527254	4653049	688651	418704	829360	3246813	1475831
5222533	4127666	929083	763682	829465	1548095	1050720
–	–	–	–	–	–	–
–	–	–	–	–	–	–
424244	30273	2026	1352	27839	9287	7843
159776	282724	10708	2922	33751	185531	10104
10337	13484	779		1473	414	111

10－07 金融机构人民币
Balance of RMB Deposits, RMB Loans

单位：万元

指 标	Item	全 市 Total		市 区 Urban District	
		2010 年	为上年(%) As Compared with the Preceding Year(%)	2010 年	为上年(%) As Compared with the Preceding Year(%)
一、年末各项存款余额	**Deposits(End of 2010)**	**168381830**	**119.8**	**154436836**	**119.1**
1. 企业存款	Deposits from Enterprises	79365395	118.0	74806040	117.4
2. 财政存款	Treasury Deposits	4706104	105.4	4171620	100.5
3. 机关团体部队存款	Deposits from Government, Groups Troops	11818088	252.3	10836661	275.5
4. 城乡储蓄存款	Agencies and Organizations from Rural and Urban	49328659	116.8	43118589	115.8
5. 农业存款	Agricultural Deposits	4284156	122.5	3483798	121.7
6. 委托存款	Entrusting Deposits	2663863	151.9	2655232	152.3
7. 其他存款	Other Deposits	16215565		15364896	
二、年末各项贷款余额	**Loans(End of 2010)**	**145029097**	**114.3**	**133023465**	**113.4**
(一)境内贷款	**Domestic Loans**	**145025435**	**114.3**	**133019803**	**113.4**
1. 短期贷款	Short－term loans	63946476	114.3	57301253	113.1
(1)个人贷款及透支	Individual loans and overdrafts	9222647	157.5	7668248	165.5
其中：个人消费贷款	in which: Loans for Individual Consumption	3093642	133.5	2619672	132.6
(2)单位贷款及透支	Unit loans and overdrafts	52194193	104.8	47233284	103.2
(3)普通并购贷款	General M & A loans	7500		7500	
(4)银团贷款	Syndicated loans	25115		25115	
(5)贸易融资	Trade finance	2497020	1718.9	2367106	1718.1
2. 中长期贷款	Medium and long Term loans	74027285	118.9	68912670	118.4
(1)个人贷款	Individual loans	23025626	124.2	20734479	122.4
其中：个人消费贷款	Loans for Individval Consumption	21170985	122.0	19158220	120.3
(2)单位贷款	Unit loans	47786644	115.5	44963176	115.5
(3)普通并购贷款	General M & A loans	121000		121000	
(4)银团贷款	Syndicated loans	2127178	153.9	2127178	153.9
(5)贸易融资	Trade finance	966836		966836	
3. 融资租赁	Finance lease	2574090	132.8	2574090	132.8
4. 委托贷款	Entrusting Loans	1705841	150.3	1705841	150.3
5. 票据融资	Note Financing	2674204	51.0	2431188	47.1
6. 各项垫款	Advance Money	97539	17.8	94762	17.8
(二)境外贷款		**3662**	**112.5**	**3662**	**112.5**

注：2010 年金融统计制度调整。

存、贷款余额(2010 年末)

of Financial Institutions(End of 2010)

(10000 yuan)

#萧山区 Xiaoshan	#余杭区 Yuhang	桐庐县 Tonglu	淳安县 Chun'an	建德市 Jiande	富阳市 Fuyang	临安市 Lin'an
22868700	**12121440**	**2129219**	**1648900**	**2095168**	**5205181**	**2866526**
8891350	4835906	592892	530266	578684	1914478	943035
169885	228007	185529	88830	86069	107668	66388
959993	998976	98911	238407	123494	281721	238894
8325107	4589929	1007085	663754	1135684	2110194	1293353
1265510	634919	156615	110061	62914	332375	138393
62507	48285			95	8536	
3194349	785417	88187	17581	108229	450208	186465
18801643	**9067780**	**1629222**	**1184510**	**1683586**	**4971548**	**2536766**
18801643	**9067780**	**1629222**	**1184510**	**1683586**	**4971548**	**2536766**
13429100	4650380	688651	417906	818896	3243939	1475831
1316577	799610	208293	203731	231703	501291	409382
310381	138561	63716	68242	91813	138980	111218
11715905	3764738	473643	204564	561572	2674883	1046247
225						
396393	86032	6715	9610	25622	67765	20203
5204987	4127666	929083	763682	829465	1541664	1050720
1323837	1478620	395656	357921	291860	797570	448140
1143133	1361649	296144	315189	229795	755320	416317
3668013	2469766	533427	405762	537605	744094	602580
213136	179280					
159776	282724	10708	2922	33751	185531	10104
7780	7009	779		1473	414	111

a) The statistical system in finance was adjusted.

10－08 城乡居民储蓄存款余额(2010 年)

Balance of Savings Deposits of Rural and Urban Residents(2010)

单位:万元 (10000 yuan)

地区	Region	总计 Total		城镇居民 Urban Residents		农村居民 Rural Residents	
		2010 年末 At the End of Year 2010	为上年(%) As Compared with the Preceding Year(%)	2010 年末 At the End of Year 2010	为上年(%) As Compared with the Preceding Year(%)	2010 年末 At the End of Year 2010	为上年(%) As Compared with the Preceding Year(%)
全　市	**Total**	**49909744**	**116.4**	**39352353**	**115.7**	**10557391**	**119.4**
市　区	Urban District	43676939	115.4	35370599	114.8	8306340	118.1
萧山区	Xiaoshan	8362016	118.9	5132129	117.4	3229886	121.2
余杭区	Yuhang	4601888	123.2	2733864	122.9	1868024	123.6
桐庐县	Tonglu	1011736	117.1	644970	115.0	366766	120.9
淳安县	Chun'an	665690	121.4	404368	119.6	261322	124.2
建德市	Jiande	1139613	122.3	822358	120.6	317255	127.1
富阳市	Fuyang	2118338	126.9	1295214	128.0	823124	125.3
临安市	Lin'an	1297428	127.5	814844	128.8	482584	125.4

注:2003 年始为本外币合并储蓄存款余额。

a) Data in this table include both RMB and foreign currency since 2003.

10－09　保险业务情况(2010 年)

Development of Insurance Business(2010)

单位:万元　　　　(10000 yuan)

指　标	Item	保险费收入 Premium	赔付金额 Indemnity Expenditure
全市总计	**Total**	**2029441**	**489816**
为上年%	As Compared with the Preceding Year = 100(%)	127.1	98.2
一、财产保险	Property Insurance	803619	344909
企业财产险	Enterprise Property Insurance	60371	22613
家庭财产险	Family Property Insurance	2251	1137
机动车辆险	Transportation Equipment Insurance	617078	271691
工程险	Project Insurance	9438	1829
责任险	Responsibilihty Insurance	13162	8207
信用险	Export Credit Insurance	63215	26297
保证险	Guarantee Insurance	6675	－136
船舶险	Shipping Insurance	8866	2888
货运险	Cargo Insurance	14311	7654
特殊风险保险	Special Pisks Insurance	2775	6
农业保险	Agriculture Insurance	4020	2663
其他险	Other	1457	60
二、人身险	Personal Insurance	1225822	144907
寿险	Life Insurance	1098284	117237
意外伤害险	Accidental Insurance	45358	8749
健康险	Health Insurance	82180	18921

主要统计指标解释

财政收入 包括:(1)各项税收。主要有增值税、营业税、土地增值税、城市维护建设税、资源税、城市土地使用税、印花税、个人所得税、企业所得税、关税和耕地占用税等。

(2)专项收入包括征收排污费、征收城市水资源费收入,教育费附加收入等。

存款 企业、机关、团体或居民根据可以收回的原则,把货币资金存入银行或其他信用机构保管并取得一定利息的一种信用活动形式。根据存款对象的不同可划分为企业存款、财政存款、机关团体存款、基本建设存款、城镇储蓄存款、农村存款等科目。它是银行信贷资金的主要来源。

贷款 银行或其他信用机构根据必须归还的原则,按一定利率,为企业、个人等提供资金的一种信用活动形式。我国银行贷款分为流动资金贷款、固定资产贷款、城乡个体工商户贷款城乡个体工商户贷款以及农业贷款等科目。

Explanatory Notes on Main Statistical Indicators

Financial Revenue It includes the following main items: (1) various tax revenues, including value added tax, business tax, land value added tax, tax on city maintenance and construction, resources tax, tax on use of urban land, stamp tax, personal income tax, enterprise income tax and tax on occupancy of cultivated land, etc. (2) Special revenues, including revenue collected from imposing fee on sewage treatment, revenue collected from imposing fee on urban water resources, and extra - charges for education, etc.

Deposit is a form of credit by which enterprises, institutions, organizations or households can put money into banks and other credit institutions for safekeeping and interest earning under the principle of free withdrawal. According to different depositors, deposits are divided into enterprise deposits, treasury deposits, deposits of government agencies and organizations, capital construction deposits, urban savings deposits, rural deposits and other deposits. Deposits are major sources of the credit funds of banks.

Loan is a form of credit by which banks and other credit institutions provide funds at certain interest rate to enterprises and individuals in the light of the principle of unconditional repayment. Loans from Chinese banks include circulating capital loans, fixed assets loans, loans to urban and rural individuals engaged in industrial and commercial business and agricultural loans.

第十一篇
CHAPTER-11

城市建设、环境保护

Urban Construction
And Environmental Protection

城市建设、环境保护
Urban Construction and Environmental Protection

主要统计指标
Major Statistical Indicators

市区建成区面积	Developed Area in Urban District	412.59	平方公里	(sq.km)
市区实有道路面积	Area of Roads in Urban District at Year-end	4754	万平方米	(10000 sq.m)
市区用电量	Electricity Consumption of Urban District	392.64	亿千瓦时	(100 million kw/h)
# 工业用电	Industrial Electricity Consumption	258.35	亿千瓦时	(100 million kw/h)
生活用电	Electricity Consumption for Residential Use	50.74	亿千瓦时	(100 million kw/h)
市区供水能力	Water-supply Capacity of Urban District	320	万吨 / 日	(10000 tons/day)
市区供水总量	Annual Volume of Tap Water Supplied in Urban District	53565	万吨	(10000 tons)
市区气化率	Percentage of Population with Access to Gas in Urban District	100	%	(%)
市区公共绿地面积	Public Green Area in Urban District	5017	公顷	(hectare)
市区工业废水排放达标率	Upto-standard Rate of Industrial Waste Water Discharge	96.37	%	(%)

11－01 主要年份市区城市公共交通

Urban Public Transportation in Main Years

指 标	Item	2000	2005	2006	2007	2008	2009	2010
年末运营线路条数(条)	Number of Operating Routes (year－end) (unit)	163	368	381	393	425	441	548
年末运营线路总长度(公里)	Length of Operating Routes (year－end) (km)	2016	4902	5172	5416	6190	6462	8594
年末运营公共汽车(辆)	Number of Public Transportation Vehicles(year－end) (unit)	1781	3997	4396	4578	5785	6150	7209
年末运营无轨电车(辆)	Number of Operating Trolleys (unit)	223	189	118	118	118	118	65
客运总量 (万人次)	Passenger Traffic (10000 person－times)	57986	70653	78027	88362	102579	112844	127967
全年票款收入 (万元)	Income of Tickets (10000 yuan)	43604	86448	98416	105773	120975	127746	150050
年末实有出租汽车数(辆)	Number of Taxis (year－end) (unit)	6300	8320	8398	8583	9167	9305	9362
年末免费公共自行车数(辆)	Number of free Public Bicycles (year－end) (unit)	－	－	－	－	－	50000	60600

注:运营线路和公共汽车数据2009年前不含萧山、余杭。

a) Data of Operating Routes and public transportation vehicles don't include Xiaoshan and Yuhang district before 2009.

11－02 主要年份市区城市供电、供水
Urban Electricity and Water Supply in Main Years

指 标	Item	2000	2005	2006	2007	2008	2009	2010
一、城市供电	**Urban Electricity Supply**							
全年用电总量（亿千瓦时）	Total Electricity Consumption (100 million kwh)	60.19	244.78	279.94	313.47	325.75	346.93	392.64
工业（亿千瓦时）	Industrial Electricity Consumption (100 million kwh)	33.52	172.56	197.61	219.92	221.28	230.20	258.35
生活（亿千瓦时）	Electricity Consumption for Residential Use (100 million kwh)	9.86	27.98	32.53	36.86	41.15	45.31	50.74
二、城市供水（自来水）	**Urban Water Supply**							
总售水量 （万吨）	Total Annual Volume of Tap Water Saled (10000 tons)	27510	58332	57518	56906	58452	59291	45666
平均日供水 （万吨）	Per Capita Daily Consumption of Tap Water (10000 tons)	92	201	177	183	187	190	147
供水能力（万吨/日）	Capacity of Water Supply (10000 tons/day)	146	253	256	274	299	320	320
供水总量 （万吨）	Total Annual Volume of Tap Water Supplied (10000 tons)	33725	73331	64734	66753	68178	69499	53565
其中：生产用水（万吨）	For Productive Use (10000 tons)	8100	27327	20258	19519	19354	16671	11479
生活用水（万吨）	For Residential Use (10000 tons)	19410	35220	33979	33682	35902	37274	30978
用水普及率 （%）	Percentage of Population with Access to Tap Water (%)	100	100	100	100	100	100	100

注：从2001年起市区数据包括萧山区和余杭区。

a) Data of urban include Xiaoshan and Yuhang district since 2001.

11－03 主要年份市区市政建设

Public Utilities in Urban District in Main Years

指 标	Item	2000	2005	2006	2007	2008	2009	2010
一、市政建设	**Urban Infrastructure**							
建成区面积（平方公里）	Constructed Area (sq. m)		314.45	327.45	344.59	367.26	392.73	412.59
年末实有道路面积（万平方米）	Area of Roads (year－end) (10000 sq. m)	1183	3175	4216	4185	4258	4485	4754
年末实有道路长度（公里）	Length of Roads(year－end) (km)	1050	1782	1942	1993	2030	2117	2194
年末实有桥梁数（座）	Number of Bridges(year－end) (unit)	291	991	857	848	917	960	1021
排水管道长度（公里）	Length of Drainage Pipelines (km)	1431	2945	2419	3115	3286	3650	3904
城市污水排放量（万立方米）	Volume of Sewage Drained (10000 cu. m)	27010	55141	44108	47952	61330	57132	43746
城市污水处理总量（万立方米）	the Total Volume of Urban Sewage Treatment (10000 cu. m)		43352	37758	36918	51808	51433	41733
二、城市液化气	**Urban Liquefied Petroleum Gas**							
供气总量 （万吨）	Total Volume of Liquefied Petroleum Gas Supply (10000 tons)	7.47	15.28	8.54	5.91	8.96	10.11	11.44
其中:家庭用气（万吨）	Supply for Residential Use (10000 tons)	5.08	9.51	5.53	3.52	6.63	6.25	5.77
三、人工煤气及天然气	**Coal Gas and Natural Gas**							
家庭用气总量（万立方米）	Total Volume of Coal Gas Consumed (10000 cu. m)	4367	3225	3101	4010	4917	7285	10053
家庭用气户数（万户）	Residential Households with Access to Gas (10000 households)	14.46	25.48	29.50	37.46	43.58	51.84	62.85
四、全社会气化率 %	**Percentage of Population with Access to Gas** (%)	95.70	99.17	100	100	100	100	100

注:从2001年起市区数据包括萧山区和余杭区。

a) Data of urban include Xiaoshan and Yuhang district since 2001.

11－04 主要年份市区园林绿化

Urban Forestation in Main Years

指 标	Item	2000	2005	2006	2007	2008	2009	2010
一、园林绿化	**Urban Forestation**							
建城区绿化覆盖面积（公顷）	The Green Areas Coveraged in Constructed Areas (hectare)	6083	11734	12490	13284	14177	15686	16483
园林绿地面积（公顷）	Total Area of Parks, Gardens and Green Areas (hectare)	6035	10774	11309	12141	12971	14366	15118
其中：公共绿地（公顷）	Public Green Area (hectare)	976	2564	2926	3486	4078	4676	5017
建城区绿化覆盖率（%）	Rate of the Green Areas Coveraged in Constructed Areas (%)	34.33	37.31	38.14	38.55	38.60	39.94	39.95
公园景点个数（个）	Number of Parks and Scenic Resorts (unit)	70	184	106	138	150	165	176
公园景点面积（公顷）	Area of Parks and Scenic Resorts (hectare)	489	997	852	1412	1430	1688	1906
二、收费公园、风景点游人量（万人次）	**Number of Visitors to Parks and Scenic Resorts (10000 persontimes)**	1916	2396	2994	2976	3726	3985	5314

注：从2001年起市区数据包括萧山区和余杭区。

a) Data of urban include Xiaoshan and Yuhang district since 2001.

11－05 工业"三废"排放及处理率(2010年)

Discharge and Disposal Rate of Industrial "Three Waste"(2010)

单位:% (%)

指 标	Item	全 市 Whole Municipality	市 区 Urban District
工业废水排放达标率	Up to－standard Rate of Indusurial Waste Water Discharge	96.88	96.37
工业废水重复用水率	Industrial Waste Water Reused	73.43	78.63
工业废水化学需氧量排放降低率	The Lower Rate of COD Emission from Industrial Waste Water	－4.34	－26.93
工业废气二氧化硫去除率	Rate of Sulphur Dioxide Removed from Industrial Waste Gas	50.96	48.43
工业废气烟尘去除率	Rate of Soot Removed from Industrial Waste Gas	97.17	97.51
工业废气粉尘去除率	Rate of Industrial Dust Removed from Industrial Waste Gas	98.58	99.1
工业废气二氧化硫排放达标率	Up to－standard Rate of Sulphru Dioxide Emission	99.19	98.73
工业废气二氧化硫排放降低率	The Lower Rate of SO_2 Emission from Industrial Waste Gas	4.57	6.8
工业废气烟尘排放达标率	Up to－standard Rate of Industrial Soot Emission	99.64	99.07
工业废气粉尘排放达标率	Up to－standard Rate of Industrial Dust Emission	99.86	99.83
工业固体废物综合利用率	Rate of Industrial Solid Wastes Utilized in a Comprehensive Way	94.13	95.23
工业固体废物贮存率	Rate of Industrial Solid Wastes Stored	0.01	…
工业固体废物处置率	Rate of Industrial Solid Wastes Treated	5.84	4.77
工业固体废物排放率	Rate of Industrial Solid Wastes Discharged	0.03	…
工业锅炉烟尘排放达标率	Up to－standard Rate of Industrial Boilers' Soot Emission	99.62	99.38
工业炉窑烟尘排放达标率	Up to－standard Rate of Industrial Furnaces & Kilns' Soot Emission	98.71	97.86
城市污水处理率	Rate of Urban Waste Water Treated	93.81	95.40

主要统计指标解释

自来水生产能力 指年底城建部门管理的自来水厂实际生产能力。

生活用水量 指居民日常生活与公共福利设施的用水量。包括居民、饮食店、旅馆、医院、理发店、浴池、洗衣店、游泳池、商店、学校、机关、部队等单位的用水量。

供气总量 指全年售给各类用户的全部煤气量。包括工业用量、家庭用量和其他用量。

年末实有道路长度 指除土路外,路面经过铺装宽度在3.5米以上的道路,包括高级、次高级道路和普通道路。

城市桥梁 指城市范围内,修建在河道上的桥梁和道路与道路立交、道路跨越铁路的立交桥,以及人行天桥。包括永久性桥和半永久性桥,不包括临时性桥、铁路桥、涵洞。

营运线路长度 指设置的固定营运线路的长度,包括郊区营运线路长度。不包括临时行驶的线路长度。

用水普及率 指城市用水的非农业人口数(不包括临时人口和流动人口)与城市非农业人口总数之比。计算公式为:

$$\text{用水普及率} = \frac{\text{城市用水非农业人口数}}{\text{城市非农业人口数}} \times 100\%$$

城市园林绿地面积 指城市公共绿地、专用绿地、生产绿地、防护绿地、郊区风景名胜区的全部面积。

公共绿地面积 指供游览休息的各种公园、动物园、植物园、陵园以及花园、游园和供游览休息用的林荫道绿地、广场绿地。不包括一般栽植的行道树及林荫道的面积。

Explanatory Notes on Main Statistical Indicators

Production Capacity of Tap Water refers to the actual comprehensive production capacity of the waterworks administered by the urban construction department.

Consumption of water for Residential Use refers to the water consumption of households for daily life and the water consumption of public welfare facilities, including the consumption of restaurants, hotels, hospitals, barber shops, public bathhouses, laundries, swimming pools, shops, schools, institutions, army units and other units.

Volume of Gas Supply refers to the total volume of gas Sold to users in a year, including the volume for industrial use, residential use and other uses.

Length of Roads at the Year – end refers to the length of roads with a paved surface, and with a width of more than 3 – 5 meters, including high quality, medium quality and ordinary roads.

Urban Bridges refers to bridges over river courses, great separated junctions and overpasses in urban areas. Permanent bridges and semi – permanent bridges are included. Temporary bridges, railway bridges and culverts are excluded.

Length in Operation refers to the length of the roads in fixed operation, including the suburb one, but excluding the tomporary ones.

Percentage of Urban Population with Access to Tap Water refers to the ratio of the urban non – agricultural population (excluding temporary and mobile population) with access to tap water to the tolal urban non – agricultural population. The formula is:

$$\text{Percentage of Poputalion with Access to Tap Water} = \frac{\text{Urban Non – agricultural Population with Access to Tap Water}}{\text{Urban Non – agricultural Population}} \times 100\%$$

Area of Urban Gardens and Green Areas refers to the total area of urban public green land, special green land, production green land, protection green land and suburban scenic spots.

Public Green Area refers to green area of various parks, zoos, botanical gardens, cemeteries, amusement parks, tree – flanked boulevards Greenland squares for tourism and relaxing. Areas with trees planted along – side the streets and boulevards are excluded.

第十二篇
CHAPTER-12

科技、教育、文化、卫生、体育

Science And Technology, Education, Culture, Public Health And Sports

科技、教育、文化、卫生、体育
Science and Technology, Education, Culture, Public Health and Sports

主要统计指标
Major Statistical Indicators

高等学校数	Number of Regular Institution of Higher Education	37	个	(unit)
高等学校在校学生数	Number of Students in Regular Institution of Higher Education	43.48	万人	(10000 person)
中等学校在校学生数	Number of Students in Secondary Schools	3999	人	(person)
高中在校学生数	Number of Students in Senior High Schools	11.70	万人	(10000 person)
初中在校学生数	Number of Students in Junior High Schools	23.60	万人	(10000 person)
小学在校学生数	Number of Students in Primary Schools	45.39	万人	(10000 person)
医疗病床数	Number of Beds in Health Institutions	4.28	万张	(10000 bed)
#医院	Number of Beds in Hospitals	3.61	万张	(10000 bed)
卫生技术人员数	Number of Medical Technical Personnel	6.11	万人	(10000 person)
#执业(助理)医师	Number of Registered (Assistant) Doctors	2.43	万人	(10000 person)
公共图书馆	Public Library	16	个	(unit)

12-01 分县(市)城镇单位年末人才资源

Trained Personnel Resource of Urban Units by Region

单位:人 (person)

地 区	Region	人才资源数 Number of Trained Personnel Resources		#专业技术人员 Technical Personnel	
		2010	2009	2010	2009
全市	**Whole Municipality**	**1341692**	**1140129**	**541569**	**482215**
市区	Urban District	1149009	988551	459257	413580
萧山区	Xiaoshan	236904	189158	77235	66000
余杭区	Yuhang	98832	83503	36557	31752
桐庐县	Tonglu	28130	24660	10986	9940
淳安县	Chun'an	21046	19381	9763	9307
建德市	Jiande	29191	23254	11976	11850
富阳市	Fuyang	67540	44887	30936	19809
临安市	Lin'an	46776	39396	18651	17729

12－02 分行业城镇单位专业技术人员(2010年末)

Technical Personnel of Urban Units by Sector(End of 2010)

单位:人 (person)

行业	Sector	合计 Total	国有 State－owned	集体 Collective－owned Units	其他 Others
全市	**Total**	**541569**	**215298**	**14200**	**312071**
农、林、牧、渔业	Farming, Forestry, Animal Husbandry and Fishery	412	143	8	261
采矿业	Mining & Quarrying	276	16	49	211
制造业	Manufacture	101354	3441	485	97428
电力、燃气及水的生产和供应业	Production and Supply of Electricity, Gas and Water	5158	2768	47	2343
建筑业	Construction	63311	4802	512	57997
交通运输、仓储和邮政业	Transportation, Storage, Post & Telecommunications	7993	3496	428	4069
信息传输、计算机服务和软件业	Information Transmission, Computer Services and Software	35793	3067	69	32657
批发和零售贸易	Wholesale & Retail Trade	24403	2499	358	21546
住宿和餐饮业	Lodging and Catering	6314	748	427	5139
金融业	Banking	35934	7305	－	28629
房地产业	Real Estate	15314	1558	251	13505
租赁与商务服务业	Renting and Business Service	10897	3257	1055	6585
科学研究、技术服务与地质勘查业	Scientific Research, Technical Service and Geological Prospecting	50605	23867	561	26177
水利、环境和公共设施管理业	Water Conservancy, Environment and Public Utility	6649	1644	120	4885
居民服务和其他服务业	Service for the Residents and Other	634	223	49	362
教育	Education	104744	95374	3822	5548
卫生、社会保障和社会福利业	Health Care, Sports & Social Welfare	57040	48409	5895	2736
文化、体育和娱乐业	Culture, Sports and Entertainment	11299	10432	32	835
公共管理和社会组织	Public Management and Social Organizations	3439	2249	32	1158

12-03 按经济类型分的城镇单位专业技术人员(2010年末)
Technical Personnel of Urban Units by Ownership(End of 2010)

单位:人　　　　(person)

地　区 Region	合计 Total	国有 State-owned	集体 Collective-owned Units	其他 Others
总计 Total	**541569**	**215298**	**14200**	**312071**
市区 Urban District	459257	175355	10780	273122
萧山区 Xiaoshan	77235	19550	3716	53969
余杭区 Yuhang	36557	14525	1736	20296
桐庐县 Tonglu	10986	6537	428	4021
淳安县 Chun'an	9763	6173	313	3277
建德市 Jiande	11976	7445	800	3731
富阳市 Fuyang	30936	11033	613	19290
临安市 Lin'an	18651	8755	1266	8630

12－04 文化事业
Number of Institutions

单位:个

指 标	Item	全 市 Total	市 区 Urban District	#萧山区 Xiaoshan
剧　　场	Theaters	12	11	–
剧　　团	Opera Troupes	21	17	1
文 化 馆	Cultural Centers	13	8	1
文 化 站	Cultural Stations	199	96	31
图 书 馆	Libraries	16	11	1
博 物 馆	Museums	65	54	8
展 览 馆	Exhibition Buildings	1	1	–

12－05 分县(市)艺术表演团体
Basic Statistics on Performance of

指 标	Item	全 市 Total		市 区 Urban District	
		2010	为上年(%) As Compared with the Preceding Year(%)	2010	为上年(%) As Compared with the Preceding Year(%)
艺术表演场所演出场次 (场)	Number of Performances in Artistic Performance Place (scene)	4773	73.5	4673	207.6
艺术表演场所演出收入 (万元)	Income of Performances in Artistic Performance Place (10000 yuan)	1460	70.8	1442	70.7
剧团演出场次 (场)	Number of Performances of Opera Troupes (scene)	7321	108.9	6263	110.8
#农　村 (场)	#Rural Areas (scene)	2688	77.4	1758	69.7
剧团演出观众人数(万人次)	Number of Spectators of Opera Troupes (10000 person－times)	685	119.1	553	124.3
剧团演出收入 (万元)	Income of Performances of Opera Troupes (10000 yuan)	6141	137.4	5741	136.6

单位数(2010 年)

for Culture(2010)

(unit)

#余杭区 Yuhang	桐庐县 Tonglu	淳安县 Chun'an	建德市 Jiande	富阳市 Fuyang	临安市 Lin'an
2	–	–	–	–	1
1	1	–	1	1	1
1	1	1	1	1	1
19	13	23	16	25	26
1	1	1	1	1	1
4	2	1	4	3	1
–	–	–	–	–	–

演出情况(2010 年)

Art Troupes by Region(2010)

#萧山区 Xiaoshan	#余杭区 Yuhang	桐庐县 Tonglu	淳安县 Chun'an	建德市 Jiande	富阳市 Fuyang	临安市 Lin'an
–	224	–	–	–	–	100
–	19	–	–	–	–	18
100	125	271	–	285	172	330
75	75	210	–	230	160	330
40	19	40	–	42	34	16
66	85	125	–	59	161	55

12-06 全市专利申请与授权情况(2010年)

Patent Application and Granted(2010)

单位:件 (item)

地区	Region	专利申请合计 Patent Applications	专利申请发明 Inventions	专利申请实用新型 Utility Models	专利申请外观设计 Designs	专利授权合计 Patent Applications Granted	专利授权发明 Inventions	专利授权实用新型 Utility Models	专利授权外观设计 Designs
全市	**Whole Municipality**	**29732**	**7766**	**13108**	**8858**	**26483**	**3238**	**11888**	**11357**
市区	Urban District	24524	7288	10998	6238	21026	3001	9443	8582
上城区	Shangcheng	1462	256	650	556	952	47	345	560
下城区	Xiacheng	2511	900	897	714	1697	379	706	612
江干区	Jianggan	4147	968	1730	1449	3395	387	1610	1398
拱墅区	Gongshu	1039	251	497	291	1016	65	497	454
西湖区	Xihu	6091	3113	2116	862	4257	1265	1946	1046
高新(滨江)区	Hi-Tech(Binjiang)	2191	954	742	495	1993	657	873	463
萧山区	Xiaoshan	3518	373	2429	716	4614	115	2087	2412
余杭区	Yuhang	3565	473	1937	1155	3102	86	1379	1637
桐庐县	Tonglu	881	61	364	456	969	37	399	533
淳安县	Chun'an	290	34	73	183	227	8	73	146
建德市	Jiande	678	64	93	521	785	24	112	649
富阳市	Fuyang	1726	151	1002	573	1814	94	1249	471
临安市	Lin'an	1633	168	578	887	1662	74	612	976

12－07 主要年份市区文化事业单位数

Cultural Institutions of Urban District in Main Years

单位:个 (unit)

年 份 Year	电影院 Cinemas	剧 团 Opera Troupes	剧 场 Theaters	文化馆 Cultural Centers	文化站 Cultural Stations	图书馆 Libraries	博物馆 Museums
1978	7	13	6	5	－	2	1
1979	8	14	7	5	27	2	1
1980	8	15	7	5	37	2	1
1981	8	17	7	6	40	2	1
1982	9	17	7	6	45	3	1
1983	9	15	3	6	46	3	1
1984	9	15	4	6	49	3	1
1985	8	16	9	6	47	3	2
1986	8	15	8	6	48	3	2
1987	8	15	9	6	38	3	2
1988	7	14	9	6	50	3	2
1989	7	14	9	6	48	2	2
1990	9	14	9	5	48	3	2
1991	10	14	8	5	48	3	2
1992	11	14	8	5	48	3	6
1993	10	14	9	5	42	3	6
1994	11	13	9	5	48	3	6
1995	11	13	9	5	67	3	6
1996	10	13	8	5	55	3	6
1997	10	13	8	5	52	3	6
1998	9	13	8	6	55	3	7
1999	9	13	6	6	52	3	8
2000	8	12	6	6	52	3	9
2001	49	14	11	8	89	5	11
2002	－	14	10	8	90	4	11
2003	19	14	11	13	92	4	11
2004	18	14	14	8	93	5	12
2005	16	15	10	8	94	7	12
2006	16	15	10	8	94	8	12
2007	16	15	10	8	92	9	12
2008	18	15	11	8	92	9	13
2009	15	16	11	8	95	11	34
2010	25	17	11	8	96	11	54

注:从2001年起市区数据包括萧山区和余杭区。

a) Data of urban include Xiaoshan and Yuhang district since 2001.

12-08 主要年份高等学校基本情况

Basic Statistics on Regular Institutions of Higher Education in Main Years

单位:人 (person)

年　份 Year	学校数(个) Number of Schools(unit)	在校学生数 Number of Students	教职员工数 Teachers and Staff	#专职教师 Number of Full-time Teachers
1978	9	13319	8966	3946
1979	12	17518	10182	4458
1980	13	23545	12400	5278
1981	13	28936	13090	5359
1982	13	25821	14363	6067
1983	14	27443	15267	6172
1984	16	31384	15889	6387
1985	20	36996	17507	7247
1986	22	40051	18968	7845
1987	21	39922	18965	7876
1988	21	40787	19582	8133
1989	21	40330	19680	8107
1990	21	39866	19495	8075
1991	21	42192	19489	7737
1992	19	43787	19841	7561
1993	19	51063	19787	7561
1994	19	59109	19903	7703
1995	20	63124	19883	7799
1996	20	66023	19693	7824
1997	20	69391	19540	7793
1998	17	76546	19320	7723
1999	18	89109	20136	8135
2000	32	122386	23791	10477
2001	33	174894	25805	11866
2002	34	224048	27307	13605
2003	35	269798	34508	18141
2004	36	313599	33325	18445
2005	36	351918	34816	19583
2006	36	373563	36929	21375
2007	36	392770	38843	23197
2008	36	409559	39762	24017
2009	36	429774	40420	24765
2010	37	434811	41582	25003

注:在校学生数包括各高校研究生。

a) Number of students include graduate students in all schools.

12－09 主要年份中等专业学校基本情况
Basic Statistics on Specialized Secondary Schools in Main Years

单位:人 (person)

年 份 Year	学校数(个) Number of Schools(unit)	在校学生数 Number of Students	教职员工数 Teachers and Staff	#专职教师 Number of Full－time Teachers
1978	26	8711	3044	1080
1979	27	11093	2601	1124
1980	26	9453	2450	1101
1981	35	7309	3122	1276
1982	37	8284	3694	1529
1983	37	10516	3716	1604
1984	42	13419	4194	1758
1985	46	16527	5095	1959
1986	50	19114	5641	2336
1987	52	20929	6081	2623
1988	51	22117	6144	2741
1989	54	23302	6602	2888
1990	55	23564	6679	2948
1991	55	23331	6584	2770
1992	55	26373	6786	2825
1993	56	30336	6732	2780
1994	57	36079	6881	2840
1995	57	42784	6851	2888
1996	58	49593	6789	2904
1997	57	51752	6731	2896
1998	56	55796	6554	2746
1999	50	52272	5023	2272
2000	28	45238	2950	1421
2001	26	32763	2053	1051
2002	14	26255	1251	566
2003	13	21735	1058	457
2004	11	21262	869	416
2005	10	20344	893	443
2006	8	12540	410	184
2007	8	8927	414	194
2008	8	5514	345	152
2009	8	4016	233	65
2010	6	3999	348	151

12－10 主要年份高中基本情况

Basic Statistics on Senior High Schools in Main Years

单位：人 (person)

年 份 Year	学校数(个) Number of Schools(unit)	在校学生数 Number of Students	专职教师数 Number of Full－time Teachers
1978	352	102815	5235
1979	182	58866	3471
1980	151	43661	3173
1981	118	34606	2825
1982	113	35136	2740
1983	111	38580	2740
1984	105	43167	2781
1985	104	47510	3016
1986	95	46379	2972
1987	92	44697	3006
1988	89	42196	2947
1989	88	39994	2898
1990	86	39829	2922
1991	82	37809	2896
1992	74	34620	2791
1993	72	32483	2641
1994	75	35720	2673
1995	72	40771	2880
1996	70	43692	3135
1997	69	47975	3388
1998	75	55688	3693
1999	82	64459	4172
2000	85	73049	4745
2001	88	79632	5262
2002	81	91635	6126
2003	77	108116	6879
2004	81	115303	7510
2005	80	120883	8041
2006	82	124177	8421
2007	80	122939	8542
2008	76	120294	8646
2009	75	118057	8751
2010	72	116983	8871

12-11 主要年份初中基本情况
Basic Statistics on Junior Middle Schools in Main Years

单位:人 (person)

年 份 Year	学校数(个) Number of Schools(unit)	在校学生数 Number of Students	专职教师数 Number of Full - time Teachers
1978	254	247209	11978
1979	363	208484	11020
1980	369	204073	10695
1981	359	194024	10015
1982	367	193135	10107
1983	370	190221	9948
1984	368	192971	9679
1985	361	196889	9799
1986	376	199638	9821
1987	385	195426	10264
1988	380	170079	10055
1989	376	151223	9825
1990	382	160111	9564
1991	387	185590	10020
1992	367	212022	10603
1993	365	203896	10876
1994	371	205388	11495
1995	373	216300	12058
1996	374	229466	12810
1997	368	227809	13370
1998	359	222191	13493
1999	339	239174	13723
2000	330	269484	14529
2001	314	285203	15685
2002	315	282951	15758
2003	316	268824	15836
2004	303	252291	16042
2005	289	241374	16205
2006	263	235527	16374
2007	262	238252	16591
2008	260	244464	16965
2009	252	241899	17317
2010	245	236014	17795

12－12 主要年份小学基本情况

Basic Statistics on Primary Schools in Main Years

单位:人 (person)

年 份 Year	学校数(个) Number of Schools(unit)	在校学生数 Number of Students	教职员工数 Number of Teachers and Staff	#专职教师数 Number of Full－time Teachers
1978	4959	605137	24103	22291
1979	4850	577811	25089	23220
1980	4781	560244	25388	22902
1981	4668	525503	22468	20832
1982	4528	479264	22213	20289
1983	4417	444301	20842	18945
1984	4345	427763	20496	18500
1985	4286	414839	20945	18415
1986	4250	413507	20796	18464
1987	4205	405856	21067	18751
1988	4137	426842	21658	19236
1989	4106	459162	22660	20177
1990	4077	460514	20542	18099
1991	3972	453055	20781	18369
1992	3654	450496	21452	19067
1993	3473	477026	22141	19775
1994	3352	504867	22751	20462
1995	3172	513988	23743	21380
1996	3006	525674	24553	22197
1997	2762	538390	25269	23022
1998	2395	532845	25718	23499
1999	1996	512874	26350	24120
2000	1659	485679	25938	23876
2001	1354	467982	25535	23179
2002	1197	456535	25425	23138
2003	1044	448969	25304	22955
2004	897	447971	25396	23066
2005	791	458942	25793	23541
2006	605	459529	26040	23848
2007	437	456152	26455	24251
2008	418	452143	26894	24743
2009	417	445132	27445	25424
2010	408	453897	27881	25709

12－13 主要年份幼儿园基本情况

Basic Statistics on Kindergartens in Main Years

单位:人 (person)

年份 Year	园数(个) Kindergartens(unit)	在园幼儿数 Number of Children	教职员工数 Teachers and Staff	#教师 Number of Full－time Teachers
1978	266	37597	2570	1439
1979	216	59245	3731	2201
1980	518	82182	4763	3398
1981	676	82808	5275	3691
1982	853	95733	6357	4269
1983	1034	95676	6271	4135
1984	1749	112095	7238	4900
1985	1743	115766	7360	5278
1986	1607	118792	7898	5659
1987	1678	133773	8622	6335
1988	1541	139883	9221	6608
1989	1397	132947	9595	6849
1990	1526	136277	9808	7167
1991	1422	150982	10472	7388
1992	1431	133773	9240	6487
1993	1328	171005	10779	7886
1994	1470	165860	10718	7891
1995	1493	149497	10102	7943
1996	1437	150587	10203	7625
1997	1504	146530	10480	7743
1998	1695	153035	10691	7956
1999	1787	156372	10719	8107
2000	2037	168414	11740	8770
2001	1249	174204	11447	7880
2002	1268	175891	11988	8086
2003	1285	176862	13702	9076
2004	1098	186472	14991	9544
2005	1188	188991	16161	10288
2006	1188	195552	17550	11053
2007	1071	212754	19330	12168
2008	1037	235867	21193	12917
2009	972	246336	22970	14211
2010	969	267352	25525	15203

12－14 高等学校

Basic Statistics on Regular

单位:人

单位名称	Item	在校学生数 Number of Students	
		2010	为上年(%) As Compared with the Preceding Year(%)
全　　市	**Total**	**395818**	**103.5**
市　　区	**Urban District**	**376333**	**103.5**
其中:1.浙江大学	Zhejiang University	22557	101.3
2.杭州电子科技大学	Hangzhou Dianzi University	16013	98.3
3.浙江工业大学	Zhejiang Univesity of Technology	21557	100.6
4.浙江理工大学	Zhejiang Sci－Tech University	16651	104.5
5.浙江林学院	Zhejiang Forestry University	13104	104.1
6.浙江中医学院	Zhejiang College of Traditional Chinese Medicine	5080	106.3
7.浙江工商大学	Zhejiang Gongshang University	14749	100.3
8.中国美术学院	China Academy of Art	8639	101.8
9.中国计量学院	China Institute of Metrology	12449	109.4
10.浙江科技学院	Hangzhou Application Engineering and Technology College	14222	102.6
11.浙江广播电视大学	Zhejiang Radio & TV University	10574	103.3
12.浙江水利水电专科学校	Zhejiang Water Conservancy and Hydroelectricity College	7125	97.8
13.浙江财经学院	Zhejiang Institute of Finance and Economics	11845	107.1
14.浙江警察学院	Zhejiang Police College	3631	123.4
15.浙江传媒学院	Zhejiang Institute of Media and Communications	9624	104.1
16.浙江树人大学	Zhejiang Shuren University	14323	102.3
17.杭州师范大学	Hangzhou Normal University	12330	109.5
18.浙江大学城市学院	Zhejiang University City College	13649	102.8

注:本表不含在校研究生。

基本情况(2010 年)
Institutions of Higher Education(2010)

(person)

本年招生数 Number of New Students Enrollment	本年毕业生数 Number of Graduates	教职员工数 Number of Teachers and Staff		2011 年预计毕业生 Number of Students Will Graduate in 2011
		合　计 Total	其中:专职教师 Full－time Teachers	
113529	**101681**	**41582**	**25003**	**108244**
108508	**97285**	**39690**	**23713**	**103494**
5619	5231	8241	2965	5839
4054	4331	1573	1108	4275
5473	5017	2659	1615	5437
4171	3464	1692	1176	4153
3494	2906	1435	935	3091
1310	995	747	571	1029
3771	3755	1646	1136	3778
2349	2073	1058	661	2323
3440	2386	1236	833	2654
3849	3025	1177	807	3146
3749	3489	231	66	4478
2844	2981	571	422	2398
3326	2472	1211	764	2843
547	879	365	245	1388
2621	2164	906	593	2482
3923	3377	790	542	3735
3740	2662	2374	1224	2727
3321	2525	991	759	3282

a) Data in this table does not contain post－graduate students.

12－15 普通中学及职业

Basic Statistics on Senior, Junior

单位：人

指 标	Item	全 市 Total	市 区 Urban District	#萧山区 Xiaoshan
高 中	**Senior High Schools**			
学校数(所)	Number of Schools(unit)	72	49	9
在校学生数	Number of Students	116983	69614	22331
为上年(%)	As Compared with the Preceding Year (%)	99.09	98.94	99.78
本年招生数	Number of New Students Enrollment	38993	23337	7589
本年毕业生数	Number of Graduates	39319	23482	7677
#专职教师	#Full－time Teachers	8871	5574	1668
2011 年预计毕业生数	Number of Students Will Graduate in 2011	38746	23164	7366
初 中	**Junior High Schools**			
学校数(所)	Number of Schools(unit)	245	150	42
在校学生数	Number of Students	236014	148648	49735
为上年(%)	As Compared with the Preceding Year (%)	97.57	100.37	98.44
本年招生数	Number of New Students Enrollment	76496	50219	16866
本年毕业生数	Number of Graduates	78379	46717	15967
#专职教师	#Full－time Teachers	17795	11464	3539
2011 年预计毕业生数	Number of Students Will Graduate in 2011	79864	48226	16182
职业中学	**Vocational Schools**			
学校数(所)	Number of Schools(unit)	37	20	4
在校学生数	Number of Students	70498	43785	14403
为上年(%)	As Compared with the Preceding Year (%)	103.19	103.71	108.18
本年招生数	Number of New Students Enrollment	25969	15930	5519
本年毕业生数	Number of Graduates	20816	12917	3912
专职教师数	Full－time Teachers	3807	2278	555
2011 年预计毕业生数	Number of Students Will Graduate in 2011	21269	13117	4147

中学基本情况(2010 年)
High Schools and Vacational Schools(2010)

(person)

#余杭区 Yuhang	桐庐县 Tonglu	淳安县 Chun'an	建德市 Jiande	富阳市 Fuyang	临安市 Lin'an
10	3	4	5	6	5
13087	7071	7533	9400	13420	9945
99.14	99.77	96.99	97.92	101.02	99.89
4324	2289	2555	3113	4441	3258
4339	2202	2753	3134	4376	3372
941	516	508	640	983	650
4347	2285	2513	2990	4400	3394
37	14	17	23	20	21
30418	13710	14753	17537	25283	16083
102.57	93.82	95.20	93.42	94.43	88.67
10313	3988	4421	5270	7794	4804
8897	4664	5048	6431	8986	6533
2414	976	1143	1247	1728	1237
9703	5046	5186	6333	9192	5881
4	2	4	3	4	4
9124	2616	4297	4394	9638	5768
100.97	99.89	94.98	105.82	106.50	100.24
3347	1159	1583	1464	3644	2189
2908	980	1654	1116	2534	1615
487	175	202	206	577	369
2616	725	1439	1445	2890	1653

12－16　小学、幼儿园及特殊
Basic Statistics on Primary Schools,

单位：人

指　标	Item	全　市 Total	市　区 Urban District	#萧山区 Xiaoshan
小　　学	**Primary Schools**			
学校数(所)	Number of Schools(unit)	408	231	80
班数(班)	Number of Classes(unit)	11833	7968	2459
在校学生数	Number of Students	453897	315731	104304
为上年(%)	As Compared with the Preceding Year (%)	101.97	104.11	102.32
本年招生数	Number of New Students Enrollment	80277	57538	18831
本年毕业生数	Number of Graduates	76126	49568	17516
教职员工数	Number of Teachers and Staff	27881	18345	4831
#专职教师	#Full－time Teachers	25709	16949	4641
2011 年预计毕业生数	Number of Students Will Graduate in 2011	73808	48776	16954
幼儿园	**Kindergartens**			
园数(个)	Number of Kindergartens(unit)	969	605	218
班数(班)	Number of Classes(unit)	8725	6183	1714
在园幼儿数	Number of Children	267352	189868	54082
教职员工数	Number of Teachers and Staff	25525	19514	5116
#教师	#Full－time Teachers	15203	11318	2884
盲聋哑学校	**Schools for the Blind, Deaf and Deaf－mute**			
学校数(个)	Number of Schools(unit)	3	2	1
在校学生数	Number of Students	721	467	125
本年招生数	Number of New Students Enrollment	80	46	15
本年毕业生数	Number of Graduates	103	85	41
专职教师	Number of Full－time Teachers	184	124	41
弱智学校	**Schools for Weaken in Intelligence**			
学校数(个)	Number of Schools(unit)	9	5	－
在校学生数	Number of Students	697	532	－
本年招生数	Number of New Students Enrollment	120	90	－
本年毕业生数	Number of Graduates	56	55	－
专职教师	Number of Full－time Teachers	156	113	－
工读学校	**Reformatory Schools**			
学校数(个)	Number of Schools(unit)	1	1	－
在校学生数	Number of Students	140	140	－
本年招生数	Number of New Students Enrollment	59	59	－
本年毕业生数	Number of Graduates	60	60	－
专任教师总数	Number of Full－time Teachers	42	42	－

教育基本情况(2010 年)
Kindergartens and Special Education(2010)

(person)

#余杭区 Yuhang	桐庐县 Tonglu	淳安县 Chun'an	建德市 Jiande	富阳市 Fuyang	临安市 Lin'an
44	23	37	27	52	38
1671	608	646	608	1241	762
70208	22230	20313	23955	42948	28720
110.58	98.01	93.54	93.92	99.07	100.36
13938	3713	3103	3570	7498	4855
9802	4190	4367	5263	7934	4804
4056	1396	1840	1572	2824	1904
3617	1227	1737	1480	2556	1760
9861	3914	4035	4917	7529	4637
70	80	61	36	109	78
1057	407	314	459	761	601
35251	12215	12992	12835	23173	16269
3102	970	583	1016	1981	1461
1971	563	401	680	1295	946
–	–	–	–	1	–
–	–	–	–	254	–
–	–	–	–	34	–
–	–	–	–	18	–
–	–	–	–	60	–
1	1	–	1	1	1
31	34	–	21	48	62
31	7	–	10	7	6
–	1	–	–	–	–
8	1	–	5	19	18
–	–	–	–	–	–
–	–	–	–	–	–
–	–	–	–	–	–
–	–	–	–	–	–
–	–	–	–	–	–

12－17 各级成人教育

Basic Statistics on

单位：人

指　标	Item	成人高等学历教育 Higher Education for Adults	职工大学 Staff and Workers College	广播电视大学 Broadcasting and Television College
全　市	**Total**			
学校数（所）	Number of Schools(unit)	4	3	1
在校学生数	Number of Students	117838	5052	10574
为上年（%）	As Compared with the Preceding Year (%)	89.98	88.99	103.3
本年招生数	Number of New Students Enrollment	49137	2576	3749
本年毕业生数	Number of Graduates	57280	2793	3489
教职员工数	Number of Teachers and Staff	600	369	231
#专职教师	#Full－time Teachers	292	226	66
市　区	**Urban District**			
学校数（所）	Number of Schools(unit)	4	3	1
在校学生数	Number of Students	115499	5052	10574
为上年（%）	As Compared with the Preceding Year(%)	89.54	88.99	103.3
本年招生数	Number of New Students Enrollment	48189	2576	3749
本年毕业生数	Number of Graduates	56700	2793	3489
教职员工数	Number of Teachers and Staff	600	369	231
#专职教师	#Full－time Teachers	292	226	66

基本情况(2010 年)
Various Adult Education(2010)

(person)

普通高校举办函大夜大 Correspondence School and Night School Held by Regular Higher Education	普通高校举办脱产班 Training Classes Be Released form Production	成人中等学历教育 Specialized Secondary Education	成人中等专业 Specialized Secondary Schools for Adults	成人中学 Secondary Schools for Adults	成人技术培训学校 Technical Schools for Adults
-	-	93	16	77	312
47609	3443	26279	24528	1751	423783
95.08	49.8	77.94	96.6	21.03	98.63
21392	-	10525	10525	-	-
23769	4572	11676	9850	1826	464841
-	-	1403	975	428	4350
-	-	893	588	305	1985
-	-	40	11	29	205
46639	3343	24893	23867	1026	348688
94.67	51.09	95.97	97.83	66.45	102.21
20981	-	10525	10525	-	-
23513	4403	10264	9518	746	382420
-	-	1084	805	279	3785
-	-	701	512	189	1568

12-18 主要年份医疗卫生机构数

Number of Health Institutions in Main Years

单位:个 (unit)

年 份 Year	全市合计 Total	#医 院 Hospitals	市区合计 Urban District	#医 院 Hospitals
1978	1361	421	689	45
1979	1390	426	696	50
1980	1381	425	675	51
1981	1476	424	749	51
1982	1540	432	798	56
1983	1540	435	800	58
1984	1574	437	807	54
1985	1582	404	787	47
1986	1636	407	826	53
1987	1693	420	865	55
1988	1710	438	878	55
1989	1721	443	882	57
1990	1738	440	890	58
1991	1789	441	889	58
1992	1767	436	885	58
1993	1730	403	882	68
1994	1717	416	882	72
1995	1712	414	883	72
1996	1712	416	893	83
1997	1711	411	891	81
1998	1491	419	757	89
1999	1530	400	789	85
2000	1599	396	853	85
2001	1496	391	1072	191
2002	1817	116	1277	88
2003	1901	99	1323	73
2004	1985	114	1396	87
2005	2196	127	1604	97
2006	2570	134	1886	107
2007	2607	138	1872	104
2008	2544	141	1813	108
2009	2687	144	1887	111
2010	2819	151	1906	113

注:从 2001 年起市区数据包括萧山区和余杭区。2002 年起医院数据不包括卫生院。

a) Data of urban include Xiaoshan and Yuhang district since 2001. From 2002, the figures of hospitals exclude health centers.

12-19 主要年份医疗病床数

Number of Beds in Health Institutions in Main Years

单位:张 (bed)

年 份 Year	全 市 Total	#医 院 Hospitals	市 区 Urban District	#医 院 Hospitals
1978	14042	11704	6588	5789
1979	15124	12682	7335	6282
1980	16317	13478	8244	6940
1981	17408	13576	9646	7185
1982	17179	14350	9194	7580
1983	17338	14584	9411	7833
1984	17694	14691	9536	7867
1985	19637	15010	11095	7933
1986	20555	16035	11657	8448
1987	21465	16770	12203	8863
1988	23394	17954	13204	9651
1989	24111	18363	13581	9773
1990	24121	18879	13219	10041
1991	24966	19444	13968	10437
1992	25606	20243	14206	10821
1993	25653	20884	14058	10982
1994	25984	20870	14231	11045
1995	26684	21360	14731	11336
1996	28141	22217	15427	12132
1997	26616	22341	15076	12190
1998	27327	23110	15530	12766
1999	26713	22952	14988	12691
2000	27166	23303	15496	13068
2001	27063	23520	20523	17770
2002	27609	22797	21200	18667
2003	29144	22036	22641	18205
2004	31738	24444	25008	20338
2005	33251	25907	26732	21931
2006	33972	27186	27172	23184
2007	36928	29987	29884	25664
2008	38114	31416	30663	26882
2009	40226	33094	32412	28031
2010	42828	36148	34693	30639

注:从2001年起市区数据包括萧山区和余杭区。

a) Data of urban include Xiaoshan and Yuhang district since 2001.

12－20 医疗卫生

Number of Health

单位:个

指　　标	Item	全　　市 Total	市区 Urban District
总　　计	**Total**	**2819**	**1906**
一、医院	Number of Hospitals	151	113
1. 综合医院	General Hospitals	80	62
2. 中医医院	Hospitals of Chinese Medicine	24	12
3. 中西医结合医院	Chinese Therapeutics with Western	3	3
4. 专科医院	Specialized Hospitals	43	35
口腔医院	Hospitals for Mouth	6	5
眼科医院	Hospitals for Eye	1	1
肿瘤医院	Tumor Hospitals	2	1
妇产(科)医院	Hospitals for Pregnant Woman	6	5
儿童医院	Children Hospitals	1	1
精神病医院	Mental Hospitals	3	2
传染病医院	Hospitals for Infectious Diseases	1	1
骨科医院	Orthopaedics Hospitals	5	3
康复医院	Healing Hospitals	6	5
整型外科医院	Plastic Hospitals	2	2
美容医院	Beauty Hospitals	4	4
其他专科医院	Other Special Hospitals	6	5
5. 护理院	Nursing Centers	1	1
二、疗养院	Sanatoriums	9	6
三、社区卫生服务中心(站)	Health Service Centers for Community	1099	756
1. 社区卫生服务中心	Health Service Centers	119	93
2. 社区卫生服务站	Health Service Stations	980	663
四、卫生院	Health Service Centers	142	25
1. 街道卫生院	Rural Township Hospitals in Subdistrict	6	-
2. 乡镇卫生院	Rural Township Hospitals in Country	136	25
五、门诊部	Clinics	227	192
六、诊所、卫生所、医务室、护理站	Other Health Care Institutions	1105	761
七、急救中心(站)	First－aid Centers(stations)	8	4
八、采供血机构	Blood Supplying Agencies	3	2
九、妇幼保健院(所、站)	Maternity and Child Care Centers(stations)	9	4
十、专科疾病防治所(所、站)	Specialized Centers for Disease Prevention and Control(stations)	7	1
十一、疾病预防控制中心	Centers for Disease Prevention and Control	15	10
十二、卫生监督所	Institutions of Public Health Inspection	14	9
十三、医学科学研究机构	Research Institutions of Medical Science	1	1
十四、医学在职培训机构	Medical Training Organization for Incumbent	7	4
十五、健康教育所(站、中心)	Education Center for Health(stations)	2	1
十六、其他卫生机构	Other Health Care Institutions	20	17

机构数(2010 年)
Institutions(2010)

(unit)

#萧山区 Xiaoshan	#余杭区 Yuhang	桐庐县 Tonglu	淳安县 Chun'an	建德市 Jiande	富阳市 Fuyang	临安市 Lin'an
462	**349**	**154**	**127**	**172**	**280**	**180**
23	7	5	5	8	9	11
17	4	3	3	5	2	5
3	1	2	2	1	4	3
–	–	–	–	–	–	–
2	2	–	–	2	3	3
1	–	–	–	–	1	–
–	–	–	–	–	–	–
–	–	–	–	–	1	–
–	–	–	–	–	–	1
–	–	–	–	–	–	–
–	1	–	–	1	–	–
–	–	–	–	–	–	–
–	1	–	–	–	–	2
–	–	–	–	1	–	–
–	–	–	–	–	–	–
–	–	–	–	–	–	–
1	–	–	–	–	1	–
1	–	–	–	–	–	–
1	–	–	–	–	3	–
226	201	92	46	36	154	15
25	22	2		2	22	
201	179	90	46	34	132	15
25	–	11	21	27	16	42
–	–	–	–	–	3	3
25	–	11	21	27	13	39
19	29	1		12	7	15
159	107	42	47	80	86	89
2	1		3	1		
1	–	–	–	1	–	–
–	1	1	1	1	1	1
–	–	–	1	1	2	2
1	1	1	1	1	1	1
1	1	1	1	1	1	1
–	–	–	–	–	–	–
1	1	–	1	1	–	1
1	–	–	–	–	–	1
2	–	–	–	2	–	1

12－21 医疗病床

Number of Beds in

单位:张

指　　标	Item	全　　市 Total	市区 Urban District
总　　计	**Total**	**42828**	**34693**
一、医院	Number of Hospitals	36148	30639
1. 综合医院	General Hospitals	23029	19124
2. 中医医院	Hospitals of Chinese Medicine	5994	4805
3. 中西医结合医院	Chinese Therapeutics with Western	1100	1100
4. 专科医院	Specialized Hospitals	6005	5590
口腔医院	Hospitals for Mouth	63	48
眼科医院	Hospitals for Eye	40	40
肿瘤医院	Tumor Hospitals	1394	1374
妇产(科)医院	Hospitals for Pregnant Woman	837	817
儿童医院	Children Hospitals	832	832
精神病医院	Mental Hospitals	1370	1200
传染病医院	Hospitals for Infectious Diseases	500	500
骨科医院	Orthopaedics Hospitals	200	130
康复医院	Healing Hospitals	333	293
整型外科医院	Plastic Hospitals	161	161
美容医院	Beauty Hospitals	81	81
其他专科医院	Other Special Hospitals	194	114
5. 护理院	Nursing Centers	20	20
二、疗养院	Sanatoriums	1313	813
三、社区卫生服务中心(站)	Health Service Centers for Community	3061	2710
1. 社区卫生服务中心	Health Service Centers	3001	2710
2. 社区卫生服务站	Health Service Stations	60	-
四、卫生院	Health Service Centers	1144	280
1. 街道卫生院	Rural Township Hospitals in Subdistrict	88	-
2. 乡镇卫生院	Rural Township Hospitals in Country	1056	280
五、门诊部	Clinics	51	51
六、诊所、卫生所、医务室、护理站	Other Health Care Institutions	-	-
七、急救中心(站)	First - aid Centers(stations)	10	-
八、采供血机构	Blood Supplying Agencies	-	-
九、妇幼保健院(所、站)	Maternity and Child Care Centers(stations)	613	200
十、专科疾病防治所(所、站)	Specialized Centers for Disease Prevention and Control(stations)	488	-
十一、疾病预防控制中心	Centers for Disease Prevention and Control	-	-
十二、卫生监督所	Institutions of Public Health Inspection	-	-
十三、医学科学研究机构	Research Institutions of Medical Science	-	-
十四、医学在职培训机构	Medical Training Organization for Incumbent	-	-
十五、健康教育所(站、中心)	Education Center for Health(stations)	-	-
十六、其他卫生机构	Other Health Care Institutions	-	-

数(2010年)
Health Institutions(2010)

(bed)

#萧山区 Xiaoshan	#余杭区 Yuhang	桐庐县 Tonglu	淳安县 Chun'an	建德市 Jiande	富阳市 Fuyang	临安市 Lin'an
4768	**3010**	**1129**	**873**	**2001**	**2521**	**1611**
4061	2078	792	661	1364	1373	1319
3393	1228	656	521	960	753	1015
608	250	136	140	194	505	214
-	-	-	-	-	-	-
40	600	-	-	210	115	90
-	-	-	-	-	15	-
-	-	-	-	-	-	-
-	-	-	-	-	20	-
-	-	-	-	-	-	20
-	-	-	-	-	-	-
-	520	-	-	170	-	-
-	-	-	-	-	-	-
-	80	-	-	-	-	70
-	-	-	-	40	-	-
-	-	-	-	-	-	-
-	-	-	-	-	-	-
40	-	-	-	-	80	-
20	-	-	-	-	-	-
60	-	-	-	-	500	-
348	732	80	-	43	228	-
348	732	20	-	43	228	-
-	-	60	-	-	-	-
280	-	177	138	254	71	224
-	-	-	-	-	14	74
280	-	177	138	254	57	150
19	-	-	-	-	-	-
-	-	-	-	-	-	-
-	-	-	-	10	-	-
-	-	-	-	-	-	-
-	200	80	74	30	229	-
-	-	-	-	300	120	68
-	-	-	-	-	-	-
-	-	-	-	-	-	-
-	-	-	-	-	-	-
-	-	-	-	-	-	-
-	-	-	-	-	-	-
-	-	-	-	-	-	-

12－22 卫生事业
Number of Medical

单位：人

指 标	Item	全 市 Total	市 区 Urban District
总 计	**Total**	**74011**	**60015**
一、卫生技术人员	Number of Medical Technical Personnel	61117	49232
1. 执业(助理)医师	Registered (Assistant) Doctor	24345	19414
执业医师	Registered Doctor	22124	18008
助理医师	Assistant Doctor	2221	1406
2. 注册护士	Registered Nurse	23418	19481
3. 药剂师	Druggist	4276	3252
4. 技师人员	Checking Member	2785	2267
5. 其他	Others	5278	4020
二、其他技术人员	Other Medical Technical Personnel	3367	2914
三、管理人员	Managerial Personnel	3969	3326
四、工勤人员	Logistics Worker	5558	4543

人员数(2010 年)
Technical Personnel(2010)

(person)

萧山区 Xiaoshan	余杭区 Yuhang	桐庐县 Tonglu	淳安县 Chun'an	建德市 Jiande	富阳市 Fuyang	临安市 Lin'an
8118	**5627**	**2329**	**1689**	**3070**	**4200**	**2708**
6886	4842	1995	1510	2572	3445	2363
2922	1828	770	660	975	1455	1071
2471	1553	615	524	836	1249	892
451	275	155	136	139	206	179
2388	1581	603	461	971	1203	699
509	364	176	155	244	236	213
300	220	95	71	121	120	111
676	761	315	130	223	360	230
367	197	78	48	34	169	124
353	194	130	43	186	191	93
512	394	126	88	278	395	128

12－23 主要年份卫生技术人员

Number of Medical Technical Personnel in Main Years

单位:人 (person)

年份 Year	全市 Total	执业(助理)医师 Number of Registered (Assistant) Doctors	注册护士 Registered Nurses	市区 Urban District	执业(助理)医师 Number of Registered (Assistant) Doctors	注册护士 Registered Nurses
1978	19059	7375	3483	10867	4346	2510
1979	20060	7539	3536	11779	4733	2632
1980	21110	8311	3885	12376	5179	2804
1981	22737	9284	4139	13697	5946	3032
1982	23558	9883	4369	14221	6204	3193
1983	24914	10833	4562	15213	6990	3352
1984	25648	11291	4817	15807	7393	3487
1985	25593	11503	5071	15840	7644	3705
1986	26489	12623	5391	16543	8239	3940
1987	27663	12369	5805	17361	8329	4156
1988	28676	13674	6938	18022	8710	4801
1989	29791	14177	7348	18619	9146	5085
1990	30990	14483	7822	19231	9374	5397
1991	32169	14858	8153	19630	9494	5610
1992	32628	14842	8417	19690	9373	5736
1993	33172	15181	8643	19708	9499	5797
1994	33964	15465	8979	19907	9472	5940
1995	34245	16465	9531	19943	9607	6249
1996	34946	16789	9794	20695	9889	6508
1997	35423	17112	10019	20728	9902	6571
1998	35857	16022	10577	21035	9452	6788
1999	35256	16668	10587	20519	9610	6856
2000	35487	16317	11186	20344	9050	7300
2001	36643	16994	11576	28293	12968	9343
2002	37193	16092	11922	28818	12332	9653
2003	39019	16614	12460	30299	12731	10161
2004	39816	16770	13248	30886	12894	10840
2005	42353	17833	14514	33206	13802	12034
2006	45375	18831	15557	35904	14689	12986
2007	49780	20701	17455	39860	16290	14601
2008	52379	21223	18702	42015	16747	15556
2009	56270	22753	20997	45219	17996	17530
2010	61117	24345	23418	49232	19414	19481

注:从2001年起市区数据包括萧山区和余杭区。
a) Data of urban include Xiaoshan and Yuhang district since 2001.

12-24 体育运动情况(2010年)

Basic Statistics on Sports Activities(2010)

单位:人 (person)

指 标	Item	2010年	为上年(%) As Compared with the Preceding Year(%)
一、体委工作人员数	**Workers in Sports Commissions**	**983**	**106.5**
#教练员	#Full-time Coaches	75	100.0
二、等级裁判员发展人数	**Number of Referees in Grades**	**280**	**144.3**
#女	#Female	110	203.7
一级裁判员	First Grade Referees	-	-
二级裁判员	Second Grade Referees	280	144.3
三级裁判员	Third Grade Referees	-	-
三、等级运动员发展人数	**Number of Athletes in Grades**	**320**	**72.6**
#女	#Female	149	111.2
一级运动员	First Grade Athlete	-	-
二级运动员	Second Grade Athlete	320	72.6
三级运动员	Third Grade Athlete	-	-

主要统计指标解释

文化事业机构 指从事专业文化工作和为专业文化工作服务的独立建制的单独核算的单位。不包括这些单位另外举办独立核算的其他机构和各部门的业余文化组织。

艺术表演团体 指从事戏曲、音乐、舞蹈、杂技等专业艺术表演，有独立帐户，实行单独核算的团体。不包括半工半艺、半农半艺和民间职业剧团。

普通高等学校 指按照国家规定的设置标准和审批程序批准举办，通过国家统一招生考试，招收高中毕业生为主要培养对象，实施高等教育的全日制大学、独立设置的学院和高等专科学校、短期职业大学。

成人高等学校 指按照国家有关规定审批，招收通过全国成人高教统一招生考试的具有高中毕业或同等学历的在职从业人员利用脱产、半脱产、业余或函授等多种形式对其实施高等学历教育，培养高等教育专科或本科毕业水平的专门人才，修业年限、课程设置和总学时数均按高等学历教育要求付诸实施的学校。包括广播电视大学、职工高等学校、农民高等学校、管理干部学院、教育学院、独立设置的函授学院等。

小学学龄儿童入学率 指调查范围内已入小学学习的学龄儿童占校内外学龄儿童总数（包括弱智儿童在内，但不包括盲聋哑儿童）的比重。计算公式：

$$小学学龄儿童入学率 = \frac{已入学的小学学龄儿童数}{校内外小学学龄儿童总数} * 100\%$$

等级运动员人数 指经考核正式批准授予等级运动员称号的人数。运动员等级分为国际级运动健将、运动健将、一级运动员、二级运动员、三级运动员、少年级运动员。

等级裁判员人数 指经考核正式批准授予等级裁判员称号的人数。裁判员等级分为国际裁判、国家级裁判、一级裁判、二级裁判、三级裁判。

卫生机构 卫生机构是指从卫生行政部门取得《医疗机构执业许可证》，或从民政、工商行政、机构编制管理部门取得法人单位登记证书，为社会提供医疗保健、疾病控制、卫生监督等服务或从事医学科研、医学教育等卫生单位和卫生社会团体。不包括卫生行政机构、香港和澳门特别行政区以及台湾所属卫生机构。

卫生技术人员 卫生技术人员包括执业（助理）医师、注册护士、药剂人员、检验和影像技师（士、员）等卫生专业人员。

执业（助理）医师、执业（中）药师和注册护士 执业（助理）医师、执业（中）药师和注册护士是指领取医师、药师执业证书和注册护士证书的人员。不包括从事管理工作的医师、药师和护士。

Explanatory Notes on Main Statistical Indicators

Cultural Institutions refer to units which have their own organizational system and independent accounting system and specialize in or serve cultural development. They exclude other establishments run by these cultural institutions and amateur cultural groups established by various departments.

Art Troupe refers to the troupe which is engaged in drama, opera, music, dance, acrobatics or other art performance, opens independent accounts with banks and has self – supporting accounting system; excluding the troupes which are engaged partly in industrial or agricultural activities, partly in art performance and the professional troupes organized by the people.

Regular Institutions of Higher Learning refer to educational establishments set up according to the government evaluation and approval procedures, enrolling graduates from senior secondary schools and providing higher education courses and training for senior professionals, They include full – time universities, colleges, high professional schools and short – term professional universities.

Institutions of Higher Learning for Adults refer to educational establishments, set up in line with relevant rules approved by the government, enrolling staff and workers with senior secondary school or equivalent education, and providing higher education courses in many forms of full – time, part – time, space – time, or correspondence for adults. Professionals thus trained receive a qualification equivalent to graduates studying regular courses at regular universities, colleges and professional colleges. Institutions of higher learning for adults include Radio and TV universities, schools of high education for staff and workers and peasants, colleges for management cadres, pedagogical colleges, independent correspondence colleges.

Enrollment Rate of Primary School – age Children refer to the proportion of school – age children enrolled at schools to the total number of school – age children both in and outside schools (including retarded children, but excluding blind, deaf and mute children). The formula is:

$$\text{Enrollment Rate of Primary School – age Children} = \frac{\text{Total primary School – age Children at Schools}}{\text{Total Primary School – age Children Both at and Outside Schools}}$$

Number of Athletes in Grades refers to the number of athletes who have been given titles through examination. The titles of athletes include international masters of sports, masters of sports, first – grade, second – grade and third – grade sportsmen and young athletes.

Number of Referees in Grades refers to the number of referees who have been given titles after examination. They are classified as international referees, national referees and referees of the first, second and third grades.

Health Institutions refers to the Institutions and Society organization that get the registered license of health and medical institution from the health adiministration department, or get the registered licence of units from civil administration department, industry and business administration and organization management department, and offers medical treatment, controlling of disease, supervision of sanitation. Health institution excludes health administration department and Institutions of Hong Kong, Macao, and Taiwan.

Medical Technical Personnel include registered (Assistant) doctor, registered nurse, druggist, checking members and photo artificer.

Registered (Assistant) Doctor, Registered Druggist and Registered Nurse refers to the personnel who get the licence of doctor, druggist and nurse, the management staff excluded.

第十三篇
CHAPTER-13

人民生活、物价、民政

People's Livelihood, Price Indices And Civil Administration

人民生活、物价、民政
People's Livelihood, Price Indices and Civil Administration

主要统计指标
Major Statistical Indicators

全市城镇单位在岗职工工资总额	Total Wages of Staff and Workers of Urban Units	933.06	亿元	(100 million yuan)
# 国有单位	State-owned Units	333.52	亿元	(100 million yuan)
全市城镇单位在岗职工平均工资	Annual Average Wages of Staff and Workers of Urban Units	48772	元	(yuan)
# 国有单位	State-owned Units	71579	元	(yuan)
市区城镇居民人均年可支配收入	Per Capita Annual Disposable Income of Urban Households of Urban District	30035	元	(yuan)
为上年	As Compared with the Preceding Year	111.8	%	(%)
农民人均年纯收入	Per Capita Annual Net Income of Rural Households	13186	元	(yuan)
为上年	As Compared with the Preceding Year	111.5	%	(%)
市区居民消费价格指数	Consume Price Index of Urban District	103.9	上年 =100	(Preceding Year=100)
市区商品零售价格指数	Commodity Retail Price Index of Urban District	103.7	上年 =100	(Preceding Year=100)
工业品出厂价格指数	Ex-factory Price Index of Industrial Products	104.9	上年 =100	(Preceding Year=100)

13-01 主要年份市区城镇住户调查情况

Basic Conditions of Urban Households in Main Years

年份 Year	调查户数（户）Number of Households Surveyed (household)	平均每户人口（人）Average Household Size (person)	平均每户就业人数（人）Average Number of Employed Persons Per Household (person)	年人均可支配收入（元）Per Capita Annual Disposable Income (yuan)	年人均消费性支出（元）Per Capita Annual Living Expenditure (yuan)	人均住房使用面积（平方米）Per Capita Living Space in City Areas (sq. m)
1978	28	4.20	2.89	338	301	-
1979	28	4.19	2.77	396	365	-
1980	28	4.18	2.79	521	491	-
1981	100	3.97	2.37	540	513	-
1982	100	3.90	2.35	532	532	-
1983	100	3.90	2.42	578	535	8.8
1984	100	3.90	2.36	729	679	9.3
1985	150	3.53	2.26	1026	908	9.7
1986	150	3.49	2.27	1169	1072	9.9
1987	150	3.42	2.25	1260	1118	10.6
1988	200	3.41	2.16	1565	1515	10.6
1989	200	3.40	2.15	1764	1615	10.6
1990	200	3.37	2.15	1985	1685	10.9
1991	200	3.40	2.20	2128	1894	10.8
1992	200	3.28	2.14	2580	2296	11.1
1993	200	3.21	2.10	3525	3183	11.2
1994	200	3.31	2.10	5249	4559	11.9
1995	200	3.20	2.05	6301	5559	11.7
1996	200	3.20	2.00	7206	6095	11.9
1997	200	3.14	1.99	7896	6766	12.4
1998	300	3.12	1.93	8465	7235	14.1
1999	300	3.11	1.92	9085	7424	14.6
2000	300	3.10	1.83	9668	7790	14.9
2001	440	2.98	1.72	10896	8968	15.5
2002	500	2.93	1.53	11778	9215	16.3
2003	500	2.92	1.51	12898	9950	17.2
2004	500	2.92	1.48	14565	11213	17.8
2005	600	2.84	1.42	16601	13438	20.7
2006	600	2.81	1.44	19027	14472	21.0
2007	600	2.72	1.45	21689	14896	21.6
2008	600	2.75	1.29	24104	16719	22.4
2009	600	2.68	1.25	26864	18595	23.1
2010	600	2.70	1.25	30035	20219	23.2

注：从 2001 年起市区数据包括萧山区和余杭区。

a) Data of urban include Xiaoshan and Yuhang district since 2001.

13－02 市区城镇居民家庭平均每人全年现金收支

Per Capita Annual Cash Income and Expenditure of Urban Residents

单位:元 （yuan）

项 目 Item	1995	2000	2005	2006	2007	2008	2009	2010
家庭总收入 Total Income	**9120.88**	**9709.45**	**18761.51**	**21367.13**	**24474.89**	**27034.76**	**30337.78**	**33810.11**
一、工薪收入 Income from Wages	6776.28	7074.79	12961.40	14427.48	16293.33	16948.94	18769.76	21074.58
1.工资及补贴收入 Bonus and Subsidy	6446.59	6702.84	12235.25	13915.20	15904.55	16572.54	18515.37	20712.77
2.其他劳动收入 Other Income of Staff & Workers From Their Working Units	329.69	371.95	726.15	512.27	388.78	376.40	254.38	361.81
二、经营净收入 Income of Staff & workers in Other－owned Units	277.48	235.69	1041.05	1101.51	2027.13	1406.95	1596.66	1650.75
三、财产性收入 Property Income	131.78	116.93	585.72	1137.67	584.11	1939.01	2147.08	2189.12
四、转移性收入 Transfer Income	1935.34	2282.04	4173.33	4700.48	5570.31	6739.87	7824.28	8895.66
#养老金或离退休金 Annuities & Retirement Pension	1705.17	1751.49	3384.69	3788.36	4461.22	5409.92	6517.65	7689.32
#赡养收入 Supporting Income	15.07	23.99	47.71	41.22	54.70	104.03	197.19	276.57
#捐赠收入 Income from Donation	118.51	230.73	353.99	473.76	474.42	676.41	563.84	377.14
其中:可支配收入 Disposable Income	9085	9668	16601	19026.86	21689.36	24103.58	26863.93	30034.99
借贷收入 Credit Income	**1680.13**	**2157.36**	**4289.05**	**5475.29**	**6882.79**	**4854.84**	**8797.72**	**23064.64**
#提取储蓄存款 Money Drawn from Bank	1464.73	1869.60	3779.11	4947.88	6044.00	4719.70	6885.49	21892.88
#借入款 Money Borrowed	85.35	62.28	118.70	302.43	228.68	36.32	110.88	17.87
家庭总支出 Total Expenditure	**6531.96**	**9169.32**	**17260.06**	**19513.14**	**21545.09**	**23289.70**	**29159.11**	**29955.68**
消费性支出 Living Expenditure	5558.62	7789.68	13437.58	14471.74	14895.75	16719.10	18594.75	20218.98
其中:服务性消费支出 Service Living Expenditure	－	－	3832.72	4230.84	4038.27	4820.91	5141.30	5426.97
非消费性支出 Other Non－Living Expenditure	973.34	1379.64	3822.48	5041.40	6649.34	6570.60	10564.36	9736.70
1.购买商品住宅及建房支出 Expenditure for House－purchasing	731.72	751.68	435.25	950.79	1565.53	947.29	4464.89	1852.46
2.赡养支出 Supporting Expenditure	54.52	108.60	345.31	557.90	756.19	722.52	871.86	1695.31
3.捐赠支出 Living Expenditure	123.79	455.76	920.25	1005.27	1246.70	1438.34	1459.77	1851.01
4.各种非储蓄性保险支出 Expenditure for Non－saving Insurance	4.99	28.80	42.99	169.95	211.19	330.88	214.92	241.83
5.社会保障支出 Expenditure for Social Security	－	－	1739.65	1924.93	2288.50	2463.66	2854.86	2963.13
#个人交纳的养老基金 Annuities	－	－	618.20	717.70	895.82	893.33	1016.32	1087.76
#个人交纳的住房公积金 Accumulated Expenditure for House－purchasing	－	－	872.86	955.39	1060.40	1201.48	1412.36	1404.53
#个人交纳的医疗基金 Expenditure for Medical Treatment	－	－	199.24	204.37	280.42	300.53	342.60	376.18
借贷支出 Expenditure for Credit	**1319.42**	**2154.60**	**4547.79**	**8215.12**	**9259.10**	**8542.02**	**10988.78**	**27961.46**
#存入储蓄款 Saving in Bank	1007.63	1658.52	3298.06	6184.50	6341.17	6993.63	9319.94	25550.75
#借出款 Money Lent	54.89	42.00	28.10	17.77	163.93	40.87	4.61	0.15
#储蓄性保险支出 Expenditure for Saving Insurance	25.99	109.80	190.63	256.15	279.31	437.27	389.03	232.59
期末手存现金 Per Capita Cash in Hand at Year－end	**512.68**	**1374.96**	**2255.52**	**1963.45**	**2770.43**	**1743.08**	**1282.59**	**783.14**

13－03　2010年市区城镇居民家庭人均现金收支(按收入水平分组)

Per Capita Annual Cash Income and Expenditure of Urban Residents in 2010(Grouped by Income Level)

单位:元　(yuan)

项　目 Item	总平均 Average	按可支配收入分组 Grouped by Disposable Income				
		20%低收入户 20% Lowest Income House－holds	20%较低收入户 20% Low Income House－holds	20%中间收入户 20% Middle Income House－holds	20%较高收入户 20% High Income House－holds	20%最高收入户 20% Highest Income House－holds
家庭总收入 Total Income	**33810.11**	**15213.18**	**23122.05**	**28095.48**	**37429.53**	**68953.11**
一、工薪收入 Income from Wages	21074.58	8500.89	12441.68	13324.53	21694.70	51964.37
二、经营净收入 Income of Staff & workers in Other－owned Units	1650.75	1040.10	809.08	504.56	2072.74	3947.11
三、财产性收入 Property Income	2189.12	908.59	1361.42	1846.88	3117.66	3963.06
四、转移性收入 Transfer Income	8895.66	4763.61	8509.86	12419.51	10544.43	9078.57
其中:可支配收入 Disposable Income	30034.99	13032.22	20640.66	25655.17	33957.68	60312.15
借贷收入 Credit Income	**23064.64**	**9540.42**	**13389.22**	**20772.63**	**21557.88**	**53260.60**
家庭总支出 Total Expenditure	**29955.68**	**14276.91**	**18410.52**	**26941.40**	**30551.42**	**63252.33**
消费性支出 Living Expenditure	20218.98	11448.59	14555.61	18404.14	21419.26	37181.61
其中:服务性消费支出 Service Living Expenditure	5426.97	2630.32	3675.67	4670.44	5120.20	11653.47
非消费性支出 Other Non－Living Expenditure	9736.70	2828.32	3854.91	8537.26	9132.16	26070.72
1. 购买商品住宅及建房支出 Expenditure for House－purchasing	1852.46	－	43.10	2557.56	377.43	6876.58
2. 赡养支出 Supporting Expenditure	1695.31	222.41	313.53	1772.80	1771.05	4795.37
3. 捐赠支出 Living Expenditure	1851.01	544.18	957.77	1718.03	3160.12	3138.88
4. 各种非储蓄性保险支出 Expenditure for Non－saving Insurance	241.83	22.21	97.60	206.38	291.96	639.18
5. 社会保障支出 Expenditure for Social Security	2963.13	1945.74	2175.05	2036.22	2900.92	5961.86
借贷支出 Expenditure for Credit	**27961.46**	**10334.41**	**17973.67**	**21846.22**	**28181.64**	**65080.94**
期末手存现金 Per Capita Cash in Hand at Year－end	**783.14**	**656.10**	**703.59**	**721.11**	**811.92**	**1050.97**

13－04 主要年份市区城镇居民家庭人均消费性支出
Per Capita Annual Living Expenditure of Urban Residents in Main Years

单位:元 (yuan)

项目 Item	1995	2000	2005	2006	2007	2008	2009	2010
消费性支出 Total Living Expenditure	**5558.62**	**7789.68**	**13437.58**	**14471.74**	**14895.75**	**16719.10**	**18594.75**	**20218.98**
食品类 Food	2774.32	3303.48	4682.40	4817.63	5526.10	6410.16	6972.89	7790.18
粮食 Grain	235.38	206.76	249.84	261.17	281.37	326.91	346.10	394.25
油脂类 Oil and Fats	49.08	56.88	72.50	77.18	118.54	162.29	137.53	149.80
肉禽及制品 Meat, Poultry and Related Products	554.87	514.56	574.29	554.89	729.53	959.13	880.45	984.02
蛋类 Eggs	57.23	43.80	55.16	52.42	65.29	73.73	79.93	99.67
水产品类 Aquatic Products	395.19	514.20	466.42	500.68	581.65	633.72	702.21	808.88
菜类 Vegetables	266.63	302.88	364.56	404.51	444.28	467.75	529.66	664.29
酒和饮料 Liquor and Beverage	146.63	192.12	298.47	259.11	308.87	381.41	439.49	485.20
干鲜瓜果类 Dried and Fresh Melons and Fruits	211.93	214.44	335.20	365.87	428.02	433.91	508.37	609.96
在外用餐 Out－dining	368.60	531.00	1232.68	1285.90	1366.37	1684.34	1820.50	2032.78
衣着类 Clothing	665.02	645.00	1298.53	1354.58	1512.81	1656.81	1818.07	2061.36
家庭设备用品及服务 Facilities, Articles and Service	491.46	626.50	673.50	584.66	678.22	762.43	1096.70	955.98
医疗保健 Medicine and Medical Service	145.11	444.12	983.06	884.82	955.53	1132.49	961.47	994.16
交通和通信 Transportation and Communication	280.01	547.51	2234.02	2876.37	2549.38	2589.77	3008.68	3909.61
教育文化娱乐服务 Education, Cultural and Recreation Service	433.13	1079.11	1970.11	2010.54	1689.63	1782.02	1956.94	2088.77
居住 Residence	488.03	701.04	1150.69	1478.91	1508.88	1814.01	2046.72	1853.18
杂项商品和服务 Miscellaneous Commodities and Service	281.53	442.92	445.26	464.22	475.20	571.41	733.28	565.73

13－05　2010年市区城镇居民家庭人均全年消费性支出(按收入水平分组)

Per Capita Annual Living Expenditure of Urban Residents in 2010(Grouped by Income Level)

单位:元　　(yuan)

项　目 Item	总平均 Average	按可支配收入分组 Grouped by Disposable Income				
		20%低收入户 20% Lowest Income House－holds	20%较低收入户 20% Low Income House－holds	20%中间收入户 20% Middle Income House－holds	20%较高收入户 20% High Income House－holds	20%最高收入户 20% Highest Income House－holds
消费性支出 Total Living Expenditure	**20218.98**	**11448.59**	**14555.61**	**18404.14**	**21419.26**	**37181.61**
食品类 Food	7790.18	5312.87	6775.61	8452.08	8284.42	10656.87
粮食 Grain	394.25	316.07	387.95	468.53	445.21	369.02
油脂类 Oil and Fats	149.80	121.14	165.35	172.05	164.76	129.06
肉禽及制品 Meat,Poultry and Related Products	984.02	810.04	1030.21	1151.54	1042.15	915.32
蛋类 Eggs	99.67	73.95	95.81	119.54	110.59	103.72
水产品类 Aquatic Products	808.88	583.76	840.78	916.03	888.12	850.59
菜类 Vegetables	664.29	534.11	691.19	824.38	692.64	604.27
酒和饮料 Liquor and Beverage	485.20	272.78	480.40	532.59	501.68	674.45
干鲜瓜果类 Dried and Fresh Melons and Fruits	609.96	355.51	542.67	696.99	671.43	834.01
在外用餐 Out－dining	2032.78	1052.82	1260.88	1930.99	2008.77	4151.63
衣着类 Clothing	2061.36	829.92	1320.59	1659.92	2209.39	4541.66
家庭设备用品及服务 Facilities,Articles and Service	955.98	347.76	610.30	818.90	968.76	2162.82
医疗保健 Medicine and Medical Service	994.16	596.01	955.18	1069.92	1025.84	1394.02
交通和通信 Transportation and Communication	3909.61	2323.87	1932.32	2782.43	4693.66	8214.66
教育文化娱乐服务 Education, Cultural and Recreation Service	2088.77	836.48	1348.81	1727.22	2111.68	4683.60
居住 Residence	1853.18	1066.38	1339.10	1500.24	1663.29	3867.95
杂项商品和服务 Miscellaneous Commodities and Service	565.73	135.31	273.69	393.44	462.22	1660.04

13－06 主要年份市区城镇居民家庭平均每百户耐用消费品拥有量
Number of Major Durable Consumer Goods Owned Per 100 Urban Households in Main Years

项目 Item		1995	2000	2005	2006	2007	2008	2009	2010
摩托车 Motorcycle	(辆) (unit)	1.50	3.60	11.00	11.67	10.02	4.89	4.78	4.51
助力电动车 Electric－bicycle	(辆) (unit)			28.67	33.33	35.96	36.05	38.78	42.37
家用汽车 Family Car	(辆) (unit)		0.70	12.83	14.00	15.44	17.84	21.65	22.83
微波炉 Micro－wave Oven	(个) (unit)		39.00	68.17	67.17	66.50	69.06	74.62	78.76
影碟机 Video Player	(台) (unit)		54.00	69.67	68.33				
普通电话 Telephone	(部) (set)		95.00	99.83	97.00	97.37	92.33	89.64	89.62
移动电话 Mobile Phone	(部) (set)		19.00	178.67	176.83	187.19	180.87	178.5	193.59
淋浴热水器 Water Heater	(台) (unit)	43.50	81.30	92.33	91.50	94.91	93.34	94.95	99.43
排油烟机 Smoke Exhauster	(台) (unit)	34.50	72.67	83.33	85.33				
洗衣机 Washing Machine	(台) (unit)	93.50	96.33	94.17	96.50	95.73	89.80	94.60	96.23
电冰箱 Refrigerator	(台) (unit)	103.50	101.67	100.00	99.50	100.82	98.15	100.30	102.28
电炊具 Electric Cooking Appliances	(个) (unit)	79.50	88.00	100.50	106.33				
家用电脑 Personal Computer	(台) (unit)		23.00	74.50	74.50	82.10	81.74	86.87	99.02
彩色电视机 Color TV Set	(台) (unit)	102.30	146.67	182.67	180.67	181.28	167.27	173.96	179.19
吸尘器 Dust Collector	(台) (unit)	21.00	23.33	20.67	20.00				
组合音响 Music Center	(套) (set)	12.00	28.67	37.83	34.83	33.00	32.27	31.15	30.00
摄像机 Video Recorder	(架) (unit)		3.33	7.50	7.00	9.03	9.20	10.31	11.09
照相机 Camera	(架) (unit)	54.00	64.67	59.00	56.67	54.02	51.50	53.73	54.76
空调器 Air Conditioner	(台) (unit)	43.00	104.00	183.33	187.83	191.30	195.53	203.87	214.61

13－07 主要年份全市农村住户调查情况

Basic Conditions of Whole Municipality Rural Households in Main Years

年份 Year	调查户数(户) Number of Households Surveyed (household)	平均每户人口(人) Average Number of Residents per Household (person)	平均每户劳动力(人) Average Number of Laborers Per Household (person)	农民人均年纯收入(元) Per Capita Annual Net Income of Rural Households (yuan)	人均生活费支出(元) Per Capita Annual Living Expenditure (yuan)	人均居住面积(平方米) Per Capita Floor Space (sq. m)
1978				162		
1979				204		
1980	60	4.72	2.93	250	287	23.3
1981	60	4.60	2.70	333	294	25.2
1982	60	4.43	2.73	405	328	26.3
1983	170	4.55	2.85	395	355	29.9
1984	170	4.44	2.81	510	416	31.7
1985	420	4.40	2.88	624	542	29.9
1986	620	4.39	2.88	675	601	31.3
1987	620	4.34	2.86	820	714	33.1
1988	620	4.26	2.87	996	925	35.5
1989	620	4.17	2.85	1117	1011	36.8
1990	620	4.16	2.89	1171	923	39.6
1991	620	4.03	2.81	1308	1018	38.0
1992	620	4.01	2.81	1493	1129	37.5
1993	540	3.91	2.76	1748	1276	37.1
1994	630	3.85	2.35	2267	1884	37.8
1995	630	3.87	2.30	3012	2373	40.5
1996	630	3.81	2.77	3482	2772	42.2
1997	630	3.87	2.86	3785	2762	42.0
1998	630	3.87	2.88	4006	2858	46.2
1999	630	3.80	2.80	4209	2851	48
2000	630	3.61	2.59	4894	3393	49
2001	630	3.57	2.53	5330	3909	52
2002	630	3.53	2.53	5708	4444	52.7
2003	670	3.48	2.53	6250	5142	54.7
2004	670	3.48	2.54	6950	5608	58.9
2005	1100	3.34	2.34	7655	6004	66.0
2006	1100	3.63	2.52	8515	6901	66.5
2007	1100	3.60	2.61	9549	7568	68.0
2008	1100	3.56	2.58	10692	8446	69.7
2009	1100	3.57	2.59	11822	9065	70.74
2010	1100	3.58	2.59	13186	10267	71.22

13－08　主要年份全市农村居民家庭人均纯收入

Per Capita Annual Gross and Net Income of Whole Municipality Rural Households in Main Years

单位：元　　　　(yuan)

项　　目 Item	1995	2000	2005	2006	2007	2008	2009	2010
全年纯收入 Net Income	**3012**	**4894**	**7655**	**8515**	**9549**	**10692**	**11822**	**13186**
1. 劳动者的工资性收入 Laborers´Remuneration	896	2045	3347	4772	5401	6318	6967	7777
2. 家庭经营收入 Income from Household Business Operation	1960	2363	3358	3011	3318	3363	3694	4049
#农业收入 Income from Farming	578	1016	1858	777	784	836	885	1005
林业收入 Income from Forestry	142	71	311	306	338	328	395	365
牧业收入 Income from Animal Husbandry	397	382	310	234	235	151	212	223
渔业收入 Income from Fishery	24	31	185	94	135	71	77	73
工业收入 Income from Industry	112	262	392	295	328	406	441	473
建筑业收入 Income from Construction	77	102	228	225	297	326	306	345
交通、运输、仓储及邮电业收入 Transportation, Posts, Storage and Telecommunication	136	163	483	334	329	367	395	517
批发和零售贸易、餐饮业收入 Income from Retail Wholesale & Trade and Catering Services	118	150	391	471	523	550	638	699
社会服务业收入 Social Serve Trade	59	73	127	125	138	146	177	210
3. 转移性收入 Transfer Income	83	312	481	346	330	419	553	719
#在外人口寄回或带回 Income of Going out to Work	5	21	93	75	41	53	72	101
农村外部亲友赠送 Present from Rural Friends and Relatives	9	7	133	13	10	31	25	23
4. 财产性收入 Property Income	73	174	469	386	500	592	609	641
#土地征用补偿收入 #Compensation for Confiscating Land	6	100	243	156	198	208	192	190

13－09 主要年份全市农村居民家庭人均支出

Per Capita Gross Expenditure of Whole Municipality Rural Households in Main Years

单位:元 (yuan)

项目 Item	1995	2000	2005	2006	2007	2008	2009	2010
全年总支出 Gross Expenditure	**3457**	**3789**	**8043**	**9308**	**9661**	**11223**	**11632**	**13439**
生活消费支出 Living Expenditure	**2373**	**3393**	**6004**	**6901**	**7568**	**8446**	**9065**	**10227**
1. 食品 Food	1213	1392	2145	2418	2636	3031	3067	3333
#在外饮食 #Out－dining	43	83	221	302	311	399	436	487
食品加工费 Food－processing	13	15	11	10	12	11	12	12
2. 衣着 Clothing	169	169	381	438	476	527	530	609
3. 居住 Residence	396	694	1143	1481	1637	1856	2157	2603
#住房 #Housing	284	509	724	1033	1103	1223	1500	1855
电费 Electricity	22	56	110	140	172	201	221	255
燃料 Fuel	53	38	77	94	108	116	102	126
4. 家庭设备、用品及服务 Household Facilities, Articles and Services	155	163	307	326	361	385	445	512
5. 医疗保健 Medicines and Medical Services	99	329	474	478	505	589	570	623
#医药卫生保健用品 #Medicines	39	99	189	170	264	264	247	252
医疗保健服务费 Medicines Services	58	64	256	292	241	325	323	371
6. 交通和通讯 Transportation and Communications	102	204	680	793	948	1065	1182	1451
#交通工具 #Vehicles	67	123	158	252	354	418	567	784
交通费 Traffic	18	36	83	79	82	88	80	90
邮电费 Postage	4	62	219	218	247	270	258	264
7. 文教娱乐用品及服务 Cultural, Educational and Recreational Articles and Services	156	318	735	823	836	828	936	934
文化教育娱乐用品 Cultural, Educational and Recreational Articles	43	70	114	167	174	176	223	227
文化教育娱乐服务 Culrural, Educational and Recreational Services	113	248	621	656	662	652	712	546

单位:元　　13－09　续表　continued　　(yuan)

项　　目 Item	1995	2000	2005	2006	2007	2008	2009	2010
#学杂费 #Tuition and Incidental Expenses	94	210	430	442	384	334	355	344
技术培训费 Technical Training Expenses	5	5	32	31	47	34	44	31
文娱费 Recreational and Cultural Expenses	11	9	22	23	33	44	53	53
8.其他商品和服务 Other Commodities and Services	84	124	139	144	169	165	178	202
家庭经营费用支出 Expenditure of Household Business Operation	**681**	**427**	**1157**	**1226**	**1017**	**1217**	**1025**	**1285**
种植业生产支出 Expenditure of Farming	199	183	245	277	283	271	220	279
林业生产支出 Expenditure of Forestry	3	10	71	99	68	62	75	87
牧业生产支出 Expenditure of Animal Husbandry	267	121	168	162	181	248	162	184
渔业生产支出 Expenditure of Fishery	4	10	116	71	32	30	28	48
工业生产支出 Expenditure of Industry	62	61	276	310	181	303	249	449
建筑业生产支出 Expenditure of Construction	3	3	35	31	39	69	92	74
运输业生产支出 Expenditure of Transportation	64	29	141	224	234	235	143	175
批发和零售贸易、餐饮业支出 Expenditure of Wholesale and Retail Trade & Catering Services	53	6	84	28	50	53	39	53
服务业支出 Expenditure of Services Trade	5	1	9	15	12	11	5	8
其他经营支出 Others	22	3	12	9	8	4	12	6
购置生产用固定资产支出 Expenditure of Purchasing Fixed Assets	**135**	**86**	**202**	**152**	**66**	**124**	**138**	**121**
税费支出 Expenditure of Taxes	**23**	**50**	**31**	**20**	**23**	**12**	**10**	**10**
其他非借贷性支出 Others Expenditure not for Loans	**235**	**206**	**649**	**344**	**383**	**712**	**710**	**1079**
#寄给和带给在外人口 Posting and Giving to People Outside	6	23	396	158	172	181	132	260
赠送农村外部亲友 Present to Rural Friends and Relatives	7	8	7	7	7	6	6	7
附:生产用固定资产累计折旧 Depreciation of Fixed Assets for Production	**63**	**79**	**218**	**235**	**–**	**–**	**–**	**–**

13-10 主要年份全市农村居民家庭平均每百户耐用消费品拥有量

Number of Major Durable Consumer Goods Owned Per 100 Rural Households in Main Years

项目		Item		1995	2000	2005	2006	2007	2008	2009	2010
自行车	(辆)	Bicycle	(Unit)	209	183	124	127	127	126	127	127
电风扇	(台)	Electric Fan	(Unit)	211	258	267	291				
洗衣机	(台)	Washing Machine	(Unit)	14	34	62	72	74	78	82	85
电冰箱	(台)	Refrigerator	(Unit)	23	46	72	83	88	91	95	98
摩托车	(辆)	Motorcycle	(Unit)	13	38	73	80	71	71	70	66
黑白电视机	(台)	Black and White TV Set	(Unit)	73	57	17	13	10	6	6	4
彩色电视机	(台)	Color TV Set	(Unit)	34	86	141	156	163	170	177	186
录像机	(台)	Video Cassette Recorder	(Unit)	3	7	7	8				
收录机	(台)	Radio Cassette Player	(Unit)	26	28	16	14				
照相机	(架)	Camera	(Unit)	4	7	14	17	17	19	22	23
抽油烟机	(台)	Smoke Exhauster	(Unit)	4	17	39	49	52	55	59	62
吸尘器	(台)	Dust Collector	(Unit)	2	3	5	6	6	6	8	10
空调机	(台)	Air Conditioner	(Unit)	1	8	12	70	83	91	100	111

13－11　主要年份全市城镇单位在岗职工工资总额

Total Wages of Fully Employed Staff and Workers in Main Years

单位:万元　　(10000 yuan)

年　份 Year	总　计 Total	国有经济单位 State－owned Units	城镇集体经济单位 Collective－owned Units	其他经济单位 Units of Other Types of Ownership
1978	43775	32730	11045	
1979	52127	38651	13476	
1980	67918	49461	18457	
1981	72896	52581	20315	
1982	75584	55325	20259	
1983	78336	57716	20620	
1984	102223	72149	29385	689
1985	130114	90643	38482	989
1986	157471	111010	45230	1231
1987	180077	127353	50512	2212
1988	230868	163863	63525	3480
1989	253956	180706	68230	5020
1990	277910	203212	70253	4445
1991	313906	227438	78827	7641
1992	377614	272098	89429	16087
1993	534537	367062	118634	48841
1994	772236	525936	159864	86436
1995	890488	598524	170638	121326
1996	973592	647327	171227	155038
1997	1073862	722182	173502	178178
1998	1112718	719249	127584	265885
1999	1180947	755073	102906	322968
2000	1267524	784396	80911	402217
2001	1481659	899920	65534	516205
2002	1614676	1026645	65820	522211
2003	1867776	1174126	64820	628830
2004	2188159	1367229	71112	749818
2005	2970200	1617671	88226	1264303
2006	3811735	1825613	99009	1887113
2007	4954813	2202920	130443	2621450
2008	6416424	2551401	149362	3715661
2009	7549145	2871075	171367	4506703
2010	9330552	3335202	201537	5793813

注:1998 年以前为全市职工工资总额。

a) Data on total wage bill before 1998 refer to wages of staff and workers.

13－12　主要年份市区城镇单位在岗职工工资总额

Total Wages of Fully Employed Staff and Workers of Urban District in Main Years

单位:万元　　(10000 yuan)

年　份 Year	总　计 Total	国有经济单位 State－owned Units	城镇集体经济单位 Collective－owned Units	其他经济单位 Units of Other Types of Ownership
1978	28256	21727	6529	
1979	34318	26164	8154	
1980	45574	33920	11654	
1981	48809	35856	12953	
1982	50959	37898	13061	
1983	52909	39848	13061	
1984	69135	51057	17498	580
1985	87774	63830	23100	844
1986	105995	77989	26936	1070
1987	121003	89233	29728	2042
1988	152859	113227	36474	3158
1989	167055	123862	38759	4434
1990	182985	139337	40061	3587
1991	209052	157279	45778	5995
1992	253653	186961	52890	13802
1993	359041	254742	63921	40378
1994	521669	360273	87807	73589
1995	615450	422101	92980	100369
1996	683244	462364	94061	126819
1997	762957	521029	84456	147472
1998	803264	532561	74852	195851
1999	864418	559707	61417	243294
2000	949872	594435	47580	307857
2001	1279749	756669	49687	473393
2002	1398222	866806	48691	482724
2003	1617504	996961	44920	575624
2004	1859164	1162299	50943	645921
2005	2584779	1380262	64558	1139959
2006	3338568	1562198	72670	1703700
2007	4317965	1882616	101388	2333961
2008	5679543	2180009	117583	3381951
2009	6665279	2425106	147894	4092280
2010	8238017	2814874	169969	5253173

注:从 2001 年起市区数据包括萧山区和余杭区,1998 年以前为职工工资总额。

a) Data of urban include Xiaoshan and Yuhang district since 2001, data on total wage bill before 1998 refer to wages of staff and workers.

13－13 主要年份全市城镇单位在岗职工年平均工资
Average Annual Wages of Fully Employed Staff and Workers in Main Years

单位：元 (yuan)

年份 Year	总计 Total	国有经济单位 State－owned Units	城镇集体经济单位 Collective－owned Units	其他经济单位 Units of Other Types of Ownership
1978	597	634	509	
1979	643	694	531	
1980	777	832	660	
1981	783	824	693	
1982	791	823	714	
1983	813	840	745	
1984	1036	1080	943	1006
1985	1266	1302	1188	1287
1986	1469	1531	1336	1561
1987	1616	1682	1469	1685
1988	1986	2063	1806	2129
1989	2173	2259	1961	2416
1990	2382	2504	2078	2582
1991	2586	2710	2252	3123
1992	3071	3236	2600	3571
1993	4220	4479	3404	4949
1994	6118	6565	4750	6936
1995	7156	7546	5604	8266
1996	7966	8336	6178	9199
1997	9108	9522	6905	10519
1998	10555	11180	7720	10826
1999	12187	12972	8938	11883
2000	14257	15441	10150	13401
2001	18319	21119	13831	15394
2002	21418	24739	15090	17685
2003	24668	29121	18154	19757
2004	28891	35507	24010	21879
2005	31069	40483	23964	24332
2006	32791	44664	21845	26641
2007	36496	53343	26095	29300
2008	40193	56802	30698	33823
2009	43947	63602	36625	36953
2010	48772	71579	42929	41378

注：1998 年以前为全市职工年平均工资。

a) Data on total wage bill before 1998 refer to average wages of staff and workers.

13－14　主要年份市区在岗职工年平均工资

Average Annual Wages of Fully Employed Workers of Urban District in Main Years

单位:元　　(yuan)

年　份 Year	全社会 Whole society	城镇单位 Urban units	国有经济单位 State－owned economic Units	城镇集体经济单位 Collective economic Units	其他经济单位 Other economic Units
1978		642	673	558	
1979		692	730	593	
1980		814	868	688	
1981		810	847	724	
1982		809	845	719	
1983		835	869	746	
1984		1071	1119	954	1012
1985		1316	1348	1235	1290
1986		1536	1589	1401	1519
1987		1690	1744	1545	1692
1988		2073	2135	4897	2119
1989		2261	2340	2031	2381
1990		2486	2587	2179	2691
1991		2706	2812	2350	3233
1992		3233	3385	2719	3658
1993		4561	4816	3565	5115
1994		6597	7024	4978	7254
1995		7786	8154	5928	8658
1996		7851	9032	6689	9888
1997		10048	10319	7624	11299
1998		11512	11865	8298	12339
1999		13225	13698	9391	13545
2000		15454	16373	10370	15017
2001	18205	18962	21916	14573	16018
2002	19749	22091	25720	15295	18279
2003	20113	25535	30334	18074	20563
2004	22235	30719	37585	24291	23488
2005	22645	32166	41977	24220	25440
2006	23581	33967	46509	21971	27751
2007	25489	37991	55675	25774	30746
2008	27863	41501	58696	31097	35252
2009	30480	45149	65118	38096	38423
2010	34330	49938	73130	43804	42850

注:市区全社会在岗职工平均工资包括所有国有、集体、股份制、三资和私营单位,但不包含个体工商户。

a) The average annual wage of fully employed workers of the whole society in urban district includes all state－owned, collective－owned, share holding, foreign－funded and private enterprises, but excludes individual businesses.

13－15 全市城镇单位从业人员劳动报酬(2010 年)

Laborers´Remuneration of Employed Persons in Urban Units(2010)

单位:万元 (10000 yuan)

项目 Item	年末单位从业人员劳动报酬 Laborers´Remuneration of Employed Persons at Year－end	在岗职工工资总额 Total Wages of Fully Employed Staff and Workers	其他从业人员劳动报酬 Laborers´Remuneration of Other Employed Persons	#在岗职工平均工资(元/人) Average Wage of Fully Employed Staff and Workers (yuan/person)
全市总计 Total	**10427958**	**9330552**	**1097406**	**48772**
其中:企业 Enterprises	7861501	6890368	971133	43759
事业 Institutions	1734352	1632170	102182	71050
机关 Agencies and Organizations	773702	755215	18486	82763
民间非营利组织 Non－profit Organizations	26576	22605	3971	31111
其他 Other	31827	30193	1633	29468
市区总计 Urban District	**9258089**	**8238017**	**1020073**	**49938**
其中:企业 Enterprises	7161266	6252205	909062	45192
事业 Institutions	1429241	1337746	91495	73436
机关 Agencies and Organizations	614836	600777	14060	87679
民间非营利组织 Non－profit Organizations	22842	18968	3874	31275
其他 Other	29903	28321	1582	30071
上城区 Shangcheng	**1099151**	**1004760**	**94391**	**69829**
下城区 Xiacheng	**1341290**	**1200636**	**140654**	**72753**
江干区 Jianggan	**537062**	**488886**	**48176**	**39022**
拱墅区 Gongshu	**692900**	**559456**	**133444**	**47469**
西湖区 Xihu	**1411078**	**1142725**	**268353**	**47757**
高新(滨江)区 Hi－Tech (Binjiang)	**951103**	**889349**	**61754**	**65404**
萧山区 Xiaoshan	**1718130**	**1641544**	**76586**	**37509**
余杭区 Yuhang	**757242**	**720027**	**37215**	**43011**
桐庐县 Tonglu	**180027**	**168632**	**11395**	**39875**
淳安县 Chun'an	**131717**	**127594**	**4123**	**44013**

项 目 Item	年末单位从业人员劳动报酬 Laborers´Remuneration of Employed Persons at Year－end	在岗职工工资总额 Total Wages of Fully Employed Staff and Workers	其他从业人员劳动报酬 Laborers´Remuneration of Other Employed Persons	#在岗职工平均工资(元/人) Average Wage of Fully Employed Staff and Workers (yuan/person)
建德市 Jiande	**172478**	**164174**	**8304**	**45432**
富阳市 Fuyang	**392257**	**351552**	**40705**	**41328**
临安市 Lin´an	**293390**	**280584**	**12806**	**39533**
按国民经济行业分组 Grouped by Sector				
农、林、牧、渔业 Farming,Forestry,Animal Husbandry and Fishery	4240	4186	55	28550
采矿业 Mining and Quarrying	8050	7456	595	30039
制造业 Manufacturing	2692556	2433820	258736	36389
电力、煤气及水的生产和供应业 Production and Supply of Electricity,Gas and Water	164606	150651	13956	80852
建筑业 Construction	1336342	972898	363444	30101
交通运输、仓储及邮政业 Transportation,Storage and Post	433364	389416	43948	52490
信息传输、计算机服务和软件业 Information Transmission Computer Service and Software	510093	468283	41810	90602
批发与零售业 Wholesale & Retail Trade	598522	543576	54945	49184
住宿和餐饮业 Lodging and Catering	195663	180480	15183	27312
金融业 Banking and Insurance	876647	805328	71319	143463
房地产业 Real Estate	271965	254176	17790	48193
租赁与商务服务业 Renting and Business Service	274378	250336	24042	39478
科学研究、技术服务与地质勘查业 Scientific Research,Technical Service and Geological Prospecting	477735	437892	39843	61272
水利、环境和公共设施管理业 Water Conservancy,Environment and Public Utility	145652	118261	27391	36128
居民服务和其他服务业 Service for the Residents and Other	25240	21318	3922	34799
教育 Education	925680	884660	41020	69556
卫生、社会保障和社会福利业 Health Care,Sports and Social Welfare	536461	490601	45861	76488
文化、体育与娱乐业 Culture,Sports and Entertainment	117003	103309	13694	67272
公共管理与社会组织 Public Management and Social Organizations	833762	813907	19855	76278

13－16　全市国有单位从业人员劳动报酬(2010 年)

Laborers´Remuneration of Employed Persons for State－owned Units(2010)

单位:万元　(10000 yuan)

项　　目 Item	年末单位从业人员劳动报酬 Laborers´Remuneration of Employed Persons at Year－end	在岗职工工资总额 Total Wages of Fully Employed Staff and Workers	其他从业人员劳动报酬 Laborers´Remuneration of Other Employed Persons	#在岗职工平均工资(元/人) Average Wage of Fully Employed Staff and Workers (yuan/person)
总计 Total	**3568249**	**3335202**	**233047**	**71579**
按隶属关系分 Grouped by Subordination				
中央属 Central	707807	642862	64945	92609
省　属 Provincial	1014821	938674	76147	72894
市　属 Municipal	535589	495922	39667	67236
县及县以下 At and below County Level	1291939	1241069	50870	65219
其他 Other	18094	16675	1419	44995
按企业、事业、机关分组 Grouped by Enterprises, Institutions and Agencies				
企业 Enterprises	1151477	1033104	118373	64609
事业 Institutions	1636404	1541551	94852	72243
机关 Agencies and Organizations	773702	755215	18486	82763
民间非营利组织 Non－profit Organizations	4875	3568	1307	35716
其他 Other	1793	1763	29	42695
按国民经济行业分组 Grouped by Sector				
农、林、牧、渔业 Farming, Forestry, Animal Husbandry and Fishery	2284	2254	31	33490
采矿业 Mining & Quarrying	237	237	0	22590
制造业 Manufacturing	98502	96984	1518	52452

项　目 Item	年末单位从业人员劳动报酬 Laborers´Remuneration of Employed Persons at Year－end	在岗职工工资总额 Total Wages of Fully Employed Staff and Workers	其他从业人员劳动报酬 Laborers´Remuneration of Other Employed Persons	#在岗职工平均工资(元/人) Average Wage of Fully Employed Staff and Workers (yuan/person)
电力、煤气及水的生产和供应业 Production and Supply of Electricity,Gas and Water	108390	95887	12503	99241
建筑业 Construction	86734	81438	5295	54499
交通运输、仓储及邮政业 Transportation,Storage and Post	239525	214832	24693	53744
信息传输、计算机服务和软件业 Information Transmission Computer Service and Software	73331	59113	14218	103056
批发与零售业 Wholesale & Retail Trade	72616	67881	4735	82420
住宿和餐饮业 Lodging and Catering	32026	28520	3506	33470
金融业 Banking and Insurance	165298	150656	14642	148342
房地产业 Real Estate	28822	27044	1779	58322
租赁与商务服务业 Renting and Business Service	102951	88043	14908	37569
科学研究、技术服务与地质勘查业 Scientific Research,Technical Service and Geological Prospecting	238827	223441	15386	73575
水利、环境和公共设施管理业 Water Conservany,Environment and Public Utility	75250	62902	12348	43303
居民服务和其他服务业 Service for the Residents and Other	14492	11690	2802	45628
教育 Education	848269	812735	35534	73809
卫生、社会保障和社会福利业 Health Care,Sports and Social Welfare	476630	438342	38288	80197
文化、体育与娱乐业 Culture,Sports and Entertainment	99999	87141	12857	71780
公共管理与社会组织 Public Management and Social Organizations	804068	786062	18006	81028

13－17 全市城镇集体单位从业人员劳动报酬(2010 年)

Laborers′ Remuneration of Employed Persons for Collective－owned Units(2010)

单位:万元 (10000 yuan)

项目 Item	年末单位从业人员劳动报酬 Laborers′ Remuneration of Employed Persons at Year－end	在岗职工工资总额 Total Wages of Fully Employed Staff and Workers	其他从业人员劳动报酬 Laborers′ Remuneration of Other Employed Persons	#在岗职工平均工资(元/人) Average Wage of Fully Employed Staff and Workers (yuan/person)
总计 Total	**213715**	**201537**	**12178**	**42929**
按企业、事业分组 Grouped by Enterprises and Institutions				
企业 Enterprises	134203	127995	6208	37703
事业 Institutions	77383	71565	5818	57380
机关 Agencies and Organizations	－	－	－	－
民间非营利组织 Non－profit Organizations	734	587	147	41028
其他 Other	1395	1391	5	36219
按国民经济行业分组 Grouped by Sector				
农、林、牧、渔业 Farming,Forestry,Animal Husbandry and Fishery	253	253	－	18079
采矿业 Mining & Quarrying	1989	1984	5	24548
制造业 Manufacturing	10622	10262	360	23892
电力、煤气及水的生产和供应业 Production and Supply of Electricity,Gas and Water	2634	2634	－	125410
建筑业 Construction	7635	6311	1324	34131
交通运输、仓储和邮政业 Transportation,Storage and Post	41720	40547	1174	58173
信息传输、计算机服务和软件业 Information Transmission Computer Service and Software	1892	1637	255	54930
批发与零售业 Wholesale & Retail Trade	7476	7255	221	39950
住宿和餐饮业 Lodging and Catering	6973	6538	435	23654
金融业 Banking and Insurance	128	128	－	55783
房地产业 Real Estate	7577	6970	607	63424
租赁与商务服务业 Renting and Business Service	37507	36788	719	29863
科学研究、技术服务与地质勘查业 Scientific Research,Technical Service and Geological Prospecting	6736	5997	739	71734
水利、环境和公共设施管理业 Water Conservancy,Environment and Public Utility	6822	6281	540	28827
居民服务和其他服务业 Service for the Residents and Other	2040	1843	197	26035
教育 Education	31425	29870	1555	63378
卫生、社会保障和社会福利业 Health Care,Sports and Social Welfare	39453	35463	3991	61965
文化、体育与娱乐业 Culture,Sports and Entertainment	312	270	42	34203
公共管理与社会组织 Public Management and Social Organizations	521	507	14	42941

13－18　全市其他单位从业人员劳动报酬(2010年)

Laborers´Remuneration of Employed Persons for Other Ownership Units(2010)

单位:万元　　　　(10000 yuan)

项　　目 Item	年末单位从业人员劳动报酬 Laborers´Remuneration of Employed Persons at Year－end	在岗职工工资总额 Total Wages of Fully Employed Staff and Workers	其他从业人员劳动报酬 Laborers´Remuneration of Other Employed Persons	#在岗职工平均工资(元/人) Average Wage of Fully Employed Staff and Workers (yuan/person)
合　计 **Total**	**6645993**	**5793813**	**852180**	**41378**
按登记注册类型分 **Grouped by Ownership**				
内资 Domestic－funded Enterprises	4489042	3876861	612181	41505
港、澳、台商投资 Enterprises with Investment from Hong Kong, Macao and Taiwan	916966	835170	81795	41088
外商投资 Enterprises with Foreign Investment	1239986	1081781	158205	41153
按企业、事业分组 **Grouped by Enterprises, Institutions and Agencies**				
企业 Enterprises	6575821	5729269	846552	41493
事业 Institutions	20566	19054	1512	49287
民间非营利组织 Non－profit Organizations	20968	18450	2517	30128
其他 Other	28639	27039	1599	28616
按国民经济行业分组 **Grouped by Sector**				
农、林、牧、渔业 Farming, Forestry, Animal Husbandry and Fishery	1703	1679	24	25704
采矿业 Mining and Quarrying	5825	5235	590	33365
制造业 Manufacturing	2583432	2326574	256858	36012
电力、煤气及水的生产和供应业 Production and Supply of Electricity, Gas and Water	53583	52130	1453	59503
建筑业 Construction	1241974	885149	356824	28887

单位:万元　　13－18　续表　continued　　(10000 yuan)

项　目 Item	年末单位从业人员劳动报酬 Laborers´Remuneration of Employed Persons at Year－end	在岗职工工资总额 Total Wages of Fully Employed Staff and Workers	其他从业人员劳动报酬 Laborers´Remuneration of Other Employed Persons	#在岗职工平均工资(元/人) Average Wage of Fully Employed Staff and Workers (yuan/person)
交通运输、仓储和邮政业 Transportation, Storage and Post	152119	134038	18081	49195
信息传输、计算机服务和软件业 Information Transmission Computer Service and Software	434870	407533	27337	89269
批发与零售业 Wholesale & Retail Trade	518430	468440	49989	46626
住宿和餐饮业 Lodging and Catering	156664	145422	11242	26539
金融业 Banking and Insurance	711221	654544	56678	142428
房地产业 Real Estate	235566	220162	15404	46838
租赁与商务服务业 Renting and Business Service	133920	125505	8415	45379
科学研究、技术服务与地质勘查业 Scientific Research, Technical Service and Geological Prospecting	232171	208454	23717	51774
水利、环境和公共设施管理业 Water Conservany, Environment and Public Utility	63580	49077	14503	30618
居民服务和其他服务业 Service for the Residents and Other	8709	7785	924	27257
教育 Education	45986	42054	3931	34022
卫生、社会保障和社会福利业 Health Care, Sports and Social Welfare	20378	16796	3582	44671
文化、体育与娱乐业 Culture, Sports and Entertainment	16692	15897	795	50661
公共管理与社会组织 Public Management and Social Organizations	29173	27338	1835	28558

13－19 主要年份市区消费价格指数

Consumer Price Indices of Urban District in Main Years

（上年＝100） （Preceding Year＝100）

年　份 Year	居民消费价格指数 General Consumer Price Index	商品零售价格指数 General Retail Price Index
1978	100.1	100.1
1979	100.4	100.9
1980	100.8	109.3
1981	102.0	102.0
1982	102.0	102.3
1983	102.1	102.3
1984	103.1	103.1
1985	117.2	117.5
1986	106.0	106.1
1987	110.5	111.3
1988	121.9	123.4
1989	117.8	118.2
1990	104.6	104.4
1991	107.5	106.9
1992	110.4	110.2
1993	121.4	117.3
1994	121.5	118.8
1995	116.5	113.3
1996	110.5	107.2
1997	106.7	102.4
1998	101.8	99.8
1999	100.4	98.2
2000	100.8	98.3
2001	99.5	95.3
2002	98.8	97.9
2003	99.5	98.1
2004	102.5	101.6
2005	101.7	100.3
2006	101.2	100.2
2007	103.5	103.1
2008	104.9	106.0
2009	98.6	98.6
2010	103.9	103.7

13－20　市区居民消费价格指数(2010年)
Consumer Price Indices in Urban District(2010)

(上年＝100)　　(Preceding Year＝100)

项　目	Item	指数 Indices
居民消费价格总指数	**Consumer Price Indices**	**103.9**
一、食品	**Food**	**107.3**
1. 粮食	Grain	117.1
2. 淀粉	Starches and Tubers	102.0
3. 干豆类及豆制品	Bean and Its Products	106.3
4. 油脂	Oil and Fat	106.9
5. 肉禽及其制品	Meal Poultry and Their Products	102.1
6. 蛋	Eggs	107.8
7. 水产品	Aquatic Products	109.7
8. 菜	Vegetables	114.0
9. 调味品	Flavoring	99.6
10. 糖	Sugar	104.6
11. 茶及饮料	Tea and Beverages	101.3
12. 干鲜瓜果	Dried and Fresh Melons and Fruits	106.5
13. 糕点饼干	Cake、Biscuit and Bread	100.1
14. 液体乳及乳制品	Milk and Its Products	107.2
15. 在外用膳食品	Outward Dinner	106.6
16. 其他食品	Other Food	102.0
二、烟酒及用品	**Tobacco、Liquor and Articles**	**101.9**
1. 烟草	Tobacco	100.8
2. 酒	Liquor	104.5
3. 吸烟饮酒用品	Articles	104.0
三、衣着	**Clothing**	**98.0**
1. 服装	Garments	97.1
2. 衣着材料	Clothing Material	107.5

项　　目	Item	指　数 Indices
3. 鞋袜帽	Shoes, Socks and Hats	100.5
4. 衣着加工服务	Clothing Processing Service	100.2
四、家庭设备用品及维修服务	**Household Facilities, Articles and Repair Service**	**103.6**
1. 耐用消费品	Durable Consumer Goods	102.1
2. 室内装饰品	Interior Decorations	101.6
3. 床上用品	Bed Articles	101.6
4. 家庭日用杂品	Daily Use Household Articles	101.6
5. 家庭服务及加工维修服务	Household and Repair Service	113.0
五、医疗保健和个人用品	**Medical Articles and Personal Articles**	**105.5**
1. 医疗保健	Medical Care	106.2
2. 个人用品及服务	Personel Articles and Service	104.0
六、交通和通信	**Transportation and Communication**	**99.8**
1. 交通	Transportation	101.1
2. 通信	Communication	97.9
七、娱乐教育文化用品及服务	**Recreation, Education and Culture Articles**	**102.2**
1. 文娱用耐用消费品及服务	Durable Consumer Goods and Recreation Service	93.4
2. 教育	Education	100.0
3. 文化娱乐类	Cultural and Recreational Articles	101.4
4. 旅游	Tourism and Outgoing	113.1
八、居住	**Residence**	**105.8**
1. 建房及装修材料	Construction and Upholstery Materials	104.0
2. 租房	House Renting	110.2
3. 自有住房	Private Owned Houses	108.0
4. 水、电、燃料	Water, Electricity and Fuels	103.4

13－21　市区零售价格指数(2010年)

Retail Price Indices in Urban District(2010)

(上年＝100)　　(Preceding Year＝100)

项　　目	Item	指数 Indices
商品零售价格总指数	**Retail Price Indices**	**103.7**
一、食品	**Food**	**107.5**
1.粮食	Grain	116.4
2.淀粉	Starches and Tubers	102.0
3.干豆类及豆制品	Bean and Its Products	106.7
4.油脂	Oil and Fat	105.6
5.肉禽及其制品	Meal Poultry and Their Products	101.9
6.蛋	Eggs	107.8
7.水产品	Aquatic Products	109.7
8.菜	Vegetables	113.4
9.调味品	Flavoring	99.5
10.糖	Carbohydrate	106.8
11.干鲜瓜果	Dried and Fresh Melons and Fruits	106.6
12.糕点饼干面包	Cake、Biscuit and Bread	100.1
13.液体乳及乳制品	Milk and Its Products	106.4
14.在外用膳食品	Outward Dinner	106.5
15.其他食品	Other Food	102.0
二、饮料、烟酒	**Beverages,Tobacco and Liquor**	**102.1**
1.茶及饮料	Tea and Beverages	101.6
2.烟草	Tobacco	100.8
3.酒	Liquor	104.4
三、服装、鞋帽	**Garments,Shoes and Hats**	**97.9**
1.服装	Garments	97.0
2.鞋袜帽	Shoes,Socks and Hats	100.5
3.其他	Other	85.0
四、纺织品	**Textiles**	**106.0**
1.衣着材料	Clothing Material	110.7
2.床上用品	Bed Articles	102.9
五、家用电器及音像器材	**Household Electric Appliances,Audio and Video Equipment**	**98.6**
1.家庭设备	Household Equipment	100.3
2.文娱用耐用消费品	Durable Consumer Goods for Entertainment	94.8

项目	Item	指数 Indices
3. 音像器材	Audio and Video Equipment	99.0
六、文化办公用品	**Stationery and Office Supplies**	**97.7**
七、日用品	**Commodities**	**100.1**
1. 日用百货	General Merchandise for Daily Use	97.7
2. 日用杂品	Sundries for Daily Use	105.1
3. 洗涤用品	Washing Articles	98.9
4. 其他日用品	Other Commodity	101.2
八、体育娱乐用品	**Sports and Entertainment Goods**	**100.5**
1. 体育用品	Sports Goods	101.8
2. 娱乐用品	Entertainment Goods	100.0
九、交通、通信用品	**Transportation and Communications Articles**	**96.4**
1. 交通运输机械	Transportation Vehicles	97.7
2. 通讯器材	Equipment of Communication	87.4
十、家具	**Funishings**	**105.2**
十一、化妆品	**Cosmetics**	**98.1**
十二、金银珠宝	**Jewellery**	**114.7**
十三、中西药品及医疗保健用品	**Chinese and Western Medicine, Health Care Articles**	**107.1**
1. 医疗器具及用品	Medical Instruments and Articles	105.0
2. 中药材及中成药	Chinese Medicinal Materials and Chinese Traditional Medicine	116.2
3. 西药	Western Medicine	101.9
4. 保健品及器具	Articles for Health Care	107.5
十四、书报杂志及电子出版物	**Books, Newspapers, Magazines and Electron Publications**	**102.8**
1. 教材及参考书	Teaching Materials and Reference Books	100.0
2. 书报杂志	Books, Newspapers and Magazines	106.5
3. 电子音像制品	Electronic Music and Film Products	100.1
十五、燃料	**Fuels**	**113.1**
1. 煤炭及制品	Coal and Coal Products	107.1
2. 石油及制品	Oil and Oil Products	114.1
十六、建筑材料及五金电料	**Construction Materials and Hardware**	**105.0**
1. 建筑装潢材料	Construction and Upholstery Materials	104.9
2. 五金电料	Hardware and Electric Materials	105.2

13－22 主要工业品出厂价格分类指数
Ex－Factory Price Indices of Industrial Products in Main Years

（上年＝100） （Preceding Year＝100）

项目 Item	1999	2000	2005	2006	2007	2008	2009	2010
工业品出厂价格总指数 Ex－factory Price Indices of Industrial Products	**96.9**	**100.3**	**103.5**	**103.1**	**103.6**	**105.9**	**95.1**	**104.9**
一、按轻重工业分 Grouped by Industries								
轻工业 Light Industry	**95.8**	**99.3**	**101.8**	**101.7**	**102.0**	**103.2**	**96.5**	**105.0**
以农产品为原料 Made from Agricultural Products	96.9	99.9	102.0	101.8	100.6	102.5	98.5	103.9
以非农产品为原料 Made from Non－agricultural Products	95.3	98.0	101.7	101.6	103.4	103.8	94.7	106.0
重工业 Heavy Industry	**98.0**	**101.1**	**105.6**	**104.9**	**105.4**	**109.2**	**93.1**	**104.7**
采掘 Mining & Quarrying Industry	－	99.5	103.0	140.0	124.0	104.9	83.5	114.0
原料 Raw Materials Industry	99.0	104.4	107.7	104.8	107.2	112.6	93.3	110.7
加工 Manufacturing Industry	97.6	98.9	104.3	102.6	103.4	108.1	93.6	102.5
二、按二大部类分 Grouped by Means of Producting and Consumer Goods								
生产资料 Means of Production	**97.9**	**101.9**	**104.8**	**103.7**	**104.4**	**107.0**	**93.2**	**106.2**
采掘 Mining	－	99.6	103.0	131.6	120.7	104.9	83.5	114.0
原料 Raw Materials	98.4	103.8	110.7	104.4	107.6	108.0	90.7	114.5
加工 Manufacture	97.7	100.3	101.6	102.2	102.8	106.8	94.4	103.9
生活资料 Consumer Goods	**95.7**	**97.5**	**101.2**	**101.6**	**101.0**	**102.8**	**100.2**	**101.0**
食品 Foods	98.8	96.4	101.6	101.8	101.0	102.2	100.2	100.1
衣着 Clothing	95.2	101.1	101.4	101.1	100.6	101.5	100.1	102.4
一般日用品 Articles for Daily Use	94.9	97.8	101.7	103.3	101.8	106.1	100.1	100.8
耐用消费品 Durable Consumer Goods	94.8	94.5	99.5	99.9	100.5	102.2	100.4	100.9

项目 Item	1999	2000	2005	2006	2007	2008	2009	2010
三、按工业部门分 Grouped by Industrial Sector								
冶金工业 Metallurgical Industry	95.6	104.0	104.8	107.2	112.9	117.3	87.0	108.0
电力工业 Power Industry	99.8	96.0	106.2	102.1	102.2	105.4	101.5	105.2
煤炭及炼焦工业 Coal and Coking Industry	99.8	107.9	102.1	101.5	108.8	99.3	-	-
石油工业 Petroleum Industry	108.1	131.6	124.7	114.0	103.1	120.7	92.3	117.0
化学工业 Chemical Industry	97.2	101.1	106.0	102.4	107.0	109.8	87.2	111.9
机械工业 Machine Building Industry	94.9	96.7	102.9	103.2	101.5	102.6	97.3	100.8
建材材料工业 Building Materials Industry	103.1	103.0	91.7	99.6	104.1	106.0	96.5	109.3
森林工业 Timber Industry	96.6	96.9	101.4	100.8	101.6	100.9	98.3	101.6
食品工业 Food Industry	98.0	95.8	100.6	101.0	101.3	102.8	100.2	100.1
纺织工业 Textile Industry	97.3	107.3	103.4	104.4	99.8	100.3	97.8	107.5
缝纫工业 Tailoring Industry	96.3	100.5	101.5	101.0	100.7	101.5	99.9	102.2
皮革工业 Leather Industry	91.6	98.0	101.4	101.3	100.3	100.2	99.7	102.9
造纸工业 Paper Industry	96.2	102.9	100.3	98.8	100.6	109.8	94.8	104.6
文教艺术用品工业 Cultural, Educational & Handicrafts Articles	90.4	98.7	99.7	98.8	99.2	103.5	98.4	97.3
其它工业 Others	101.1	103.6	102.2	108.5	103.3	103.4	101.7	104.7

13-23 主要原材料、燃料、动力购进价格分类指数

Purchasing Price Indices of Raw Materials, Fuels and Power in Main Years

(上年=100) (Preceding Year=100)

项目 Item	1999	2000	2005	2006	2007	2008	2009	2010
原材料购进价格指数 Raw Materials Purchasing Price Index	**97.2**	**107.4**	**106.9**	**106.1**	**104.6**	**110.8**	**92.2**	**112.1**
燃料动力类 Fuel and Power	103.0	108.0	116.4	107.4	104.5	126.1	91.5	111.3
黑色金属材料类 Ferrous and Metals	96.3	102.7	105.2	94.2	109.7	123.9	83.6	108.6
1. 钢材 Rolled - steel	94.9	103.2	104.9	94.2	108.6	120.3	82.9	108.2
2. 其它 Other	98.2	101.0	105.7	94.0	114.0	137.4	86.2	113.0
有色金属材料及电线类 Non-ferrous Metals and Electric Wire	97.6	108.0	111.2	129.8	113.4	95.6	85.2	129.3
化工原料类 Chemical Raw Materials	97.6	111.0	110.1	106.3	108.1	106.3	88.5	113.3
木材及纸浆类 Wood and Paper Pulps	95.5	104.5	101.0	102.7	106.6	104.4	91.4	106.4
建筑材料及非金属类 Building Materials	98.2	100.6	102.3	98.9	103.6	114.8	98.5	108.8
其它工业原材料及半成品类 Other Industrial Raw Materials and Semi-products	97.2	111.0	103.6	110.5	102.5	107.3	96.1	109.8
农副产品类 Farm and Sideline Products	95.0	104.0	103.9	112.2	100.2	107.6	101.5	114.1
纺织原料类 Textile Raw Materials	89.4	104.7	99.9	103.3	98.5	99.2	96.6	110.4

13－24 房地产销售价格指数
Sales Price Indices of Houses in Main Years

(上年＝100) (Preceding Year＝100)

项目	Item	2000	2005	2006	2007	2008	2009	2010
总计	**Total**	**104.9**	**109.7**	**102.6**	**107.3**	**108.6**	**102.8**	**110.3**
一、新建房	**New Building**	**105.7**	**110.1**	**102.9**	**107.8**	**110.0**	**102.0**	**110.8**
(一)住宅	**Residential Buildings**	**104.7**	**109.7**	**103.2**	**108.3**	**109.9**	**102.1**	**111.4**
1.经济适用房	Economical and Livable Living Houses	99.5	100.0	100.0	100.0	100.0	100.0	100.0
2.普通住宅	Common Residence	104.9	112.1	103.0	108.3	107.8	102.1	114.7
(1)多层住宅	Multi－layer Residence	106.2	115.5	103.0	106.1	108.2	98.9	106.8
(2)高层住宅	Higher Level Residence	101.2	110.6	102.8	108.3	107.8	102.4	115.2
3.高档住宅	Luxury Buildings	105.6	110.2	105.5	114.0	123.7	103.5	103.3
(1)别墅	Villas	105.6	112.9	103.5	－	100.1	100.1	98.8
(2)高档公寓	Flats	－	109.8	105.6	114.0	123.7	104.1	104.6
(二)非住宅	**Non－residential Buildings**	**110.5**	**111.0**	**102.0**	**105.9**	**110.9**	**101.6**	**107.3**
1.办公楼	Office Buildings	103.1	112.6	102.5	106.6	114.7	102.9	108.9
2.商业营业用房	Buildings for Commercial and Entertainment Use	117.1	105.3	101.2	105.4	107.1	99.2	104.6
3.其他用房	Other	－	113.2	102.8	101.3	100.0	101.9	107.5
二、二手房	**Second－hand Housing**	**107.1**	**108.4**	**102.0**	**106.0**	**104.2**	**104.6**	**109.4**
(一)非住宅	Non－residential Buildings	－	110.6	104.0	106.9	102.2	102.0	102.5
(二)住　宅	Residential Buildings	107.1	107.6	101.6	105.8	104.5	105.3	111.1

13－25 房地产租赁价格指数

Rental Price Indices of Houses in Main Years

(上年＝100)　　(Preceding Year＝100)

项目	Item	2000	2005	2006	2007	2008	2009	2010
总　计	**Total**	**103.3**	**102.4**	**101.1**	**102.7**	**102.5**	**101.8**	**103.4**
一、住宅	**Residential Buildings**	**118.8**	**101.1**	**101.0**	**102.2**	**106.0**	**101.9**	**103.4**
(一)廉租房	Low－cost Housing	119.0	－	－	－	100.0	87.5	95.8
(二)商品住宅	Commercial Residential Buildings	98.8	101.1	101.0	102.2	106.3	102.5	103.9
二、非住宅	**Non－residential Buildings**	**103.4**	**101.0**	**102.0**	**104.2**	**101.2**	**101.8**	**103.4**
(一)办公楼	Office	106.5	101.2	102.2	105.8	102.7	103.8	101.1
(二)商业营业用房	Commercial Business Buildings	110.3	103.2	100.6	102.5	100.5	100.7	106.4
(三)其他	Else	99.5	101.2	100.0	100.0	100.0	100.0	100.1

13－26 社会办福利院情况(2010年)
Basic Statistics on Welfare Homes(2010)

指标
Item
	单 位
	(个)
	Homes
	(unit)
		年末职工人数
		(人)
		Staff and Workers
		(person)
			年末床位数
			(张)
			Beds
			(bed)
				年末在院人数
				(人)
				Persons Housed
				(person)
					#老 人(人)
					Seniors(person)

全 市 Total	**216**	**2056**	**23215**	**12437**	**11162**
市 区 Urban District	118	1620	16276	8351	7292
#萧山区 Xiaoshan	31	272	4489	1823	1627
余杭区 Yuhang	24	164	2402	657	584
桐庐县 Tonglu	12	78	1071	965	933
淳安县 Chun'an	21	59	1216	764	747
建德市 Jiande	15	97	1494	829	815
富阳市 Fuyang	24	87	1243	678	594
临安市 Lin'an	26	115	1915	850	781

13－27 优抚对象

Number of Persons Enjoying

单位:人

指　　标 Item	全　市 Total	市　区 Urban District	#萧山区 Xiaoshan
享受定期抚恤金人数 Number of Persons Receiving Periodical Commiseration	643	197	90
烈属 Number of Martyr Kinsfolk	295	76	32
牺牲军人家属 Number of the Sacrifice Soldiers	107	32	12
病故军人家属 Number of Kinsfolks of the Illness－died Soldiers	241	89	46
享受定期补助人数 Number of Persons Enjoying Regular Subsidies	13971	3318	1491
其中:红军失散人员 Number of Persons be Scattered of the Red Army	2	－	－
在乡复员军人 Rural Demobilized Soldier	3937	1209	465
抗日 The War of Resistance Against Japan	37	20	2
优待优抚对象带病回乡退伍军人 Number of Rural Veterans with Illness Receiving Subsiders	5651	790	551
优待优抚对象户数 Number of Households Receiving Subsiders	24162	10502	3303
优待军属户数 Number of Households Sacrifice Soldiers	6661	3573	1167

人员情况(2010年)

Public Subsidies(2010)

(person)

#余杭区 Yuhang	桐庐县 Tonglu	淳安县 Chun'an	建德市 Jiande	富阳市 Fuyang	临安市 Lin'an
56	96	90	87	112	61
21	40	51	54	40	34
11	22	7	11	28	7
24	34	32	22	44	20
1244	1513	1573	2000	3045	2522
–	–	2	–	–	–
545	535	481	384	674	654
3	5	–	1	1	10
207	602	937	1152	590	1580
2508	2288	2510	3238	4382	1242
822	533	525	646	763	621

13－28 市、县级社会

Basic Statistics on Institutions and

单位:个

指　　标 Item		全　　市 Total	市　　区 Urban District	#萧山区 Xiaoshan
合　　计	**Total**	**2258**	**1536**	**226**
按活动区域分	**Grouped by Region**			
地级社团	City－level Societies	633	633	－
县级社团	County－level Societies	1625	903	226
按性质分	**Grouped by Category**			
科技与研究	Technology and Research	149	95	－
生态环境	Ecological Envirenment	22	8	2
教育	Education	73	54	4
卫生	Health	91	60	13
社会服务	Social Services	262	174	14
文化	Culture	209	135	32
体育	Sport	169	137	8
法律	Law	16	12	－
工商业服务	Industry and Business Services	418	271	21
宗教	Religion	34	19	5
农业及农村发展	Agricure and Rural Development	168	57	23
职业及从业组织	Vocational and Business Organizations	195	105	1
国际及涉外组织	International and Foreign Organizations	6	－	－
其他	**Other**	**446**	**409**	**103**

团体机构情况(2010 年)

Organizations at County Level(2010)

(unit)

#余杭区 Yuhang	桐庐县 Tonglu	淳安县 Chun'an	建德市 Jiande	富阳市 Fuyang	临安市 Lin'an
218	**126**	**107**	**167**	**180**	**142**
–	–	–	–	–	–
218	126	107	167	180	142
4	11	4	13	13	13
3	2	2	7	2	1
15	3	3	7	1	5
7	6	6	8	5	6
63	21	30	16	19	2
8	12	6	20	28	8
21	3	3	14	8	4
2	–	1	1	2	–
85	30	10	19	42	46
2	5	3	2	4	1
6	16	28	8	41	18
2	17	11	38	4	20
–	–	–	4	2	–
–	**–**	**–**	**10**	**9**	**18**

13－29　社会保障分县(市)情况(2010年)
Social Security by Region(2010)

单位:万人　　　　(10000 persons)

指标 Item	城镇基本养老保险参保人数 Number of Persons in the Basic Pension Program	基本养老保险参保职工 Number of Employed Persons in the Basic Pension Program	基本医疗保险参保人数 Number of Persons in the Basic Medical Insurance Program	工伤保险参保人数 Number of Persons in the Work－injure Insurance Program	生育保险参保人数 Number of Persons in the Bear Insurance Program	职工失业保险人数 Number of Persons in the Unemployment Insurance Program
全　市 Total	**383.97**	**325.88**	**345.24**	**314.95**	**228.53**	**243.98**
市　区 Urban District	316.47	268.37	290.09	255.32	193.02	213.40
#萧山区 Xiaoshan	78.02	70.32	49.21	61.42	41.90	41.92
余杭区 Yuhang	39.30	34.09	36.18	35.17	22.34	24.14
桐庐县 Tonglu	10.48	8.85	8.65	9.12	5.31	4.43
淳安县 Chun'an	7.59	6.32	7.33	6.93	3.62	3.18
建德市 Jiande	12.79	10.08	8.46	8.22	6.05	6.13
富阳市 Fuyang	23.04	20.48	18.62	23.32	13.53	13.02
临安市 Lin'an	13.60	11.78	12.09	12.04	7.00	3.82

13-30 近年来社会保障情况

Social Security in Recent Years

单位:万人 (10000 persons)

指标 Item	2000	2005	2006	2007	2008	2009	2010
城镇登记失业人员 Number of the Registered Unemployed Persons in Urban	5.6	6.09	6.30	5.96	5.45	5.64	4.85
城镇登记失业率(%) The Registered Rate of Unemployment in Urban (%)	3.48	3.71	3.46	3.21	3.02	2.99	2.19
失业人员再就业 The Re-employed Persons of Unemployment	14.69	13.09	12.08	13.1	12.59	15.56	15.54
城镇基本养老保险参保人数 Number of Persons in the Basic Pension Program in Urban	123.69	227.58	253.34	280.49	318.11	342.24	383.97
#基本养老保险参保职工 Number of Employed Persons in the Basic Pension Program	81.96	185.32	208.87	233.15	267.6	288.29	325.88
失业保险参保人数 Number of Persons in the Unemployment Insurance Program	96.66	118.36	145.77	170.09	202.41	215.68	243.98
基本医疗保险参保人数 Number of Persons in the Basic Medical Insurance Program	-	187.71	208.5	237.74	274.59	298.31	345.24
工伤保险参保人数 Number of Persons in the Work-injure Insurance Program	47.86	111.03	132.09	201.64	245.82	274.15	314.95
生育保险参保人数 Number of Persons in the Bear Insurance Program	63.99	96.41	128.89	155.64	181.68	199.80	228.53
城乡居民参加医疗保险人数 Number of urban and rural residents participated in medical insurance	-	350.6	370.65	369.7	369.18	346.95	408.32

注:城乡居民参加医疗保险人数:2009年前为参加新型农村合作医疗的人数。

a) Number of urban and rural residents participated in medical insurance: before 2009, it was the number of people who participated in new rural cooperative medical insurance.

主要统计指标解释

从业人员劳动报酬　指各单位在一定时期内直接支付给本单位全部从业人员的劳动报酬总额。

在岗职工工资总额　指各单位在一定时期内直接支付给本单位全部在岗职工的劳动报酬总额。

工资总额的计算原则应以直接支付给职工的全部劳动报酬为根据。各单位支付给本单位全部职工的劳动报酬,不论是计入成本的还是不计入成本的,不论是以货币形式支付还是以实物形式支付的,不论是单位自筹的资金还是上级(或政府财政部门)下拨的资金,不论是厂级单位筹集的资金还是下属车间(科室)及附属经营单位筹集的资金,均应列入工资总额计算的范围。

在岗职工平均工资　指各单位的在岗职工在一定时期内平均每人所得的货币工资额。它表明一定时期内在岗职工工资收入的高低程度,是反映在岗职工工资水平的主要指标。计算公式为:

$$在岗职工平均工资=\frac{报告期实际支付的全部在岗职工工资总额}{报告期全部在岗职工平均人数}$$

城镇居民家庭总收入　指被调查的城镇居民家庭全部收入。包括经常或固定得到的收入和一次性收入,不包括周转性收入。如:提取银行存款、向亲友借入款、收回借出款以及其他各种暂收款。

城镇居民家庭可支配收入　指被调查的城镇居民家庭在支付个人所得税、个人交纳的社会保障支出之后,所余下的实际收入。

计算公式为:可支配收入=总收入-个人所得税-个人交纳的社会保障支出

城镇居民家庭消费性支出　指被调查的城镇居民家庭用于日常生活的全部支出,包括购买商品支出和文化生活、服务等非商品性支出。不包括罚没、丢失款和缴纳的各种税款(如个人所得税、牌照税、房产税等),也不包括个体劳动者生产经营过程中发生的各项费用。

农村居民家庭纯收入　指农村常住居民家庭总收入中,扣除从事生产和非生产经营费用支出、缴纳税款和上交承包集体任务金额以后剩余的,可直接用于进行生产性、非生产性建设投资、生活消费和积蓄的那一部分收入。它是反映农民家庭实际收入水平的综合性的主要指标。农民家庭纯收入,既包括从事生产性和非生产性的经营收入,又包括取自在外人口寄回带回和国家财政救济、各种补贴等非经营性收入;既包括货币收入,又包括自产自用的实物收入。但不包括向银行、信用社和向亲友贷款等属于借贷性的收入。

计算公式为:

纯收入=总收入-家庭经营费用支出-生产用固定资产折旧-税收-上交集体承包任务

离休、退休、退职人员　指正式办理了离休、退休、退职手续,并享受相应的离休、退休、退职待遇的人员。

保险福利费用　指企业、事业、机关单位在工资以外实际支付给职工和离休、退休、退职人员个人以及用于集体的劳动保险和福利费用。

社会福利事业单位　指集中收养社会孤、老、残、幼的机构。包括由民政部门管理的社会福利院、儿童福利院、精神病人福利院和城镇集体办的福利院,以及农村集体举办的敬老院。

社会福利事业单位收养人数　包括民政部门管理和城镇及农村集体举办的社会福利事业单位中收养的老人,少年儿童,缺乏生活自理能力的残疾人员和精神病人。

商品零售价格指数　是反映城乡商品零售价格变动趋势的一种经济指数。零售物价的调整变动直接影响到城乡居民的生活支出和国家的财政收入,影响居民购买力和市场供需平衡,影响消费与积累的比例。因此,计算零售价格指数,可以从一个侧面对上述经济活动进行观察和分析。

居民消费价格指数　是反映一定时期内城乡居民所购买的生活消费品价格和服务项目价格变动趋势和程度的相对数。是综合了城市居民消费价格指数和农民消费价格指数计算取得。利用居民消费价格指数,可以观察和分析消费品的零售价格和服务价格变动对城乡居民实际生活支出的影响程度。

工业品出厂价格指数　是反映全部工业产品出厂价格总水平的变动趋势和程度的相对数。其中除包括工业企业售给商业、外贸、物资部门的产品外,还包括售给工业和其他部门的生产资料以及直接售给居民的生活消费品。通过工业生产价格指数能观察出厂价格变动对工业总产值的影响。

Explanatory Notes on Main Statistical Indicators

Labour Remuneration refers to total payment by various units to their employees during a certain period of time, including total wage bill of permanent workers and staff and remuneration payment to other employees.

Total Wages of Fully Employed Staff and Workers refer to the total remuneration payment to fully employed staff and workers in various units during a certain period of time. The calculation of total wages is based on the total remuneration payment to the staff and workers. Therefore, all the wages and salaries and other payments to staff and workers are included in the total wages regardless of their sources, category, and forms (in kind or cash). (Total wages of staff and workers in this yearbook include only total wages of fully employed staff and workers, excluding the living allowances distributed to those who have left their working units while keeping their labour contract/employment relation unchanged).

Average Wage of Fully Employed Staff and Workers refers to the average wage in money terms per person during a certain period of time for fully employed staff and workers in enterprises, institutions, and government agencies, which reflects the general level of wage income during a certain period of time and is calculated as follows:

$$\text{Average Wage of Fully Employed Staff and Workers} = \frac{\text{Total wages of Fully employed staff and workers in Reference Period}}{\text{Average Number of Fully employed Staff and workers in Reference period}}$$

Total Income of Urban Households refers to the total actual income of the sample households, including regular or fixed income and occasional income. The income of a circulating nature such as withdrawal from bank deposit, loans borrowed from relatives or friends, repayment of loans received and various temporary collection of many is excluded.

Disposable Income of Urban Households refers to total income minus income tax, personal contribution to social security and subsidy for keeping diaries in being a sample household. The following formula is used:

Disposable Income = total households income – income tax – personal contribution to social security

Expenditure for Consumption of Urban Households refers to total expenditure of the sample households for consumption in daily life, including expenditure for various commodities and expenses for non – commodity items such as culture and service, etc., but excluding fines and confiscation, loss, tax payments (such as income tax, license tax, real estates tax, etc.) and various expenses by individual laborers for business purposes.

Net Income of Rural Households refers to the total income of the permanent residents of the rural households during a year after the deduction of the expenses for productive and non – productive business operation, the payment for taxes and productive constriction, for consumption in daily life and for savings deposit. It is a comprehensive indicator to show the actual level of the income of the peasants' household. The net income of the rural households includes not only the income from the productive and non – productive business operation, but also the income from the non – business operation, such as the money remitted or brought back by the members of the household who are in other places, the government relief payment and various subsidies. It includes not only the money income, but also the income in kind. But the income from borrowing from banks, friends and relatives is excluded.

Retired and Resigned Person refers to the persons who have form ally gone through the formalities for their retirement or quitting work and enjoy the corresponding treatments.

Insurance an d welfare Funds refers to labour insurance and welf are funds paid by enterprises, organizations and institutions to their staff and workers as well as retired and resigned persons in addition to their wages and salaries.

Social Welfare Institutions refer to institutions taking care of old people without children, handicapped people and orphans. They include social welfare institutions run by civil affairs departments, children welfare institutions, social welfare institutions for mental patients, and collective – owned old people's home in rural areas.

Number of People Taken in by social welfare Institutions refers to the number of old people, children, totally dependent handicapped people and mental patients taken in by social welfare institutions run by civil affairs departments and those run by collective units in urban and rural areas.

Retail price Index reflects the general change in retail prices of commodities. The change and adjustment in retail prices directly affect the living expenditure of urban and rural residents, government revenue, purchasing power of residents and the equilibrium of market supply and demand, and the ratio of consumption to accumulation. Therefore, the calculation of retail price index is useful to analyze the changes of the above economic activities.

Consumer Price Index reflects the trend and degree of changes in prices of consumer goods and services purchased by urban and rural residents, and is a composite index derived from the urban consumer price index and the rural consumer price index. Consumer price index can be used to analyze the impact of consumer price change on actual expenditure for living cost of urban and rural residents.

Ex – factory price index of Industrial Products reflects the trend and degree of changes in general ex – factory prices of all industrial products, including sales of industrial products by and industrial enterprise to all units outside the enterprise, as well as sales of consumer goods to residents. It can be used to analyze the impact of ex – factory prices on gross industrial output value.

中国统计出版社最新图书简目

(仅供参考,以最后出书为准)

统计资料

中国统计年鉴-2011
中国统计摘要-2011
国际统计年鉴-2011
2011中国发展报告
中国第三产业统计年鉴-2011
中国区域经济统计年鉴-2011
中国劳动统计年鉴-2011
中国社会统计年鉴-2011
中国城市统计年鉴-2009
中国建筑业统计年鉴-2011
中国人口和就业统计年鉴-2011
中国工业经济统计年鉴-2011
中国商品交易市场统计年鉴-2011
中国房地产统计年鉴-2011
中国能源统计年鉴-2011
中国民政统计年鉴-2011
中国贸易外经统计年鉴-2011
2011中国地区经济监测报告
中国科技统计年鉴-2011
中国农村统计年鉴-2011
中国农产品价格调查年鉴-2011
中国高技术产业统计年鉴-2011
中国教育经费统计年鉴-2010
中国农村贫困监测报告-2011
全国农产品成本收益资料汇编-2011
中国科学技术协会统计年鉴-2011
工业企业科技活动资料-2011
大中型批发零售和住宿餐饮企业统计年鉴-2011
中国城市(镇)生活与价格年鉴-2011
中国县(市)社会经济统计年鉴-2011
中国农村住户调查年鉴-2011(中、英文)
中国农村全面建设小康监测报告-2011
第二次全国R&D资源清查资料汇编-综合卷
第二次全国R&D资源清查资料汇编-工业企业卷
中国零售和餐饮连锁企业统计年鉴-2011
2010年中国第六次人口普查公报

2011年省级综合统计年鉴系列

北京 天津 河北 山西 内蒙古
辽宁 吉林 黑龙江 上海 江苏
浙江 安徽 福建 江西 山东
河南 湖北 湖南 广东 广西
海南 重庆 四川 贵州 云南
西藏 陕西 甘肃 青海 宁夏
新疆 新疆生产建设兵团

2011年市(县)级综合统计年鉴系列

天津滨海新区
石家庄 唐山 邯郸 太原 大同
长治 阳泉 晋城 朔州 晋中
运城 忻州 临汾 呼和浩特
包头 沈阳 大连 长春 吉林市
四平 哈尔滨 黑龙江垦区
上海浦东新区
苏州 无锡 常州 徐州 南通
盐城 镇江 江阴 丹阳
杭州 宁波 绍兴 台州 温州
金华 嘉兴 衢州
福州 福州经济技术开发区
厦门经济特区 南昌 上饶
济南 青岛 潍坊 郑州
洛阳 三门峡 南阳 武汉 宜昌
十堰 荆州 咸宁 长沙 广州
东莞 惠州 深圳 桂林 南宁
柳州 来宾 河池 海口 成都 绵阳
贵阳 昆明 庆阳 西安
兰州 银川 乌鲁木齐

“十一五”规划教材

非参数统计 医学统计学
概率论与数理统计 统计学
现代金融投资统计分析
多元统计分析 经济计量学教程
应用时间序列分析
统计指数理论及应用
统计数据处理概论
质量管理统计方法 社会统计学
多元统计分析实验
企业经营管理统计
市场调查与预测
统计学原理(非统计专业使用)
统计学:从数据到结论
国民经济核算教程(国民经济统计学)
概率论与数理统计(经济、管理类专业使用)

重点图书

挑大学选专业2011—高考志愿填报指南
挑大学选专业2011—考研择校指南